ITALIAN LITERATURE AND THOUGHT SERIES

The Italian Literature and Thought Series makes available in English some of the representative works of Italian culture. Although it focuses on the modern and contemporary periods, it does not neglect the humanistic roots of Italian thought. The series will include new scholarly monographs, anthologies, and critically updated republications of canonical works, as well as works of general interest.

Images *of* Quattrocento Florence

Selected Writings in Literature, History, and Art

EDITED BY STEFANO UGO BALDASSARRI AND ARIELLE SAIBER

Yale University Press   *New Haven and London*

Designed by Rebecca Gibb.
Set in Bembo type by Keystone Typesetting, Inc.
Printed in the United States of America

Library of Congress Cataloging-in-Publication Data
Images of quattrocentro Florence : selected writings in literature, history,
and art / ed. Stefano Ugo Baldassarri and Arielle Saiber
p.   cm. — (Italian literature and thought series)
Includes bibliographical references and index.
ISBN 0-300-08051-4 (C) — ISBN 0-300-08052-2 (P)
1. Florence (Italy)—Civilization.   I. Baldassarri, Stefano Ugo.
II. Saiber, Arielle.   III. Series.
DG735.6.I86 2000
945'.51—dc21   99-052702

A catalogue record for this book is available from the British Library.

The paper in this book meets the guidelines for permanence and dura-
bility of the Committee on Production Guidelines for Book Longevity
of the Council on Library Resources.

10   9   8   7   6   5   4   3   2   1

CONTENTS

v

Contents

Contents

FOREWORD

Vico's *New Science* is an archaeology of history, a long meditation on the "principles" (which are origins, beginnings, causes, and foundations) shaping the "nature of nations," two words that designate births and begetting. Origins, Vico argues, are uncertain, hazy, and unknowable. They are even dangerous, because human beings invest myths of beginnings with the concerns of the present, and, thus, they may manipulate or falsify them.

As a genealogist of knowledge, Vico retrieves ancient wisdom about beginnings. Plato's commentary in the *Timaeus* tells the story of a war between Atlantis and Athens. Plato admonishes the Athenians—who are said to have been children of the earth—to forget the harshness of their origins, in order not to be tempted by them. In reality, Plato knew that human beings weave fables about their beginnings, and that in doing so, they seek to live up to them and re-create them. The same insight shapes Aristotle's maxim in his *Politics,* "Every beginning contains its ending"—to wit: fables of origins determine the inexorable unfolding of history.

If origins are obscure, new beginnings are feasible. Accordingly, Vico turns into an original theorist of new beginnings. His science of beginnings and new beginnings had powerful models: Virgil's *Aeneid,* with its account of Aeneas' quest for a new city and nostalgia for the old Troy; but above all the rich historiography of the Renaissance, which, as the present volume shows, is a vast, conscious trope for the possibility of rebirth.

The early humanist historiographies record concerns about the human or divine origins of cities such as Rome and Florence. These concerns, however, are thoroughly treated by such poets as Dante (who dramatizes at length the question of the origins of Mantua) and Boccaccio, a man whose personal history is marked by the problem of legitimacy and uncertainty about his own origins. Boccaccio's *Ninfale fiesolano,* moreover, is a reflection on the founding of Florence—metaphorically refracted into issues of poetic authority and originality—and on natural origins. Boccaccio argues that it was Atlas, the mythic astronomer, who founded the city of Fiesole; and in his *Ninfale* he refers to Charlemagne's restoration of the city of Florence after its destruction by the barbarians.

Boccaccio's representation of Florence's origin in the rationality of science and its restoration by the first French Holy Roman Emperor anticipates and crystallizes Florence's vital political mythology in the succeeding centuries. One may recall Lorenzo de' Medici's emblem: it features a young woman (Astraea), the Sun, and a rainbow, and it bears the inscription "Le tems revient."

The emblem's references are clear: the myth of Saturn, god of time and the astrological sign of Lorenzo; the Platonic-Pythagorean-Ficinian rationality of the stars; Virgil's Fourth Eclogue, which announces the return of Saturn's golden age and of justice ("Iam redit et virgo"); the mysteries of the cosmos attendant on the city's destiny; the biblical sign of peace and of the reconciliation of man, nature, and God; time's periodic returns.

Nothing illustrates Lorenzo's political vision better than this emblem and his villa at Poggio a Caiano. Jacopo Pontormo decorated this building with the story of Vertumnus and Pomona; the frieze by Andrea del Sansovino, with its figuration of the seasons, the cave of eternity, memory and forgetfulness, the months, and the ever-green laurel, which signals the enduring remembrance of Lorenzo's name, contained complex allegories of time.

Roughly at the same time, Machiavelli, while in exile, wrote the poem "Serenata." An adaptation of an Ovidian myth, the poem tells of the blissful union between the goddess of cultivation and Vertumnus, who seduces the virgin by fraud. It comes through as a Vichian fable: its overt political allegory concerns the union of Florence and the house of the Medici, and thus it conveys Machiavelli's sense of Florentine politics and, generally, of city government as an art of prudent cultivation of nature. The Renaissance historiographers of the myth of Florence—its art, its literature, its religious fervor, its scientific achievements, and its harsh politics—constantly return to these issues. Just as the mythology of Florence echoes that of Athens and Rome, so the mythology of the major European cities (London, Paris, and so on) recasts the rhetoric of the humanists of the quattrocento.

Giuseppe Mazzotta

ACKNOWLEDGMENTS

We would like to express our sincere gratitude to the mentors and colleagues who have helped us develop and refine this anthology. Many, many thanks go to Professors Giuseppe Mazzotta, David Quint, Vincent Ilardi, Riccardo Fubini, and Giuliano Tanturli.

We are grateful to the following colleagues for their careful readings of early drafts: J. Davidson, C. Dolan, D. Friedman, J. Houston, H. Lieberman, E. Lintz, J. Luzzi, A. Miller, L. Nalencz, D. Pascale, S. Roush, R. Ruquist, K. Solomon, A. Steinfels, C. Von Zastrow. We are particularly indebted to Julia Boss and Susan Abel for their thoughtful, meticulous comments.

Finally, we wish to thank Jonathan Brent, Cynthia Wells, and Susan Abel of Yale University Press for their encouragement and enthusiasm throughout our work on this book.

As if she were the queen of Italy, Florence sits between the
Tyrrhenian and Adriatic Seas. She is located in a salubrious
and pleasant climate, not far from either plains or mountains, surrounded by fertile fields on one side and by delightful hills on the other. A river runs through her circle of
walls, enhancing her beauty and supplying her with even
greater utility. Within the city one can find astounding
riches, unparalleled splendor, magnificent architecture, and
exquisite amenities. The villas around her, moreover, offer
stupendous and unheard-of delights; with supreme joy,
affability, and elegance they possess an unearthly charm. Indeed, Florence's splendor eclipses not only all Italian cities,
but those of the entire world.

LEONARDO BRUNI, *Laudatio florentinae urbis*

Crucial to all works of human invention is the complex relationship between novelty and tradition or, more precisely, the juxtaposition of elements
the author views as original with various familiar traditions. We must especially bear this in mind when studying the Italian humanists, whose "tradition"
was far from univocal. Their pioneering studies were instead based on a new
interpretation of two extremely rich cultural legacies, the Christian and the
classical. A case in point is Leonardo Bruni's innovative *Panegyric of the City of
Florence* (ca. 1404). When Bruni—then one of the most promising pupils of the
Florentine chancellor Coluccio Salutati—began his *Panegyric,* he drew from a

centuries-old tradition, promoted by artists and writers alike, depicting the city of Florence as a fascinating, virtuous woman.

Amid dramatic changes—artistic trends, political upheaval, and religious movements whose influence on the history of modern Europe can hardly be overstated—Florentines of the fifteenth century strove to develop and shape anew the myth and the identity of their city. It is precisely this process of self-mythification that this book aims to document. We present a variety of texts—most hitherto unavailable in English translation—to illustrate the spectrum of fifteenth-century Florentine views of the city's origins, history, and accomplishments. We thus hope to recapture the process through which, during a transformative period in Italy's history, a pivotal center of culture created and re-created its own myth.

In selecting texts, we have followed three main principles. First, especially in regard to humanist writings, we have drawn from the works that proved most influential. Second, the majority of texts included in this anthology belong to the genre of epideictic literature, which relies upon fixed rhetorical patterns and a common set of images. This style is inherently repetitious, and it may be hard for modern readers to perceive the nuances that render each text an important and singular piece of literature. We have therefore generally included only the most significant passages of the original documents, rather than translate them in their entirety. Recalling Leonardo da Vinci's well-known criticism of those who do not strive to know all the parts of a subject they love, we hope that readers will move from this selection to the original documents. Third, we made our selection partly according to subject matter. To demonstrate best the shaping of Florence's image throughout the quattrocento, we have divided the anthology into six parts: "Origins"; "History and Society"; "Literature"; "Art"; "Religion"; and "Florence Through Foreigners' Eyes."

Clearly our selection omits certain other aspects fundamental to the cultural development of a city, such as the sciences. There is, however, a sound historic justification for this omission. Although such noteworthy figures of quattrocento Florence as Paolo da Pozzo Toscanelli, Leonardo, Leon Battista Alberti, and Luca Pacioli pursued the study of science, it did not become a significant component of the city's identity until the second half of the following century. It was only then that the Medici grand dukes began to consider scientific studies as worthy of their patronage as literature, philosophy, and the visual arts, which they had been fostering for more than a hundred years. Numerous fifteenth-century sources praise these scientists and commend such thriving local industries as map-making, but we can find these encomiums only in long lists of activities said to illuminate Florence. Ugolino Verino's poem on the unparalleled splendor of his city and Luca Pulci's *Driadeo* are valuable examples. The sciences never constituted the central topic of any written work bent on celebrating fifteenth-century Florence, but they were often mentioned as part of the city's interdisciplinary culture. Most texts of the Florentine quattrocento represent the full range of experiences inside and outside the city walls and for that reason offer both a wealth of subjects for contemplation and fruitful points of departure for future research. In this light, even omissions, being historically determined, give us insights into the culture of the time. Marginalized members of society, such as women and Jews, were not active in the body politic, or in contributing encomiums or critiques of the city of Florence. They are thus seldom mentioned in the sources included in our anthology.

In translating these documents, we have tried to render faithfully the stylistic features of each text, without imposing on those which are less refined a rhetorical veneer absent from the originals. The translations of documents 1, 2, 5, 6, 7, 17, 18, 19, 22, 23, 27, 33, 34, 36, 38, 39, 40, 41, 42, 43, 45, 46, 47, 49, and 50 are by Stefano Ugo Baldassarri; the translations of documents 3, 4, 8, 9, 10, 11, 12, 13, 14, 15, 16, 20, 21, 24, 25, 26, 28, 29, 30, 31, 32, 35, 37, 44, 48, and 51 are by Arielle Saiber.

ORIGINS

The image of a city, whether earthly or celestial, has always evoked a strong emotional response. Accounts of a city's origins, moreover, retain great political significance, as they often inspire citizens to emulate the virtues of their celebrated founding fathers. This is the spirit that animated the numerous mythographies on the origins of Italian towns, myths first elaborated during the late Middle Ages. At that time the communes of the peninsula started to grow in economic and military power, and the expansion gave birth to edifying accounts of the origins of the city.

The political import behind these myths and texts concerning the foundation of the city was most astutely perceived by the renowned Renaissance Florentine Niccolò Machiavelli. In *The Prince* Machiavelli proposes to train the novice ruler in the art of governing—through emulation of the ancient founders of the Western world. That this text was written at the beginning of the sixteenth century indicates that the debate on the city's origins flourished in quattrocento Florence, where Machiavelli was born and raised. Before focusing on this debate, however, we wish to discuss medieval theories concerning the foundation of Florence, and in the process to describe how the myth of Florence—that is, a myth of a modern city founded by men independently of any divine intervention—was continually modified to meet the changing circumstances of its history and the mutable identity of its society.

Like many medieval Italian centers, Florence claimed to have been founded by the Roman emperor Julius Caesar. According to the thirteenth-century chronicle of the Florentine notary Sanzanome, Caesar founded Florence immediately after the war against the notorious conspirator Catiline, which would mean around 62 B.C. Sanzanome linked the foundation of Florence to the destruction of Fiesole, the town overlooking the River Arno. Having supported Catiline, Fiesole was besieged and eventually razed to the ground by Roman soldiers. Various accounts written in the late thirteenth and early fourteenth centuries relied on Sanzanome's chronicle, at times adding unfounded details to his account. By the second half of the thirteenth century, Florentines commonly considered their city "the most beautiful and renowned daughter of Rome," as Dante wrote in his *Convivio* (1.3.4). The city's ties with the French royal house, strengthened by the political supremacy of the Guelph faction, gave rise to a number of local legends that credited Charlemagne with having rebuilt the walls believed to have been destroyed by the barbarian horde of Totila, king of the Ostrogoths.

In the first half of the fourteenth century, the merchant and historiographer Giovanni Villani read through the various accounts of the origins of Florence and subsequently penned what came to be the version most commonly accepted until the birth of the humanist movement. In the initial passages of his famous *Cronica,* Villani recounts how King Atlas built the city of Fiesole—which, as Sanzanome had reported, was eventually destroyed by Caesar's army. In Villani's version, Caesar ordered that the rebellious Fiesole be replaced by a new center modeled on Rome. To this purpose, the senate sent officials to the banks of the Arno for the founding of the city. As Villani writes, it was to be named Floria, after Fiorino, a Roman general killed during the siege of Fiesole, and the lily was chosen as its symbol. With the diffusion of the Tuscan vernacular, the chronicler explains, the name was eventually transformed into Fiorenza, or "flowery sword."

By the beginning of the fifteenth century, Villani's account in *Cronica,* 1.38, no longer satisfied a society transfigured by a long war against Milan and by the innovative spirit of the humanist movement. The victory against the Milanese lord Gian Galeazzo Visconti in 1402 and the appearance of the first humanist writings contributed to Florence's perception of itself as the Italian defender of liberty. Soon after Gian Galeazzo's death, the first traces of this momentous shift appeared in important works such as the *Invective,* written by the Florentine chancellor Coluccio Salutati against the Milanese secretary Antonio Loschi. In this work, rejecting Villani's account of Caesar's founding of Florence, Salutati ardently defends the theory of the city's Roman origins against Loschi's accusations. The numerous archaeological remains to be seen all over Florence, Salutati writes, clearly attest to its Roman origins, even though, as with most cities, it is not possible to indicate the exact date of foundation. Salutati's version cleared the way for new myths on the origin of Florence; the next step was to trace the city's "republican" heritage. It was Leonardo Bruni who provided such an account in the initial passages of his *History of the Florentine People,* begun around 1415. Relying on the works of Cicero and Sallust, as well as on Salutati's *Invective,* Bruni asserts that Florence had been founded by Sulla's veterans after the end of the Social War (around 80 B.C.). According to this account, the building of the city had been the work not of Caesar, but of the Roman Republican soldiers. Florence came into being well before the death of Cicero and the subsequent establishment of the Roman empire. With this myth, Bruni not only provided Florence with a glorious republican past but also linked the city to the peerless cultural heritage that, in the humanists' eyes, had characterized the society of classical Rome before tyrannical rule led to decadence.

Bruni's version gained immediate respect in early fifteenth-century Florence. Even conservative intellectuals such as Giovanni Gherardi—utterly opposed to most of the daring theories proposed by the humanist movement—could not help employing the revised legend in their eulogies of the city. Some local historians even exceeded Bruni in their anti-imperialist spirit. Giovanni Cavalcanti, for instance, not only reported that Florence, contrary to Villani's assertions, had been founded by Sulla's veterans; he also drew on compromising passages of Suetonius' *Life of Caesar* to deride the Roman emperor. The humanists introduced the study of the Etruscans (who inhabited the region now known as Tuscany), together with the interest in classical archaeology. The scholars' findings further contributed to the myth of Tuscany as the cradle of republicanism and high culture in the Italian peninsula. Well into the second half of the fifteenth century, Florentine intellectuals continued to rely on classical sources in celebrating Etruria's republican magistratures, military power, economic primacy, superiority in the arts, and outstanding piety—the last confirmed by the many lavishly decorated sarcophagi that remained scattered throughout the Tuscan countryside.

In the last decades of the quattrocento, the Medicis' increasing control over the city forced acceptance of a version of Florentine origins more consistent with the propaganda of the new regime. During the crisis that the ruling faction faced after the death of Lorenzo the Magnificent, Angelo Poliziano published a letter in support of the political claims of Piero de' Medici. In this work, he proposed a new account of the city's origins. Poliziano relied on the anonymous *Libri regionum,* which he erroneously believed to be Frontinus' *De agrorum mensuris,* to celebrate the founding of Florence by Octavian and other members of the second triumvirate. He thus proudly extolled Florence as "the only city in all of history that has been built by three generals, one of whom was to become Emperor Augustus." The humanist image of Florence as the sole heir to the republicanism of classical Rome was thus superseded by a new version that emphasized the city's imperial origins—a version necessarily different from Villani's earlier myth. By the end of the quattrocento, Medicean propaganda succeeded in imposing on Florence a new and enduring identity. Poliziano's account far outlived Piero's short rule and served the political ends of the Medici well into the sixteenth century, when they regained control of the city.

HISTORY AND SOCIETY

Humanist literature and merchants' memoirs are two basic sources for learning about the cultural setting of quattrocento Florence. The product of an urban society eager for political and cultural change, humanism is generally believed to have developed first in Florence toward the end of the fourteenth century. The movement spread to other cities of the peninsula via the works and exemplary teachings of figures such as Coluccio Salutati, Leonardo Bruni, Poggio Bracciolini, Roberto de' Rossi, and Cencio Rustici. It is not surprising that an intellectual movement rooted in the lay and urban world would transform the medieval way of envisioning and praising cities. In this respect, Bruni's *Panegyric* played a decisive role not only in its description of the arts, architecture, economy, and government of Florence, but also in its definition of her political role in Italian history as the staunch defender of republican liberty against all forms of tyranny. The enduring success of Bruni's text is evident, for it served as a model for future descriptions of Florence and for eulogies of European cities well into the sixteenth century. Both Marin Sanudo's *Praise of the City of Venice* (1493) and the description of London in Polydore Vergil's *History of England* (1523) are strongly indebted to the Florentine humanist's work.

Merchants' memoirs—in which the record of private matters generally alternates with the account of momentous historical events—are by contrast a peculiarly Florentine genre. One can draw few comparisons with writing produced in other mercantile cities of this period, whether in Italy or elsewhere in Europe. Both the classicist rhetoric of the humanists and the crisp prose of these diaries vividly convey the Florentines' pride in their city by underscoring three main elements: Florence's thriving economy, her expanding dominion, and the organization of her government.

Let us first address the city's economy. When the new system of tax assessment, the *catasto,* was introduced in 1427, Florence was by far the largest city in Tuscany, having an urban population of approximately 38,000 inhabitants. Pisa, the second largest city of the Florentine territory, had no more than 7,000 residents, while the population of Florence's entire dominion amounted to some 240,000 people. In fifteenth-century Florentine dialect, *contado* meant "countryside." It also referred to the countryside of Florence's dominion (roughly one third of today's Tuscany). When we use terms such as "Florentine dominion" and "Florentine territory," we refer to the cities that were then subject to Florence (such as Pisa and Arezzo) and their surrounding countryside. Both "dominion" and "territory" indicate cities and territories that Florence conquered from the eleventh to the fifteenth century. In 1427, the citizens of Florence possessed 66 percent of the wealth of the state, although they represented only 16 percent of the whole population. Over the preceding century, Florentine merchants had controlled the finances of many European courts and had been in charge of collecting papal taxes all across the continent. By the beginning of the fourteenth century Boniface VIII had called the Florentine merchants the "fifth element of the universe" because of their extensive trade. Almost two hundred years later, after reporting the pope's famous saying in his proem to the first edition of Dante's *Commedia,* the humanist Cristoforo Landino praised the thriving Florentine economy, comparing the merchants of Florence to a swarm of industrious bees determined to return to their beehive with the wealth taken from each flower. Equally laudatory, the wool merchant Goro Dati in his *Istoria di Firenze* (1410) expressed a belief shared by his fellow citizens: "A Florentine who is not a merchant, who has not traveled the world over, seeing foreign nations and peoples before returning to Florence with riches, is a man who deserves no esteem whatsoever."

The numerous technical innovations—such as the new accounting system known as the *partita doppia* and the bill of exchange—introduced by the Florentines during the late medieval and Renaissance periods further attest to the crucial importance of economics in their society. As one might expect, numerous texts in praise of Florence proudly mention innovative business practices among the distinctive merits of the city. The successful merchant and versatile writer Benedetto Dei inserted into his *Chronicle* a glowing description of the city to serve as a guide for foreign businessmen. Dei's panegyric is largely devoted to a celebration of the city's exceptional wealth. Florence's many trading companies, the efficiency of the fiscal system, the lavish festivals, and the pageants performed throughout the year all testify to the unremitting industry of its citizens.

Dei did not limit his "guide" to the glories of the city center, as fifteenth-century Florentine writers generally did; instead, he included in his description a discussion of the splendor of the countryside. He strongly believed that the magnificent villas and the rich estates outside Florence's walls deserved mention as proof of the citizens' virtue and wealth. Poets, especially those at the court of the Medici, also rendered the fertile countryside an exceptional feature of quattrocento Florence's image. To celebrate the Medici estates, such authors as Luca Pulci, Naldo Naldi, Angelo Poliziano, and Ugolino Verino transformed the Tuscan Apennines and the Arno Valley into the scene of etiological myths. Lorenzo himself tried his hand at this popular genre: the myth narrated in his *Ambra,* a text composed shortly after he purchased the estate of Poggio a Caiano, illustrates the origins of toponyms in that area of the Florentine contado, where he was soon to start building what would become his favorite villa.

Many renowned writers and artists who distinguished themselves in fifteenth-century Florence originally came from towns and villages that fell within the city's sway. Moreover, as the case of the Medici themselves demonstrates, the distinction between urban and rural patriciates was not as clear-cut in Florence as it was in other regions of Italy or in northern Europe. Above all, however, the importance that so many fifteenth-century writers assigned to the territory outside the town walls must be viewed as a consequence of Florence's expanding dominion. Between the end of the fourteenth and the beginning of the fifteenth centuries, the Florentine Republic grew considerably, as Florence seized Arezzo (1384), Pisa (1406), Cortona (1411), and Leghorn (1421). The conquest of Pisa provided Florence, for the first time in history, with direct access to the sea. This had particularly significant consequences both for the city's economy and for the shaping of her image in the course of the fifteenth century. Dati, for instance, does not hesitate to present the victory over this age-old enemy as an epic deed, and Bruni boldly compares it with the wars between Rome and Carthage. Florentine maritime trade increased, thanks to the officials entrusted with the development of a mercantile fleet, whose galleys reached the main Mediterranean seaports as early as 1422. Coupled with the successful resistance to repeated Milanese attacks between 1390 and 1402, this notable expansion of Florentine trade further promoted the image of Florence as a growing military power. In 1447, moreover, the death of Filippo Maria Visconti finally brought the conflict with Milan to a close; only three years later, the daring political strategies of Cosimo de' Medici (the unofficial ruler of the city since 1434) culminated in the conquest of the Lombard capital by Francesco Sforza, Florence's chief ally. Once free from the threat of the Visconti, Florence was able to consolidate her position as the main power in Tuscany. In 1472, for example, the sack of Volterra served as an admonition to all the towns of the Florentine state that contemplated rebellion against the capital. Outside the Tuscan borders, Lorenzo the Magnificent relied on careful diplomacy, rather than military intervention, to conduct Florentine politics during the second half of the fifteenth century.

In the quattrocento, however, the events that had the greatest influence on the identity of Florence occurred within the city itself. Cosimo's successors were not as skillful as the "Pater Patriae" at stifling internal uprisings against the family regime. The 1466 conspiracy against Piero de' Medici, foiled by the unexpected intervention of his seventeen-year-old son Lorenzo, is just one example of increasing opposition to the ruling faction. The Pazzi conspiracy of 1478, in which assassins wounded Lorenzo the Magnificent and killed his younger brother, Giuliano, inside the cathedral of Florence, marked the dramatic outbreak of hatred toward the Medici—shared by many more citizens than Poliziano's propagandistic account of the conspiracy would lead us to believe. Countless Florentines imbued with the ideals promoted by the early humanists now regarded the government of the early fifteenth century as a model. In the writings of such figures as Alamanno Rinuccini and Donato Acciaiuoli, the period immediately after the war against Gian Galeazzo Visconti is praised as a golden age in Florentine history: a time when republican institutions flourished and citizens enthusiastically performed their civic duties. Throughout the quattrocento, Florentines took great pride in the equity and efficiency of their administrative system. As early as 1410, Dati provided a remarkably detailed description of the Florentine magistratures in the last book of his *History of Florence from 1380 to 1405.* This depiction of governmental offices is unprecedented in its clarity and thoroughness. It bears witness, as do many other texts of the period, to the high level of political consciousness attained by the citizens of Florence. Dati's accomplishment was unequaled until the end of the fifteenth century, when Marin Sanudo's two descriptions of the Venetian magistratures appeared.

The government of fifteenth-century Florence was far from democratic by today's standards. Only members of the twenty-one city guilds enjoyed the right to hold office—provided they were age thirty or over, solvent, and, obviously, male. This meant that not only all women but also the thousands of laborers in the textile industry were ineligible for public office, as were those workers whose professions did not qualify them for guild membership. The Ordinances of Justice (1293), moreover, prevented the descendants of noble families from occupying the highest executive posts. Subsequently, in late fourteenth- and early fifteenth-century Florence, only a minority of eligible citizens—roughly one third—ever assumed administrative positions.

After the banishment of the main representatives of the Albizzi faction in 1434, Cosimo de' Medici worked aggressively to consolidate his power. By directly controlling the officials in charge of voting procedures (the *accoppiatori*), he made sure that only his supporters were appointed to the key positions of the city government—a technique frequently used in quattrocento Florentine politics. In addition, Cosimo and his descendants further strengthened their rule by creating special executive commissions *(balìe)* whenever their power seemed to be at risk. The balìe passed laws and made crucial decisions regarding the fiscal system, the commune's foreign politics, and the administration of the law. The establishment of new councils controlled by members of the ruling party diminished the republican character of the Florentine government and intensified discontent among the opponents of the Medici. Modern scholars have rightly described the Council of Seventy as a sort of life senate. It was created by Lorenzo the Magnificent in 1480 and held Florentine politics in check until Piero de' Medici's fall in 1494. But this pattern of Medicean interference in the government of Florence helps explain why in his dialogue *On Liberty,* composed shortly after the Pazzi's attempt to overthrow the Medici, Alamanno Rinuccini commends the conspiracy as a glorious act. He believed that the conspirators deserved the highest praise, for they had tried to restore the citizens' liberty, which Lorenzo, "the tyrant of Florence," had usurped.

Familiar with Rinuccini's views on the politics of quattrocento Florence,

Machiavelli (*The Prince,* 1.3) would point out that cities with a republican history possessed "greater life, greater hatred, and more desire for revenge, as the memory of ancient liberty does not let them and cannot let them remain quiet." When Lorenzo the Magnificent died in 1492, he passed on to his son the rule over a city that, although no longer a republic, had not yet become a principality. Self-promoting intellectuals in the Medici court had celebrated Lorenzo's government as the culmination of early quattrocento humanist civic ideals; yet Florentines perceived that behind the republican façade held up by official propaganda, their liberty had been significantly restricted by the Medicean regime. It need not surprise us that within a city disappointed by the betrayal of long-shared ideals, Savonarola's movement met with enormous success. During the last decade of the quattrocento, many citizens followed Savonarola's call not only in response to its religious appeal, but also in the hope of seeing their political aspirations for a free city realized at last.

LITERATURE

The most illustrious Florentine writers, as one would expect, contributed much to the myth of their city. The intellectual and moral teaching of the "three crowns"—Dante, Petrarch, and Boccaccio—profoundly influenced the culture of quattrocento Florence. Their impressive and unparalleled literary output not only allowed Florence to proclaim itself the center of Italian literature and the cradle of the Italian vernacular but also provided it with a unique paradigm of civic and scholarly life.

In the opening years of the fifteenth century, humanists such as Niccoli, Bruni, and Bracciolini opposed the conservative intellectuals' generous appraisal of the so-called three crowns of Florence. This debate produced Bruni's *Dialogi* and the conservative Cino Rinuccini's *Invective Against Slanderers of Dante, Petrarch, and Boccaccio.* The Florentine humanists, however, soon abandoned their excessively classicist ideals in favor of sincere admiration of their city's literary geniuses. Thus in 1436 Bruni himself composed a laudatory biography of Dante and Petrarch on the model of Plutarch's *Parallel Lives.* The political value of the text is worth noting, for Bruni wrote it at the request of the city government when Florentine liberty was once again threatened by the army of Viscontean Milan. Even more important, however, is that Bruni's biography presents his two illustrious fellow citizens not only as the greatest representatives of two different genres (Dante of vernacular poetry, Petrarch of

Latin prose), but also as eminent models of two kinds of life, the active and the contemplative. Dante, as Bruni writes, not only fought gallantly for his country at the Battle of Campaldino but showed dedication in his work for the city government. Endowed with a great sense of civic duty, Dante performed many noble and difficult tasks for Florence before he was banished by his opponents. "Moreover," Bruni adds, "although constrained by exile and poverty, Dante never abandoned his distinguished studies, managing to complete his beautiful work [the *Commedia*] amid numerous difficulties." Though the example offered by Petrarch is different, as one of solitary contemplation and study, Bruni deems it equally praiseworthy, especially considering how beset Petrarch was with hardships on a daily basis.

In the first half of the quattrocento the influence of civic humanism led most Florentine intellectuals to esteem Dante's strenuous activity in the service of his country more highly than Petrarch's solitary life of study and meditation. A noteworthy example is Matteo Palmieri's *Civic Life* (1438–1439), which focuses on the education of the perfect citizen. Palmieri concludes with the narration of a vision, modeled on a famous passage in Plato's *Republic* and on the passage from Cicero known as Scipio's Dream, which illustrates the heavenly rewards awaiting the man who faithfully serves his country. The vision is "miraculously" reported to Dante by a friend killed during the Battle of Campaldino, where Dante himself was fighting. Because of his courage and military valor, Dante is granted the privilege of hearing this account from the mouth of the slain friend himself. After having heard that eternal bliss is granted to all who strive to defend their country, Palmieri writes, Dante solemnly pledges to continue serving Florence.

The anecdote reported in Palmieri's book sheds light on the political import that fifteenth-century Florentines attached to the study of their own literary tradition. Numerous authors emphasized the usefulness of the vernacular to a city's identity, a notion that grew as knowledge of classical culture spread. Scholars such as Bruni, Manetti, Landino, and Poliziano drew heavily on the writings of the ancient orators as tools for city politics. They encouraged Florentine orators to resort to the refined techniques of Cicero and Demosthenes when speaking either in the sessions of the Florentine government or before foreign authorities. Translating the classics also lent richness and polish to vernacular Italian, as Landino asserted in the proem to his version of Pliny's *Natural History* (1474). Throughout the quattrocento, Florence distinguished itself as the center for the translation of classic authors, as well as for the authorship of highly original treatises—for instance, Bruni's *De interpretatione recta*

(1420) and the fifth book of Manetti's *Apologeticus* (1456), the first texts in modern literature devoted to the art of translating.

The humanists' faith in the utility of classical scholarship for civic life brings us to another significant factor in the image of fifteenth-century Florence: the study of Greek. First actively pursued by Petrarch and Boccaccio and then by the local pupils of Manuel Chrysoloras, the knowledge of ancient Greek language and culture was repeatedly praised by Florentine writers throughout the quattrocento. The rediscovery of Greek civilization received great attention from such writers as Giannozzo Manetti. Although indebted to Bruni's biography of Dante and Petrarch, Manetti's *Lives of the Three Illustrious Florentine Poets* was the first text to discuss at length the short yet admirable history of Greek scholarship in Florence. As Manetti proudly points out, Chrysoloras' lectures in the Tuscan city from 1397 to 1400 marked the crowning contribution to Petrarch's and Boccaccio's pioneering efforts to propagate the study of Greek in the Western world. After Manetti, all intellectuals of the fifteenth century, both in Florence and elsewhere, would consider Chrysoloras' university instruction a watershed in the history of modern culture. Italian humanists generally used the revival of Greek to establish a clear and convenient boundary between what they called the Dark Ages and their own epoch of dramatic cultural renewal.

It is common knowledge that the idea of a renaissance first appeared in the works of the humanists themselves. The documents we have selected for Part 3 emphasize the concept of renaissance as the rediscovery of classical eloquence and scholarship first promoted in the philological studies of Petrarch and Boccaccio. Equally important is the periodization of Western culture conceived of by the humanists to elaborate the first comprehensive overview of the history of vernacular literature. In the early quattrocento, rigorous assessments of the literary style and the personal merits of Dante, Petrarch, and Boccaccio significantly contributed to an increased respect for the vernacular. The 1441 Certame Coronario in the cathedral of Florence—an event at which authors were asked to compose poetry in the vernacular on the topic of friendship—is a case in point. This ennobling of the vernacular, in turn, inspired the compiling of the first exhaustive anthologies of vernacular literature. The first noteworthy example is the well-known *Raccolta Aragonese,* assembled by Angelo Poliziano in 1477 at the request of Lorenzo the Magnificent. The *Raccolta* presents works of authors, including Lorenzo himself, from the thirteenth century on—underscoring, as one might expect, the continuous and unparalleled success of Florentine literature, from the time of Dante to that of the Medici court poets.

Finally, in this section on literature, we wish to stress the association increasingly made between Florence and ancient Athens, rather than Rome, in the second half of the quattrocento. This gradual yet continual change was not solely the result of the rediscovery of Greek scholarship after Chrysoloras' arrival. The influence of this crucial event should not be overlooked, nor should the coming of another famous Byzantine professor, Joannes Argyropoulos, in 1457. The parallel with ancient Athens was, for example, present in Bruni's works—most notably in his *Panegyric,* based on Aelius Aristides' *Panathenaicus,* a celebrated second-century laudation of Athens—and in his funeral eulogy for Nanni Strozzi, which was indebted to the renowned oration of Pericles reported by Thucydides in his *History of the Peloponnesian War.* That Florentine scholars of the later fifteenth century embraced classical Athens as their model city, rather than republican Rome, should, however, be attributed primarily to the propaganda of the Medicean court. It was principally in the new climate of Ficino's Platonic Academy and Poliziano's studies in Greek philology that Florence began to be praised explicitly as a new Athens. To support their regime, the Medici substituted a new set of models for those of republican Rome. Cicero ceased to be regarded as the exemplary statesman and was replaced by Plato. The latter better suited the Medici's aim of presenting themselves as the "philosopher-rulers" of Florence. Ficino's translation of the Platonic corpus soon affected the way people read the city's greatest writers, Dante and Petrarch. As early as 1468, in the proem to his vernacular translation of Dante's *Monarchia,* Ficino celebrated his illustrious fellow citizen as "divine by fatherland, Florentine by dwelling, angelic by race, and a poetical philosopher by profession." Thirteen years later, Landino diverged from the medieval notion that Dante was primarily an encyclopedic and accomplished versifier to claim that Dante's masterpiece was the work of an inspired philosopher, theologian, and prodigious poet whose genius served to enlighten the city of Florence. Landino's commentary on the *Commedia* of 1481 is both a milestone in the history of Dante studies, and a sincere tribute to the Neoplatonic teaching of Marsilio Ficino.

ART

Authors who compared Florence to ancient Athens celebrated not only the rebirth of classical literature but also the development of the visual arts in the city. In the case of the arts, however, laudatory parallels with the capital of ancient culture derived not from Medicean propaganda but from other features peculiar to the Florentine society of the early quattrocento. Among these were the growing interest in the study of antiquities, the development of new techniques, and the elaboration of innovative theories in the fields of architecture, sculpture, and painting.

Giotto occupies an especially prominent place in the early quattrocento literature extolling Florence as the fountain of artistic renewal. In the *De origine civitatis Florentiae et eiusdem famosis civibus* (1390–1405)—a voluminous work on the history of Florence and its illustrious citizens—Filippo Villani first credits Giotto with reviving the elegance of classical art after centuries of oblivion. About forty years later, Lorenzo Ghiberti's highly original *Commentaries* elaborated the same notion. The very structure of this work reveals the innovative spirit so conspicuous in the artistic milieu of quattrocento Florence. Book 1 of the *Commentaries,* which focuses on classical art, relies heavily on Vitruvius and Pliny. In Book 2, Ghiberti discusses the development of artistic style from late antiquity to his own time and in the process gives us the first autobiography by an artist. Book 3, which Ghiberti left unfinished, contains discussions of scientific topics useful to the artist, such as optics and anatomy. The *Commentaries* highlight the key features of the artistic myth of quattrocento Florence. Ghiberti introduces the concept of periodization in art, as had been done for literature, by praising the Florentine authors who shaped the rebirth of classical style. Comparing Giotto's technique to the groundbreaking study of Greek undertaken by Petrarch and Boccaccio, Ghiberti celebrates the artist's work as a decisive improvement on a tradition characterized by stylistic rudeness. Like most innovations introduced by fifteenth-century artists, the new periodization of art history proposed by Florentines such as Ghiberti and Alberti exerted a lasting influence on scholars and artists alike. For example, the distaste for the art of the so-called Dark Ages would last well into the nineteenth century.

Another similarity between the humanists' periodization of literature and the artist-authors' treatment of the history of art should be underscored. Like their fellow citizens, Florentine artists considered the study of ancient models crucial to the dramatic progress in the visual arts in their city. By the second half of the fourteenth century, Petrarch and Boccaccio had judged the elevated quality of Giotto's art to be a result of his excellent education, which they deemed utterly superior to that of all other artists of his time. The spread of humanist ideals in quattrocento Florence led to a focus on the link between an artist's studies and his mastery of style. Antonio Manetti draws this connection in his *Life of Brunelleschi*. He describes Brunelleschi's and Donatello's early archaeological excavations in Rome, arguing that Brunelleschi's rigorous study of classical architectural styles, and his unique acquaintance with ancient art, had helped make him the greatest architect of his time.

This emphasis on the study of ancient models should not, however, overshadow the importance of originality to Florentine artist-authors. We do not have to look far to find harsh criticism of mere *imitatio* in Ghiberti's *Commentaries,* for example, in the famous sculptor's condemnation of Byzantine art for its failure either to improve on its models or to break away from them. A more important testimonial to artistic innovation can be found in one of the most influential texts in the history of art literature, Alberti's *On Painting.* Alberti broke with custom by dedicating the Italian version of this treatise—a true monument to the Florentine artistic Renaissance—to the artist Filippo Brunelleschi, rather than to a wealthy patron. In the dedicatory preface, Alberti expresses his amazement at the great dome of the cathedral of Florence, which he deems "an exceptional feat," because of its novelty. The work Alberti extols as the foremost symbol of Florence's artistic achievements stands out precisely by virtue of its brilliant departure from tradition.

Artists earned greater respect in Florentine society than in any other city of the period, whether in Italy or abroad. As Florentines highly valued the originality of their scholars, so too they believed that their artists were deserving of praise for their masterpieces. In quattrocento Florence, as we have seen, many artists devoted themselves not only to reading literature, but also to writing. Although it is a well-known feature of fifteenth-century Italy as a whole, "art literature" saw its greatest production in Florence. Artists contributed substantially to the shaping of Florentine identity through their celebration of the city in monuments and texts. Documents like the anonymous *Notable Men in Florence Since 1400* and the poem by Verino that we include in Part 4 rank artists' contributions to the glory of Florence above those of humanist scholars, jurists, and theologians. Understandably enough, moreover, Florence became one of the first Italian centers to offer detailed guides to its monuments. Albertini's *Memoriale* is a valuable example.

Further evidence for the crucial role of artists in quattrocento Florentine society comes from the political value of the works they were commissioned to produce. City officials were actively involved in the adornment of Florence and the surrounding region. In his book on the Florentine magistratures, Dati describes the tasks of the *ufficiali delle castella* and the *ufficiali della torre,* two councils specifically responsible for the maintenance and the improvement of

public buildings in the city and countryside nearby. There were countless public debates over the best way to embellish Florence. On April 20, 1406, for
example, the city council ordered each guild to finance a sculpture of its patron
saint to be placed in the appropriate niche outside Orsanmichele. Throughout
the quattrocento the council sponsored public contests in the decoration of
Florentine monuments; the competition for the baptistery doors that was won
by Ghiberti is one of the most renowned. It is important to heed the political
implications inherent in these competitions, in the commissioning of the art,
and in its symbolism.

Whether they were the product of public or private commission, Donatello's *Judith,* Gozzoli's *Procession of the Magi,* and the decorations of the Palazzo
della Signoria were all meant, more than anything else, as political propaganda.
The many grand palaces commissioned by private citizens during the second
half of the century prove how valuable the contributions of renowned artists
could be in the struggle for power. The intense competition for economic and
political supremacy that characterized quattrocento Florence brought about a
significant change in the landscape of the city, punctuating it with stately symbols whose elegant architecture expressed underlying political aims. Lacking
absolute power, and desiring to appear respectful of the city's republican tradition, the Medici were unable to develop any town planning project comparable to the Sforzas' for Vigevano or Ercole d'Este's for Ferrara.

The same limits on the power of the Medici help to explain the compara-
tive absence of utopian literature and architecture in quattrocento Florence.
Unlike the other great Italian powers, Florence did not foster any significant
utopian tradition before the establishment of the grand duchy. Only in 1598,
under a government noticeably different from that of the previous century,
would Giorgio Vasari the Younger dedicate his treatise *The Ideal City*—certainly a more serious approach to utopianism than Doni's sardonic vision in the
Mondi (1553)—to Grand Duke Ferdinando de' Medici. The civic ideal of quattrocento Florence was far from utopian. It was firmly grounded in the economic and social reality of the city, whose wealth visitors could perceive from
afar in the outstanding majesty of its buildings. As with Dei's guide, the flourishing arts and increasing wealth of Florence seem to be at the core of Francesco Rosselli's famous *Map with the Chain* (ca. 1472)—the first panoramic
urban view independent of medieval iconography. Threats of war and internal
discord further dictated the direction of art and literature and made it impossible for the Florentine society of the time to conceive of utopian projects.

Utopian visions found a much more suitable social and intellectual climate in principalities dominated by a single ruler—as Leonardo himself clearly understood when he submitted his sketches for the perfect city to the Milanese duke Ludovico Il Moro, rather than to the Medici.

RELIGION

The image of the city in Christian thought is often marked by its inescapable earthliness. The Bible tells of humankind's divine origin, but of the city as a product of human effort. In Apocalypse (21:2), St. John envisions the Holy City as "the new Jerusalem, coming down out of heaven from God, prepared as a bride beautifully adorned for her husband." The earthly city, however, occupies an ambiguous position in the works of Christian thinkers. St. Augustine's notion that the origin of earthly cities lay in the violence of self-interest had a lasting influence on Western culture. Yet paradoxically, Christianity first established itself among urban populations in the Roman empire; the term *paganus* ("rustic" in classical Latin) bears witness to the difficulties Christians met with in attempting to spread their creed to the countryside.

Unlike Christian thinkers, prominent Latin and Greek philosophers had viewed happiness as the result of life spent in a well-ordered city. Only within the urban sphere, they claimed, could man fully attain the happiness deriving from the practice of virtue. It is precisely this search for the greatest good within the city that leads the Stoic interlocutor in Cicero's dialogue *On the Nature of the Gods* to state that civic society mirrors the way in which the gods themselves associate. He also partakes of the classical view that the universe itself is no more than "the common dwelling place of gods and men, the city that belongs to both" (2.31.78–79).

Both Christian and Greco-Roman interpretations of the origin and nature of urban society must be kept in mind when considering the way in which fifteenth-century Florentines looked at the religious tradition of their city. As we have pointed out, a variety of viewpoints—some from antiquity, others utterly new—contributed to shaping the image of quattrocento Florence. Humanism embraced the Greco-Roman view of the city as the place where moral virtue and piety could best express themselves. Moreover, for all the scholarly emphasis on the elitism of humanistic thought, its influence on the popular religiosity of fifteenth-century Florence should not be overlooked. Also crucial to the religious identity of Florence during the first half of the century was the city's privileged relationship with the papacy. Finally, in Florence's rich millenarian tradition, the city appears as the capital of spiritual and political rebirth.

Regarding the city's special relationship with the Roman Curia, we should recall that in the quattrocento, Florentine bankers managed the collection of papal taxes and were in charge of the pontiff's finances. For most of the century, the Medici carefully maintained their role as papal bankers—and profited politically from this valuable connection. Cosimo succeeded in establishing a strong link with Pope Eugenius IV in 1434 after the pope took refuge in Florence's Santa Maria Novella from a rampaging mob in Rome. Eugenius IV would spend most of his pontificate in Florence. Soon people were referring to the Dominican church as "the Florentine Lateran," an epithet recalling that Martin V had also resided there in 1420. Eugenius IV, to secure Medici financial support, helped Cosimo prevail over the Albizzi faction and thereby gain control of the city. So began the strong alliance between the Curia and Medicean Florence. Among the momentous consequences of this relationship was the transfer of the council for the union of the Eastern and Western churches from Ferrara to Florence early in 1439. This important event, at least until the July pronouncement came that the two churches had united, temporarily turned Florence into the center of Christendom. For the occasion, Cosimo de' Medici managed to be elected standard-bearer of justice, the highest office of the Florentine Republic. In that prominent role he entertained the papal Curia and Byzantine authorities, including the emperor John Paleologus and the patriarch of Constantinople.

This was not the first time the unofficial ruler of the city had used his familiarity with the pontiff to enhance his own status. Many documents report Cosimo's involvement in the solemn consecration of the cathedral of Florence by Eugenius IV on March 25, 1436. Among the sources describing this episode, Belcari's brief account is particularly important. In it he observes that the pontiff granted—at Cosimo's request—an extraordinary number of indulgences to the Florentine crowd attending the consecration and yet duly stresses that Eugenius had previously disregarded similar petitions for indulgences from other city officials and important prelates. Nevertheless, the Medici's political goals did not always coincide with those of the papacy, and the league between Cosimo and Eugenius IV would eventually sour. Tensions arose from the election of Antoninus as bishop of Florence in 1445 over the objections of the leading family and, two years earlier, from the pope's choice of the Viscontean condottiere Niccolò Piccinino as leader of the papal forces. The Medici's exceptional influence on the Curia did not, however, cease after Cosimo's rule. In 1488, Lorenzo the Magnificent would succeed in marrying his daughter Maddalena to Franceschetto Cibo, son of Pope Innocent VIII, and a year later he would have his thirteen-year-old son Giovanni appointed cardinal.

The Medici's patronage exerted considerable influence on the religious life of quattrocento Florence through the family's intensive financing and restoration of religious buildings in both the urban area and the surrounding countryside. The Church of San Lorenzo, the abbey of Fiesole, and the convent of San Marco are among the best-known examples. It is hardly surprising, then, that many documents celebrate the Medici for their patronage of religious institutions. Authors linked to the Medicean court commended their patrons for adorning the city with churches and monasteries. Thus developed a new literary genre that coupled Florence's artistic beauty with its citizens' piety and the patronage of the Medici. Belcari—one of the most important religious writers of fifteenth-century Florence—dedicated many of his works to members of the powerful family. His pageants, whose propagandistic intent cannot be overestimated, are particularly notable for their praise of the Medici's devotion. Another valuable example of this genre is Domenico da Corella's *Theotocon,* which was dedicated to Piero de' Medici. In this long poem, the prior of Santa Maria Novella describes the Florentine churches and praises the citizens' great piety, underscoring the unique nature of the Tuscan city said to be the main center of Christendom after Rome.

Florence's relationship with Rome also influenced Florentine religious literature. Many fifteenth-century prophecies, for example, emphasize the close ties between the Tuscan city and its Roman mother. These visions—often seemingly products of a Franciscan milieu close to Joachimite millenarianism—outline a central role for Florence in the imminent spiritual cleansing of the entire world. As such, they employ the usual striking array of allegorical and apocalyptic language. Like many other writings of this kind, the authors of the two texts we have included in our anthology—one an anonymous writer, the other a Franciscan friar from Rieti—expect that Florence will join forces with the king of France to free Rome from the corruption of the ecclesiastics. The prophecies declare that the two powers, after having defeated all the enemies of the Christian faith, will bring about an age of peace under their just rule. In the anonymous text, Florence becomes the new papal seat and the capital of all Western countries; political aims are clearly central to visions that announce so forcefully the goals of a Franco-Florentine hegemony. This tradition of religious exaltation of Florentine centrality in a coming age of bliss helps to explain Girolamo Savonarola's immense and rapid success in the Tuscan city during the last decade of the century. Savonarola's exhortations to repent were more effective because they were coupled with the promise of a universal rule soon to be established by Florence and its age-old ally, the royal house of France.

Savonarola's indebtedness to strains of Florentine culture and devotion, therefore, is fundamental to understanding not only the nature of his preaching but also his enormous influence. The same is true of the works by his unlettered followers and those who readapted erudite forms of piety to the new climate of late quattrocento Florence. Within this last category, Girolamo Benivieni may be cited as one of the most salient representatives of the Savonarolan movement. Before becoming an ardent follower of Savonarola and the translator of several of his works, Benivieni had been a valued poet at the Medici court and a member of Ficino's Platonic Academy. Traces of his typically Florentine education are clearly visible in the religious poems he wrote in support of Savonarola's promised spiritual renewal: he fuses Ficinian mysticism, moral righteousness, and visionary language to celebrate Florence as "the new Jerusalem, the city that God loves most."

Humanist ideals were also absorbed into the message of "renovation" emerging at the end of the fifteenth century. Savonarola himself drew from the political tenets of the Florentine humanists in his *Treatise on the Constitution and Government of the City of Florence*. This famous work, composed during the last months of his life, attests to Savonarola's participation in the debate on the restructuring of the Florentine government after the downfall of the Medici. It also reveals the care he took in founding his political program on the republican principles upheld by the local humanists in the first half of the quattrocento. Borrowing from Salutati, Bruni, and others, Savonarola argued that it was impossible to establish any type of political system in Florence other than a popular government open to as many citizens as possible. Hoping to create a Florentine Republic respectful of people's liberty, Savonarola has no qualms about depicting the previous Medicean rule as a form of tyranny utterly in contrast to Florence's praiseworthy libertarian tradition. Such republicanism is also present in the works of less erudite followers of the Savonarolan movement, as we can see in Luca Landucci's diary and in the writings of Piero Bernardo, the leader of the friar's *fanciulli* and one of Savonarola's most radical and influential supporters. In his letter to the fanciulli, the Florentine children whom Savonarola had appointed to eradicate vice from the city, Bernardo often quotes from the preacher's prophecies on the renovation of the Church and the fight against the infidels. Nor does Bernardo forget to mention the practical consequences of their religious movement, whose success clearly depends on a policy of action. Even while addressing such a young crowd, this unlettered layman cannot help picturing a radiant future for Florentine religious and political primacy. Thus it need not surprise us that the most eminent Florentine intellectuals of the sixteenth century, beginning with Machiavelli and Guicciardini, will often focus on religion as a means of obtaining power.

FLORENCE THROUGH FOREIGNERS' EYES

Much research still needs to be done on the presence of foreigners in quattrocento Florence. Medieval and Renaissance travel literature, apart from pilgrims' diaries, still awaits in-depth study. We use the term "foreigner" to describe all people who were not born within Florence's dominion. Except in one instance, the texts included in Part 6 of our anthology are by Italians, most of them humanists. Since the humanists were usually accomplished orators inclined by nature and profession to travel and to write elegant accounts of their experiences, most texts translated here belong to the genre of epideictic literature.

Official visits to Florence provided foreigners with an immediate opportunity to comment on the city's appearance. A valuable example of this type of travel literature comes from an anonymous Russian clerk—a member of the retinue of Bishop Abraham of Suzdal—who attended the Council of Florence in 1439. On the day of their departure from Russia, the clerk began to record his impressions of the numerous places he was visiting. On his arrival in "the glorious and magnificent city of Florence" he was impressed with its vast population, clean and spacious streets, numerous markets, and local products. As did most visitors to the Tuscan city, he praised its majestic churches and numerous monasteries. The Florentine hospital of Santa Maria Nuova, in its orderliness and size, seemed to astonish him more than anything else.

Italian visitors' descriptions of the Tuscan city, by contrast, maintain a constant emphasis on Florence's high culture and style. The celebration of the city's artistic and literary primacy is a recurrent feature of such texts, especially in travelogues composed by humanists. It is not surprising to encounter in fifteenth-century Italian literature numerous eulogies of Florence's polished vernacular and its revival of classical rhetoric. Despite his hostility toward the Medici, the humanist Pope Pius II commended the Florentines for choosing accomplished and learned rhetoricians as chancellors of their republic, while other Italian cities selected lawyers lacking any knowledge of ancient history and classical eloquence. The same admiration appears in a letter by Ludovico Carbone, the official orator of the Este court, to his patron Ercole I. En route to Naples to escort Ercole's future wife, Eleonora of Aragon, back to Ferrara with the rest of the ducal retinue, Carbone stopped in Florence. There, in a lavishly decorated hall of the Palazzo della Signoria, Carbone delivered an oration in front of the Florentine government—which, as he writes in the letter, seemed to him as imposing and honorable as the Roman senate. The praise he received on his oration thrilled him, because he believed Florentines to be "the fathers of all eloquence." Carbone considered Florence equally noteworthy for its poets and scholars and proclaimed the city the most suitable place for humanist study.

Another important component of the favorable image of Florence offered by the family's Italian allies is the praise which visitors to the city lavished upon the Medici. Included in this collection is an excerpt from Galeazzo Maria Sforza's letters to his father Francesco, the duke of Milan, written during his first stay in Florence in 1459—during the very days when Pius II also visited the Tuscan city. The fifteen-year-old Sforza expressed sincere admiration for the city and appreciation for his reception there. He offers valuable insights into the life of the Medici court by describing an evening of song and dance in his honor at Cosimo's Villa Careggi. It is likely that, once back in Milan, the young son of Francesco Sforza tried to introduce to the Milanese court the types of entertainment he described in his letters.

It was not uncommon for foreigners to emulate Florentine trends, literary and artistic models, and political thought. Two significant and well-documented cases are those of Pandolfo Collenuccio and Stefano Porcari.

Collenuccio, a respected jurist and humanist, recited a long poem in Latin in praise of Florence during the ceremony for his election as podestà of the Tuscan city on November 1, 1490. His *Panegyrica Silva* is important not only as a eulogy of Florentine justice by a foreigner about to undertake the local administration of law, but also in its attempt to imitate the literary style peculiar to the circle of Lorenzo the Magnificent. The presence of Lorenzo and intellectuals from the court of the Medici at Collenuccio's induction ceremony inspired him to compose a poem whose refined syntax and wealth of sources would demonstrate great erudition. To achieve this purpose, he created a new myth of the Tuscan city, drawing on the works of the most renowned Florentine authors. Collenuccio opens his *Silva* by recounting the River Arno's divine origin and by narrating the myth of the nymph Florence, born of Mars and Ianthe. He then reports the city's founding by Roman soldiers at the end of the Social War, before ending his poem with a celebration of Florence as the "moral capital" of Italy, eternally defending justice and liberty. Praise of Florence's justice and Roman heritage also characterizes the orations that Stefano Porcari delivered while serving as *capitano del popolo* (captain of the people) in 1427–1428.

Whereas Collenuccio's intention to flatter Lorenzo the Magnificent might make the sincerity of his statements suspect, Porcari's words unequivocally demonstrate his deep admiration for the Florentine government. Imbued with the republican ideals promoted by the first humanists, Porcari—himself a descendant of a noble Roman family—viewed Florence as the sole heir to the teaching of classical Rome. Following the example of Salutati, Bruni, and other Florentine writers, he commended Florence both for its military success against Milanese tyranny and for the popular character of its political system. Echoing the remark that the Queen of Sheba made to King Solomon on visiting his country, Porcari insisted that the splendor of Florence and the equity of its government were much greater than one could imagine. The lasting consequences of Porcari's stay in Florence are evident in the many orations he delivered as podestà in various Italian cities, and, more significantly, in his unsuccessful attempt to establish a republic in his native Rome. Finding Roman dignity oppressed by the treachery of the Curia, Porcari hoped to overthrow the pope and create a libertarian government modeled on the one he had observed in Florence. His conspiracy against Pope Nicholas V was immediately discovered, and the aborted revolution ended with Porcari's hanging. Porcari's short-lived revolution is a testament to the powerful inspiration the works of Florentine authors represented for thinkers in other parts of Italy.

By the middle of the quattrocento, the development of the myth of Florence had already reversed the relationship between the Tuscan city and its ancient mother. For the first time, it was Florence that gave Rome the language and the ideals to shape its own myth anew, as it would continue to do for other Italian cities throughout the Renaissance.

CLASSICAL ABBREVIATIONS

Here, listed alphabetically, are the classical authors and works cited in this anthology, followed in each case by the English title (in parentheses) and the abbreviations used in the notes. Wherever the notes cite *PL* and a number, the reference is to the volume in *Patrologia Latina*.

Aristotle, *Ethikon Nikomakeion* (*Nicomachean Ethics*): Arist., *Eth. Nic.*
——, *Politikon* (*Politics*): Arist., *Pol.*
Augustine, *Civitas Dei* (*The City of God*): Aug., *Civ. Dei.*
Aulus Gellius, *Noctes Atticae* (*Attic Nights*): Au. Gell.
Cicero, *De fato* (*On Fate*): Cic., *De fato*
——, *De finibus bonorum et malorum* (*On the Supreme Good and Evil*): Cic., *De fin.*
——, *De natura deorum* (*On the Nature of the Gods*): Cic., *De nat. deo.*
——, *De officiis* (*On Moral Obligation*): Cic., *De off.*
——, *De oratore* (*On the Making of an Orator*): Cic., *De orat.*
——, *De republica* (*The Republic*): Cic., *Rep.*
——, *Epistulae ad familiares* (*Letters to His Friends*): Cic., *Fam.*
——, *Oratio pro Archia poeta* (*On Behalf of Archias the Poet*): Cic., *Pro Arc.*
——, *Orationes in Catilinam* (*Speeches Against Catiline*): Cic., *Cat.*
——, *Paradoxa Stoicorum* (*Paradoxes of the Stoics*): Cic., *Par.*

——, *Tusculanae disputationes* (*Tusculan Disputations*): Cic., *Tusc.*

Demosthenes, *Peri tou stephanou* (*On the Crown*): Dem., *De cor.*

Diogenes Laertius, *Bioi* (*Lives of the Philosophers*): Diog. Laert.

Dionysus of Halicarnassus, *Romaikes archaiologias* (*Roman Antiquities*): Dion.

Florus, *Epitome* (*Epitome of Roman History*): Flor., *Epit. Hist.*

Hesiod, *Astronomia* (*Astronomy*): Hes., *Astr.*

Jerome, *Epistulae* (*Epistles*): Jer., *Epist.*

Juvenal, *Saturae* (*Satires*): Juv., *Sat.*

Livy, *Ab urbe condita* (*From the Founding of the City*): Liv.

Ovid, *Fastorum libri* (*Fasti*): Ov., *Fas.*

——, *Metamorphoseon libri* (*Metamorphoses*): Ov., *Met.*

Paulinus, *Vita sancti Ambrosii* (*Life of St. Ambrose*): Paul., *Vita Ambr.*

Plato, *Politeia* (*The Republic*): Pla., *Rep.*

Pliny, *Naturalis Historia* (*Natural History*): Pliny, *Nat. Hist.*

Procopius, *Upon ton polemon* (*History of the Wars*): Pro., *Hist.*

Propertius, *Elegiarum libri* (*Elegies*): Prop.

Ptolemy, *Geographikon* (*Geography*): Pto., *Geo.*

Sallust, *Bellum Catilinae* (*The Conspiracy of Catiline*): Sal., *Cat.*

——, *Bellum Iugurthinum* (*The Jugurthine War*): Sal., *Bel. Iug.*

Seneca, *Epistulae* (*Epistles*): Sen., *Epist.*

Silius Italicus, *Punicorum libri* (*Punica*): Sil., *Pun.*

Strabo, *Geographikon* (*Geography*): Stra., *Geo.*

Suetonius, *Vita Julii Caesaris* (*Life of Julius Caesar*): Sue., *Caes.*

Tibullus, *Elegiarum libri* (*Elegies*): Tib.

Varro, *De lingua latina* (*On the Latin Language*): Var., *Ling. Lat.*

Virgil, *Aeneis* (*The Aeneid*): Vir., *Aen.*

——, *Eclogae* (*The Eclogues*): Vir., *Ecl.*

——, *Georgica* (*The Georgics*): Vir., *Geo.*

SWITZERLAND

D. OF MILAN

D. OF SAVOY

Milan

VENETIAN REPUBLIC

Venice

D. OF FERRARA

Mantua

Parma

M. of Saluzzo

R. OF GENOA

Genoa

Modena

Bologna

OTTOMAN EMPIRE

DALMATIA

LIGURIAN SEA

Pisa

Leghorn

R. OF FLORENCE

Florence

Urbino

Ancona

Siena

Elba

R. OF SIENA

ADRIATIC SEA

Ragusa

CORSICA

PATRIMONY OF ST. PETER

ABRUZZI

Rome

SARDINIA

TYRRHENIAN SEA

Capua

Naples

APULIA

Bari

KINGDOM

Otranto

OF THE

TWO SICILIES

CALABRIA

Palermo

Messina

SICILY

M = Marquisate, D = Duchy, R = Republic

CITY PLAN OF

LATE QUATTROCENTO FLORENCE

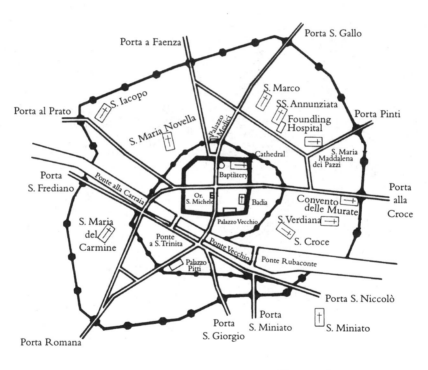

City plan showing churches, palaces, gates, and bridges of late Quattrocento Florence, including Porta a Faenza, Porta S. Gallo, S. Iacopo, Porta al Prato, S. Marco, SS. Annunziata, Porta Pinti, S. Maria Novella, Palazzo Medici, Foundling Hospital, Cathedral, S. Maria Maddalena dei Pazzi, Baptistery, Porta S. Frediano, Ponte alla Carraia, Or. S. Michele, Badia, Convento delle Murate, Porta alla Croce, Palazzo Vecchio, S. Verdiana, S. Maria del Carmine, Ponte a S. Trinita, Ponte Vecchio, S. Croce, Ponte Rubaconte, Palazzo Pitti, Porta S. Niccolò, Porta S. Giorgio, Porta S. Miniato, S. Miniato, Porta Romana.

1334 Walls
1175 Walls
Roman Walls

1397

January: The Byzantine Manuel Chrysoloras accepts Chancellor Coluccio Salutati's and Palla Strozzi's invitation to hold the first
chair in Greek at a European university since late antiquity. He
will serve at the University of Florence until 1400.

February: Gian Galeazzo Visconti once again wages war against Florence. Giovanni di Bicci de' Medici establishes the first branch
of the family bank.

1399

February 19: Milan purchases Pisa from its lord, Gherardo d'Appiano.

August 3: The Viscontean army seizes Siena.

1400

July 21: Perugia acknowledges Gian Galeazzo Visconti as its lord.

1401

February 2: Duke Robert of Bavaria is elected king of the Romans in
Frankfurt.

February 22:   Florence sends an ambassador to King Robert of Bavaria to persuade him to come to Italy to receive the imperial crown and help the Florentines fight against Milan. Having been promised 400,000 florins, Robert finally accepts and leaves for Italy on September 25.

October 24:   Near Brescia, the Milanese forces effortlessly defeat Robert of Bavaria's troops; this rout puts an end to the German king's intervention in Italy in support of the Florentines.

1402

June 26:   The Viscontean army defeats the Florentine forces at Casalecchio and seizes Bologna.

September 3:   Gian Galeazzo Visconti dies.

1403

September 3:   Papal troops free Bologna from Viscontean rule.

October 25:   Papal troops free Perugia from Viscontean rule.

1404

April 6:   Liberation of Siena from Viscontean rule enables Florence to regain access to the seaport of Talamone.

1406

October 9:   The Florentines conquer Pisa after a thirteen-month siege.

1408

April 21:   King Ladislas of Naples occupies Rome.

1409

March 27–
August 7:   Council of Pisa is organized to repair the Great Schism. The council fails to fulfill its purpose. Both the Avignon pope, Benedict XIII, and the Italian pope, Gregory XII, reject the council's decision to depose them. Far from putting an end to the Great Schism, the election of Alexander V on June 26 further weakens the papacy.

April:	Ladislas invades Tuscany and on June 3 takes Cortona.
June 27:	Florence joins the league created by Louis of Anjou, Siena, Pope Alexander V, and Cardinal Baldassarre Cossa, legate of Bologna, to fight Ladislas and claim the kingdom of Naples.

1410

May 3:	Alexander V dies. Cardinal Baldassarre Cossa, supported by the Medicean bank, becomes pope, taking the name John XXIII. The antipopes Benedict XIII and Gregory XII both refuse to acknowledge Cossa's election.

1411

January:	Two new councils are introduced into the Florentine political system: the Consiglio dei Duecento and the Consiglio dei Centotrentuno. Their creation is promoted mostly by conservative forces, to hamper any reform in favor of the lower classes.
January 4:	A peace treaty between Florence and King Ladislas of Naples is signed. Florence purchases Cortona from Ladislas on January 18.

1413

April 27:	A peace agreement is signed between Genoa and Florence, which enables the latter to regain full control of the important seaport of Porto Pisano.
June:	New war between Ladislas and the partners of the league is declared in June 1409.

1414

June 22:	A peace treaty is signed between Florence and Ladislas.
August 6:	Ladislas dies. Florence thereafter enjoys ten years' respite from foreign invaders.
November 5:	A council formed to remedy the Schism begins in Constance; it will last until 1418, up to the election of Martin V. The council decides, among other things, that ecumenical meetings are to be held at regular intervals and that the council is to

be acknowledged as the supreme authority for the Church, even greater than the pontiff himself.

1415

Statutes of the Florentine Commune is published, with the aim of reorganizing the laws accumulated over the past two centuries of Florentine history and resolving legal entanglements and redundancies.

1416

Piero de' Medici, Cosimo's eldest son, is born.

1417

October 2: Maso degli Albizzi, leader of the ruling Florentine oligarchy, dies. He is replaced at the head of the oligarchic faction by his son Rinaldo.

1419

December: The newly elected pope, Martin V, comes to Florence and is lodged at the convent of Santa Maria Novella, where he will reside for almost a year. There the pontiff is reconciled with the former antipope, John XXIII. Martin V's long stay in Florence brings about the re-establishment of the crucial alliance between the city and the Roman Curia.

1420

February 8: After several months of negotiations, Filippo Maria Visconti and Florence sign a peace treaty.

September 30: Pope Martin V enters Rome for the first time since his election. The papal Curia finally returns to Rome after the so-called second Babylonian captivity and the Great Schism.

1421

June: Florence purchases Leghorn from Genoa for a hundred thousand ducats.

The reorganization of the Florentine maritime trade is undertaken, entailing the election of six new officials known as consuls of the sea, two of whom must reside in Pisa. Among their tasks are presiding over the building of a fleet of galleys and assuring that regular convoys are sent to the main Mediterranean seaports.

June 3:   Giovanni di Cosimo de' Medici is born.

November 3:   Filippo Maria Visconti conquers Genoa.

1422

The first Florentine galleys arrive in Alexandria.

1424

April: In contravention of the 1420 peace treaty signed with Florence, Filippo Maria Visconti occupies Forlì, in the region of Romagna, thus instigating a new war on Florence.

July 28:   The Milanese army defeats the Florentines at Zagonara, near Faenza.

1425

October: In Tuscany, the Milanese forces prevail over the Florentines, first in Anghiari on October 9, then in La Faggiola on October 17.

December 4:   Florence and Venice agree to a ten-year anti-Viscontean alliance.

1426

March: Venice wages war on Milan and invades Lombardy. On March 17, Brescia falls to the Venetians, who plunder the surrounding countryside.

December 30:   A peace treaty ends the war of the Venetian-Florentine alliance against Milan. Of the three parties, only Venice profited from the war.

1427

May 27: The *catasto,* a new system of tax assessment, is introduced in Florence.

1429

February 20: Death of Giovanni di Bicci de' Medici. His son, Cosimo, had already taken over the responsibility for directing the family bank nine years earlier.

November: Florence starts an unsuccessful military campaign to conquer Lucca. The enterprise will be finally abandoned in 1433.

1431

March 3: The Venetian Cardinal Gabriele Condulmer is elected pope and assumes the name of Eugenius IV.

December 7: The first session of the Council of Basel takes place. Fearful of having his recent election contested, Eugenius IV does not attend the council, and through the bull of December 18, he orders it dissolved. Opposing the pope's decision and in accordance with the principles sanctioned at Constance, the council proceeds with its sessions, which will continue until 1443, despite unremitting strife with the pontiff and the official condemnation promulgated by Eugenius IV at the Council of Ferrara and Florence.

1433

September 7: At the order of the oligarchic government, Cosimo is arrested. On September 28 he is sentenced to ten years of exile in Padua.

December: The condottiere Francesco Sforza occupies the papal territory of the Marches.
The beginning of Cosimo's friendship with Francesco Sforza dates to this period. In order to lend him financial support without openly opposing the papal Curia, the Medici open a branch of their bank in Ancona.

1434

June 4: An angry mob, manipulated by certain Roman families (the Colonnas in particular) allied with the Visconti, forces Pope Eugenius IV to leave Rome. With the help of Rinaldo degli Albizzi and the anti-Medicean faction, the pontiff takes refuge in Florence, where he will remain, with few interruptions, until 1443.

October 5: Cosimo returns to Florence from exile. In the hope of receiving from the Medici the financial support necessary to reconquer his territories in the Marches, Eugenius IV helps Cosimo overthrow Rinaldo degli Albizzi. Rinaldo is then banished, together with the most influential opponents of Cosimo's new regime, most of whom take refuge in Siena before moving on to Milan. There follows the creation of a *balìa,* which allows Cosimo's family to rule over the city by retaining direct control over the electoral system.

1435

December 27: A popular revolt frees Genoa from Milanese rule.

1436

March 25: Eugenius IV consecrates the cathedral of Florence. Begun in 1420, Brunelleschi's dome is now completed, except for the lantern, which will be placed at its pinnacle by 1461.

1437

Cosimo de' Medici commissions Michelozzo to restore the Dominican convent of San Marco in Florence, which he will later endow with a vast collection of manuscripts, thereby rendering it one of the greatest libraries of religious texts in Europe at the time.

1438

January: The council for the union of the Greek and Roman churches opens in Ferrara.

1439

January: After a few months of unsuccessful deliberations, the ecclesiastical council leaves Ferrara for Florence, thus yielding to the requests of Cosimo de' Medici and his brother Lorenzo. Cosimo manages to be appointed standard-bearer of justice of the Florentine Republic in time for the welcome of the pontiff and the Byzantine authorities; his only previous election to this post was in 1435. The main sessions of the council proceed from February to August. Before leaving, Emperor John VIII Paleologus grants the Florentines the same commercial privileges and fiscal exemptions for trading in the Byzantine empire as had been granted to the merchants of Pisa in the thirteenth century. Upon their return to Constantinople, however, the Byzantine ecclesiastics and the emperor are forced by the enraged populace to revoke the agreements signed at the Florentine council on July 5, 1439.

1440

June: Spurred on by promises of success from Florentine exiles at the Milanese court, the Viscontean troops led by the condottiere Niccolò Piccinino invade Tuscany and occupy a location close to the Mugello Valley. On June 29, the Florentines defeat the Viscontean army in Anghiari. This crucial victory consolidates the Medici rule in Florence and definitively shatters the exiles' hopes of returning to power with the help of Milan.

1441

October 22: The Certame Coronario is held in the cathedral of Florence.

1442

February 2: Rinaldo degli Albizzi, Cosimo de' Medici's greatest opponent, dies in Ancona, where he had settled after his unsuccessful attempts to return to Florence and to regain control of the city with the help of Filippo Maria Visconti.

1443

September 19: Welcomed by a cheering crowd, Pope Eugenius IV returns to Rome.

1444

Michelozzo starts building the vast palace of Cosimo de' Medici in the Via Larga, near the cathedral of Florence, where the powerful family will reside from 1452 onward. In the eyes of fifteenth-century Florentines, the Medici Palace will immediately replace the Palazzo della Signoria as the symbol of the city government.

1445

September– Cosimo de' Medici succeeds in having himself elected
October: standard-bearer of justice for the third time, in order to pass laws aimed at strengthening his faction's control over the Florentine government.

1447

August 13: Filippo Maria Visconti dies, leaving no heirs to his rule. There follows the institution of the Ambrosian Republic.

1449

January 1: Lorenzo is born to Piero di Cosimo de' Medici and Lucrezia Tornabuoni.

1450

February 27: Francesco Sforza puts an end to the Milanese republic and gains control of the Lombard capital, thanks to the support of Cosimo de' Medici.

1452

January 30– Frederick III visits Florence on his way to Rome to be
February 6: crowned emperor. He will stop in the Tuscan city again on his return trip to Germany.

February 21: The treaty of Montil-les-Tours is signed, obliging France to come to the help of Florence and Milan should they be attacked and, in return, assures the French king Charles VII that neither one of those Italian powers will interfere if he decides to move against Naples. In response to this treaty, Venice and Naples declare war on Florence and Milan.

May 16: Venice invades Lombardy, while Ferdinand of Aragon marches on Tuscany with his army.

1453

January 5: Stefano Porcari's conspiracy against Pope Nicholas V fails; Porcari is captured and is executed four days later.

May 29: Constantinople falls to the Turks.

August 1: Summoned by the Florentines, René of Anjou departs from Marseille with an army to combat Ferdinand's invasion of Tuscany.

August 15: The Milanese inflict heavy losses on the Venetians at Ghedi, near Brescia. This episode is the first of a series of victories that in the autumn of 1453 will force the Venetian troops to retreat and to abandon most of the territories conquered in Lombardy.

1454

April 9: The Peace of Lodi is concluded, along with a pact establishing the so-called Italian League, which was to be observed for the next twenty-five years between Florence, Naples, Milan, Venice, and the papacy.

1455

March 25: Death of Pope Nicholas V. He is succeeded by Calixtus III (Alfonso Borgia).

1457

February: The Byzantine scholar Joannes Argyropoulos begins his tenure as professor of rhetoric at the University of Florence, a post he will keep until 1471.

1458

August 10:   Under pressure from Cosimo, the Florentine government creates a special executive committee, thus further assuring the Medici's power. This balìa, in fact, introduces the measures proposed by the Medicean party regarding the revision of the catasto and the system for election to public office. It also creates a new political body, the Consiglio dei Cento, entrusted with the task of supporting the previous councils in the administration of finances and in matters of war.

August 19:   The humanist Enea Silvio Piccolomini, as Pius II, succeeds Calixtus III on the papal throne.

1459

April 17–
May 5:   Pius II and the fifteen-year-old Galeazzo Maria Sforza visit Florence at the same time and are welcomed with great festivities.

1462

August: Cosimo de' Medici gives the villa at Careggi to the twenty-nine-year-old scholar of Greek Marsilio Ficino. This villa will soon become the seat of the celebrated Platonic Academy.

1463

April: Marsilio Ficino dedicates to Cosimo his Latin version of texts ascribed to Hermes Trismegistus. At his patron's request, Ficino begins a translation of Plato's dialogues, which he will complete five years later.

1464

April 13:   Milanese troops enter Genoa and take possession of the city. Until 1478, the Sforzas, Florence's main allies, will hold this seaport, crucial for both its strategic and commercial position.

August 1:   Cosimo de' Medici dies. Piero takes charge of the family bank and, unofficially, becomes the head of the Florentine government.

August 15:   Pope Pius II dies at the seaport of Ancona, while waiting in vain for the arrival of military support from the Italian states to start his crusade against the Turks. The Venetian Pietro Barbo succeeds to the papal throne under the name of Paul II.

1465

March 15:   By public decree, the title Pater Patriae (Father of the Country) is conferred on the late Cosimo de' Medici.

1466

March 8:   Francesco Sforza dies and is succeeded by his son, Galeazzo Maria.

August 27:   The conspiracy of Luca Pitti against Piero de' Medici is foiled, thanks to the intervention of Piero's son Lorenzo.

1467

January 4:   An anti-Venetian league is formed between Milan, Florence, and Naples.

July 25:   Near Faenza, the condottiere Count Frederick of Urbino, hired by the Florentine government, defeats Bartolomeo Colleoni, the captain-general of the Venetian republic.

1469

February 7:   The tournament celebrated by Luigi Pulci in his *La Giostra di Lorenzo de' Medici* is staged.

June 2–7:   The marriage of Lorenzo de' Medici with Clarice Orsini, a Roman noblewoman, is celebrated in Florence.

December 2:   Piero de' Medici dies.

1471

February 15:   Piero, Lorenzo's eldest son, is born.

March: Galeazzo Maria Sforza and his wife, Bona of Savoy, visit Florence.

1472

June 19:   Count Frederick of Urbino, hired by Lorenzo the Magnificent to suppress Volterra's rebellion against dominion by the Medici, enters the small town and plunders it. Lorenzo intends this violent reprisal to serve as a warning to all the other towns of the Florentine state. To legitimate the tactic, Lorenzo has numerous intellectuals of his court write propaganda in support of it.

December 22:   For economic reasons, Lorenzo transfers the Florentine university to Pisa.

1474

November 2:   Florence enters into a defensive league with Milan and Venice.

1475

January 29:   A tournament in honor of Giuliano de' Medici is held in Florence in the Piazza Santa Croce. To celebrate this event, intended officially to mark Florence's recent alliance with Venice and Milan, Poliziano starts the *Stanze per la giostra,* which he will leave unfinished after Giuliano's untimely death.

June 15:   With a papal bull, Sixtus IV officially founds the Vatican Library, first organized by the humanist pope Nicholas V.

December 11:   Giovanni, Lorenzo de' Medici's second son, is born.

1476

December 26:   In Milan, Galeazzo Maria is stabbed to death on his way to church. His only heir is his seven-year-old son Gian Galeazzo Maria. The Milanese duchy is left temporarily in the hands of Galeazzo Maria's wife, Bona of Savoy, who declares herself regent, and of the secretary Cicco Simonetta.

1477

The so-called Raccolta Aragonese is composed. Lorenzo de' Medici gives the anthology of poems to Frederick of Aragon,

King Ferdinand's son. Prefaced by a dedicatory letter by Poliziano, this is the first anthology of Italian literature in the vernacular.

1478

April 26:   Supported by Pope Sixtus IV, the Pazzi, a rich Florentine family, try to overthrow the Medici. The conspiracy fails, but Giuliano is murdered in the cathedral of Florence, and Lorenzo is wounded. Most of the conspirators are immediately captured and executed.

June 1:   Sixtus IV excommunicates Lorenzo de' Medici.

June 4:   The pope pronounces an interdict against Florence and wages war against the Tuscan city with the support of the kingdom of Naples. To counter the papal decision and legitimate the conduct of the Florentine government, Lorenzo has the principal humanists of his court write propaganda in his defense.

1479

September 7:   The forces of the Neapolitan-papal coalition defeat the Florentines at Poggibonsi, near Florence, then plunder the Tuscan countryside in Val di Chiana and Val d'Elsa.

September 8:   Summoned by Bona of Savoy, Ludovico Il Moro enters Milan peacefully; this marks a crucial step toward his ultimate seizure of the duchy.

December 6:   Without an armed escort, Lorenzo goes to Naples in hope of convincing King Ferdinand of Aragon to remain at peace.

1480

March 13:   A peace treaty is signed at last between Lorenzo and Ferdinand of Aragon.

April 10:   Less than a month after his return from Naples, Lorenzo manages to introduce the Consiglio dei Settanta into the Florentine political system so as to strengthen his own control on the election of the signoria. The Settanta also receive the authority of choosing from among their members both the officials of the Otto di Pratica appointed to take care of the city's foreign politics, and the Dodici procuratori, entrusted with the administration of the revenue.

July 25: A league is formed between Milan, Florence, and Naples to counter the alliance signed between Sixtus IV and Venice on April 16.

August 11: The Turks take the southern Italian seaport of Otranto, in Apulia.

December 3: Sixtus IV withdraws the interdict against Florence pronounced on June 4, 1478.

1481

Shortly before his death, Charles of Anjou makes King Louis XI of France sole heir to his dominion and possessions. This decision leads to a considerable increase in the power of the French royalty, but also to future French claims to the throne of Naples.

August 30: The first edition of Dante's *Commedia* is printed in Florence, with a commentary by Landino and drawings by Botticelli.

1482

May: The Venetians invade the Ferrarese territory, marking the beginning of the so-called War of Ferrara, which pits Florence, Milan, and Naples against Venice and the papacy.

August 30: King Louis XI of France dies. He is succeeded by Charles VIII.

1484

August 7: The Peace of Bagnolo puts an end to the "War of Ferrara."

August 29: Pope Sixtus IV, Florence's greatest enemy, dies. He is succeeded by Innocent VIII, the Genoese Cardinal Giovan Battista Cibo.

November: The philosopher Giovanni Pico della Mirandola arrives in Florence and immediately becomes one of the most active members of Ficino's academy.

1486

May 7:   The league created by Milan, Florence, and Naples in July 1480 defeats the papal troops in Montorio, in the territory of the Orsini family. This loss necessitates the pope's signing of a peace treaty on August 11 and induces him to give up his attempt to set the southern Italian barons against the house of Aragon.

1487

March: Lorenzo de' Medici's son Piero is married to Alfonsina Orsini. The marriage is seen as a means of strengthening the relationship with this powerful Roman family.

June 22:   Florence defeats the Genoese on the Ligurian border and seizes the important stronghold of Sarzana.

July 10:   The Sforzas regain control of Genoa.

1488

January 20:   Lorenzo the Magnificent's daughter, Maddalena de' Medici, marries Franceschetto Cibo, son of Pope Innocent VIII.

June 9:   The Florentine army seizes Faenza, whose lord, Galeotto Manfredi, has been murdered a few days earlier (May 31).

1489

March 9:   Lorenzo de' Medici succeeds in having his thirteen-year-old son Giovanni elected cardinal, the youngest candidate—as his father proudly points out—on whom such honor has ever been conferred. Giovanni will become pope in 1513, taking the name Leo X.

1490

June: The friar Girolamo Savonarola returns to Florence (where he has previously stayed in 1482–1484) and on August 1 starts preaching in the Dominican convent of San Marco. For a whole year he will lecture on Revelations.

1491

July: Savonarola is elected prior of the convent of San Marco.

1492

April 8:   With Pico, Savonarola, and Poliziano at his bedside, Lorenzo the Magnificent dies in his villa at Careggi. The Medicean oligarchy officially acknowledges his son Piero de' Medici, known as the Unfortunate, as the new ruler of Florence.

August 11:   The Spanish cardinal Roderigo Borgia is elected pope and takes the name Alexander VI.

1494

August 22:   Led by King Charles VIII, the French troops march on Italy to conquer the kingdom of Naples, which the French sovereign, as heir to Anjou, claims as his due.

September 2:   The French army crosses the Alps.

November 9:   Piero de' Medici is driven out of Florence. All his family's possessions are confiscated.

November 17:   King Charles VIII of France enters Florence and is welcomed by a cheering crowd.

November 26:   King Charles VIII signs an agreement with the Florentine government in which he is given a loan of 120,000 florins to continue his military campaign against southern Italy. In return, the king is to yield to Florence Pisa and all the other Tuscan strongholds he has occupied. He also swears not to help Piero de' Medici return to Florence.

November 28:   Charles VIII leaves Florence.

December 2:   A popular meeting abolishes the councils that the Medici have introduced in the course of the preceding decades to control the Florentine government. A temporary council of twenty men is entrusted with the task of preparing lists of citizens eligible to participate in the next signoria. These changes mark the beginning of a more republican form of government, after seventy years of Medicean rule.

December 24:   The Florentine Great Council is instituted, by a large majority of votes.

1495

February 22:   Charles VIII enters Naples with his army and conquers the kingdom.

March 31:   Milan, Venice, Pope Alexander VI, Emperor Maximilian, and King Ferdinand of Spain join together to fight Charles VIII. Florence refuses to enter the league.

May 20:   Abandoned by his allies Ludovico Il Moro and Pope Alexander VI, Charles VIII is forced to leave Naples and head back to France.

June 10:   As Charles VIII is marching north toward the Po Valley, the duke of Orleans leads his forces to seize Novara. This unexpected victory, which offers the French an opportunity to take all of Lombardy, prompts Venice to intervene.

July 6:   The Battle of Fornovo takes place near Parma between Charles VIII and the troops of the anti-French league. Although outnumbered, the French army manages to resist. Nonetheless, Charles VIII has little choice but to continue his retreat to France. He has failed to claim any territory on the peninsula, including the kingdom of Naples.

July 21:   The pope summons Savonarola to appear before the Roman Curia.

October 9:   Ludovico Il Moro and Charles VIII sign the Treaty of Vercelli. The duke of Milan promises to provide the king with military support the next time he undertakes an expedition to conquer the kingdom of Naples. This agreement marks the end of Charles VIII's campaign in Italy.

October 16:   Alexander VI forbids Savonarola to continue preaching and requests him to appear in front of the Curia to discuss his alleged gift of prophesy.

1496

French officials, ignoring the treatise signed by Charles VIII, surrender Pisa to the Pisans, rather than giving it back to the Florentines. To reconquer this crucial post, Florence begins a campaign that will last until 1509.

August 20:   For the second time, the Florentine signoria refuses to join the

anti-French league and does its best to delay Emperor Maximilian's ambassadors, who have come to sue for support in
their fight against Charles VIII.

November 16: The fleet of Emperor Maximilian, anchored outside Leghorn
since October, is seriously damaged by a storm, which many
Florentines regard as a miracle.

1497

February 7: One of the largest processions of Savonarola's *fanciulli* through
the streets of Florence culminates in a bonfire of the vanities in
the Piazza della Signoria.

April 27: Piero de' Medici's attempt to return with an army to Florence
is foiled.

May 5: The signoria, now composed mostly of anti-Savonarolans,
prohibits all forms of preaching in Florence.

May 13: Pope Alexander VI excommunicates Savonarola.

1498

February 11: Savonarola resumes preaching.

March 17: The pope issues an interdict against Florence for not having
taken strict measures to silence Savonarola. He also orders that
all Florentine merchants in Rome be arrested and their goods
be confiscated.

March 18: Savonarola delivers his last sermon in the Church of San
Marco. On the same day, the Florentine merchants in Rome
write to the signoria urging the signori to take action against
Savonarola.

April 7: King Charles VIII dies. His successor, Louis XII, immediately
reasserts the family's right to the throne of Naples and prepares
a new campaign in Italy.

April 8: Yielding to pressure by the pope and the anti-Savonarolan
party, the Florentine authorities arrest the Ferrarese preacher.

May 23: Following the torture of the Dominican friar and a two-day
summary process conducted by the papal officials, Girolamo
Savonarola is executed. During the period from 1498 to 1502,
a republican government is established to preserve the institu-

tions created on December 2, 1494. Responsibility for directing the government, however, will fall on the Standard-bearer for life, a newly created post that will be held by Piero Soderini. The Florentine Republic will collapse in September 1512, upon the Medici's return to the city with the help of the Spanish army.

PART ONE

Origins

I

A Defense of the Roman Origins of Florence

COLUCCIO SALUTATI

Coluccio Salutati (1331–1406) is commonly thought to have had a seminal influence on the passage from medieval culture to humanism started by Petrarch. Some of the most momentous cultural events of the second half of the fourteenth century are linked to Salutati, who was chancellor of Florence from 1375 until his death. Thanks to him and Palla Strozzi, for instance, Manuel Chrysoloras, the famous Byzantine scholar, came to the University of Florence in 1397 to hold the first chair in Greek at a modern European university, an event duly recorded and celebrated by many fifteenth-century writers. Another sign of the profound cultural change taking place in Florence at that time is Salutati's polemic against the Dominican Giovanni Dominici. On this occasion, Salutati defended the merits of classical literature and poetry against the accusations of conservative ecclesiastics, who thought such humanist interests incompatible with Christian piety. He participated in the discussions organized by Luigi Marsili in the Florentine church of Santo Spirito, and intellectuals from all over Italy turned to him for advice on literary and philosophical topics. Among Salutati's renowned students were the humanists Leonardo Bruni and Poggio Bracciolini; some of their early writings, however, reveal ideas at odds with those of their teacher, whose mentality, despite his vast erudition, came to seem old-fashioned to his innovative pupils.

Salutati's numerous works are also notable for their meticulously detailed treatment of diverse subjects. His extensive collection of private letters and the series of official documents he wrote on behalf of the Florentine Republic bear witness to his rhetorical skill and intense intellectual activity. Filippo Villani considered Salutati's De saeculo et religione *(1381) the equal of Plato's* Phaedo *as a paean to the contemplative life. As for his other works, the erudite yet unfinished* De laboribus Herculis *is a monument to the medieval search for allegorical meaning in classical mythology, and* De nobilitate legum et medicinae *continues Petrarch's defense of the superior value of literary studies by comparison with the limitations of the scientific method.*

Either directly or indirectly, much of Salutati's literary output served political aims, as illustrated in the text we include here, the famous Invective Against Antonio Loschi of Vicenza. *Salutati wrote this piece against the Visconti secretary, a fellow humanist, shortly after the end of Florence's victorious war against Milan in 1402. He reports Loschi's accusations against the republic and rebuts them systematically by resorting to examples drawn from the history of the city. The Ciceronian structure of the text itself emphasizes the Roman origins of Florence and its unique cultural heritage, and Salutati explicitly discusses the foundation of the Tuscan city. In this respect, it is noteworthy that Salutati preferred not to follow Giovanni Villani's traditional version: Florence was certainly built by Romans, as numerous archaeological remains and ancient authors attest, but it is impossible to indicate the precise date or identify the founders. The hybrid nature of this work, in which medieval attitudes and nascent humanistic tenets are intermingled, also characterizes much of the rest of Salutati's thought. We present an excerpt here.*

Source: Coluccio Salutati, *Invectiva in Antonium Luschum Vicentinum,* in *Prosatori latini del Quattrocento,* ed. Eugenio Garin (Milan: Ricciardi, 1952), pp. 8–22.

INVECTIVE AGAINST ANTONIO LOSCHI OF VICENZA

Who could bear to stand aside and let strangers shamefully slander our home-land, to which we owe everything? I would like to bring this case before a prince and argue it in the presence of our enemies themselves. I would like to listen to them speak, in order to understand the reasons for their lies and see what sort of evidence and arguments they bring forth. I dare say I would so thoroughly give them what they deserve that they would never again hurl their insults at that city which they have been unable to defeat—and, by God, they never will defeat us—not even with those mighty forces of which you [Antonio Loschi] boast. Since I am a citizen and a member of this community, and no longer a stranger, I intend to plead the cause of my homeland, which every-one should strive to defend with all his might. I entreat those who read my words to listen to me with benevolence as I speak in defense of truth, justice, and my homeland. Since you, my readers, have managed to suffer my opponent's irreverence—with reluctance, I imagine—I beg you to be patient with me and listen to my words.

I wish to start by quoting my opponent's words, one after the other, exactly as he wrote them, and I shall then reply separately to each one of his assertions. You, Loschi, began your venomous speech as follows: *Someday, wretched citizens who have destroyed your country and disrupted peace in all Italy, you will finally suffer the just punishment for your crimes and pay the penalties you deserve. Someday your followers will be so horrified at your tremendous corruption as to fear their own ruin on account of their misdeeds. Your fall, therefore, will be not only a legitimate vindication but also a useful example. Someday your scheming, in which your entire force lies, will finally be discovered and revealed to all, thereby showing your opponents' wisdom and, by contrast, your depravity and utter wickedness.*

At the very beginning of your oration, as your words attest, you seem to express three wishes. Like a raging madman with a harsh tongue, you invoke the Furies' aid, a sign of extreme desperation, in making the Florentines suffer base and undeserved punishments. You wish their ruin to be an example to all; to terrify all with the Florentines' misfortune. You wish, thus, that a due vindication would also become a useful example. You wish our plots to be discovered, and others to appear wise, while the Florentines seem wicked, as you think they truly are. I shall now briefly explain how foolish the beginning of your oration is and what it really conveys to readers. Is there any prince or lord against whom these same accusations could not be hurled, if one let himself get carried away by wrath? If these words were pronounced against your lord, O Loschi, who could assert that they were spoken unjustly? What else would one need do, apart from substituting the word "tyrant" for "citizens" and replacing the plural with the singular? But let us leave out your lord and all the dead, to whom one should always show greater respect than to those who are alive. Tell me, if you will: Is it not true that your words prove you a fierce and deadly enemy of the Florentines? Answer, if you please: Are you acting as prosecutor or witness? If the latter is the case—namely, if you claim to be a witness and act as such, while at the same time you openly confess to being an enemy of those you are accusing—how can you hope to be considered the least bit trustworthy? Was there ever an efficacious prosecutor who merely asserted the veracity of his accusations or hurled invective at the accused? Without bringing forth any evidence, one can never convince the court to convict the accused, be the prosecutor Cicero, Demosthenes, the virtuous Cato, Antony, Crassus,

Aeschines opposing Demosthenes, or any other accomplished orator speaking in the senate or a court of law, or even all these figures put together.

Recognize your ignorance, therefore, and acknowledge your mistake; learn, you mad and foolish beast, that before both the senate and the people no trust is or should be granted to the accuser and witnesses if they prove to be enemies of the accused, even if the judges, whether senators or the people, happen to be ill disposed toward the accused, as is often the case. Each time the accuser or the witnesses asked to testify show this rage and aversion which you demonstrate so candidly, they either unwittingly behave like madmen or consider the members of the court stupid. They believe they can convince the audience that their insane statements are true, and they strive to induce the judges to commit an obvious folly or a shameful injustice. Who, in fact, would be so mad and naive as to trust an accuser or a witness who openly demonstrates his hostility or confesses himself an enemy of the accused?

You call the Florentines "wretched citizens who have destroyed your country and disrupted peace in all Italy." "Wretched citizens," you say. If your aim is to insult the Florentines, what you say is an outright lie. The term "wretched citizens" may, in fact, apply to those who squander their possessions and lead a wicked life, committing immoral acts and all sorts of sins; truthfully speaking, however, the Florentines who do not deserve to be dubbed wretched are far more numerous. You must confess that, by consensus, many of them should and must be acknowledged as good citizens, not wretched ones. At any rate, it does not behoove our enemy to complain about this; we [not you] are the ones who should deplore wicked citizens, for it is in our interest to have good and useful citizens who help our republic.

This is a matter of concern to us, but what you said regarding those of us who have destroyed your country also concerns us. What does it mean to destroy a country, if not to ruin it? Now, if you are referring to our country [Florence], you should not deplore it, but wish it to happen. If, on the other hand, you are referring to Liguria, Romagna, and Veneto, oppressed by your lord's yoke, I urge you to be distressed about it, for far from inveighing against those you call the destroyers of your enemies' country and lamenting the fate of the rest of Italy, you should wish to have them as the rulers of your own region. In Italy there are many people who are not subject to your lord; they rule their own territory, have freedom of speech, and know how to use it. Have rulers or citizens of these regions ever complained about the things of which you are now accusing us? If, as you assert, we disrupted the peace of all Italy, all Italy would be our enemy. This is not the case, but, on the contrary, wherever the serpent[1] that hates justice has not imposed his yoke and spread his venom, the Florentines are allowed to dwell, and people love them for their mercantile activities. Is it not clear, thus, that your assertions counter this factual evidence and that the word "fraud," which you use to accuse the Florentines, should rather be employed to describe you? I suppose you use the word "plot" in the meaning of "hidden fraud"; you would not wish to expose all these things, in fact, if you did not believe such plots to be secret. But who taught you to accuse your enemies of such things? Who has ever cared whether his enemy's actions were fraudulent or virtuous? At any rate, please tell me: When has the Florentine Republic ever plotted against either your lord or anyone else? When has it ever attacked anyone other than its enemies? Nothing keeps you from throwing these insults at anyone you wish; but it is not enough to utter such things, you must also provide proof of your statements.

Let us listen once more, however, to this new, furious prophet of ours: *We shall see,* you say, *your famous Roman steadfastness and strength in defending your shameful liberty, or, should I say, your most fierce tyranny. You always pride yourselves on claiming descent from the Romans, but I shall explain at another time the greatness of your impudent behavior.*

We shall see, you say, but, in truth, you have already seen, as you do now and will again in the future, the steadfastness and the fortitude of the Florentines, superior even to that of the Romans, in defending their most beloved liberty; a divine gift, as the saying goes, more precious than all the money in the world. All Florentines are firmly committed to using their riches and their weapons to protect their lives, as well as this priceless blessing that they have received from their elders. They actually prize it even more than life itself, and wish to pass it down to their sons, by God's will, intact and pure. Great is our love for the liberty that you, most foolish of all men, call shameful; only those who have never experienced it, like yourself, fail to appreciate it and to understand its value. The people of Lombardy alone—I do not know if it is due to their nature, or their lifestyle, or both—seem neither to desire nor to love liberty. You are the only one, however, who considers this, God's greatest gift, to be a vile and despicable thing. I truly doubt that you will find anyone who shares your opinion, not even among those who live with you under the rule of your Lord, since the love of liberty is something completely natural. I think you should be called servant of the servants,[2] not on account of your humility, but because of your vice. But why do I even call you servant, since you enjoy your servitude to the point of not refraining from calling liberty shameful, considering it a most fierce tyranny, which is a sign of even greater insanity? I am sure your definition will make many people laugh, but I find it truly detestable. Have you ever known any form of liberty, either in Italy or abroad, which can be said to be greater and purer than Florentine liberty, or even [to be] its equal? Is the tyranny that oppresses you so tremendous that it forces you to consider Florentine liberty a form of tyranny? I know that to abide by the law in order to preserve one's freedom can be hard; it can even look like a kind of slavery, especially to a reckless young man, always eager to fulfill his material desires and yield to passion. I can easily understand how you and people like you not only fail to appreciate the value of liberty, but even abhor its very name and its effects as something awful. Livy, too, substantiates this, in his usual expressive style, when he writes about the attempt to bring monarchy back to Rome. "There were Roman youths," he writes, "born into well-off families, who—being of the same age as the Tarquins, and their friends—had grown used to a regal lifestyle, since they had enjoyed complete license under the monarchy. They considered equality of rights as lack of order and lamented that the liberty of all had led to their enslavement."[3] Since human beings are curious about the things they desire, they naturally dedicate themselves to pursuing them; I suppose, thus, that you have read the above-mentioned words and other similar passages by this excellent author and have finally come to the conclusion that liberty, the sweetest of all things, is a fierce tyranny and something despicable. I would gladly leave it up to you to judge how foolish and inane your statements are; but since you do not speak for yourself alone, but on behalf of others, I must make your opinion known to all my readers.

Among other things, you do not believe that the Florentines descended from the Romans. Tell me, if you will, where have you found proof to the contrary? Why do you want to deny what all Italy grants us, what everyone, except you, horrible beast, holds to be true, what even Rome herself and the Roman princes have always admitted by considering and calling us their sons, flesh of their flesh, bones of their bones, unique honor and glory of their name? To make you feel ashamed of your foolishness in having doubted all this, I want to relate what I believe is the origin of our great city, using authors I can cite. Since you promised to show how impudent we are in claiming to be the offspring of the Romans, my account will acquaint you with the truth, and prevent you from ranting any further.

Regarding the origin of Florence, a difficult subject buried in antiquity, I would certainly be disposed to believe that this glorious people and famous city derive from a small yet noble source. Nevertheless, there is no doubt that Florence has a more illustrious origin than one might expect. It is known, in fact, that the ancient people of Fiesole moved to our city. Tradition has it that they came to our city after having been defeated in war, although some hold that the people of Fiesole, being mountain dwellers, were inspired to move simply because of the beauty of the land. It is not surprising that we do not know precisely how things actually happened. Who knows, for instance, the exact origin of Rome, not to mention the origin of other cities? We read that, having reached Italy with the gods' help and at Carmentis' bidding, Evander and the Arcadians went up the Tiber and arrived at a city called Valentia, at the exact site where Rome was later founded.[4] By looking at the etymology of the name, the Arcadians translated the Latin *Valentia* into "Rome." This is why some believe the Arcadians to be the ones to have named the city Rome, not Romus. The founder of the city, in fact, was called Romus, not Romulus, as is clearly attested by the name of the city itself, Roma, not Romula. Varro, for instance, writes "Romus."[5] Where can we find information on the ancient author of the name Valentia and the foundation of that city? We have also inherited from the Romans the tradition that the precise origins of our city remain unknown, as is the case with Rome herself, which is further proof to the ancient foundation of Florence.

As for the founders of our city, there is precise evidence attesting to the fact that Florence was built by the Romans. In the center of Florence, there is a capitol building with a forum right next to it; there is, moreover, the so-called Parlascio or amphitheater, as well as places called Terme, Capacia, and a neighborhood called Parione.[6] There is a temple that was once consecrated to Mars, whom pagans believed to be the father of the Roman people. It must be noted that this temple is built in a style not Greek or Etruscan, but utterly Roman.[7] I also want to mention another element confirming our Roman origin, although it no longer exists: until the third decade of the fourteenth century after the incarnation of Christ (mediator between God and mankind) an equestrian statue of Mars stood on the Ponte Vecchio. People preserved it as a testimonial to our entirely Roman origin, but the flood that destroyed three of Florence's bridges swept it away seventy years ago November 4. Many people still alive today saw it and remember it.

We still possess, moreover, the arches and other remains of the aqueducts built in ancient Roman style that brought fresh water to the city for public use. Since all these Roman ruins are still to be found here today, together with Roman names and the customs of that ancient people, who would dare say, against such strong evidence of our illustrious origins, that the authors of such things were not the Romans? Anyone who has ever seen the round towers and

9

the ruins of the city gates, which are now attached to the bishop's palace, would not only suspect but actually swear that they were built by the Romans—and not merely because of the material out of which they are made, namely tiles and bricks, but because of the style itself.

It need not surprise us, therefore, if, relying upon such solid elements, the Florentines have always maintained the belief that our city was built by the Romans in order to oppose Fiesole. Strong evidence of the people of Fiesole's deep hatred for the Romans is provided by writings on the Social War,[8] a conflict in which Fiesole and many other cities were razed to the ground. It is thus complete folly to doubt the Roman origin of Florence. In Sallust, a most trustworthy historian, we read that Catiline sent a certain Caius Manilius to recruit an army in the territory of Fiesole. The people of Etruria "were eager for a revolution," he writes, "because of both poverty and the wrong they had suffered, having lost their fields and all their possessions under Sulla's rule. Manilius thus managed to recruit a vast army by assembling all the many criminals of various sorts who lived in that region and some of the settlers sent by Sulla, who, because of their debauchery and lack of restraint, had soon squandered all the wealth they had amassed through great plunderings."[9]

Let us return, now, to your accusations: *We shall see the vain and foolish arrogance of the Florentines and their insolence,* you say, *and find out how much truth there is in the abundance of praise they unjustly receive.*

You accuse the Florentines of a vain and foolish arrogance. Who would say that the Florentine government has boasted of anything in its letters, sent all over the world? Arrogance is a characteristic that is preoccupied with the future, and we leave such behavior to you and people like yourself. It is typical of the Florentines' seriousness, in fact, not to make bold claims about the future, as you do with your foolish prophecies. But we shall discuss this later. If, as I believe, by "arrogance" and "insolence" you mean the taking of pride in one's own merits, there are no lords in Italy, nor nations in the world that can more deservedly and rightly take pride in their deeds in war and peace than the Florentines, who, however, boast little indeed. After all, there is no glory more complete than that which proceeds from true merit. I do not mean to offend anyone, but would it not be proper to remember, for example, the deeds carried out by this free people in wars fought either to defend its own liberty, as it has often done, or to maintain an agreement, as it has always done? Is it some kind of vain and foolish arrogance to pride oneself on what is true? If I wanted now to collect all your lord's deeds and sayings, since I ignore your own, Loschi, and those achievements of which he boasts, I am sure that the Florentines could hardly be accused of such boasting in either public or private, unless one attacked them, as is your custom, with false accusations. But let us now move on to investigate the truth of your other assertions.

1. The symbol of Milan.
2. Salutati employs sarcasm in this biblical expression (*servus servorum Dei*), which has been used by the papal Curia to sign its official documents since the ninth century.
3. Liv., 2.3.1–3.
4. See Ov., *Fas.,* 1.461–586.
5. See Var., *Ling. Lat.,* 5.33.
6. Most of these names are still in use today, though no longer to indicate neighborhoods or particular sites, but rather streets.
7. On the alleged Roman origin of the Florentine baptistery, see Bruni's account (document 2).
8. On the Social War and its consequences, see Bruni's account (document 2).
9. Sal., *Cat.,* 28.4.

The Republican Legacy

LEONARDO BRUNI

Because the Historiae *by Leonardo Bruni, the chancellor of Florence, have strongly affected modern historiography as a whole, it would be hard to overestimate their import. Bruni's text influenced later historians for many reasons and in a variety of ways. In inaugurating a monographic style of historiography, he abandoned the universalistic, encyclopedic outlook of medieval chroniclers, who merely listed the significant events from the creation of the world up to their own time. Moreover, Bruni's subtle eloquence, along with his astute use of sources, reveals the character of an intellectual whom various scholars have rightly considered a forerunner of Machiavelli.*

These features of Bruni's writing are also apparent in his version of the origins of Florence, another area of interpretation on which, as can be easily understood, the chancellor had a lasting influence. After Tacitus, Bruni was the first historiographer to criticize the Roman Empire not from a religious point of view but from a genuinely political one. Contrary to the opinion of medieval authors, who considered Caesar's coming to power the most glorious moment in the history of Rome, Bruni saw in the event not only the ruin of the Roman Republic but also the ruin of the noble ideals it had fostered. In contrast to such thinkers as Giovanni Villani, Bruni believed that the city had been founded by veterans of Sulla's army around 80 B.C., well before Cicero's death and Caesar's rise to power. In his account of the origins of Florence, Bruni significantly reworked the thesis expressed some fifteen years earlier by his teacher Coluccio Sa-

lutati, the late chancellor, in the invective composed against the Visconti secretary An-
tonio Loschi.

Source: Leonardo Bruni, *Historiarum Florentini populi libri XII*, ed. Emilio Santini, in *Rerum italicarum scriptores* (Città di Castello: Lapi, 1914), 19.2–3, pp. 3–6.

PREFACE

For a long time I have debated with myself whether or not to record the history of the Florentines: their civil discord, their struggles against foreign enemies, and their glorious deeds in peace and war, the awesome nature of which enticed me to engage in such a project. The Florentines first faced civil discord and upheaval, then fought bravely against their neighbors, and finally attained such great power in our time that they could stand up to both the potent duke of Milan and the bellicose King Ladislas, making all Italy, from the Alps to Apulia, tremble under the clash of arms, and even causing kings and mighty armies from France and Germany to cross the Italian borders. Additionally, the Florentines have seized Pisa, which—because of the differing nature of the two cities or their rivalry, or on account of the outcome of the war—should be rightly called, I believe, another Carthage. The attack on and final capture of Pisa, in which both the vanquished and the conquerors showed an equal tenacity, are such memorable events that they do not seem of lesser merit than those great ancient deeds that we are accustomed to admire in our readings.

I certainly find these things worthy of being recorded in a book, and I recognize that knowledge of them would be useful to one's private and public life. For if we believe older men to be wiser by virtue of their greater experience in life, how much more wisdom can history offer us, provided that we read it carefully? In it, we see the deeds and the teachings of many centuries, such that one can easily decide which examples to follow and which to eschew, and thus be inspired by the glory of excellent men to act virtuously.

On the other hand, the magnitude of the task discouraged me, as did the lack of information regarding certain periods, the incompleteness of the documents, the very rudeness of the names (so unresponsive to the polishing of eloquence),[1] and a slew of other difficulties. After having pondered all this for a long time, I finally came to the conclusion that any form of writing was preferable to idle silence. Thus I started to write, fully aware of my own limitations and the difficulty of the task. I hope God will favor my enterprise and help me persevere in it. If my ability does not suffice for the work I have undertaken, I hope He will benevolently assist one who strives and endeavors. If only our ancestors, whatever their education and eloquence, had written the history of their time rather than remaining silent! The main task of the learned, if I am not mistaken, is to prevent the principal episodes of their age from being forgotten and to pass them on to posterity through writing. I believe, however, that there have been as many reasons for remaining silent as there have been men: some men were held back by the arduous nature of the task, some by their lack of ability; others preferred other forms of writing to history. One can easily compose a booklet or a letter, for example, without too much effort. With history, however, it is necessary to write a long and orderly account, to provide an exact explanation of every single fact and its causes, and to comment upon each one of them. The immense magnitude of the enterprise is such that it may overwhelm the writer; it is, in fact, as dangerous to promise a work of history as it is difficult to complete it. Consequently, as everyone is fundamentally concerned only with his own tranquillity or reputation, the public good is neglected and the memory of great men and important deeds vanishes.

I have therefore resolved to report the documented history of this city, concerning not only this present age but also times as far back as the available documents permit. This will necessarily lead me to discuss Italian history as well, for nothing worth recalling has taken place in Italy for a long time without the intervention of the Florentine factions. Moreover, in explaining why embassies were either sent out or received by this city, I shall have to detail the affairs of other nations. Before addressing the period that is the main topic of my work, however, I intend to follow the example of some historians[2] and state what I consider the correct account of Florence's foundation and origins. In doing so, I shall refute some of the fables believed by the majority. This will facilitate the reader's understanding of the events I shall narrate in the following pages.

BOOK ONE

The founders of Florence were Roman settlers sent to Fiesole by Sulla. They were veterans of his army who, as a reward for their excellent deeds both in the campaigns and during the civil war, received part of the territory of Fiesole, the town itself, and dominion over the old inhabitants. The Romans used the term "colony" to indicate the relocation of citizens and their allotment of land. This meant that the settlers received fields to cultivate and on which to establish themselves.[3] To better understand what happened, it is necessary to explain why these new settlers had been sent there in particular. A few years before Sulla's dictatorship, almost all the people of Italy rebelled simultaneously against Rome. They protested because they had not been allowed to share in the spoils, after having fought alongside the Romans on many occasions and having undertaken hardship and danger to expand the empire. Having often lamented this situation, they finally resolved to appoint legates and send them to Rome to request a share in the honors and the offices of the empire, which was tantamount to asking to be made Roman citizens. The question was raised during the tribunate of Marcus Drusus, and the final decision, repeatedly postponed, remained uncertain for a long time. Once the petition was finally rejected, however, the people of Italy immediately started an open revolt against the Romans and waged war, wishing to punish them for what they held to be ingratitude. Since this war was fought by Rome's former allies, it is known as the Social War.[4] The Romans eventually won the war and inflicted heavy damage on the provinces that had led the revolt. In the Marches and in Tuscany, they treated the population unusually harshly; they sacked Ascoli, the most flourishing center in Piceno, and razed the Tuscan city of Chiusi to the ground. Besides the damage and the losses caused by war, the people of Arezzo and Fiesole also suffered tremendous calamities at the hands of the Romans: many properties were confiscated, many people were forced to flee, and the cities were left with few inhabitants.

Thus, after Sulla became dictator, he had the opportunity, or rather free rein, to reward his veterans with these lands. Many settlers, upon arrival in Fiesole, felt that it was unnecessary to live in a city located on top of a steep mountain, especially since the area around the mountain was securely defended by the Roman Empire. They thus moved down to the valley and began to construct their houses along the banks of the rivers Arno and Mugnone. Since this new city was located between two rivers, they first named it Fluentia,[5] and its inhabitants were called Fluentini. This name remained in use for quite some time, as the city developed and became considerably larger. "Fluentia" was eventually replaced by "Florentia," either because, as often happens, the word was simply corrupted, or because the city was flourishing.

In their writings, Cicero and Sallust—those most excellent Latin authors—mention these settlers.[6] Cicero asserts that they were worthy and valiant Roman citizens who displayed no frugality whatsoever once they found themselves unexpectedly and suddenly enriched by Sulla in the aftermath of the civil war. They thoughtlessly spent money on buildings, numerous slaves, sumptuous banquets, and great spectacles. Consequently, they ran up such great debts that to free themselves from this situation they would have needed to raise Sulla from the dead. In regard to these settlers, I wish to attach great importance to what the father of Latin eloquence [Cicero] writes about the buildings they erected, for it leads me to believe that this city must have been magnificent from its very inception. Even now, amid the splendor of today's Florence, there are some ancient remains truly worthy of admiration. There is the aqueduct, which brought water to the city from sources seven miles away. There are the ruins of the large theater where performances were held to entertain the masses; in ancient times this building was located outside the circuit of walls, whereas today its remains are to be found within the city in an area occupied by private residences. The baptistery itself was built on top of an ancient and exquisite temple that the pagans had consecrated to Mars.[7]

It seems that the settlers, inspired either by nostalgia or by love of their native country, wanted to model the city after places and buildings in Rome. They utilized elements of Roman architecture to build the capitol and a forum—one next to the other—both of which we can still see today. They also constructed public baths and an arena for athletic games. In the same spirit of emulation, they built the temple of Mars, as this god—according to the fables of their religion—was considered the patron of the Roman people. The desire to model the new city on Rome was so ardent that it led them to imitate even buildings of lesser functionality without heed for the cost. They built, for instance, an aqueduct which brought water to the city from sources seven miles away; this structure would have certainly been appropriate in Rome, where the water is chalky, but it was superfluous in Florence, whose urban area is rich in pure spring water. Finally, although there are not as many ruins of private homes, I tend to believe that the magnificence of the residences was equal to that of the public buildings, whose remains, as I have said, are most remarkable indeed.

1. Bruni has in mind the barbarian kings and tribes that invaded Italy after the fall of the Roman Empire.

2. Bruni is referring sarcastically to Giovanni Villani. At the same time, he is announcing his intention of emulating the classical historians, especially Livy, who began his celebrated history of Rome with the story of its founding.

3. The Latin term *colonia* ('colony') comes from *colere* ('to cultivate').

4. From the Latin *socii* ('allies').

5. From the Latin *fluere* ('to flow').

6. See Cic., *Cat.,* 2.9.20 and Sall., *Cat.,* 28.4.

7. Contrary to Bruni's statement, the baptistery, the most important example of Romanesque architecture in Florence, was not built on the ruins of a Roman temple. Archaeological excavations in that area have uncovered mosaic pavements of a private house dating from the first century A.D. It is worth noting that the Roman heritage of the Florence baptistery, on which construction probably started in the seventh century, is further corroborated by the construction of its vault, which had a central opening like that of Rome's Pantheon.

3

Inquiry into the Origins of Florence

GIOVANNI GHERARDI

Giovanni Gherardi da Prato's narrative, Paradise of the Alberti, *stands out as one of the most important examples of the Florentine traditionalists' struggle against humanist ideology. The action of Books 3–5 takes place in the villa owned by Antonio Alberti on the outskirts of Florence, where prominent guests alternate between storytelling and erudite discussions of various philosophical, historical, and political topics of relevance to contemporary Florence. Among the interlocutors are some notable fourteenth-century Florentines, such as the famous preacher Luigi Marsili, the musician Franceso Landino, and the chancellor of the republic, Coluccio Salutati. It is worth noting, furthermore, that among the participants in the gathering are various distinguished intellectuals from cities other than Florence, such as the Averroist Marsilio of Padua (doctor to Gian Galeazzo Visconti and professor at the universities of Padua and Bologna) and the philosopher Biagio Pelacani of Parma. Their presence at the villa indicates that Florence had become an outstanding cultural center.*

Composed in 1425, set in 1389, Gherardi's narrative represents the last of the eulogies of Florentine culture to show no connection with humanist style and tenets. Its structure and prose, in fact, were strongly influenced by Boccaccio's works, mostly the Decameron *and the* Filocolo, *though the views expressed by the author through the characters of his narrative are close to those held by Rinuccini in his* Invective Against Slanderers of Dante, Petrarch, and Boccaccio. *As regards the origins of Florence, however, Gherardi feels obliged to follow Bruni's version at a time when the republican-*

ism proper to this account had become a fundamental feature of Florentine culture. We should also point out that Gherardi felt the need to put the narration of the Roman origin of the Tuscan city in the mouth of the conservative Augustinian Luigi Marsili, one of the cultural beacons of trecento Florence soon to be supplanted by the members of the humanist movement.

Source: Giovanni Gherardi da Prato, *Il Paradiso degli Alberti,* ed. Antonio Lanza (Rome: Salerno, 1975), pp. 307–315.

After the peace of the night came gentle breezes. The songs of countless birds resounded through branches laden with new flowers. Apollo, the longhaired and glorious god, had begun to radiate within his wondrous chariot. The noble guests left their rooms and gathered by the fountain abundant with cool water to find refreshment and relief before proceeding devoutly to the chapel. Having attended mass with sincere reverence, they all agreed to return to the fountain, where they were to start a conversation. Many things were said in praise of our most glorious city, until Master Marsilio [of Padua] finally inquired about its origin. He admitted to being interested in knowing who the true ancestors of the Florentines were and whether they were really descended from the Romans, as most Florentines believed. He claimed, however, that he had never found any evidence that such was the case, either in chronicles or in other worthy sources, and thus he wondered whether this ancestry was a mere invention to exalt and ennoble the city. The main cause of his suspicion, he explained, was a Florentine chronicle he had come across that was filled with unreliable and false information. He then turned to Salutati and said:

"Please, if you would, satisfy my curiosity: tell me if this story is worthy of credence, for I am truly eager to know."

Salutati welcomed his question and thought Master Luigi[1] would be the best person to discuss the matter, as he was both a good historian and an excellent orator. He therefore invited Master Luigi to share what he knew about this subject, in the belief that his answer would satisfy all present.

Having listened to the request, Master Luigi thus started to speak:

Distinguished fathers, I shall obey your order, although for many reasons, especially the lack of genuine sources, I would rather be among the listeners than be the speaker on this topic. If I did not have any reliable and clear material to bring forth, I would certainly keep silent and confess my ignorance. I shall be glad to speak about it, however, as I have no doubt that the Florentines are descendants of the Romans.

Before discussing the origins of Florence, I would like to enumerate those ancient buildings whose ruins are extant. Such costly monuments must have certainly been built by a great power. I shall begin by mentioning the only ancient building still intact, namely the temple of Mars, as it was called by the Ancients who erected it in honor of this god. As good Christians following the true religion, the Florentines later dedicated it to John the Baptist, our patron saint.

This, as anyone can see, is a temple of outstanding beauty, built in the Roman style. Look at it carefully and you will realize that there is no other example, either in Italy or indeed in all Christendom, that can compete with its extraordinary elegance. Look at the uniform columns inside it; notice how the extremely refined architraves, works of great art and genius, support the considerable weight of the vault and make the floor appear both larger and more attractive. Look at the columns and the walls sustaining the ceiling up above, with the spaces neatly insinuated between the vaults. Look at it carefully inside and out; and you will agree that this work of architecture is functional, delightful, durable, and perfect like no other in even the most glorious and fortunate time.

Let us proceed, now, to discuss the magnificent works of public utility: Who cannot see the greatness of the ruins and the massive circumference of the amphitheater? There, in ancient times, our pagan ancestors staged their games and their plays. Just look at the buildings located between the palace of the Peruzzi and the house of the Tolosini near Piazza Santa Croce. You can see that from the Pozzo all'Anguillara the diameter of the theater extended almost as far as the above-mentioned piazza. Can you also see the marvelous foundations of the stadium where equestrian sports were played? Even today that place is called Il Guardingo.[2] At one time, the stadium occupied all the space between the house of the Sacchetti and the Church of San Piero Scheraggio. One can still admire its lavish walls by the Palazzo della Mercatantia.[3]

What can I say regarding the Capitol, whose foundations are still visible? What about the extraordinary aqueduct, whose magnificent arches collected all the cool spring waters from Mount Morello and brought them to the city, almost eight miles away? What about the pavement which decorated the city and made it look unusually tidy? As all the ruins of these monuments are still visible, who could deny that great sums must have been spent to build them? I shall not even bother to mention things of lesser importance whose origin is clear. I want to underscore, instead, how powerful Tuscany was in ancient times, even before the founding of Rome. It could boast many powerful cities, twelve of which are explicitly mentioned in the sources.[4] Of these cities, some have been destroyed, others remain. None of the extant buildings can be said to be as magnificent as the ones we see in Florence, except for the remains of the labyrinth.[5] Some of the ancient authors mention it, and it can still be seen in Chiusi, in Valdichiana. What else? We can assert, therefore, that in all likelihood Florence was founded by men of outstanding wealth, distinction, and military power. In order to prove it, I shall now turn to the most famous among the Latin authors who witnessed the foundation of this glorious city and the erection of its buildings.

As narrated by the famous historian Sallust in his work on Catiline, Sulla, during his dictatorship, sent a group of people to a village near Fiesole.[6] One of them, a certain Manlius, eventually tried to start a revolt among his fellow settlers in Tuscany, who, having squandered all their money, were eager for a revolution. It is well known that Fiesole, like many other cities during the Social War, was razed to the ground. The war was followed by struggles between the factions of Marius and Sulla in Rome. After his victory, Sulla sent a number of excellent and valorous Romans to the territory of Fiesole. There, drawing on their considerable wealth, they erected extraordinary buildings and founded the city on the banks of the River Arno; their lives were luxurious, thanks to their grand houses, their properties, the continuous feasts they celebrated, and the numerous slaves they possessed. Soon, however, they lost their entire fortunes and grew eager for new spoils. They were in such a wretched state that only the return of Sulla himself from Hell would have made them rich again. Many of them, hoping for new booty, joined Catiline's faction. If you read Cicero's second oration against Catiline, you will see that what I say is true.[7] There Cicero describes to his Roman audience the sorts of people who had joined the conspirator. When Cicero begins talking about the third group, he reports all the things I have said above and much more. Although not attested in any ancient chronicle, it is thus obvious that Florence was founded, erected, and adorned by powerful, rich, strong, and valorous Roman citizens, who provided it with beautiful buildings and a circuit of walls. At any rate, the foundation of the city and all the other things I have mentioned are also confirmed by contemporary accounts of the two renowned authors I have mentioned.

I think I have said enough to satisfy your request. If only God had preserved Livy's books, especially those of the last two decades, in which I believe he discussed these things! I point this out in order to reproach the Latins for having lost these works, which were more divine than human. Most of them—being trapped in their despicable idleness and their insatiable, infectious avarice—ridiculed, censured, and derided every noble study and virtue.

He thus ended his speech.

Everyone praised him for his convincing and sound words, and for his mockery of various chroniclers whose foolish assertions and deceptions show them to be not only ill informed, but utterly ignorant of these things. He showed, in fact, how their complete unfamiliarity with even a single ancient and important source led them to use unreliable information, mere delusions deserving of derision. During this part of Master Luigi's discussion, Master Biagio contributed a comment:

"Reverend master, many reasons, especially the authority of such famous and renowned authors, make us believe your account, by which, I must confess, I have been fully satisfied. I would like to hear something, however, also on the origin of the name Florence, for I find it actually corresponds to Florence itself. I have never known any other city, in fact, as beautiful and as flourishing, let alone as remarkable." Having said this, he lapsed into silence.

Master Luigi immediately replied:

"I shall leave aside, dear master, many unacceptable opinions of unreliable historians on this subject. Even one of the most famous historians, Pliny, in his *Cosmography,* refers to the city as Fluentia, not Florentia.[8] Considering the time in which he wrote, namely, when Trajan was emperor, it is highly plausible that an error of the scribes changed the name Florentia to Fluentia. I base this notion also on the fact that after him, Ptolemy, an author who is particularly meticulous in his *Geography* with regard to names and places, and whose books always offer extremely precise information on both the Romans and the Greeks, calls it Florentia, not Fluentia.[9] If Ptolemy had found the name Fluentia in Pliny, he would have called it that. Therefore, in the end, I hold that a name which has been used for such a long time must be the one originally assigned to the city. Many reasons, not just one, lead me to believe this, especially in light of the fact that very few cities or communities have origins similar to that of Florence. If one studies the origins of other cities, he will notice that they generally started out small, and even those which were powerful from the very beginning could not boast of great riches. In examining the facts, one realizes how wealthy and powerful the founders of Florence were, for they soon managed, as I have said earlier, to fill the city with magnificent buildings. These first citizens were excellent and valorous Romans, who had accumulated their fortunes under Sulla during the Social War. Bold and valiant, they founded a truly glorious city with Rome as a model, and strove to advance their own glory by surpassing that of Rome itself. The name was assigned to this mighty city upon its achieving such a respected and magnificent position within such a short time. This is the reason it is called Florence, underscoring that it was able to flourish so quickly, like no other of nature's creations.

"One might also think that the city derived its name from the condition of the land itself, for it is fertile and full of flowers, especially lilies. It is plausible that the abundance of such flowers on the banks of the River Arno is behind the origin of the name Florence.

"For the time being I cannot think of anything else to add regarding the origin of Florence's name. I would be pleased indeed if my answer even partially satisfies your query. If not, the lack of written sources and the negligence not only of the past generations, but of all Latins, is to blame. I shall end here."

1. Luigi Marsili, an Augustinian friar, a friend of Petrarch, and a prominent figure in the Florentine culture of the fourteenth century. The famous discussions he organized at the Church of Santo Spirito were attended by such notable future representatives of the humanist movement as Roberto de' Rossi and Niccolò Niccoli.
2. From the Italian *guardare,* 'to watch'. Contrary to Gherardi's assertion, the name Guardingo derives from a watchtower which was built there during Lombard rule, around the end of the sixth century.
3. On the east side of the Piazza della Signoria. The Palazzo della Mercatantia was built in 1359, and its interior was decorated with frescoes by Taddeo Gaddi.

4. The main classical source on the twelve Etruscan cities, among which is also Fiesole, is Dionysius of Halicarnassus' *Roman Antiquities,* 6.75. For information on the Etruscans, however, Gherardi relies mainly on the first book of Livy's *Histories.*

5. He refers to the tomb of the Etruscan king Porsinna, a famous monument also described by Alberti in *De re aedificatoria* and by Filarete in his *Trattato di architettura.*

6. Sall., *Cat.,* 28.4.

7. Cic., *Cat.,* 2.8.20.

8. From the Latin *fluere,* 'to flow', and not from 'florere', 'to flourish'. See Pliny, *Nat. Hist.,* 3.5.52.

9. See Pto., *Geo.,* 3.1.43.

4

So Depraved a Man as Julius Caesar Should Not Be
Deemed the Founder of Florence

GIOVANNI CAVALCANTI

Not much is known about the life of Giovanni Cavalcanti (1381–ca. 1451), a descendant of the Florentine family to which the dolce stil nuovo *poet Guido belonged. Giovanni was appointed to various offices in the city government, such as captain of the Guelph party in 1422, but near the end of the 1420s he was sentenced to ten years for insolvency and imprisoned in the notorious jail of the Stinche. During his detention, Cavalcanti wrote his first and most famous work, the* Istorie fiorentine, *in fourteen books, addressing the main happenings in the city from 1420 through 1440. Cavalcanti was highly critical of the faction led at the time by Niccolò da Uzzano and Rinaldo degli Albizzi, Cosimo de' Medici's opponents. In his* Istorie, *Cavalcanti contrasts the citizens' mercantile activities with the socially disruptive craving for power of the political leaders.*

In his second work, Nuova opera, *Giovanni Cavalcanti also describes the contrast between the industriousness and peace-loving nature of the citizens and the wickedness of their rulers. Unlike his* Istorie, *Cavalcanti's second chronicle, which covers the years from 1441 to 1447, directly attacks Cosimo de' Medici and his supporters. In the author's opinion, far from protecting the liberty of the common people, the Medici regime, now firmly established, commits the same crimes as its predecessors in the attempt to keep the city under complete control. This accounts for the strongly moralistic tone of the* Nuova opera, *a text which the author himself defines as a "satire" on the vices of contemporary Florentine society.*

The polemical spirit of the Nuova opera *can be seen immediately in its initial passages, which discuss the origins of Florence. Here Cavalcanti imagines he is conversing with a personification of Genius, who answers all of his questions concerning the city's history. In narrating the origin of Florence, Genius sneers at the medieval accounts, including Giovanni Villani's, that ascribed the founding of the city to either Caesar, the Roman general Florinus, or the French paladins. The true version, Genius says, is that offered by the humanists: Sulla's veterans were the founders of Florence. Cavalcanti, however, goes even further in his condemnation of Julius Caesar by citing the most defamatory passages from Suetonius' biography of the Roman emperor.*

Source: Giovanni Cavalcanti, *Nuova opera,* ed. Antoine Monti (Paris: Université de la Sorbonne Nouvelle, 1989), pp. 17–19.

As attentive to the melodious harmony of eloquence as to the truths of the extraordinary foundation of our city of Florence, I said [to Genius]: "Since these spreaders of lies request better evidence to prove that Giovanni Villani's mendacious assertions are not as reliable as the texts we cite, I beg you to clarify the stories told of Caesar, King Rinaldo, Renzo, and Fiorino. With equal fervor I pray that you reveal to me who erected the temples [of our city] and to which gods they were first consecrated. I should also like to know if, at that time, the River Mugnone followed its ancient course, namely from the [houses of the] Pecori through Calimala[1] to join the Arno, where Ponte Vecchio is today."

The golden image [of Genius] then fulfilled my wish and started to speak:

If everything said regarding these issues had to be proved more rigorously than is usually done,[2] no greater truth could be found than in the present case, for both the proof and the author of the work are tied to one and the same master. Zeal, who is the author of this work, merely carried out my orders. I have now, and I shall always have, the same power as I had when the world was created. You must understand, therefore, that not only was I present when all things were said, but I was the one who gave the orders which Zeal fulfilled.

Using arguments that satisfy those who believe in the ancient texts and simple truth, I should like to state that Caesar was the most conceited and arrogant man of his time—his shameful acts and the exploits by which he earned fame are duly recorded. According to Suetonius and other authors who report his most despicable actions, he was "every woman's man and every man's woman," and the king of Bithynia used him for a time as a depraved concubine. In a debate with the king he responded shamelessly. On that same occasion, a member of the court tried to offend Caesar by saluting him with the words: "Welcome, Queen Caesar!" Caesar, far from being ashamed, with even greater boldness retorted, "Semiramis, too, was a queen."[3]

If we have recorded evidence of Caesar's vices, then we might expect his glorious deeds to fill even more pages. There is no better means of judging how well-deserved glory is than through its longevity. What can be more enduring than the foundation of a city? But if his shameful actions were recorded, whereas his exploits are not, one must assume that the latter did not exist. Caesar, consequently, did not found Florence, for at the time of Sulla's famous dictatorship he had not even become a knight yet; as a matter of fact, he was still so young that Sulla called him "the ill-girt boy," a definition proving that he was then no more than an adolescent.[4] Just as Caesar did not figure among the founders of Florence, neither does Renzo, Fiorino, or Rinaldo deserve this glory.

Furthermore, in order to emphasize how significantly Roman customs differed from those of the people of Fiesole, the Roman settlers resolved to build a temple unlike that of the Fiesolans. Because they had won numerous battles and had seen the expansion of Roman domination, they chose to venerate Mars, the god of war. They thus dedicated a temple to him, which is now consecrated to St. John the Baptist, on the banks of the Mugnone. Being that the city was surrounded by a circuit of walls, they deflected the course of the river [Mugnone] outside the gates and made it flow into the Arno, right at the city's perimeter where the Ponte alla Carraia is today.

Now, my readers, you should note that every year, during the month named after Mars, the settlers celebrated the feast of this god with much pomp. For the entire month, no one went to work, and the city organized a wonderful fair. To the word "fair"[5] they added the genitive ending "-enze" which eventually yielded the name Firenze. This is similar to what happens to the names of famous and praiseworthy men—one syllable of their name is changed, but the root remains the same.[6] At any rate, the noble Romans usually called the city by its common name, that is, Firenze. It is now up to you, my readers, to choose

which of these versions you prefer, since everyone has his own explanation for
the origin of the name of Florence.

1. The area in the center of Florence where the cloth merchants—whose guild was called
   the Arte di Calimala—had their warehouses. It is probable that the name Calimala is a
   corruption of the Roman *Callis Maior* (Main Street).
2. That is, by Giovanni Villani and other Florentine historians before Bruni.
3. Sue., *Caes.*, 52 and 49.
4. Ibid., 45.
5. *Fiera* in the original.
6. See Bruni's "The Lives of Dante and Petrarch," document 21.

5

The Original Site of Florence Contrasted with Its Present Splendor

CRISTOFORO LANDINO

Cristoforo Landino (1424–1498), teacher of Lorenzo the Magnificent, Poliziano, Ve-
rino, and Ficino, was a professor at the University of Florence from 1458 until the year of
his death. He is rightly regarded as one of the most important humanists of the fifteenth
century. His first literary work is Xandra, *a collection of Latin poems in three books.*
These verses, rich in classical overtones, were composed and carefully revised by Landino
between 1443 and 1458. As he was deeply influenced by his close friendship with Ficino,
Landino came to embrace philosophy, which guides the writing of his most renowned
work, the four books of Disputationes Camaldulenses *(1472–1473). Book 1 reports a*
dialogue between Leon Battista Alberti and Lorenzo the Magnificent on the worth of the
active life as opposed to the contemplative life, a topic much debated in Florence at the
time. Book 2 treats the topic of the utmost good, and the last two books are an allegorical
reading of Virgil's Aeneid.

Among the interlocutors of the Disputationes *is Antonio Canigiani, a close friend*
of both Landino and Ficino. Ficino dedicated three works to him—De virtutibus
moralibus, De voluptate, *and* De quattuor sectis philosophorum—*and sent him*
a long letter known as De musica. *Canigiani was a member of the Platonic Academy*
and an important political figure (he was elected standard-bearer of justice in 1484, and
later podestà of Pisa). Landino dedicated the elegy De primordiis urbis Florentiae
*(*Xandra, *3.3) to him, a text containing descriptions of Florence and its surroundings. In*
De primordiis *the villas of the Medici figure prominently as magical places that were*

once peopled by nymphs and gods, a favorite topos among the literati of Florence. We find valuable examples of this epideictic genre, which gave rise to mythological reinterpretations of the entire Florentine region, in poems by Verino, Naldi, Poliziano, Luca Pulci, and Lorenzo de Medici himself. The poem by Landino we have included here, however, presents neither mythological figures nor Ovidian metamorphoses. In order to sing of the Roman founding of Florence and celebrate the daughter city's noble destiny, Landino instead sets forth the striking contrast between the original bleakness of the site where the city was founded and its present splendor. Drawing on well-known classical sources (Virgil, Ovid, Tibullus, Propertius) describing the site where the capital of the empire was later erected, Landino praises the first Roman settlers for their zeal and enterprising spirit, the same qualities which made it possible for their descendants to transform Florence into a city of outstanding beauty. The poem ends by praising the Medici for their strenuous defense of Florentine liberty and for their glorification of the city through their patronage of the arts.

Source: Cristoforo Landino, *Carmina omnia*, ed. Alessandro Perosa (Florence: Olschki, 1939), pp. 86–88.

TO ANTONIO CANIGIANI:
ON THE FOUNDING OF FLORENCE

All these rich buildings, both sacred and profane, rising before your eyes and rendering you speechless, could not have been imagined by Sulla's soldiers when they first settled in the territory of Fiesole. The beautiful cultivated fields that you now see were once covered by the Arno's dark, swampy waters, whose rapid course was obstructed by a massive rock and turned here into a stagnant pond.[1] The ground could not be trodden by man, nor was the lake navigable; the river was not suitable for fish, nor the grass for cattle. It was not yet possible for the traveler to look at these four wonderful bridges and use one of them to cross the river without wetting his feet. Water was not yet brought to our city by aqueducts channeling it from distant springs. Where today the high tower of the senate rises, the fishermen built their huts; and where the holy fonts of the baptistery now stand was a marsh that resounded with the croaking of frogs. Who could foresee, back then, the Church of Santa Croce, the marble works of Alberti, the Florentine courthouse, or the piazza surrounding the noble senate? Where massive buildings now reach up toward the sky, there was once nothing but a revolting swamp.

The first settlers—the veterans of Sulla's army—abandoned the inhospitable mountains and diligently cultivated the fields on which we now dwell. They carved a straight course for the River Arno, guiding all waters nearby to flow into its bed. Satisfied, they then started to inhabit the valley and build this noble city. They gave Roman names to the palaces they erected; they built both a forum and a senate building like those of Rome. They then consecrated to Mars a temple with high columns of variegated marble. Lastly, they built large theaters near the city walls whose remains, worn away by the centuries, can still be seen today.

This is the noble origin of our city, which was founded under a good omen. A century later it expanded, thanks to the people of Fiesole who moved there after abandoning their old houses on the mountain and increased its affluence through their possessions. Among those initial Fiesolans, O Antonio, was the progenitor of your family, the Canigiani. In memory of your ancient homeland, your family's coat of arms thus displays a bronze moon on a white marble shield—the moon being the ancient symbol of Fiesole.

1. This description of the old course of the Arno is reminiscent of the main classical sources already mentioned in the introduction to this text. For descriptions of the area where Rome was to be founded, see especially Virg., *Aen.,* 8.97–101; Ov., *Fas.,* 1.243–246; Tib., 2.5.23–28; Prop., 4.2.7–8 and 4.9.1–20.

6

The Only City Founded by Three Roman Generals

ANGELO POLIZIANO

Angelo Ambrogini, known as Poliziano, was born in Montepulciano, near Siena, in 1454. He was one of the greatest philologists of the quattrocento. As a professor at the University of Florence, Poliziano taught many well-known humanists. His fame, however, is primarily linked to the numerous works he composed in the course of his long stay in Florence during the reign of Lorenzo the Magnificent, whose sons he tutored. His support of the Medici faction led him to write the well-known, although unfinished, Stanze per la giostra, *in which he celebrates the victory of Giuliano, Lorenzo's brother, in the joust of 1475. To sustain the Medici's propaganda after the Pazzi conspiracy in 1478, he wrote an account of the tragic episode, presenting Lorenzo as the legitimate ruler of the city and the defender of Florentine liberty, under attack from a band of rebels.[1] Around 1479 Poliziano's relationship with the powerful patron soured, however. This deterioration led to his departure for Mantua, where his* Fabula d'Orfeo *was first staged. By the end of 1480, Poliziano was back in Florence, where he resumed his studies and published the* Miscellaneorum centuria prima, *a true monument to classical learning and philology.*

Poliziano's use of philology and the classics to support the pro-Medici propaganda characterizes the letter to Piero de' Medici that we have translated here. It is a significant document, as it is the first letter in his epistolary collection. Written shortly after Lorenzo's death (April 8, 1492), this brief yet fundamental text offers a new thesis on the origins of Florence and reveals how profoundly the political ideals of the city had changed during the second half of the quattrocento. Poliziano directly opposed the republican view expressed at the beginning of the century by such humanists as Leonardo Bruni. He believed that Florence was founded not by veterans of Sulla's army, but rather by the generals of the second triumvirate in 43 B.C., Augustus, Mark Antony, and Lepidus. When Poliziano wrote this letter—like nearly all humanist correspondence, not intended to remain private—Piero had just succeeded his deceased father, Lorenzo, as ruler of Florence. This young Medici had to face an unstable political situation, and opposition to the regime was stronger than ever. Poliziano's letter aims to legitimate Piero's rule by underscoring its consistency with the imperial origins of the city. The account aims to show that the Medici's control over Florence simply expresses what was already inherent at the very founding of the city.

Source: Angelo Poliziano, *Opera omnia* (Venice: Manuzio, 1498), folios 3v–5.

Angelo Poliziano sends greetings to his dear Piero de' Medici. You have often heard me say that this city, in which you are now deservedly the ruler, as your elders were before you, has an origin other than what our historians write. Thus you have asked me, with your usual gentility, to write what I know about the topic. You have mentioned that Florence would be extremely grateful to me if I showed it who its fathers were, especially since these men were such that if one had wanted to select them from a history book, he could have found no one better. Therefore, my dear Piero, in order to give a gift to this city, which has always been kind and loving to me, and to satisfy a request that comes from you, whom I hold dearer than anyone or anything else in the whole world, I shall briefly illustrate what I have found in the literary works regarding the founders of this city. I shall also touch upon a few things concerning the name of Florence, and since a number of inhabitants of Fiesole were accepted into the newly founded city, I shall also explain what I believe to be the origin of Fiesole's name.

The colony of Florence was founded by the triumvirs: Caius Caesar (who later took the title of Augustus), Mark Antony, and Marcus Lepidus, who then held the office of pontifex maximus. The settlers who moved to this new colony were soldiers of Caesar; they were granted two hundred *jugera* to mark out the foundations of the city. I get this information from Julius Frontinus' *De agrorum mensuris,*[2] a text of which you have a very old copy at home, Piero. Florence, therefore, is the only city in all of history that has been built by three generals—one of whom was to become the greatest emperor of all, and another, the pontifex maximus.[3] The first Florentines, moreover, were men of such virtue that they were able to overcome all clash of weapons, fortresses, and armies.

Having discussed the origins of Florence, let us now investigate the development of its name. It is a known fact that Rome had three names: the first one can be considered the common one; the second is the ancient one from which the poet[4] took the name Amaryllis, that is, "love," for his bucolic; and the third is the one used specifically in sacred ceremonies. From the third derives the name used for celebrating the goddess Flora—Anthusa in Greek—as attested by the learned Philadelphus, from whose work I have gathered this information.

The Latin form of this name can be either Florens, Flora, or Florentia. We know that the Romans developed their colonies as small models or imitations of their own city. Clearly, given the name Capitol that is still used in the city and the names of some neighborhoods, Florence was also modeled on Rome. Both Philadelphus and the most learned Eustace write that the name Anthusa had also been given to Constantinople, the new Rome. The name of the city and its origin, therefore, were one and the same thing. In Pliny,[5] the term *Fluentini* rather than *Florentini* is probably due to an error of the scribes or, perhaps, to the fact that in olden times the people who lived by the banks of the River Arno were so called. After the settlers arrived and founded the city, they joined the Florentines to live with them. Their name Fluentini in the edict of the Lombard king Desiderius can be traced back to one of the two abovementioned reasons. At any rate, there is no doubt that Ptolemy, as reported in several manuscripts, calls this city Florence;[6] Pliny himself does so in Book 14 of his *Naturalis historia,*[7] although this passage is corrupt and survives only in unreliable manuscripts. Paulinus, Ambrose's disciple, also speaks of "Florence" in a passage that bears witness to the holiness of our bishop Zenobius.[8] The same name appears in Procopius,[9] who shows how strong and powerful this city already was at that time, repeatedly managing to resist the Goths' attempts to seize it. One can still see in Florence the remains of a superb ancient monument: the temple which was originally consecrated to Mars and is now dedicated to St. John the Baptist. Caesar's soldiers, conquerors of the whole world, were particularly devoted to Mars, the father of the Roman race. Augustus, the primary founder of your city, also venerated Mars and to such a degree that it was he who in the middle of the Roman forum consecrated the temple to Mars Ultor. It need not surprise us, therefore, that the Florentine youths—despite their dislike of weapons, as is customary among their people—have always defeated even the most expert soldiers in jousting tournaments. But I must refrain from speaking of the many tournaments you have won in just a few days, dear Piero, lest someone think that I write this letter merely to praise you.

Finally, let us consider Fiesole, which was founded by the divine Atlas, according to an ancient tradition supported by Boccaccio,[10] one of the most erudite authors of his time. In order to uphold his authority, I want to quote Hesiod, the ancient poet who writes that Fiesole was not only one of the nymphs who feature in the Hyades constellation, but the most important among them. The Hyades are called *Suculae* in Latin, and their position is indicated by the moon. This is why the moon is still the symbol of Fiesole, although it is also possible that its inhabitants adopted this symbol because the last one of the wandering stars is very close to the top of Atlas, who holds up the heavens. Here are the verses of Hesiod's *Astronomy* taken partly from the authoritative Theon, and partly from the outstanding Byzantine grammarian Tzetzain's commentary on Theon's letters:

> . . . nymphs like the Graces,
> Fiesole, Coronis, and beautifully crowned Cleeia,
> Exquisite Phaeo and long-robed Eudora,
> Whom the mortals on earth call the Hyades.[11]

Hesiod calls Fiesole the most important of the nymphs, as does Eustace, but owing to the terrible state of the manuscripts, one finds the word "Esole" rather than "Fiesole." The grammarian Ammonius, moreover, includes Fiesole among Bacchus' wet nurses. The Hyades were Atlas' daughters, and whoever possesses even a small amount of education knows the names of Bacchus' wet nurses. The town of Fiesole had renowned augurs who practiced the ancient Etruscan art of interpreting thunderbolts, as Silius wrote in the following passage:

> Fiesole, too, was present, able to interpret
> The winged thunderbolt of the heavens.[12]

I have never understood why other cities have received more praise than this one. I cannot fail to mention, in fact, that all Italy owes its safety to the people of Fiesole, for it was in their mountain pass that, by God's will,

Radagasius—the terrible king of the Goths who was devastating the whole world with his army of more than two hundred thousand men—was finally surrounded, captured, and executed.[13]

This, dear Piero, is what I have found regarding Florence and Fiesole in the historical works of our writers and in other, less accessible but trustworthy authors. I hope that you and our fellow citizens will be pleased to receive these bits of information. As a man of letters, I could offer no greater gift to those who have invited me to this city than to endeavor to acquaint you with your illustrious but little known and much neglected ancestors.

1. See document 18 of the present anthology.
2. The anonymous *Libri regionum,* not Frontinus' text, is the source of this passage. Poliziano's misunderstanding of this source was due to an error of the scribe, as shown by Nicolai Rubinstein in "Il Poliziano e la questione delle origini di Firenze," p. 106.
3. August and Lepidus, respectively.
4. Virg., *Ecl.* 1.
5. Pli., *Nat. hist.,* 3.5.52.
6. Pto., *Geo.,* 3.1.43.
7. Pli., *Nat. hist.,* 14.4.36.
8. Paul., *Vita Ambr.,* 50.1 (*PL,* 14.44).
9. Pro., *Hist.,* 7.5.1–5.
10. In the last section of his *Ninfale fiesolano.*
11. Hes., *Astr.,* frag. 291.
12. Sil., *Pun.,* 8.476–477.
13. Radagasius invaded Italy in 405, leading an army of Germans, mostly Ostrogoths. After having sacked northern Italy, he besieged Florence, but the Roman general Stilicho came to rescue the city and compelled Radagasius to withdraw to Fiesole, where he was captured and finally executed on August 23, 406.

PART TWO

History and Society

7

Panegyric of Florence

LEONARDO BRUNI

As we pointed out in the introduction, Bruni's Laudatio florentinae urbis *is a text of fundamental importance to the history of Renaissance epideictic literature. Modeled on Aelius Aristides'* Panathenaicus—*the panegyric of Athens in which the second-century Greek orator praises the city as the savior of Greece in the Persian wars—Bruni's* Laudatio *differs considerably from the typical medieval* laudes civitatum. *As Hans Baron notes, before Bruni no one had ever tried to offer such an exhaustive view of a city: its geography, history, culture, architecture, politics, and specific mission in Italian society.*

Scholars tend to regard this work, composed shortly after the Florentine victory in the 1402 war against Gian Galeazzo Visconti, as a manifesto of civic humanism. Throughout the text, Bruni credits the Florentines with a political awareness superior to that of all other Italians. He presents the Tuscan city and its dominion as the crowning achievement of a people continually striving to defend its own liberty and to shape a society on par with that of ancient republican Rome. In military valor, literature, art, and commerce, Bruni writes, Florence is the greatest heir to the Roman tradition.

In 1436, most likely at the government's request, Bruni would once again circulate the Laudatio, *accompanied by his* Lives *of Dante and Petrarch, in order to oppose the* Panegyric of the City of Milan *written by the Viscontis' secretary Pier Candido Decembrio and to promote Florence as a candidate to host the upcoming council for the union of the two churches. From Bruni's long panegyric we have chosen to translate the first paragraphs and the passage concerning the Florentine victory over Milan.*

Source: Leonardo Bruni, *Laudatio florentinae urbis,* in *Opere letterarie e politiche,* ed. Paolo Viti (Turin: UTET, 1996), pp. 569–647.

I wish that God immortal would bestow upon me an eloquence worthy of the city of Florence, of which I am about to speak, or at least an eloquence that equals my love and zeal for it. One form of eloquence or the other would, I believe, suffice in revealing the magnificence and splendor of this city. Nothing more beautiful or more splendid than Florence can be found anywhere in the world. I must confess that I have never been more willing to undertake anything than the present task. I have no doubt whatsoever that if my wish for either type of eloquence were granted, I would be able to describe this illustrious and beautiful city in an articulate and dignified manner. Since, however, not all our wishes can be fulfilled, I shall do my best, thereby showing that I was lacking not in will, but rather in talent.

The splendor of this city is so remarkable that no eloquence could begin to describe it. We know that a number of distinguished and righteous men have dared speak about God Himself, whose glory and infinite nature a man's words, no matter how eloquent they may be, can never come close to capturing; but regardless of God's ineffable superiority, they still attempt to employ all their rhetorical skills in speaking about such infinitude. I, on the other hand, shall have fulfilled my task of praising Florence if I make adequate use of all the knowledge I have acquired through my ardent study, although I know full well that my ability cannot ultimately apprehend such an extraordinary city.

I now must face something most orators face, namely, that they do not know where to begin their speech. In my case, however, this is not owing to a lack of words, but to the subject matter itself—and not only because of the many things that are relevant to one another, but also because they are all so remarkable that they seem to compete for excellence among themselves. It is, thus, not easy to decide which topic should be discussed first. If you consider the beauty and the magnificence of the city, you would think that there is nothing more deserving with which to begin a speech. If, on the other hand, you take into account its power and wealth, you would think it right to start an oration with these topics. Furthermore, if you look at its deeds both in the present and in the past, nothing could appear more important than to begin here. But if you focus on its customs and institutions, nothing could seem more worthy of distinction. With all this to think about I am uncertain where to begin; and when I am about to commence with a certain topic, another catches my attention and I cannot resolve which to discuss first. Nonetheless, I shall begin at what I find to be the most logical starting point, although I do not consider the other subjects less worthy of attention.

As it sometimes happens that a son's resemblance to his parents is immediately noticeable, so the Florentines resemble their most noble and illustrious city to such a degree that one is led to believe that they could have never lived anywhere else, nor could Florence ever have had any other kind of inhabitants. Just as these citizens far excel all other people by virtue of their natural genius, prudence, wealth, and magnificence, so Florence, whose site was most carefully chosen, is superior to all others in splendor, beauty, and cleanliness.

First of all, let us note the signs of its wisdom. For one, Florence has never done anything ostentatiously; it has always preferred to reject dangerous and foolish arrogance in order to pursue a state of peace and tranquillity. It was not built on top of a mountain, to show off its greatness; nor, by the same token, was it built in the middle of a plain and open on all sides to attack. Instead, with the discerning prudence of its citizens, Florence attained the best of both situations. They [the Florentines] knew that it was impossible to live on mountaintops without being subjected to the harshness of the elements—strong winds and heavy rains—which are uncomfortable and hazardous to the inhabitants. They also recognized that a city placed in the middle of plains, correspondingly, is necessarily disturbed by the dampness of the soil, the impurity of the air, and fog. Attempting to avoid all these risks, and acting as wisely as always, they built Florence midway between two extremes: it lies far from the discomforts of the mountains and free, at the same time, from the inconveniences of the plains. It has the best of both situations, and a good climate, too. To the north, the mountains of Fiesole, like a kind of fortification, ward off severe cold and the furious gusts of northern winds. To the south, smaller hills protect it from the less violent winds that blow from that direction. In the other areas surrounding the city are sunny fields open to gentle breezes. Florence sits peacefully in an ideal location and climate; when you move away from it in any direction, you will meet with more severe cold or more intense sun.

From the hills to the plains, moreover, the entire city is surrounded by a splendid circuit of walls which are not so excessively imposing to make it appear fearful and dubious of its power; nor, on the other hand, are they so small or neglected to give the impression of being conceited or indiscreet. And what can I say of the multitude of inhabitants, of the splendid buildings, of the richly decorated churches, of the incredible wealth of the whole city? Everything here, by Jove, is astonishingly beautiful. . . .

Bruni continues his praise of Florence, describing its unparalleled cleanliness, the Arno spanned by impressive bridges, the magnificent palaces before which throngs of people from all over the world gather, the marvelous churches, and the grand villas in the well-cultivated countryside surrounding the city. All these features lead Bruni to assert, "Indeed, the very hills seem to smile and to convey a sense of joy. No one could ever tire of such a sight. This whole region could rightly be considered a paradise whose beauty and joyful harmony are unparalleled anywhere in the world."

He then relates a single fact, which, he believes, suffices to prove the greatness of Florence.

I now wish to mention an aspect of Florence that, I believe, demonstrates the greatness of this city. It fought innumerable wars, opposed mighty enemies, and vanquished threatening powers at the peak of their strength. Through wisdom, wealth, and great courage it has managed to overcome enemies that no one could have ever believed it could have conquered or resisted. It has been vigorously fighting a powerful and rich enemy [Gian Galeazzo Visconti] for the past few years and has earned everyone's admiration. That duke, whose resources and might have filled the people north of the Alps and the rest of Italy with fear, was elated by his victories and hopeful of more, attacking and seizing all places with incredible ease, like a storm. Only Florence opposed him and not only managed to resist his invasion and hamper the course of his conquests but even defeated him after a long war. I shall soon devote time and space to the other deeds of Florence, so let us now return to the topic at hand.

Everyone was so astonished by the scope and duration of the conflict that they wondered how this single city could find so many troops, such massive resources, and so much money to continue the war. Such amazement, however, seizes only those who have not seen Florence and are ignorant of its magnificence. Once they have visited it, all such perplexities and doubts cease. This is what everyone experiences, and no one who has ever been to Florence denies it. As soon as anyone has before his very eyes such marvels, such architecture, the towers, the marble churches, the basilicas, the palaces, the turreted walls, the villas, the charms, and the elegance of this city, he immediately changes his mind and is no longer astonished by Florence's victories and glorious deeds. On the contrary, he deems it capable of conquering and ruling the entire world. All this helps understand how exceptionally admirable Florence is—a city whose magnificence cannot be adequately imagined or described.

8

The Structure of the Florentine Government

GORO DATI

Gregorio Dati (1362—1435), brother of Leonardo Dati (general of the Dominican order), did not go into the clergy but continued in the trade of his father, a silk merchant. Consequently, Goro (short for Gregorio) had to spend several years abroad, mostly in Spain, as we know from his diary, the Libro segreto *(1388—1434). Unlike such other famous Florentine merchants of the quattrocento as Buonaccorso Pitti and Giovanni Morelli, Dati preferred to keep his personal memoirs separate from his account of the momentous public events he witnessed. Dati's* Istoria di Firenze *narrates Florence's foreign politics from the first war against Gian Galeazzo Visconti (1388) until the Florentine conquest of Pisa in 1406. The* Istoria *is divided into nine books and structured in the form of a dialogue. The first eight books outline Florence's struggle to defend its liberty and the expansion of its dominion in Tuscany. The author's indebtedness to medieval historiography helps to explain the* Istoria's *moralistic bent. The* Istoria *also demonstrates the influence contemporary writers such as Salutati and Bruni had on Dati's account. Drawing on the texts of these and other early humanists, Dati honors Florence as the main arbiter of Italian politics and the defender of peace on the peninsula. He also celebrates its economic primacy and the industriousness of its citizens, wisely supported by a well-ordered government.*

The praise of the Florentine political system culminates in Book 9 of the Istoria, *which is devoted entirely to a detailed description of the magistrates appointed to govern the city and its expanding territory. According to Dati, the efficient organization of the*

Florentine state attests to the virtue of its citizens and to their sincere effort to guarantee liberty and peace. Probably composed in 1410, one year after the rest of the work, Book 9 of the Istoria *shows the high level of political consciousness the Florentines had attained by the beginning of the quattrocento. It is an extremely innovative text; a few well-known verses from Antonio Pucci's* Centiloquio *offer the only precedent of any consequence. To read an account of the Florentine political system as detailed as Dati's, one must turn to the works of the great city historians of the sixteenth century, such as Benedetto Varchi and Donato Giannotti.*

Source: Goro Dati, *Istoria di Firenze dall'anno MCCCLXXX all'anno MCCCCV,* ed. Giuseppe Bianchini (Florence: Manni, 1735), bk. 9, pp. 132–144.

ON THE ORGANIZATION OF THE DISTRICTS AND THE *GONFALONI,* ON THE *SIGNORI, PRIORI,* AND ALL OTHER OFFICES CONCERNING BOTH THE CITY GOVERNMENT AND THE ADMINISTRATION OF THE FLORENTINE TERRITORY; ON THE *RETTORI* AND THAT WHICH PERTAINS TO THEIR OFFICE

One must certainly believe and give heed to what the Bible says in the words of the Psalmist, "Unless the Lord watches over the city, the watchmen stand guard in vain."[1] No matter what we may say about the just and magnificent government of our city, we must always remember that it is the Lord—by His grace and by the prayers of both the glorious Virgin Mary (whose name is more venerated in Florence than anywhere else in the world) and St. John the Baptist, patron of this city—who governs our state and bestows virtues upon men, as well as the rewards they earn. In order to explain this fact, I shall begin by pointing out that our city possesses active virtue, which pertains to the many occupations that we have already mentioned in the course of our discussion. Like the efforts of Martha,[2] this virtue requires prudence. Florence is also, however, endowed with the virtue of contemplation, which brings us closer to God. Mary achieved this proximity to God on account of its charitable acts, and thereby received God's protection and help. I shall first speak of the active life, for clarity and order are fundamental to a better understanding of the whole subject.

The city is divided into four districts, called *quartieri:* Santo Spirito, Santa Croce, Santa Maria Novella, and San Giovanni. Each district is divided into four *gonfaloni* (sixteen altogether), each with its own symbol (one need not list them). Next come the twenty-one *arti*,[3] whose names I shall list here, for it will help us understand many things I shall soon be discussing. The first guild is the Guild of Lawyers and Notaries, which has a proconsul ranked above its consuls; it is a powerful guild and can be said to be Christendom's center for the notary profession. The great masters, teachers, and authors who have written on this subject have all been from Florence. The center for lawyers is Bologna; that of notaries is Florence.

Next in importance is the Guild of Cloth Merchants. There are more cloth merchants in our city than in any other, and they export large quantities of goods outside Florence.[4] The third guild is that of the moneychangers, and one can duly say that all the currency of the world passes through the hands of the Florentines, for they have managers who exchange money in all the important economic centers of the world. Then comes the Guild of Wool Merchants, the members of which produce wool cloth of unrivaled quality and quantity; they are respectable citizens and experts in their field. The fifth guild is that of silk workers, which includes those who deal in silk and gold-embroidered cloth; goldsmiths [are also part of this guild]. The products of this guild are spectacular, especially the cloths. The sixth guild is that of apothecaries, doctors, and shopkeepers; it is a guild which boasts a large number of members. The seventh and last of the "major guilds" is that of the furriers.

Then come the fourteen so-called minor guilds, each one organized according to the specific activity of its members. Only one of the minor guilds combines two occupations: those of tailors and linen dealers. Each of the other occupations, correspondingly, has its own guild: shoemakers, blacksmiths, grocers, butchers, wine merchants, hotel owners, leather dealers, tanners, armorers, locksmiths, masons, carpenters, and bakers.

The term *signori* refers to the *priori* of the guilds and the gonfaloniere di giustizia.[5] There are eight priori, two for each district, and one standard-bearer of justice, elected in turn from one of the four districts. During the year, each district chooses an experienced, worthy citizen from among them for the position of standard-bearer. The standard-bearer is the head of the priori and walks in front of them. Only men forty years of age and older are eligible for this post. The morning on which the standard-bearer assumes his office, he receives the Standard of Justice, a large banner of white cloth with a red cross that he must keep in his temporary residence.[6] When necessary,[7] he must hold the standard while riding, and everyone must follow him and obey his orders.

There are eight priori, six of whom belong to the major guilds and two to the fourteen minor guilds. Two brothers or two relatives from the father's side may not simultaneously be elected to this office. Once the member of a family has been elected, none of his relatives is eligible for one year. Moreover, whoever has been appointed must wait three years from the end of his term of office before being re-elected. The first term of office starts on January 1 and lasts for two months; the second term of office, consequently, begins on March 1, and this is the schedule followed for the whole year, so that each year the *signoria* changes six times. On the morning the new officials assume their offices, all shops in the city are closed and everyone goes to the piazza to meet the old officials, who return to their houses, each one of them accompanied by his family, friends, and relatives. Two days before the end of their appointment, the old priori meet with their successors and bring them up to date on the business they have carried out.

During their two months of office the priori reside in the government palace, where they eat, sleep, and assemble each day to discuss and decide the good of the commune. One of them, in turn, holds the office of *proposto* for three days; all the other priori must obey the orders of the proposto, who walks in front of them next to the standard-bearer. During those three days nothing can be carried out without the proposto's approval, for he is the one entitled to propose actions and ratify the council's decisions.

The signori vote using black and white beans. A friar acts as secretary, collecting the beans in a bag that he receives from the hand of each voter without letting the others see its color. The black bean means "yea," the white one "nay." In order for a proposal to pass, two thirds of the beans must be black.

Each member of the signoria is assigned a room in the government palace according to his rank and the district from which he comes; the best room is reserved for the standard-bearer. All the signori have a servant who helps them with whatever they may need in their room, during meals and so forth. There are nine servants altogether—very courteous and well-mannered youths who reside in the palace throughout the year. Each member of the signoria, moreover, has two subordinates whom he sends to act as legates. Altogether, the signoria has a hundred subordinates in its service. They wear green uniforms, and they must carry certain banners of the commune during processions, some of them walking in front of the signori, some behind. They must escort citizens before the signoria whenever ordered to do so. These one hundred officials are commanded by a foreign captain whose title is *capitano dei fanti;* he is highly esteemed, being the head and the general supervisor of so many men. The minor officials of the signoria are also respected, so much so that when one of them is appointed to escort someone who has been sentenced to exile or is convicted for insolvency, no one—either the *rettori,* the other members of the government, or the private citizens—would ever dare do or say anything against that convict. Upon assuming office, the signori have the authority to decide whether to keep these minor officials or to replace them.

No one sits at the table of the signoria except the signori themselves and their secretary. Guests, foreign authorities, or ambassadors of foreign lords and communes are [however] sometimes invited to dine at the table. On special occasions, such as religious feasts or the welcoming of important guests, the rettori and certain city officials are allowed to have lunch with the signoria, whose table is said to be well appointed, elegantly served, and orderly, as befits the highest authorities of a government. Each month three hundred florins are spent on the signori's meals. They also enjoy the company of the commune's fifers, musicians, jesters, jugglers, and all sorts of entertainers, though they can rarely indulge in such activities, being continually summoned by the proposto to discuss the needs of the state. They never lack for things to do.

They have a secretary in their service who stays in the palace for two months and sits at their table; his only task is to record the signoria's deliberations. There is also another secretary, however, who, by contrast, is elected for life. His aid is requested only when needed, and he is appointed to write down and learn all the laws issued by the signori and the councils of the *collegi.* They have a chancellor who lives in the palace and whose job it is to write all the letters and official documents that the commune sends to princes and governments all over the world. This office is always held by men of great erudition who are also expert in poetry. Both the secretaries and the chancellor need numerous subordinates to see to their orders.

The signori have unlimited power and authority. While holding office, they can do whatever they see fit in emergency situations; normally they simply enforce the commune's laws. Once their term of office is over, they cannot be charged with anything they have done while in service, except for embezzlement or simony. A special official who must come from outside Florence, the *esecutore degli ordini,* is entrusted with the task of verifying any such accusation. If there is not an esecutore in service at the time, it becomes the duty of the podestà.

The sixteen gonfalonieri have a term of office that starts on January 8 and lasts four months. There are three elections a year to the position. The gonfalonieri must appear before the signori whenever requested, which basically means every day, and give their advice, just as the cardinals do with the pope.

On the morning they assume their office, all the city shops are closed and the signori stand with the rettori by the *ringhiera*[8] outside the palace. Then one of the rettori steps up to another ringhiera, or rather, pulpit, and delivers a beautiful oration in honor of the said signoria and the gonfalonieri. Each gonfaloniere is given his own standard, and to the sound of trumpets and fifes they return to their homes, congratulated by the crowd. All citizens follow the gonfaloniere of their own district, whose standard he carries. He is accompanied by three men carrying smaller district banners that have been handed over to them in the course of the ceremony; all they have to do is follow the gonfaloniere whenever necessary.

Another council is the Dodici buoni uomini, which holds office for three months and is composed of twelve citizens, three for each district. The first term of office starts on March 15 and lasts until the beginning of the summer. In the middle of June, when the days start to become shorter, the new officials assume their position and remain in service until the day lasts as long as the night. They proceed in such a manner until the following March, when, and I am not sure why, the day lasts again as long as the night. They must be constantly ready to appear before the signori and give advice. The laws of the commune state that important decisions cannot be made by the signori without the consent of the Dodici. These two councils, the gonfalonieri and the Dodici, are called the collegi and are held in high esteem by the signori.

Next comes the Consiglio del popolo, composed of ten citizens per *gonfalone,* the consuls of all the guilds, the signori, the collegi, and a few other officials, for a total of 250 members. The Consiglio del popolo discusses the laws, the statutes, and the orders proposed by the signori and the collegi. If in a vote by the consiglio the black beans do not outnumber the white ones by two thirds, a law cannot be passed. The deliberation of the Consiglio del popolo must, in turn, be discussed by another council, called the Consiglio del comune which consists of about two hundred members including the signori and the collegi. Similarly, two thirds of the votes must be in favor of the proposal in order for it to be accepted. Good, useful, and honest proposals, however, are generally accepted and become communal laws.

The officials of the *Dieci di balìa,* who are elected by an open vote instead of by private ballot, are upright, experienced, and distinguished citizens brought into office only in time of war. These men are given full power from both the signori and the whole commune to make all necessary decisions concerning the war.

The council of the *Otto di guardia* keeps watch over the citizens and detects anyone who may be trying to damage or plot against the government, the city, or the communities of its territory. The Otto (the eight officials) do not have the authority to punish suspected instigators; they must hand them over to the rettori.

There are six officials called *regolatori* who take care of all revenue and income of the commune, seeing to it that the accounts are properly handled and recorded. Their other duties are to make sure that the commune is free of fraud, to check the treasurers' accounts, and to collect on debts. Other officials, once called governors of the entrance tolls, and now called customs officials of salt, wine, and contracts, try to prevent tax frauds against the commune.

The *capitani di Parte Guelfa* are held in high esteem and great respect, more for the virtuous deeds once performed by the Guelph party than for the office itself. They manage large amounts of money and spend it to the honor of the Guelph party.[9]

Another important council is the *Dieci di libertà,* consisting of learned and experienced men whose duty it is to listen to the numerous complaints of those against whom a lawsuit has been filed. The accused claim to be innocent, swear that they have already paid the debt, state that they should not be judged in such a manner, or claim to have been victims of deceit and fraud. The task of these officials, therefore, is to see whether it is possible for the two parties to come to an equitable and just agreement. These officials are of great help to the poor, who cannot afford to spend money on lawsuits, judges, and lawyers.

The *ufficiali dell'abbondanza* are elected only in time of famine in order to supply the city's poor with enough wheat. They come up with clever solutions in times of crisis.

The *ufficiali di grascia* must see to it that the millers of the surrounding countryside do not defraud the commune; they also control the activity of all those who do not belong to any guild.

The *ufficiali di pupilli e vedove* are appointed to take care of orphans and widows. They are elected by an open vote, and are all good, honest, God-fearing, charitable men. They look after orphans until they reach maturity.

The *ufficiali di castella* check the condition of all the castles, strongholds, and fortresses in the Florentine countryside. They must renovate the buildings as needed and, taking care of the maintenance, supply, and defense of such places, see to it that the castles' wardens have a sufficient number of subordinates in their service.

The *ufficiali della torre* maintain and restore the bridges and the walls of the city as well as those in the surrounding countryside. They also make sure that damaged streets get repaved. They must also check the condition of roofs and balconies and take care of all public works of restoration.

It is the *ufficiali di condotta*'s job to recruit and replace the commune's soldiers.

For brevity's sake I shall not list the many other communal officials, such as the accountants and the treasurers, who all have their seats in the city.

Then come the *Consoli delle Arti*. Each guild has its own seat in a beautiful and richly decorated palace where the members of that guild assemble at least twice a week to confer, hear lawsuits, and decide cases. Some guilds have eight consuls, others six, and some only four, depending on their rank. The consuls' verdict cannot be appealed. Each guild has the authority to judge lawsuits filed against one of its members, as well as the lawsuits filed by its members against someone who does not belong to a guild.

The *Ufficio della Mercanzia* consists of a scholar of civil law from outside of Florence and six counselors chosen from the most distinguished, wisest, and most experienced citizens, five of whom must be members of the above-mentioned major guilds, and one drawn lots from the fourteen minor guilds. The guild of the lawyers and notaries, in fact, and that of the dealers in fur do not join the other major guilds on this occasion, although the latter participates in this election as one of the minor guilds. The reason for this is that the members of those five guilds, namely cloth merchants, moneychangers, wool merchants, silk dealers, and apothecaries, are all devoted to mercantile activities.[10] Only few citizens are appointed to this office, but once they are elected, their power is considerable, for they must judge each and every important cause involving people from all over the world, lawsuits concerning doings on sea and on land, contracts, bankruptcies, foreclosures, and all sorts of cases.[11] The Mercanzia thus appoints qualified judges, whose verdicts are fair and cannot be appealed. The council has its seat in a large, distinguished, and lavishly decorated building. The six counselors have a three-month term of office, whereas the foreign official remains in service for six months, during which time he must reside in the palace together with his secretaries and subordinates; neither his wife nor his children are allowed to stay there with him.

We cannot forget to mention the three main rettori: the podestà, the capitano, and the esecutore. They must come from a place at least sixty miles outside Florence. Their office lasts six months and neither they nor their subordinates can be re-elected for ten years after the conclusion of their term of office, unless otherwise decided by the commune with the councils' approval, which seldom happens. These measures are adopted to prevent any of the rettori from favoring a relative, friend, or acquaintance and to induce them to put all their efforts into enforcing the communal orders and laws which they themselves are obliged to observe. They have great power and are held in the highest esteem.

The podestà has four judges—all of whom are doctors of civil law—and sixteen notaries in his service. All sorts of civil lawsuits are debated in his court, such as inheritances, wills, dowries, acquisitions, and sales. [The notaries] must, therefore, be versed in jurisprudence and be able to judge cases. The podestà must bring with him a large number of subordinates and horses. He receives a stipend of 2,300 florins for the six months of his term of office and resides in a beautiful palace. Each person elected either podestà or capitano of Florence must be Guelph [by political affiliation] and either a count, a marquis, or a knight. The esecutore, too, must be a Guelph but, unlike the other two, he can be a man of the people. The podestà, the capitano, and the esecutore have complete power over convicts, exiles, and all those who have committed murder, theft, forgery, or any other crime. The captain's full title is capitano del popolo, and his duty is to defend the city, the government, and the whole state—he is in charge of dealing with anyone who tries to harm the government in any way. The esecutore, instead, has authority in cases that concern the defense of the common people against noblemen. He was entrusted with this power in olden times to repress the potentially dangerous ambitions of the most influential citizens.

This is all I have to say regarding the officials who serve within the city of Florence. The offices held outside the city, however, are the ones that allow the citizens a considerable potential for advancement and offer them the largest salaries and benefits.[12] The most important of all are the offices of the capitano of the following cities: Pisa, Arezzo, Pistoia, and Volterra. These officials serve for six months, at which time their position automatically grants them full power to adopt the measures necessary to defend these cities. Next in importance come the podestà of Pisa, those of Arezzo and Pistoia, the capitano of Cortona and that of Borgo San Sepolcro, the podestà of Prato and those of Colle [Valdelsa], San Gimignano, Montepulciano, and various other cities. They all must hear civil and criminal suits. They are also obliged to bring their own judges and subordinates with them. Then we have the following: the *vicario* of San Miniato, those of Val di Nievole, Pescia, Firenzuola, and Anghiari, the three vicarships of the area of Pisa [Vicopisano, Valdera, and Lari], the capitano of the mountains of Pistoia, those of Romagna and Castrocaro, the vicario of Poppi and all Casentino, the podestà of Castiglione Aretino,[13] and finally the podestà of Maremma di Pisa,[14] who is also called capitano. It would take too long to name the many podestà of all the other towns. The best and wisest Florentine citizens are appointed to these posts; they want to assume office either to acquire honor or to increase their patrimony, and some of them for both reasons. The elected officials often achieve their goals, either fully or partially, but the contrary also happens, namely that they shame and damage themselves, for their actions cannot remain hidden when the eyes of so many people are upon them. Who acts well, therefore, is rewarded, whereas the committer of unlawful deeds is immediately discovered, convicted, and punished, both to enforce the law and to serve as an example for others. When these officials return to Florence at the end of their appointment, their activities are carefully examined and each is thereupon rewarded as he deserves. By virtue of this just policy, the righteous are always inspired to act well, whereas the bad and the wicked are punished and deterred from carrying out their plans. Good thus prospers while evil is vanquished; harmony thrives in Florence among the citizens of all classes—high, middle, and low—for each one is rewarded according to his station and his merit. This produces so sweet a melody that even heaven hears it and the saints are inspired to love this city and protect it from whoever might want to disrupt such a tranquil and peaceful state.

There are, moreover, as I mentioned at the beginning of this discussion, many good men and women who, through prayers and alms, beseech God's mercy for those who live in vice—as no city is without them. And so it has happened that, by virtue of the prayers of the good people, God has protected and preserved this city, seeing to it that it flourishes more than any other in all Italy. Amen.

1. Psalms 127:1.
2. See Luke 10:38–42 regarding the episode of the two sisters, Martha and Mary.
3. The guilds.
4. Often called *Arte di Calimala,* after the street behind Orsanmichele where its storehouses were situated, it dealt mostly in foreign cloths and wool; these materials were imported from northern Europe in an unfinished state, to be refined and then exported to foreign markets.
5. Standard-bearer of justice.
6. As Dati will soon explain, all the signori, immediately upon their election, were required to leave their homes and move into the Palazzo della Signoria, where they had to remain throughout their term in office.

7. During official ceremonies and processions.
8. A tribune with an iron bar where the officials appeared to speak to the crowd.
9. In the fifteenth century, the Guelph party gave to the poor part of the wealth it had amassed from the defeat of the Ghibellines.
10. The actual reason for the exclusion of these two major guilds from the *Ufficio della Mercanzia* is that they did not participate in its foundation.
11. After having been elected standard-bearer of justice in 1429, Dati would also serve as one of the six counsellors of the Mercanzia in 1434.
12. Dati himself would be elected to many such offices in the years between 1417 and 1427.
13. Today called Castiglion Fiorentino.
14. Today's Campiglia.

9

The Beauties of the Florentine Countryside

GIOVANNI MORELLI

Though Giovanni Morelli (1371–1444) was born into a family of wealthy merchants and continued in the family business, he also participated fervently in the city govern-ment. He supported the Medicean faction, and was elected prior in 1426, and standard-bearer of justice in 1441.

Morelli began his Ricordi, a vivid diary of personal and public events, in 1393. The memoirs are a notable example of the typically Florentine genre of libri di famiglia. He divides his book into two sections, spanning the years 1348 through 1411. The first section focuses on the author's family: their origins in the Florentine countryside and transfer to the city, where they eventually started a business in the wool trade. In the second section, devoted to a reconstruction of fourteenth- and early fifteenth-century Florentine history, the author's political leanings are evident. Understandably, Morelli's account is disjointed, mingling memories of family life (births and deaths, marriages, his affection for his sister Bartolomea, financial successes and failures) with the account of historical facts, such as the plague of 1348, the Ciompi revolt, and the war between Florence and Milan. As is characteristic of libri di famiglia, moreover, Morelli expresses his moral convictions and his teachings on various subjects, from the value of classical culture to the importance of not overdisciplining children.

The following passage, which is from the beginning of Book 1, is a delightful descrip-tion of the Mugello Valley. Here Morelli shows the pride proper to so many of his fellow citizens whose families had come to Florence from the villages just outside the city. The celebration of the countryside around Florence—with its well-cultivated fields, elegant villas, and castles where people could find shelter in times of danger—is an acclamation of the values of order and efficiency that the city encouraged to spread and thrive beyond the circuit of its walls.

Source: Giovanni Morelli, *Ricordi,* ed. Vittore Branca (Florence: Le Monnier, 1956), pp. 87–104.

The origin of our family dates back a long time, some five hundred years or more. Our ancestors were first noted for their properties and possessions in the beautiful Mugello Valley, more precisely in the area of San Cresci, in the parish of San Martino a Valcava. Not only is this distinguished and pleasant region the place where our family originated, but it has passed down the virtues of our ancestors. It would be most ungrateful not to mention the numerous noble qualities of this region. In order not to begin something my humble intellect cannot finish, and in order to avoid verbosity, I shall focus merely on three main aspects of the Mugello: its beauty, its fertility, and the shape and extent of its land. For the sake of clarity, I shall insert a brief introduction to each one of these topics, followed by three short paragraphs.

I must start by saying that the Mugello is the most beautiful area of our countryside, as most of our fellow citizens, if not all of them, agree. Although this alone could suffice, I still wish to glorify the Mugello even more by describing it in greater detail, offering further evidence of its beauty. To demonstrate this claim properly, I shall select three categories that include other elements pertaining to this topic. Having done so, I shall illustrate them as follows: first I shall describe the inhabitants and the rulers of this region; then I shall divide my discussion of the territory into two parts—the nature of the soil and the style of the houses. This is the pattern I intend to follow in the next three short paragraphs.

One can immediately observe the beauty of the Mugello through looking at its inhabitants, for many live there who, though peasants, are honorable, polite, and honest people. The women are attractive, friendly, pleasant, amorous, merry, and constantly dancing and singing. All year round, moreover, noble citizens come to the Mugello, both men and women, to hunt all sorts of animals and birds, to hold parties, and to organize elegant gatherings, filling the region with a constant resounding of joyous voices and beauty.

The fields are magnificent, offering all you could ever want. They are located in the middle of a cultivated plain covered with luscious fruits and are as well maintained as the garden of a private house. A shimmering river and numerous streams and torrents flow through the fields descending from the beautiful mountains which surround the plain. Hills and slopes delicately garland the fields. Some of these hills can be easily climbed, though the higher ones are just as attractive. Some are partly tilled and partly uncultivated; others are neither, but something in between—quite beautiful indeed. The fields close to the houses are tilled and well cultivated, adorned with fruits and vineyards, abounding in wells and fresh spring water. As you move toward the hills, the land is less cultivated and you find vast forests and woods of chestnut trees, which produce a large quantity of delicious nuts. In the same woods is a great variety of animals, such as wild boar, deer, bears, and many more. Close to the houses there are groves of young oak trees—many of them planted merely for pleasure. The soil there is so nicely kept, like a garden, that one can walk barefoot without being afraid of getting hurt. You will then see large areas covered with broom, where many hares, pheasant, and various types of game can be found. Proceeding toward the mountains, one comes to vast clearings filled with all sorts of fragrant herbs, such as wild thyme and juniper, and exquisite springs supplying the area with water. This area is also abundant in partridge, gray-coc, pheasant, quail, and especially hares. Hunting here is truly great fun.

This third section of our description, as I mentioned earlier, is devoted to the buildings of the Mugello, which are large, solid, well positioned, made of expensive materials, vast, and spacious. People live in rich and elegant houses, provided with delightful gardens in which to enjoy all sorts of entertainment. In order to illustrate this section dedicated to the Mugello's buildings in the same orderly way as I did the last two, I want to start by saying that in the center of this region—where the heart, the head, and the government are located— are six distinguished walled towns built by the Florentine commune to guard and protect the territory. These well-constructed towns are centrally located in the plains, about three miles apart from one another. As you approach them, you see impressively wide, deep moats. Each town has large, solid walls supporting strong and elegant towers reinforced by beams. Inside the circuit of walls, there are exquisite houses in beautiful quarters and all sorts of workshops run by skilled men who know how to host and honor foreign visitors. For about two or three miles, the hills and slopes around these towns are dotted with villas owned by Florentine citizens. These residences are located in charming, elevated sites from which one can enjoy a panoramic view of the cultivated plains. Adorned with gardens and orchards, these exquisite homes have wells that provide extraordinarily fresh and pure water in abundance. Their rooms and large halls are elegantly decorated, as befits their distinguished guests. About six or eight miles outside these walled towns, toward the higher mountains, are large castles owned by noble lords who win the local people's support by granting them honors and offices. The lords thereby manage to convince the local residents to live near the castles and will support them when necessary. In the less populated areas, our commune provides soldiers to protect many beautiful castles that support the local population. Twelve pages would not suffice to describe all the beauties of this country; I shall, thus, stop here and be satisfied with having touched on only a few of them.

As promised, in the second section of this discussion I shall speak about the Mugello's gifts. In order to carry out my task, I shall follow the same pattern I adopted previously to discuss the region's beauties. By this token, therefore, I shall begin by saying that the Mugello's gifts are immediately visible in its people. The people of the Mugello are as devout and pious as people can be in their condition. They have built numerous houses of worship which are still active, such as the hermitage of Mount Senario, inhabited by pious hermits and, not far from there, the [Franciscan] monastery of Bosco, which is a center of great devotion. The people of the Mugello have often shown themselves to be faithful to the commune of Florence and to the Guelph party. They succeeded, for instance, in driving out the tyrannous Ubaldini—a Ghibelline family hostile to the Guelphs and opposed to the city of Florence—by joining forces with our commune.[1] These fights caused many a death and financial loss to our relatives who lived in the Mugello. By refusing to accept the solicitation and gifts of the Ubaldini, the people of the Mugello have shown their steadfast loyalty to the commune of Florence, whose policy has always been to fight that family. Only the people of the Mugello, thus, are appointed to protect and guard this territory and its villages, for throughout the ages they have zealously followed our commune's triumphant banner and the pious standard of the venerable Guelphs. These people are particularly loyal to the Florentines, and they prove to be honest and trustworthy, diligent, well-mannered, agreeable, respectful, and courteous. They skillfully entertain noblemen in the sports of hunting and fishing. Whatever the nature of your request, they are always ready to satisfy it. The women of the Mugello, just like the men, are well-mannered, pleasant, honest, experienced, diligent, and endowed with all those qualities which country folk should have.

We can see in their fields and in their rich harvests the Mugello's other gifts. The plains, in fact, possess the best and most fertile fields of all our countryside; people harvest two or even three times a year, and each time the crop, always of excellent quality, provides in great variety all the fruits one could ever want. On the hills you will find well-cultivated land that produces grain, fruit, and olive oil in abundance. The grape harvest is also bounteous, and there is plenty of wood, especially chestnut. They have so many cows that Florence is said to receive one third of its meat supply from the Mugello. The Mugello also produces a great quantity of cheese, wool, and poultry; and it provides game in profusion. The quality of all these things is superior to that of any other region of the Florentine countryside.

We now come to the third section, in which we intend to investigate the characteristics and the utility of the Mugello's buildings. We shall first consider the aforesaid five[2] walled towns that lie in the middle of the plains. Moats and very solid walls and towers protect them [the towns] so well that they do not fear any army in the world. Within the walls' compass, the buildings are so well made that they can hold, if necessary, an extensive crowd of people together with all their crops and cattle, keeping everything safe and dry. In accordance with a precise schedule, every fifteen days one of these towns holds a market, to which people flock from all over the Mugello, either to buy or to sell their merchandise. You can find plenty of anything you might desire. A Florentine citizen is put in charge of each one of these towns in order to take care of any problems that might arise. His task is to administer justice and judge the cases involving people in his jurisdiction. These courts are the best regulated and the most efficient in all our countryside. As mentioned earlier, throughout the Mugello, both in the plains and on the hills, there are many beautiful houses that are well built, comfortable, located on sites with a breathtaking view, and also have numerous pigeon coops, wells, and all sorts of other useful and profitable things. There are, moreover, many castles that can easily repel any assault and are built in such a way as to satisfy every possible need. Whenever necessary, these castles serve all the people who live in a given area, for they can provide shelter not only to them but to their possessions as well.

In order to fulfill my original promise, I shall briefly mention a few more items, although we have already touched upon them in the foregoing pages. The Mugello has a large population, so large that, I believe, even fifty years ago it would have been possible to recruit ten thousand soldiers from its soil. The population here has probably decreased just as it has everywhere else, for many people have died in war, while others, being unable to pay their debts, have been forced to leave in order not to be put in jail. I think today some six or eight thousand men[3] live here, most of whom are comfortably well-off.

Now, as promised, I shall address the size and shape of the Mugello. This region stretches for a great distance: it is about twenty-five miles from San Gaudenzo up to Vernio and down to Barberino. Its width is also considerable, since it stretches from Uccellatoio to the pass in the Apennines that was once controlled by the Ubaldini, although some say that its border is even farther away. At any rate, the Mugello is said to be at least eighteen miles wide. One can find very few areas in our countryside which are superior to the Mugello either in size or in anything else. We have already shown how well furnished it is with fortresses, castles, buildings, and houses, and we have also mentioned its six large walled towns. One might rightly say that Dicomano and Barberino cannot be considered among these towns since they lack a circuit of walls, but they are as large and populated as the others. They have no walls, moreover, simply because they do not need them, for they are located in a sheltered position that is difficult to attack. One should also consider that, besides these towns, there are copious fortresses built by the commune, more than twelve, if I recall correctly. Because there are also numerous castles and houses owned by private citizens, as mentioned earlier, this region's safety and large population is undeniable.

1. In the thirteenth century, the Ubaldini controlled the region of the Apennines that divides Tuscany from Emilia Romagna. The Florentines repeatedly defeated them, destroying many of their castles from 1358 to 1373.
2. A mistake by the author, who previously wrote six. Branca also notes this error on p. 93 of his edition.
3. Morelli is referring to the population of adult males living in the Mugello, whose number was calculated from tax assessments.

A Letter to Bartolommeo Cederni on Gambling at the Feast of St. John

FRANCESCO CACCINI

In the introduction to a recent volume on Bartolommeo Cederni (1416–1482), Francis W. Kent emphasizes what he calls Cederni's "un-Florentine," even "un-Renaissance" characteristics. "In a society and a historiography strewn with so many improvers and achievers," Kent writes, "the life of this mediocre bank employee stands out only for its uncharacteristic modesty and lack of achievement." Despite his scanty official recognition, Cederni attracts the attention of scholars because of his two volumes of essays and the several hundred letters addressed to him by both famous personalities and ordinary citizens of fifteenth-century Florence. These documents not only convey the image of a devout and respected person, but give an incredible amount of information on the Florentine society of the time.

The letter we have included here is a good example of such informative historical material. In June 1454, Cederni was in Venice as Giannozzo Pandolfini's assistant on a diplomatic mission. Francesco Caccini, one of Cederni's closest childhood friends, writes to him of the recent feast of St. John the Baptist—Florence's patron saint—providing him with a short yet vivid description of the events Cederni had missed. This feast was one of the most important annual social events in fifteenth-century Florence, and it has rightfully been the subject of various detailed studies. Celebrations for the feast of St. John that Caccini describes started on the morning of June 23 with an exhibition of jewels,

tapestries, fine glass, and all sorts of costly wares. This was followed by a solemn proces-
sion of the clergy through the city. Confraternities put on biblical plays and organized
floats for the parade. On the morning of the 24th, both the urban population and the
subjects of the Florentine dominion brought offerings to the patron saint inside the
baptistery, and by the afternoon the events concluded with a horse race. Despite its
brevity, Caccini's letter to Cederni reveals the pride fifteenth-century Florentines took in
this festival, whose rituals became a means of showing the city's wealth and power not
only to the patron saint himself but to the peoples of the republic and to foreign visitors.
Devotion and solemnity, however, gave way to greed and other vices when gambling on
the horse race started.

Source: *Bartolommeo Cederni and His Friends: Letters to an Obscure Florentine*, ed. Gino Corti
and Francis W. Kent (Florence: Olschki, 1991), pp. 95–96.

Florence, June 26, 1454

On the twentieth of this month I wrote you a letter and prepared a box containing six pairs of eyeglasses—three for shortsightedness and three for far-
sightedness.[1] On the same day I asked Pandolfo Pandolfini to send you both
things immediately, but, as he later told me, it was not possible to find a cou-
rier. Since then I have received two letters from you, one from June 16, and the
other from the 18th. I am happy to read that everyone there is doing fine. Praise
be to God. In this letter, I want to tell you about the feast of St. John.

On Friday a wonderful *mostra*[2] was set up, attended by many foreigners, especially people from Perugia, Bologna, and Siena. On Saturday morning there
was a parade—quite a spectacle, as most of the floats in it were new. All went
well, except that they started late and finished only at 1 P.M.[3] The signori
invited the duke to the loggia, where he stood to the left of the standard-bearer
[of justice]. After him, in order of importance, came the podestà, then the
proposto, Messer Michele, and finally the lord of Faenza, who was so enraged
at having been assigned a place inferior to Michele's that he decided to leave,
saying that he was not feeling well. He did not show up later in the day when all
the officials went to give offerings.

On Sunday morning there was a procession of six hundred flagellants, priests,
and friars with sacred ornaments and relics; here people had the opportunity to
see beautiful paraments. In the afternoon it was the gonfalons' turn to give

offerings. On the morning of St. John's Day there were the usual ceremonies, with three hundred and one Sienese, sixty-eight trumpeters, ten *barbereschi*,[4] three prisoners, and one woman[5] to give offerings.

In the afternoon was the *palio*.[6] People gambled large quantities of money and all sorts of things on the horses. Bets on Mirabello's victory were first set at 40 percent, then at 16 percent; they said it was going to rain and the track would be so filled with puddles that the horses would have to swim rather than run. The following bet was set at 3 percent, and they kept saying that the race was not going to start and that even if it did, it would be impossible to finish. Because they waited for the rain to come, the race did not begin until 7 P.M. They drew lots to pick the starter. At the city gate, Andrea della Stufa's Leardo[7] was first, and he led the race as far as Borgo Ognissanti, whereupon Giannino d'Asti took the lead, followed by the marquis's Cecco. Mirabello was third, then came Andrea della Stufa on Leardo, and Duke was fifth, eventually moving into fourth place because of Andrea's fall, and this was the order in which they crossed the finish line. Pandolfo lost eighteen florins, Pierfrancesco and Piero de' Pazzi fifty florins. Andrea della Stufa also lost, as did others. Because of the rain, Matteo Rinaldi lost eighty-four florins, and so did Pierleone, along with a lot of other people.[8]

1. Florence was the Italian center for the production of eyeglasses during the Renaissance. It is likely that Cederni had asked for eyeglasses to give or sell to Venetian officials during his diplomatic mission.
2. The mostra is the exhibition of wares mentioned in the headnote.
3. The fifteenth-century Florentine clock started at sunset and thus varied with the seasons. In June, "le ore 17" (as Caccini wrote in his letter) corresponded to 1 P.M. in our system. In both this document and all that follow we will always translate the hour into our modern clock.
4. The equerries entrusted with the care of the horses that were to run the race in the afternoon.
5. Offerings to St. John on the last day of the feast were also made by representatives of Florentine institutions (the Guelph party and the communal mint), by the jockeys who were to ride in the horse race that afternoon, and by prisoners the government had freed.
6. The horse race. The name derives from the cloth (*palio*) that is given to the winner.
7. A horse, as Cecco and Mirabello are here.
8. The last seven lines of the letter concern private matters which have no connection with the rituals of the feast day.

A New Rome

VESPASIANO DA BISTICCI

Vespasiano da Bisticci (1421–1498) was the most famous Italian bookseller of his time and one of the last great manuscript makers before the introduction of the printing press. A good many kings and intellectuals commissioned him to produce elegant manuscripts of their favorite texts. By virtue of his profession, Vespasiano knew the most notable figures of fifteenth-century politics and culture personally. Among his distinguished customers was Cosimo de' Medici, who was a close friend, as we can assess from the laudatory and affectionate biography of the Florentine "Pater Patriae" included in his Vite, *a collection of more than one hundred biographical sketches celebrating the cultural innovations of quattrocento Florence.*

A deep sense of the moral and educational value of literature is palpable throughout Vespasiano's work. He was influenced by the Greco-Roman biographical tradition— which the Florentine humanists of the early fifteenth century had revived—and wanted to underscore how the Roman heritage of Florence was apparent in the noble conduct of its citizens, whose achievements, he believed, deserved to be emulated. According to Vespasiano, the supremacy of Florentine historiography is indicative of the city's cultural primacy, which he sees as evident in the works of accomplished writers such as Poggio Bracciolini. After a long and honored career as papal secretary, Poggio, probably the greatest fifteenth-century discoverer of classical texts, succeeded Carlo Marsuppini as chancellor of the Florentine Republic and extended Bruni's History of Florence *up through his own time. The two passages translated here—one from the preface to the lives*

of members of the Strozzi family and the second from the biography of Bracciolini—
demonstrate Vespasiano's belief that the actions and accomplishments of Florentines such
as these indubitably confirm the city's direct descent from Rome.

Source: Vespasiano da Bisticci, "Proemio a Filippo Strozzi nel commentario della vita di
messer Palla, di messer Marcello, Matteo e Benedetto degli Strozzi," in *Le Vite,* ed. Aulo
Greco (Florence: Istituto Nazionale di Studi sul Rinascimento, 1976), vol. 2, pp. 429–433,
and "Vita di Messer Poggio fiorentino," vol. 1, pp. 547–550.

PROEM TO THE LIVES OF PALLA, MARCELLO, MATTEO,
AND BENEDETTO STROZZI, DEDICATED TO
FILIPPO STROZZI

The Roman Republic increased to the point of becoming a great empire,
dominating the whole world during the time in which its founding fathers
virtuously governed it and considered it to be more important than anything.
By choosing justice as their fundamental principle, they followed the precept
of the divine Plato, who stated that justice should be the soul of a republic, for,
as he said, a republic cannot endure without justice, just as the body cannot live
without the soul. The founders of the Roman Republic wished to be rich in
honor and glory, and poor in material possessions, as was demonstrated by the
first and the second Brutus (liberators of Rome), Horatius Cocles, Marcus
Furius Camillus, the Curii, the Fabii, the Pauli, the Marcelli, the Torquati, and
the Scipiones, all of whom accomplished great and glorious deeds for their
country. Because the Romans maintained justice, their empire grew. Then war
broke out between the Romans and the Carthaginians, followed by peace. The
Romans maintained their integrity, fearing that the Carthaginians, who were
very powerful, would not respect peace and would start the war again. This
uncertainty regarding the possibility of hostile fortune induced the Romans to
uphold this integrity and follow their virtuous principles. Scipio's advice was
in fact quite wise, for he suggested that the Romans not destroy Carthage after
conquering it, in order not to alter [their] good fortune. His advice was excellent, and blessed would that republic have been if it had followed it! The Romans eventually seized Carthage and razed it to the ground, following the
advice of Cato and others, who certainly did not know what Scipio had clearly
known, as the events that ensued demonstrate. Immediately after the destruction of Carthage, a bloody civil war broke out; the Gracchi and their followers
were killed. The civil struggles brought about greed and ambition, while other

vices stemmed from prosperity. This most noble and beautiful city thus became utterly wicked; the consuls themselves, who were the main officials of
the government, became evil and replete with vice. The corruption of the
consuls and the magistrates, who were the heads of the republic, was copied by
that of the other citizens. The first to be corrupted were the elder citizens,
who set a bad example, followed by the youth, so that the whole city in turn
became corrupt. It is clear that excessive prosperity brought all these evils to
the city. Justice fell and inequity rose. Marius, Sulla, and then Julius Caesar
were born and nurtured by this wickedness. They despised law and justice,
and using weapons wet with the blood of their citizens, they subjected the
Roman Republic to civil discord, just as had happened in Athens, the capital of
Greece.

This is why, in his *City of God*, St. Augustine writes that as soon as kingdoms, empires, and republics succumb to internal struggles, they can no longer
endure.[1] They must fall, he asserts, because the ones who rule them should
have aimed at securing harmony for all. Just as the ears cannot tolerate the
sound of an organ, or that of any other instrument, out of tune, so it is with the
governments of cities once they are not working together for the common
good; the harmony of voices becomes corrupt. Hence, one can understand
how empires, republics, and kingdoms cannot endure when lacking in excellent rulers and citizens, as these men are the means by which they are maintained. For this reason, and for the good they ultimately bring, these excellent
men deserve to be admired and honored. The city of Florence shows how
much it has increased in power because of the presence of these virtuous men—
men who, through their wise council, dealt with one of the most powerful
princes of Italy, and equally with the republic of Venice, and won great respect
for doing so.[2] I have no doubt, therefore, that if these distinguished citizens of
Florence had been commemorated in writing, they would appear very similar
to the ancient Romans. But among the famous families of our city, the Strozzi
are very worthy of regard, for they gave to the government of the republic
remarkable men, and they defended their city through wisdom, riches, and
their very persons. Such being the case, I wish to commemorate the Strozzi in
a brief commentary, thereby ensuring that the fame of such noble men not be
lost, as has happened with innumerable others.

The first Strozzi I shall consider is Palla di Nofri Strozzi, a most honorable,
virtuous citizen, who not only elevated a family like yours, but could have
brought prominence to any worthy city. Marcello will follow, a most estimable
citizen, both in the city and outside it. It will then be the turn of Matteo

Strozzi, your father, who possessed many of the noblest virtues. The life of Benedetto di Piero Strozzi will come next, as he certainly deserves to be remembered among these others.

As you are one of the prominent members of your house, bringing honor to it no less than did your ancestors, thanks to the wisdom and the prudence that have governed you up to the present day, I have decided to send you these "lives" of mine, which I have composed in solitude. Please accept this product of sleepless nights with a charitable heart. I cannot otherwise show you my affection, for, if I could, I would be glad to do so. And if these lives meet with your satisfaction, I shall send you more of them, having no greater means of pleasing you than immortalizing your family through the written word.

FROM THE 'LIFE OF POGGIO BRACCIOLINI'

Since Poggio had, by then, spent a long time in Florence, the Florentines decided to honor him by making him one of the signori. Once his term of office in the signoria was over, he remained in the chancellery carrying out the same work he had done at the Roman Curia, where he had served the papacy by writing letters to authorities all over the world. It was then in Florence, however, that certain people—always ready to criticize and find fault with everything—plotted to drive him out of the chancellery and put someone else in his office, manipulating Cosimo de' Medici, who was a close friend of his. We should note how dangerous it is for a man's fortune to depend on the judgment of a crowd that is torn between contrasting opinions. Realizing that it was impossible for him to fulfill so many requests from different parties, Poggio resolved, as he was already aged, to abandon his office and be replaced. This would give him the opportunity to rest and to pursue his studies, and this is exactly what he did, observing the city's present state and knowing that he would be totally unfit for such a life. Cosimo, who cared for him deeply, would have preferred that he not leave his post, but seeing that Poggio was immovable in his decision, Cosimo resolved to abstain from discussing this matter any further, in order not to hamper the replacement in the chancellery. Poggio was very wealthy by then, having spent a long time at the court of Rome. He did not need to make money, for he already had a great deal: estates, houses in Florence with handsome furniture and fittings, and numerous precious books.

After retiring from his office in the government, Poggio had a good deal of time at his disposal, and consequently started to write his *History of Florence,* picking up where Leonardo Bruni had left off and carrying it through to his own time. Florence valued this work highly.

By paying a certain annual sum, Poggio could exempt both himself and his children from Florentine taxation. This privilege, however, went unused, and he was required to pay two hundred florins in taxes, like all residents of his status. When Poggio was informed of this, he was furious, seeing that his previous exemption had been nullified in his own lifetime. Had it not been for Cosimo, who managed to mitigate his anger, he might have done something rash, for Poggio thought that his labors should be rewarded and that he should not be treated like this. The city, in fact, and all Latin scholars were greatly indebted to him, for, together with Leonardo Bruni and Ambrogio Traversari, he was among the first to bring back the Latin tongue after so many centuries of oblivion; he was indeed one of the many learned men of this golden age.

Among the other debts the city of Florence owes to Leonardo [Bruni] and Poggio is that, ever since the time of the Roman Republic, there has not been a king, a republic, or a popular government in Italy as celebrated as the city of Florence. This city has had its history written by two worthy authors— Leonardo and Poggio—who managed to unearth facts that had previously been hidden. If the exploits which the Venetian republic carried out both by land and sea had been recorded by the many learned men it has produced throughout the ages, its present fame and repute would be even greater. Like- wise, the deeds of Galeazzo Maria, Filippo Maria, and all the other Visconti would be better known than they are today. If, contrary to what usually hap- pens, virtuous acts received the reward they deserve, not so much would be lost to oblivion. Every republic should reward its writers for recording its history. Look at Florence, where, before Leonardo and Poggio, there was not a single work in Latin that illustrated the history of the city and the deeds of its people. Poggio continued Leonardo's history, also in Latin. Giovanni Villani wrote a universal history in the vernacular, reporting things that occurred all over the world, including the activities of Florence through the ages. Picking up where Giovanni left off, Filippo Villani did the same. They alone are the historians who have made Florence famous through their writings.

1. Aug., *Civ. Dei*, 2.21.1.
2. Vespasiano refers to the long struggle against Gian Galeazzo Visconti and the numerous wars Florence fought against Venice after 1450.

12

A Critique of Cosimo's Florence

MARCO PARENTI

In many respects, Marco Parenti (1421–1497) can be said to exemplify the Florentine merchant of his time. A wealthy silk dealer, he was always careful not to show his political affiliation openly (he gives no outspoken opinions on the important events of his time in his almost one hundred private letters). In 1448 Parenti enhanced his station in life by marrying Caterina Strozzi, daughter of the humanist Matteo and the celebrated noblewoman Alessandra Macinghi, but this did not gain him more recognition within the city government. Although he was appointed to various posts, his political career cannot be said to have been successful, a fact certainly due to his anti-Medicean spirit. Not much is known about Parenti's education, though he is praised for his erudition by Donato Acciaiuoli, Francesco Filelfo, Cristoforo Landino, and Vespasiano da Bisticci.

Because of his familiarity with important humanists and the most influential citizens of the time, Parenti's account of the history of Florence is a valuable document. Most diaries by Florentine merchants, like Parenti's Ricordi, mingle private and public events. His Memorie, however, offers a more interesting historiographic analysis. The Memorie is a fragmentary work that covers only four years in detail, starting with the death of Cosimo in the summer of 1464 through the aftermath of the Pitti conspiracy. The other pages contain a retrospective on the lives of Cosimo de' Medici and Francesco Sforza, whose careers the author considered exemplary for their time. While Cosimo succeeded in increasing his father's wealth and in seizing political control of the city, Sforza struck Parenti's imagination, as a man of humble origin who, through military valor and well-chosen alliances, managed to become duke of one of Italy's strong-est regions.

Parenti's memoirs show his ambivalent attitude toward the hegemony of the Medici and the events of these crucial years, an ambivalence that was shared by many of his fellow citizens. In the passage we have included here, Parenti focuses on the prosperity of Florence during Cosimo's time and the rejoicing that took place upon this ruler's death. He then mournfully goes on to explain that Cosimo's death did not bring about the hoped-for renewal of liberty; his descendants, Parenti points out, have gone on to follow the Pater Patriae in the establishment of a similar political regime. It is at this point in his Memorie *that Parenti briefly explains why the facts he records become fragmented: he was upset by seeing Florence fail to obtain the liberty its citizens desired and was frus-trated by the ambiguous and secretive government.*

Source: Marco Parenti, *Memorie,* Florence: Biblioteca Nazionale Centrale, MS. Magl. 25.272, fols. 68–70.

Florence had not seen such prosperity in a long time. People spent great sums on sumptuous feasts, jousts, pageants, weddings, balls, and banquets. Innumer-able women in pearls, jewels, and rich silk clothes decorated with lavish em-broidery attended these feasts, as did youths in costly livery of diverse kinds. On ordinary work days, men of all ages wore elegant clothes of rose, scarlet, or black, and silks of every color with luxurious linings. Florence's archi-tects constructed magnificent buildings both inside and outside the city walls. Cosimo accomplished greater feats than anyone else, on account of his im-mense wealth, such as constructing beautiful and expensive buildings—an ac-tivity continued by his sons. Though his own home was elegant and civilized, it was not dissimilar to that of a common citizen. Likewise, many distinguished Florentines possessed attractive residences appropriate to their station, with furnishings, servants, horses, and the like.

Our city remained in this joyous, affluent state until August 1, 1464. Al-though the city's prosperity was due to the fortunate situation of the time—given that the league had brought peace to all Italy[1]—Cosimo strove hard to preserve this situation and turn it to the advantage of Florence, using the au-thority he had in the city government. Nevertheless, the love and desire for liberty was such that everyone rejoiced at his death. People felt, in fact, that the way he ruled had imposed upon them a sort of servitude, and they imagined they would regain their lost liberty after his death. Their possessions and comfortable lifestyle notwithstanding, they longed more for liberty than for any-thing else.

What followed Cosimo's death I have already reported at the beginning of this book, thinking that, from then on, I was to record the deeds of citizens and the events of a free city, which would have improved upon the release from their previous servitude. Since things did not go this way at first, I remained patient, waiting for this liberty to come; it did approach, but it never arrived, and thus was lost. I was deeply saddened by this, and as it was difficult to know the workings of the new government, owing to the secrecy of those who ruled the state, I decided to stop trying. This is why certain parts of my memoirs are not written with great care and do not report in chronological order every episode that occurred in Florence during these years—sometimes they are more detailed, sometimes less.

1. The Peace of Lodi.

13

A Merchant's Praise of Florence

GIOVANNI RUCELLAI

Like his friend Cosimo de' Medici, Giovanni Rucellai (1403–1481) was a patron of the arts and a successful merchant. Rucellai was born into one of the wealthiest and most distinguished Florentine families, and became Palla Strozzi's son-in-law. After Cosimo's return from exile, Rucellai joined the Medici party, and his new political affiliation was sanctioned by the marriage of his son Bernardo with Nannina de' Medici, Piero de' Medici's daughter. Rucellai was a great patron of the arts, particularly known for his support of Leon Battista Alberti. Rucellai commissioned Alberti to build his palace in Via della Vigna Nuova, the loggia in front of the palace, the Holy Sepulchre *in the nearby* Church of San Pancrazio, *and the magnificent façade of Santa Maria Novella.*

Rucellai's cultural interests were not limited to art, as we can see in his Zibaldone quaresimale *(1457–1471), a peculiar diary in which excerpts from Alberti's* Libri della famiglia *and Palmieri's* Vita civile *mingle with the author's personal notes and moral precepts. The reader of the* Zibaldone *is immediately aware of Rucellai's versatile personality and multitudinous interests through the variety of topics and impressions animating the pages. This heterogeneity also characterizes the passage we have included here, which was composed in 1457 and is a celebration of what Rucellai considers to be the most splendid period of Florentine history. His panegyric embraces topics as divergent as Florence's military victories and the city's unmatched wealth and urban development. Though Rucellai praises the Florentine scholars and artists, he considers the city's economic growth as perhaps the most valid grounds for civic pride. He frames his discussion of*

Florentine economics with tributes to the two famous bankers Palla Strozzi and Cosimo de' Medici, whom he considers two of the four most illustrious men of fifteenth-century Florence.

Source: Giovanni Rucellai, *Zibaldone,* ed. Alessandro Perosa (London: Warburg Institute—University of London, 1960), vol. 1, pp. 60–62.

Most people believe that our age, from 1400 onward, is the most fortunate period in Florence's history. I shall now explain why this is so. It is commonly believed that since 1400 the Italians have been superior to all other nations in the art of war, whereas before 1400 the northern Europeans were thought to be peerless. Thanks to their intelligence, astuteness, cunning, and strategic ability, the Italians are now the best at seizing cities and winning battles. In this age, moreover, there are more outstanding scholars of Greek, Latin, and Hebrew in Florence than ever before. An elegant and pure Latin eloquence, the likes of which has not flourished since Cicero's time, has finally returned to refine our literature. Our men of letters have revived the elegance of the ancient style that has long been lost and forgotten. Those who have participated in the government of the city since 1400 have surpassed all their predecessors. Likewise, the dominion of Florence has considerably expanded since 1400, controlling more land than ever before: it [Florence] has conquered Pisa, Cortona, Borgo San Sepolcro, and Poppi, as well as many other towns of the Casentino.

The city and its countryside have also augmented in beauty—they are now embellished with new churches, hospitals, buildings, and palaces with elegant façades and lavishly decorated interiors. Beautiful Roman worked stones—that is, stones worked in classical Roman style—adorn these constructions. Lately, in fact, we have had a great number of excellent architects, sculptors, woodcarvers, and stone-cutters who have adorned all Italy with their talent. There have not been such accomplished masters in joinery and woodcarving since the days of antiquity: they are able to produce such skillfully designed works in perspective that a painter could not do any better. The same can be said of our masters in painting and drawing, whose ability, sense of proportion, and precision are so great that Giotto and Cimabue would not even be accepted as their pupils. Similarly, we cannot forget to mention our excellent tapestry makers and goldsmiths.

Never before have men and women dressed in such expensive and elegant clothing. Women wear brocade and embroidered gowns covered with jewels and saunter through the streets in their French-style hats that cost at least two hundred florins apiece. Neither the city nor the countryside has ever had such an abundance of household goods: there are plenty of tapestries and materials to cover chairs and chests, and more female servants than ever before.[1] The production of textiles has never been greater, nor have such precious silk clothes luxuriously adorned with golden embroideries ever been made. We first started embroidering with gold after 1400, and now the best golden embroideries in the world are ours, and the same goes for our fustian. Since 1400, the Florentines have used massive ships to transport their products by sea—an innovation which has brought great profit to our city, besides making its name world-renowned. It is also at this time that the government created the Monte to help young women assemble their dowry,[2] a charity that turned out to be very profitable not only to the citizens, especially those who are needy, but to the commune itself. From 1400 on, dowries have been larger than ever before.

This age has also had four notable citizens who deserve to be remembered. The first one is Palla di Nofri Strozzi, who possessed all seven of the things necessary for a man's happiness: a worthy homeland, noble and distinguished ancestors, a good knowledge of Greek and Latin, refinement, physical beauty, a good household, and honestly earned wealth. Rarely do we find in a single man so many things conducive to happiness. Then we have Cosimo de' Medici, probably not only the richest Florentine, but the richest Italian of all time. Cosimo was born into a distinguished family and became a powerful citizen supported by many followers. In the whole of our history, no one has ever been as honored as Cosimo both in Florence and abroad. Suffice it to say that he managed to control the city government as if it had been his private property. The third citizen I shall mention is Messer Leonardo di Francesco Bruni. Although he was born in Arezzo, he was an honorary citizen of Florence.[3] He had a unique knowledge of and expertise in Greek, Hebrew,[4] and Latin and was more famous than any rhetorician after Cicero. Bruni revived Latin eloquence and refined it, as he did with the humanities and ancient rhetoric, which he rescued from oblivion. Finally, Filippo, son of Ser Brunellesco, was a master architect and sculptor. He was an accomplished geometer and was endowed by nature with great intelligence and an artistic genius superior to any since the time of the Romans. He is the one who rediscovered ancient Roman building techniques.

The earnings of the Florentine commune are now greater than ever. In this period, both in our city and in its countryside, people have witnessed tremendous wars and political upheaval, the like of which were never seen in the past.

Churches and hospitals are richer than ever, better supplied with gold and silk paraments and precious silver. There are numerous friars and priests caring for these places, which the faithful visit constantly. Men and women attend Mass and other religious ceremonies with greater devotion than ever. I shall but mention the lauds, the gospels, and the rhymed laments that are skillfully sung with sweetness and devotion throughout the whole year, especially during Lent. The citizens perform exquisite mystery plays, especially during the feast of St. John the Baptist.

I must also add that very recently, in October, the government issued a law decreeing that the citizens of Florence were to be free of all taxes for a period of ten years; it would certainly be a wonderful thing to have this law enforced.

Until a few years ago, it was fashionable, not so much among rich and distinguished men, but rather among middle-class citizens, to wear hoods of fine scarlet cloth while riding or relaxing in the countryside. The citizens have never had so much wealth, merchandise, and property, nor have the Monte's interests ever been so conspicuous; consequently, the sums spent on weddings, tournaments, and various forms of entertainment are greater than ever before. Between 1418 and 1423 Florence's wealth was probably at its height. At that time, in the Mercato Nuovo and the streets nearby, there were seventy-two exchange banks. I believe that at that time the Florentines possessed some 2,000,000 florins in money and merchandise alone. When the government first established the catasto[5] in 1427, it was estimated that the citizens had only 1,000,000 florins left, as the terrible war fought between 1423 and 1427 was horrendously expensive and drained many family patrimonies. In 1451, moreover, they decided to impose heavy taxes on all kinds of transactions, a maneuver that brought in 750,000 florins altogether. By now, that is, in 1457, I think the Florentines' wealth has doubled this amount, so that in money and merchandise they must possess 1,500,000 florins. Because of this fiscal abundance, between 1418 and 1423 the accounts in the communal bank bore nearly a 3¾ percent interest rate, giving 61 florins for each 100. Good banks did not request a deposit as a guarantee, and despite all the expenses, their accounts always had a 5 percent interest rate, so that even apothecaries, wool workers, storekeepers, and the like, deposited their money there.

1. The importing of young women from foreign countries (especially Eastern Europe) to serve as maids was a widespread practice in late medieval Florence and lasted well into the seventeenth century.

2. The Monte delle Doti.

3. Bruni was granted Florentine citizenship in 1416.

4. Bruni did not study Hebrew. Giannozzo Manetti, another Florentine humanist and an admirer of Bruni, however, became one of Italy's first experts in the language.

5. This was a system of tax assessment based on the amount of property each Florentine citizen owned.

14

On the Celebrations for Pius II's and Galeazzo Maria Sforza's Visits to Florence

FRANCESCO FILARETE

Other than the record of his humble descent, we have no information about the youth of Francesco di Lorenzo di Jacopo (ca. 1419–ca. 1506). His father, a barber by profession, bore no last name, and Filarete is most likely a nickname that Francesco took in later years. A close friend of Benedetto Dei, he was probably also well acquainted with Cristoforo Landino and participated in the meetings of the Platonic Academy. He was interested in topics as diverse as astrology, poetry, art, and architecture. Among his works are an ode to Count Frederick of Urbino upon his capture of Volterra in 1472 and a poem entitled Della rinnovazione della libertà *composed in 1494, after the Medici were driven from Florence. He achieved fame as an artist in his own time, and he is known to have proposed models for the renovation of various city buildings, such as the Palazzo della Signoria and the cathedral façade.*

Despite his intellectual versatility, however, at age thirty-three Filarete was still merely a respected servant of a distinguished Florentine family. His ascent began in 1456 when he was elected mayor and herald of the Florentine Republic. In 1475, the signoria appointed him to write the Libro cerimoniale—*a record of the ceremonies in honor of distinguished visitors to Florence from 1450 onward. This work (continued by Filarete's son-in-law, Angelo Manfidi, from 1515 through 1522) is an invaluable description of Florentine diplomacy in the fifteenth century. It shows how important people were welcomed into the city and what honors they received, depending on changing Florentine politics. Filarete's* Libro *also reveals the commune's political alliances and enmities through the insertion of brief digressions on various episodes, such as the one we have selected to include here. In this passage, Filarete describes Pius II's stay in Florence on his way to the Diet of Mantua in 1459 (where the project of a crusade against the Turks was to be debated), and the simultaneous visit of the fifteen-year-old Galeazzo Maria Sforza, son of Francesco Sforza, whose friendship with the Florentines had begun in the 1430s and continued, to the advantage of both parties, until the death of the Milanese duke.*

Filarete diverges somewhat from his official task in remarking with asperity on the alleged incivility of members of the papal entourage, but his barely disguised indignation renders this excerpt one of the most readable of the whole book. In his Commentaries, *Pius II would resort to his well-known sarcasm to repay the Florentines for the lukewarm welcome he received on that occasion, whereas an enthusiastic letter by Galeazzo Maria to his father bears witness to his comfortable stay and positive impressions of Florence and the Florentines.[1]*

Source: Richard C. Trexler, *The "Libro Cerimoniale" of the Florentine Republic by Francesco Filarete and Angelo Manfidi* (Geneva: Droz, 1978), pp. 75–78.

For the illustrious prince Galeazzo Maria's arrival [in Florence], the officials of our government appointed many distinguished citizens and a great many youths to welcome him; they were all richly dressed, accompanied by their servants in elegant uniforms and more than three hundred beautifully caparisoned horses. The foreign officials of the Florentine government, namely, the podestà and the capitano, were there to receive the noble prince, and, like everyone else, they went to great lengths to honor his arrival. The city musicians and the herald of our republic presided over the prince's entry into the city. Gian Galeazzo's retinue included noblemen, princes, and officials, who were all received with great honor by our distinguished citizens, while the Florentine youths paid homage to the equerries who walked in front of them in the procession. The priori of our city headed the procession, followed by the group of distinguished citizens, the court of the most noble Count Galeazzo Maria, the trumpeters, the Florentine youths with the count's equerries, the pipers and the herald with the prince and our authorities, the horsemen with other honorable foreigners, and then all the other members of the prince's court, each arranged according to his dignity and office, and accompanied by the rest of the worthy people of Florence. Finally, the procession left the Canto alla Paglia, passed in front of the Tornabuoni Palace, went through Borgo Santi

Apostoli, and arrived in the Piazza della Signoria, accompanied by the sound of trumpets and church bells. It was a truly marvelous spectacle. The signori and a number of respected citizens were waiting on the tribune platform outside the government palace as the illustrious prince arrived; the signori walked toward him, meeting him at the palace's entrance. Having exchanged greetings with them, the prince remounted his horse and rode as far as the house of Cosimo de' Medici, accompanied by the procession arranged in the order described above. This is what took place on April 17, 1459.[2]

As I mentioned earlier, the supreme pontiff arrived in Florence on April 25. His arrival was celebrated as follows: the glorious, Catholic heads of the Guelph party along with the officials of the collegi welcomed the supreme pontiff just outside San Gallo and, carrying their banner, escorted him through the San Gallo city gate to meet the Florentine signori who were waiting for him there. The Holy Father was sitting on the papal chair[3] and would have liked to be carried by our signori, but they resolved not to comply with his wish. He was eventually carried, however, by the lords and the princes of Romagna, some of whom were in Florence at the time while others happened to be members of the pope's retinue on that occasion. Among them there were Sigismondo [Pandolfo Malatesta], Astorre [Manfredi II, lord of Faenza], [Taddeo Manfredi] the lord of Imola, and others. The pope was escorted by our distinguished signori and the officials of the collegi carrying the standard of our republic, under which he passed through the city gate. They headed the cortege with the banner of the Guelph party and, below it, the Eucharist. All the minor magistrates were present, and the procession of the ecclesiastics was duly solemn, arranged meticulously and with great respect. It is not my duty to describe either the order of the papal procession or that of the lord cardinals and the princes following the papal court, for I am entrusted with the task of recording only what pertains to our republic. In this regard, the parade was headed by the large group of distinguished citizens who had been appointed to welcome the supreme pontiff; then came the Florentine authorities, followed by the foreign princes and, behind them, the cardinals. The ranks of the ecclesiastics followed, then the princes and the horsemen who traveled with the Roman court, accompanied by Florentine youths, other fellow citizens, and horsemen who had been sent to receive our pastor. The last group of the cortege was that of the minor magistrates of our city. The only layman who took part in the procession of the ecclesiastics was the most illustrious Count Galeazzo Maria, who met the pope at the city gate. The pope invited the count to ride next to him in front of the cardinals and all the other prelates, an invitation that our distinguished citizens prized. The procession passed in front of the government palace in the piazza and culminated at Santa Maria del Fiore to give thanks to the Almighty.

I cannot refrain, now, from reporting something that, at the time, deeply upset me. I saw many of our excellent signori—who, as is customary among our highest authorities on rainy days, were heavily clad—pushed and thrown into the mud by the ecclesiastics escorting the pope. The pope, in my opinion, was not surrounded by ecclesiastics, but by a gang more befitting a suspicious tyrant than a pope. Their band consisted of mercenaries and henchmen armed with crossbows, spears, and other weapons more proper, as I said, to a tyranny founded on distrust. They were disrespectful, violent, and arrogant people, who had no consideration for the orders of the mace-bearers, the guards, or any other minor official of our excellent signori. Upon giving thanks to the Almighty, the procession went on much faster than before, for the original arrangement had already been disrupted by the time they entered the church. One can easily imagine how difficult it must be on a rainy day for a cortege to go from the houses of the Carnesecchi through Piazza Santa Maria Novella and Via della Scala. I was riding, and I found it to be more a travail for our distinguished signoria than any kind of celebration. When the procession arrived at the church,[4] I saw the crowd pushing our signori as they ascended the steps, looking more like exhausted servants than the highest authorities of our city. Some of them, in fact, were still in the first hall when the pope had already reached the lodging prepared for him. I think it is my duty to report such things, especially for the benefit of good people. Amid these difficulties, however, we finally arrived at the pope's lodging, where he kindly thanked the signoria and gave it permission to go after having given his blessing.

The following morning our standard-bearer, accompanied by a magnificent cortege of citizens, visited the pope. I cannot relay what they said during the meeting, for, not having been present, I am not certain. Before leaving, our signori gave the pope a gift, as is customary.

In order to make this happening even more eventful, the city decided to have a tournament in Piazza Santa Croce on April 29. They also organized an exceptional feast at the Mercato Nuovo, to which all the most distinguished girls and women of our city were invited and received by the most courteous and honorable young men. I shall not describe the great opulence there, other than to note that both men and women were dressed in elegant and precious clothes with exquisite embroidery, and that the abundance of pearls and daz-zling jewels gave all those present the impression of being among angels rather than on earth. The foreigners were especially astonished by the great number of distinguished women, the politeness of the young people, and their harmo-nious way of dancing and celebrating together, just as citizens should do. An abundance of delicious sweetmeats were served, not only on plates, but in full baskets, which made the delicacies look more like rough provender than sweetmeats.

As a final homage to the guests, our city constructed a fence of tall wood panels all around the main piazza, and sixteen of our lions,[5] or maybe more, were released into the piazza along with a multitude of prey, such as calves, bulls, horses, and wolves: it was quite a spectacle. On the morning of the same day, our magnificent signori invited the illustrious prince Galeazzo Maria to lunch—a delicious banquet with all kinds of excellent food and wines, as befits such a prince. Following the order of the illustrious prince, we prepared three tables to be filled with other princes and notable lords. I shall not list the numerous courses, the excellent wines, and the many sweetmeats the city served, nor shall I describe the seating order, since everything was arranged according to the prince's wishes. After lunch, the guest observed the hunting event I mentioned above.

On May 2, the newly elected signori paid a visit to the supreme pontiff.[6] On Thursday, May 3, the most noble Prince Galeazzo Maria and his court left, saluted with great warmth by many noble Florentine citizens. The day before, our signoria had presented him with two large trays, two jugs, boxes of sweet-meats, and cups. I have found no records of these gifts, and therefore I cannot describe them.

On Saturday, May 5, the supreme pontiff left for Mantua with the same ceremony and magnificence as had been organized for his arrival. At his depar-ture, the Florentines gave gifts to all the cardinals, as well as to certain princes. The total cost [of the ceremonies and the gifts] amounted to 13,626 florins and £48,091.

1. See documents 47 and 51.
2. In a passage of the *Libro Cerimoniale,* Filarete explains that when an author describes an event, the ceremonies should always come first, followed by the date on which the event took place, and finally by the total cost.

3. He was unable to walk because of gout, as Pius II himself writes in his *Commentaries*.

4. Santa Maria Novella.

5. Well into the seventeenth century, the Florentine authorities displayed caged lions, the symbol of the city, behind Palazzo Vecchio to impress notable guests and released the animals for spectacles like the one described here.

6. The signori were elected every two months on the first day of the month, starting January 1. These signori, therefore, had just started their term of office.

15

The City's Unparalleled Economic Prosperity

BENEDETTO DEI

Thanks to his numerous travels and multifarious activities, Benedetto Dei is one of the most intriguing figures of fifteenth-century Florence. He was a member of the silk merchants' guild in 1440, and of the wool dealers' two years later. Not much is known about Dei's youth, although his Cronica *informs us that he started traveling in his early twenties: he visited the branches of the Medici bank in Rome and Venice between 1433 and 1440, although he does not specify what his tasks were on such occasions. Economic problems, which vexed him throughout his life, brought him to accept office in several towns of the Florentine dominion. He was also appointed to important diplomatic missions around the time of the Peace of Lodi (1454). He never succeeded, however, in obtaining influential posts within the city government, and it was probably because of this that he decided to travel to Tunisia, Greece, and Turkey in the 1460s. As he writes in his chronicle, he resided in Constantinople from 1462 to 1464, where he had the opportunity to meet the Ottoman Emperor Mohammed II and the most influential members of his court. Laden with exotic gifts and animals, he returned to Italy in 1467, and was welcomed at the seaport of Pisa by his friend Luigi Pulci. In the following years, Dei's relationship with the Medici faction and with Lorenzo the Magnificent himself deepened. In 1480 he moved to the Milanese court of Ludovico Il Moro, and spent a whole decade at the service of lords such as the Bentivoglios in Bologna and the Estes in Ferrara, always alternating his mercantile occupation with the role of informer and ambassador. He finally returned to Florence in 1492, where he died on August 28 at the age of seventy-four.*

Like his friend Luigi Pulci, Dei possessed substantial knowledge of vernacular litera-
ture and had a natural tendency to fill his writings with long, interesting enumerations.
We find a good example of Dei's literary style in his description of Florence in 1472, the
initial passages of which are included here. The panegyric offers a picture of the city's
economy, which was thriving, in contrast to those of the other main commercial centers of
Italy. This view can be legitimately compared with that of Florence by Francesco Rosselli
in his famous Map with the Chain *(Figure 4). In both cases the Tuscan city appears as*
a precious jewel, a masterpiece produced by the citizens' diligent application in all fields,
from art and architecture to commerce and war. A deeply patriotic spirit animates Dei's
description, particularly apparent in the phrase he repeats again and again, "Flor-
entie bella."

Source: Benedetto Dei, *La Cronica dall'anno 1400 all'anno 1500,* ed. Roberto Barducci (Florence: Papafava, 1985), pp. 77–79.

1472

Let all Italy know, and all Christendom too, of the power, the strength, and the
glory that the Florentines have at present in Tuscany. May this record benefit
the peoples of Venice, Milan, Rome, Naples, Siena, Ferrara, Mantua, Lucca,
Bologna, Perugia, Ancona, and Romagna who do not know what Florence
looks like and have never been here. In order for them to learn, understand,
consider, and appreciate what this city is like, I, Benedetto Dei of Florence,
shall speak at length about the city's location, size, buildings, citizens, towns
governed (while specifying their names, number, and previous rulers), origins,
and ancestors. I have resolved to do this out of love for my friends, the Giustiniani and the Pattei, who are members of the Maona of Chios,[1] and have
chosen this year, 1472, the year the government of Venice sentenced Francesco
Bembo to hanging.

Beautiful Florence has preserved its liberty since its founding 1,545 years
ago, never changing its political stance, currency, or banner. The origin of the
city dates back to seventy-two[2] years before the birth of Christ, as can be noted
in the baptistery—a temple consecrated to Mars before the inhabitants of Florence were converted to Christianity. There is further evidence of this at the top
of the baptistery dome, which is enameled with letters in Chaldean, Moorish,
Turkish, and Arabic.[3]

Beautiful Florence is laid out in a circular fashion and has a diameter of five miles, each mile consisting of three thousand *braccia*.[4] It does not have a moat or a fortified citadel, nor does it have drawbridges, checkpoints, a fortress, sentinels, a standing army, or a stronghold; but atop its circuit of walls are eighty towers made of solid stone and lime from which one can launch an assault or defend the city from invaders. A river flows through the city, crossed by four marble bridges, and there are many mills within the city walls that satisfy the inhabitants' needs throughout the year.

Beautiful Florence rules over 406 walled towns, whose gates are opened each morning and closed at night. These towns and castles once belonged to the people of Arezzo, to the Roman Church, to Genoa, Milan, Pisa, Siena, Volterra, San Miniato, Lucca, the lords of Romagna, Naples (I refer to Cortona and Prato), the Ubaldini family, the lords of Battifolle (who ruled over Casentino), the counts of Orciatico and those of Pistoia, as well as other Tuscan lords. I shall not even count the people who live in unwalled hamlets, or those who dwell in the villas of the Florentine countryside no further than eight miles outside the city.

Beautiful Florence has organized its Monte[5] in an original way, managing its loans in the Venetian manner, and its deposits in the Genoese. The Monte takes fifteen florins from each of its citizens and after a fifteen-year period it gives back one hundred florins to the citizens and the subjects who need to raise a dowry for their daughters. There is no doubt that this institution, the Monte delle Doti, has been an excellent measure adopted by the city of Florence and has turned out to be very profitable for its people. Nothing like this is to be found in Venice, Genoa, Rome, Siena, or Lucca.

Beautiful Florence has an annual revenue of 360,000 florins deriving from taxation, salt and wine gabelles, and from the fees for drawing up contracts. Thanks to these resources, the Florentine government manages to meet all its expenses and give the citizens the interest they have accrued at the Monte. There always remains enough money to finance a war or, when necessary, to purchase cities or villages. Today, in 1472, the Monte is solvent, whereas the Venetians, as they themselves openly confess, are fifteen years behind in payments and are suffering a budget deficit.

Beautiful Florence has a total of thirty square miles of land within twenty miles outside its walls. This land, dotted with churches, monasteries, and religious sites, belongs to Florentines who reside in the city. The estates and farms provide great wealth and large quantities of wheat, forage, wine, olive oil, wood, meat, cheese, saffron, fruit, and vegetables all year round. It has an income of thirty gold florins for each of the said products, which amounts to a total of nine hundred thousand florins a year, not counting the constant surplus of wheat and olive oil. The Bolognese, the Genoese, the Lombards, and the people from the regions of Bologna and Romagna know these facts quite well.

Beautiful Florence has another source of income apart from the annual 360,000 gold florins deriving from taxes and the 900,000 gold florins provided by its land. It has the forced loan, the catasto,[6] as well as the *balzello,* the *ventina,* the *decina,* the *denaro per lira,* the *settina,* the *novina,* and the *cinquina.*[7] When necessary, such taxes are imposed once, twice, or three times a month, according to the government's needs and the expenses resulting from ongoing or recently ended wars. Let it be known to the people of Venice, Lombardy, Naples, Siena, and Lucca that every year more than five hundred thousand *fiorini larghi d'oro* are collected in addition to all other taxes.[8]

Beautiful Florence has 3,600 villas within a five-mile radius beyond the city walls. All of these houses are built with worked stones and are surrounded by beautiful fields plowed with the help of cattle. These villas have halls, private rooms, loggias, wells, springwater, farms, orchards, gardens, sheds, cellars, vaults, oil mills, vineyards, dovecotes, lodgings, and all sorts of furniture and fittings, both grand and small. Each villa is worth more than four thousand gold ducats, a sum equal to the cost of a large Genoese merchant ship.

Beautiful Florence has 108 churches within the city proper, which hold both morning and evening Mass. The churches are meticulously maintained and exquisitely furnished with cloisters, chapter houses, refectories, infirmaries, sacristies, libraries, bell towers, relics, crosses, chalices, silver items, gold and silver paraments, and velvet and damask clothes, as is well known to the foreign friars who come to preach in Florence for Lent. Theologians from Venice, Milan, Rome, Genoa, Naples, and Siena can confirm that what I am saying is true. All this is an amazing thing to contemplate.

Beautiful Florence has twenty-three palaces inside the city walls that host the guild leaders, their subordinates, secretaries, accountants, notaries, servants, and other minor officials. In these palaces are the seats for the twenty-three local guilds, whose presence is necessary in an ideal city; a place that lacks them cannot consider itself a city. Pay close attention to what follows, dear reader: the tribunals located in the said seats may hear cases and pass sentences that cannot be appealed. Another council, called the Mercanzia, presides over these twenty-three guilds.

Beautiful Florence has all seven of the fundamental things a city requires for perfection. First of all, it enjoys complete liberty; second, it has a large, rich, and elegantly dressed population; third, it has a river with clear, pure water, and mills within the circuit of walls; fourth, it rules over towns, castles, lands, people, and communes; fifth, it has a university, and both Greek and accounting are taught; sixth, it has masters in every art; seventh and last of all, it has banks and business agents all over the world. Venetian, Milanese, Genoese, Neapolitan, Sienese, try to compare your cities with this one!

1. The Maona of Chios was a company established in 1349 by twenty-six Genoese families to control the monopoly of the main products of that Greek island after its conquest by Genoa.
2. Actually, it was sixty-two years. "Seventy-two" was probably a scribe's error; Barducci's diplomatic edition of the manuscript reports seventy-two.
3. Dei probably refers to the fact that the baptistery dome originally had an opening modeled on that of the Roman Pantheon. This opening was closed and the dome assumed its present structure only in the sixteenth century.
4. A Florentine *braccio* was equivalent to about fifty-eight centimeters (twenty-three inches).
5. On the Monte delle Doti see document 13 and n. 2.
6. The system of tax assessment introduced in 1427; see document 13, n. 5.
7. Apart from the catasto, all the assessments here mentioned by Dei were occasional levies named after the number of members in the Florentine councils that were responsible for them; the *decina,* for instance, was imposed by the council of the Dieci di balìa. The balzello was also a type of forced loan. The levy called denaro per lira, by contrast, consisted in the payment of a *denaro di picciolo* for each lira of taxable income.
8. According to the Florentine law in Dei's time, all important commercial transactions had to be carried out in fiorini larghi d'oro, more valuable than the regular *fiorini d'oro*—always minted full weight—and the so-called *fiorini di suggello,* which had by then dropped in value.

16

Lorenzo the Magnificent's Utopian State

LUCA PULCI

Modern scholars have given Luca Pulci (1431–1470) much less attention than they have to his two younger brothers, Luigi and Bernardo. Although he was forced by bankruptcy to leave Florence in early 1465 and was arrested for insolvency upon his return, Luca managed to distinguish himself as a prominent author of bucolic and chivalric poems. In 1464 he, much more than Luigi, seemed destined to become the official Medicean vernacular poet. Pulci started the Ciriffo Calvaneo, *which turned out to be more successful in later times than in his own. His brother Luigi continued it, and, on Lorenzo the Magnificent's command, Bernardo Giambullari saw to its completion. The* Ciriffo *presents many similarities to the* Morgante, *though was not read nearly as much. Luca's two other works met with greater success. Dedicated to Lorenzo the Magnificent, his seventeen* Pìstole, *modeled on Ovid's* Heroides, *were highly esteemed in the Medicean literary circle. An even greater success was his* Driadeo, *an etiological poem that was reprinted at least nine times before the end of the fifteenth century.*

Luca's Driadeo *(1464–1465) possessed all the characteristics of a best-seller in the Florentine society of the late quattrocento. He modeled it on Boccaccio's* Ninfale Fiesolano, *and drew liberally from Ovid's* Metamorphoses. Driadeo *narrates the story of the satyr Severe's love for the nymph Lora. The tale takes place in the Mugello, a valley in the Florentine countryside, which was the birthplace of the Medici and where the Pulci family had a number of small estates. Like Naldo Naldi, Cristoforo Landino, Ugolino*

Verino, Angelo Poliziano, and others, Pulci celebrates the Medici by situating his tale in the spot where the ruling family built its villas.

The inclusion of Lorenzo the Magnificent among the characters, moreover, brings out the laudatory nature of the poem. Richly appareled, accompanied by a splendid retinue and by his younger brother Giuliano, and riding a white horse, the future leader of Florence carries on a poetic contest with the shepherd Taviano to win the love of the nymph Estura, whose name resembles that of Etruria (Tuscany). In telling Estura of the city he rules, Lorenzo describes its marvels and its riches and declares that she would be its adored princess. Florence thus takes on the appearance of a city similar to those which will soon fill the imagination of Thomas More and other sixteenth-century utopian writers.

Source: Luca Pulci, *Driadeo,* ed. Paolo E. Giudici (Lanciano: Carabba, 1916), pp. 96–98.

BOOK 3

(79)   Lauro[1] spoke thus: "My beautiful nymph, I wish you to dwell with me in the city that is queen of all other cities, enriched by property and castles, a university, a seaport,[2] and divine liberty. Inhabited by a great people, it boasts experts in many arts and is perfect in all respects. I shall now briefly describe her seven virtues to you.

(80)   "While on a rock by the river, you may happen to see fish in the waves, Clymene crying,[3] and wild beasts fleeing from bold hunters in the environs of the city and within the circle of walls. My city has a worthy, noble, and undefeated people, civilized and pious, hostile to all crime. The citizens unite to protect their beloved country and travel the world over.

(81)   "Its countryside is fertile and rich, dotted with villas and sacred temples. The vines of Minerva and Bacchus cover the soil, a soil which also abounds in other fruits, woods, and springs and has a temperate climate. Ceres lavishes food on the inhabitants of this region. Here you will find a variety of plants and all sorts of orchards, fine gardens, and sweet-scented flowers.

(82)   "The greatest eloquence could not help me recount to you these people's skills, nor the means of becoming rich that they have discovered. Some of them make a living by working iron, others weave clothes; no one dares waste time. Neither Daedalus nor the men who first breasted the waves aboard the Argus—not even their very captain—could be deemed as illustrious as these citizens.

(83)   "This entire city espouses, like a creed, noble, sincere, and untainted

liberty. It fosters sacred orders and just laws; it sentences convicts to death and banishes forgers, blasphemers, and thieves. By contrast, it rewards the worthy with appointments and high offices. It elevates the humble and answers their prayers, repays good deeds and punishes evil.

(84) "Here you will find an academy, a circle of bucolic poets who read verses from manuscripts, and schools of moral philosophers and Stoics. Cosmographers draw maps of the whole universe, while geometers elaborate precise rules. There are grammarians, orators, and historians, as well as musicians, those who track the motions of the stars, and doctors and surgeons to heal the body.

(85) "Often you will see, immediately upon their arrival at the city gates, distinguished visitors, sovereign pontiffs, and emperors being welcomed amid great joy by all the conscript fathers, our senators, and parades with princes, lords, knights, soldiers, standard-bearers, heralds, and jugglers.

(86) "You will also see the beautiful sandy river which flows through the city, where goods are loaded to be taken to the seaport. You will see men who, leaving their wives and homes, put all their merchandise on board to sail to a distant island, always consulting the North Star in tracing their route. They do not linger in seaports during their voyage; some return, some do not, as Fortune wills.

(87) "Various instruments and bells within the city mark the hours and beat the time of everyday life.[4] One can hear diverse and praiseworthy things: some explain God's actions to the common people, clarifying their meaning; the lawyer explicates the case to his customer in great detail; others compose verses to the sound of a lyre and sing of poets, the philosophic life, and prophets.

(88) "Our holy temples and sacred oracles are open to the faithful, to heretics, and Jews; they are without any restriction whatsoever. Both laymen and priests piously attend church services, their devotion strengthened by the many miracles they witness. The floors are inlaid with porphyry, the vaults with mosaics: all the heavenly signs are painted there, from Taurus to the other ten, and Gemini too.

(89) "In beautiful, lavish, and grand palaces, I shall introduce you to the most distinguished citizens. All your commands will be fulfilled, just speak and you will see. You will wear oriental gems and golden jewels and taste the most exotic food. Is there more? Happy in our heavenly choir, from balconies and within theaters you will watch games, festivities, tournaments, and jousts."

1. Lauro ('Laurel') was a name used frequently to refer to Lorenzo the Magnificent in fifteenth-century Medicean poetry.
2. Here he is referring to Pisa's seaport, which was then under Florentine rule.
3. The mother of Phaeton, who, having being allowed by his father, Apollo, to drive his chariot, died in his attempt to control it. See Ov., *Met.,* 1.750–2.328.
4. A passage reminiscent of Cacciaguida's description of Florence in Dante's *Par.,* 15.97–99.

17

The Glories of a New Golden Age

UGOLINO VERINO

Born in Florence in 1438, Ugolino de' Vieri (Verino is the vernacular form of the Latin Verinus) was a notary by profession, yet at an early age he showed an inclination for writing Latin verse. In 1464, he completed the Flametta, *a collection of poems patterned after Landino's* Xandra. *On Cosimo de' Medici's death, he composed the* Paradisus, *a Neoplatonic poem in honor of the Florentine Pater Patriae, thereby declaring both his devotion to the Medici family—whose patronage he would constantly seek—and his indebtedness to the poetic and philosophical theories promoted by his master Landino and Ficino's Platonic Academy.*

In the 1470s and the decade that followed, Verino's literary output remained steady, although it did not receive the hoped-for support from Lorenzo de' Medici. In 1480, he finished Carlias, *a chivalric poem about the Carolingian court, which he later dedicated to Charles VIII of France. In 1485 he unsuccessfully sought the patronage of King Matthias Corvinus of Hungary by sending him the seven books of his* Epigrams. *Two years later, Verino lost his son Michele, who had already attained considerable fame as a poet himself. This loss was one of the main factors in Verino's decision to devote the rest of his life to writing religious poems. He was close to Savonarola and his Piagnoni, as we can see in his dedication of* Carmen de Christianae religionis ac vitae monastichae felicitate *to Savonarola in 1491.*

Though Verino's poetic inspiration cannot be considered among the most original of the Italian quattrocento, his work is important. In his prolific writings one can find the most ordinary and therefore characteristic features of late fifteenth-century Florentine literature: an erudite use of classical sources; imitation of Greek and Roman authors; epideictic compositions; and a versatile poetic style. Verino celebrated the main figures of his time, especially his most generous patron, Piero de' Medici, and the humanists Cristoforo Landino, Angelo Poliziano, and Marsilio Ficino. The poem from his Flametta, *translated here in prose, is a good example; the couplets are dedicated to Andrea Alamanni—a friend of many humanists and one of the founders of the Florentine academy—and praise all forms of study thriving in quattrocento Florence. We have omitted verses 1–68, in which Verino speaks of his friendship with Alamanni and the nature of poetry.*

Source: Ugolino Verino, *Ad Andream Alamannum de laudibus poetarum et de felicitate sui saeculi* (*Flametta*, 2.45), in *Poeti latini del Quattrocento*, ed. Francesco Arnaldi, Lucia Gualdo Rosa, and Liliana Monti Sabia (Milan: Ricciardi, 1964), pp. 860–864.

TO ANDREA ALAMANNI: IN PRAISE OF POETS AND ON THE SPLENDOR OF HIS TIME

I am delighted indeed to have been born in this fortunate time, a time in which men are rewarded according to their merits, and excellent deeds receive excellent recognition. Glory now advances the liberal arts and laboring brings joy, for no one is left uncompensated for his efforts; now is a great moment to devote one's efforts to the art of poetry. In Italy, these studies have been ignored for a thousand years, ever since barbarian races invaded our soil. It was many years later that the great Tuscan Dante finally brought poetics back for the people of Italy to celebrate. Other arts were also rediscovered and began to flourish, when you, O Tuscan lion, vanquished your neighboring tyrants with the help of Mars and your fame started to grow day by day, together with your power. Eloquence and rhetoric also began to prosper, and today there are an immense number of erudite men in the city. Some know the laws of nature, some know the stars: how the wrath of old Saturn is curbed by Jove; how the light of the sun mitigates the influence of Mars; and how Mercury's burning star favors the birth of thieves and rhetoricians.[1] Some know the size of the ocean, how the earth remains suspended between two heavens, and how sunlight alternately touches the antipodes, despite Christianity's condemnation of such theories.[2] Many even strive to comprehend the nature of God, although this exceeds human capability.[3]

Today we also have a man of high morals and principles, which he offers to his city and family and puts into practice himself; he is a man of such worth that I pray God will not take him away from us too soon.[4] There are some who, through subtle dialectics, lead their opponents to grant things that they would never hold themselves, not even if forced to do so. Nowadays we see innumerable arts flourishing which have been absent from Italy for ten centuries. Zeuxis himself has returned; he who painted those grapes which often attracted you, O birds, so real did they seem. Now a new Phidias is among us, and a new Apelles too, whose paintings seem to be alive. There are those who carve a breathing face out of Parian marble, others who cast bronze statues, still others who make bowls. Many other arts without a name, moreover, are prospering—increasing the wealth of those persons who cultivate them.

May I say it without offending you, O men of ancient times: the Golden Age is inferior to the time in which we now live. Was there ever more justice or more respect for the law? Has either piety or faith ever been more honored? Cruel wars are no longer fought, since the neighboring peoples have been vanquished. Has any time ever enjoyed greater peace? By virtue of its citizens, Florence has become paramount among Italian cities. Who, in fact, has ever equaled the honesty, intellect, and nobility of Cosimo de' Medici and his two sons? Who has ever made use of his own abundant wealth with greater generosity? These are among the things which make us equal to the gods. Men praised by the Ancients for their merits were later believed by posterity to be gods. That is why Lemnos worshipped Vulcan; Naxos honored you, O Bacchus; the people of Attica, Minerva; the Cretans, Jove; the Phrygians, Hyperion; and you, Rome, venerated Mars, who was the originator of the house of Sulla. From Mars came your family, Alamanno, and the Medici as well; maybe you, too, have an ancestor who was born into the family of Julius Caesar.

The noble and pious house of the Medici has seen to the consecration of numerous temples to the Virgin. Many needy girls have married thanks to the generosity of the Medici, and preserved their virtue, the greatest of all gifts.[5] But you, Piero, noble offspring of the magnanimous Cosimo, you deserve to receive the greatest praise. A new Maecenas born on Tuscan soil, you are a man of culture who protects the learned. You are, O Piero, the greatest glory of the Tuscan people, for, as long as you live, scholars will always be well provided-for.

Through his wealth and patronage, Piero has supported poets, and, being a poet himself, poets are of great concern to him. You, therefore, fellow scholars, who sing with a might greater than mine, help me celebrate this man.

1. In classical mythology Mercury was thought to be the patron of both thieves and rhetoricians.
2. The theory of antipodes, condemned by the Church Fathers (see, for instance, Aug., *Civ. Dei,* 16.9), was commonly accepted in the fifteenth century.
3. An allusion to Ficino's Platonic Academy.
4. He probably refers to Matteo Palmieri and the precepts of his *Vita Civile* (1438–1439).
5. Verino refers to the Monte delle Doti.

18

The Pazzi Conspiracy

ANGELO POLIZIANO

Poliziano wrote his account of the Pazzi conspiracy within three months of the actual event. His text—which explicitly celebrates the Medici as the defenders of civic liberty and deliberately omits details about the social and political factors behind the conspiracy—is part of an extensive program devised by the Medici to counter the propaganda issued by the papal Curia. Pope Sixtus IV supported the conspiracy, which on April 26, 1478, injured Lorenzo the Magnificent and caused the death of Giuliano, his younger brother, while the two were attending Mass inside the cathedral of Florence. The Medici's response to the Curia was to have lawyers declare the pope's excommunication of their family invalid. Lorenzo also sought the help of his former tutor, Gentile Becchi, and of the chancellor of the republic, the humanist Bartolomeo Scala, to write in his support; which they did, respectively producing the Synodus Florentinus *and the* Excusatio Florentinorum. *All the prominent intellectuals of the Medici faction, Poliziano included, attempted to serve the ruling family in whatever way they could during this moment of extreme crisis.*

One of the main purposes of Poliziano's text is to show how the Florentines played a decisive role in these tragic events by bravely and steadfastly defending the Medici. Poliziano reports that the citizens of Florence assaulted the conspirators who, immediately after murdering Giuliano and wounding Lorenzo, tried to get the populace to overthrow the Medici. The author names the Pazzi involved in the plot, describes their traits, both physical and moral, and compares them to the most notorious conspirators of classical times. He punctuates the whole account with passages after the style of famous excerpts from Tacitus and Sallust. Poliziano presents the dismemberment of the conspirators' bodies by the Florentines, although horrifying in its cruelty, as an act of justice. The people of Florence, Poliziano explains, could not leave unpunished any attempt to destroy the harmonious social order the Medici had constructed. Once the tumult was over, the citizens and the subjects from the surrounding countryside paid homage to Lorenzo, rejoicing in his safety and celebrating him as the legitimate ruler of the Florentine state. The excerpt we have translated reports the conspirators' tragic fate and the Florentines' testimonial of loyalty to the ruling house.

Source: Angelo Poliziano, *Coniurationis commentarium,* ed. Alessandro Perosa (Padua: Antenore, 1958), pp. 43–65.

Meanwhile, people flocked to the Medici palace with incredible passion and love, demanding that the traitors be executed and that they be shown no mercy until they had been dragged to their punishment. The house of Jacopo Pazzi was barely saved from looting, and Piero Corsini's men, overcome by fury, took the naked and wounded Francesco Pazzi off to be hanged. Francesco was nearly dead before he reached the gallows, for it was impossible to curb the wrath of the multitude. Soon afterward, they hung the Pisan leader[1] from the same window as Francesco Pazzi, right above the latter's corpse. Once his body was lowered, something occurred which I think must have astonished everyone; it became known throughout the city almost immediately. Either by chance or out of rage, Francesco Salviati sank his teeth into Francesco's corpse, and even after the rope had choked him, he held on with his teeth to the other's chest, eyes frozen in an angry stare. After that, ropes broke the necks of the two Jacopos of the Salviati family.

By the time the situation had quieted down, I went to the square myself, and I remember seeing many corpses strewn about,[2] bearing signs of the contemptuous abhorrence of the furious crowd. Florentines loved the Medici house and condemned the murder of Giuliano, saying it was an outrage. They claimed that these men, who had no reason for such a heinous act, had resorted to crime, deceit, and treason to murder a most worthy young man, the favorite of all Florentine youth. A miserable and sacrilegious family, they said, abominable to both God and men, had committed this offense. The memory of his [Giuliano's] worth inflamed the people's hatred. A few years earlier, Giuliano had shown his remarkable valor in a jousting tournament; he had won it, and this is a deed that usually endears one to the multitude.[3] The outrageous nature of the crime added to all of this, for they said that it was impossible either to describe or to conceive of such a wicked, atrocious act. They trembled with rage at the thought of a pious and innocent lad being cruelly slain inside a church, during Mass, right before the altar. They considered it most hideous that hospitality[4] and religion had been violated, that a sacred place had been polluted with human blood, and that the very same Lorenzo—on whom alone the whole Florentine Republic depended and in whom lay all the hopes and the power of the people—had been attacked by armed men.

From all the villages of the surrounding countryside, large crowds of armed men began to gather in the main square, in the city streets, and especially at the Medici palace,[5] all of them eager to show their support. Citizens brought their children and acquaintances to offer their service and riches, saying that both the private and public welfare of Florence depended on Lorenzo alone. Day after day, weapons, meat, bread, and all sorts of provisions were brought to Lorenzo's residence. Neither the wound nor fear nor the profound grief he felt at his brother's death prevented him from performing his duties. He welcomed all citizens, thanking them one by one. At times, he appeared at the window so that the crowd below, anxious to know about his health, could see him. The people would sing his praises and wave their hands, rejoicing and celebrating his well-being.

Meanwhile, it was reported that Giovanni Francesco da Tolentino, the prefect of Forlì, had invaded our territory, crossing the border with a troop of specially trained horsemen. At the same time, numerous letters and dispatches informed us that Lorenzo Giustini had left Città di Castello and was about to attack us from the border which divides Florentine territory from that of Siena. Our troops, however, forced them both to retreat. Sentries were posted at night throughout the city; Lorenzo's house was diligently guarded, and armed men were stationed at the crossroads, in the main square, and all over the city. The following day, Giovanni Bentivoglio, a knight of Bologna and that region's lord, closely linked to the Medici family, came to the Mugello offering several squadrons of horsemen and infantry divisions. The city was soon filled with foot soldiers, but the Committee of Eight[6]—fearing that the soldiers, who were eager for booty, might start a riot—appointed men to guard the city and then ordered everyone else who arrived in the city either to return home or to go wherever he thought he would be of use.

In the meantime, Renato Pazzi, who the day before the conspiracy had retreated to his villa in the Mugello and had gathered soldiers there, was captured along with two brothers, Giovanni and Nicola. Giovanni Pazzi, Guglielmo and Francesco's brother, was caught in a garden near his house. The pursuers captured Jacopo, who was now abandoned by all his men, in the village of Castagno. The first one to reach him was a certain Alessandro, a farmer who was about twenty years old. As soon as he caught him, Jacopo offered him seven pieces of gold, pleading with him to let him kill himself then and there, but he did not manage to persuade him. Since he continued and even increased his pleas, Alessandro's brother hit him with a stick. The fearful man then understood the truth of the saying: "Fate guides the willing man and drags the unwilling."[7] He was later escorted to Florence and brought to the signoria by a patrol provided by the Committee of Eight to prevent the crowd from tearing him apart. He confessed his crime without the application of torture, and a few hours later he was hanged. Even as he neared the moment of his death, Jacopo never abandoned his raging and furious nature, shouting that he was giving his soul over to the devil. After that, Renato's death sentence was pronounced, and his brothers were bound in chains. The youngest of them, Galeotto, still an adolescent, was seized with terror and tried to flee, disguised as a woman. He was immediately recognized and thrown into prison with the others. Shortly afterward, Andrea Pazzi, Renato's brother, was caught while trying to escape, and imprisoned as well.

During his flight, Bandini met Giustini and succeeded in escaping to Siena by joining his troops. With the help of the knight Piero Vespucci, meanwhile, Napoleone Franzesi saw to his own escape. A few days later, Giovanni Battista Montesecco was executed. Antonio of Volterra, the one who had wounded Lorenzo, and Stefano[8] remained hidden for several days in a Florentine monastery. As soon as the hiding-place was discovered, the people gathered at the monastery, barely restraining themselves from assaulting the monks who, in accordance with the rule of their order, had not reported the men's presence. They [the crowd] caught the murderers and began viciously to tear them apart. Having confessed their crime, they were finally dragged to the gallows with their noses and ears cut off, after already having received countless blows. The herald later announced that rewards had been set by the government for anyone who could either kill Bandini and Napoleone or capture them alive. Guglielmo Pazzi, relying on their family tie,[9] had rushed to take shelter in Lorenzo's house, but was sent with his children into exile between five and twenty miles outside the city.

When the Florentines discovered that Piero Vespucci had helped Napoleone, he, too, was immediately taken captive. Since his adolescence, he had squandered his father's patrimony, and his father had thus decided not to bequeath him anything in his will. As he was extremely poor, deeply in debt to people outside Florence, and dissatisfied with the present government, he was eager for a revolt. His nature was so impulsive and reckless that immediately after Giuliano's murder he started extolling the crime committed by the Pazzi. As soon as he realized, however, that all the people were on Lorenzo's side, he rushed to loot the Pazzi's palace. There he met soldiers greedy for loot, and he would have caused great danger to the whole city, to both its secular and religious institutions, had Piero Corsini, a worthy young man, not opposed this ferocious man. The violent and rabid Vespucci incited the crowd and all the soldiers to plunder. He, too, was finally thrown into jail, and his son Marco was sent into exile at least five miles outside the city.

Many more deaths followed. Of all the conspirators, some were killed, and the rest were either put in chains or banished. When the news reached Rome, there was great sorrow; embassies were sent from different places, and all rejoiced at Lorenzo's safety. Giuliano was given a solemn funeral, the obsequies being celebrated in the Church of San Lorenzo. Many youths were in mourning. He had suffered nineteen wounds and died at the age of twenty-five.

A few days later, after heavy rains, people from all over the countryside began to arrive. They claimed that it was a despicable thing to have buried Jacopo Pazzi in sacred ground, and the reason it had rained so much was precisely that, contrary to all human and divine laws, such an evil man as he, who even at the time of his death had shown no respect for either religion or God, had been buried in a church. According to an old peasant superstition, such a burial was harmful to the grain crop, which was just then beginning to grow. As is bound to happen with these sorts of things, this belief started to spread among the citizens, and people swarmed over Jacopo's tomb to unearth the body, and bury it outside the city walls.

What happened the following day could be considered something of an abomination. It was as if a large crowd of children had been inflamed by the mysterious torches of the Furies. These children unearthed Jacopo's body once again, nearly stoning to death a person who tried to stop them. Around the corpse's neck they retied the rope with which he had been choked, and proceeded to drag it through every street of Florence, insulting him the whole way. Some went ahead, in jest ordering the people they met to move aside to let the distinguished knight they were escorting pass; others, instead, hit the body with sticks and goads, urging him not to be late, as the citizens were waiting for him in the main square. Once they arrived at his house, they knocked on the door with his head, yelling "Is anyone in? Who will welcome the knight who has just returned home with his great escort?" Since they were not allowed to enter the main square, they went to the banks of the Arno River and deposited the body. As it floated along, a crowd of peasants followed, shouting obscenities. Someone said that Jacopo's dreams would have come true if, during his life, he had had the popular following he was now enjoying in death.

Recalling this momentous upheaval has often led me to think about the vagaries of fortune. I have been especially struck by the incredible sorrow everyone felt at the death of Giuliano, whose physical appearance, personality, and habits I shall briefly describe. He was tall and robust, with a large, muscular chest, shapely and brawny arms, strong joints, flat stomach, solid thighs, full calves, lively eyes with excellent vision, darkish skin, and thick, long black hair, which he combed back to keep his forehead visible. He was an experienced rider and archer, excelling at sports of all kinds, and extremely fond of hunting. He was magnanimous and steadfast, pious and just, particularly versed in painting, music, and refined pursuits of every kind. He was a gifted poet, composing verses in the vernacular which were profound and rich in moral teachings. He also enjoyed love poetry and read it often. He was eloquent, prudent, and not at all impulsive. He loved wit, and he himself did not lack for it. He especially hated liars and men who bear grudges. Although he did not dress to excess, he was incredibly elegant and well groomed. He was agreeable, gentle, and respectful of his brother, and he admired strength and virtue. During his lifetime, these and other qualities made the Florentines and his relatives love him; they also make the memory of this distinguished youth sad and most bitter for us all. Still, we pray to Almighty God that he may grant "at least this youth to help a devastated age."[10]

1. Francesco Salviati, archbishop of Pisa, who took part in the conspiracy. His body and that of Francesco Pazzi were hung from a window of the Palazzo della Signoria, the seat of the Florentine government.
2. The corpses of the conspirators, which, as described in the preceding passages, were mutilated by the enraged Florentine multitude.
3. Poliziano is referring to the well-known tournament held in 1475, which he celebrates in his *Stanze per la Giostra,* an unfinished work precisely because of the young Medici's death in the Pazzi conspiracy.

4. At the beginning of his account, Poliziano relates how, before the conspiracy, the Medici family—"always splendid and magnificent in its style, . . . especially in entertaining distinguished visitors"—had hosted some of the conspirators at their residence in Fiesole.

5. The palace (Figure 14) that Cosimo de' Medici, Lorenzo's grandfather, had Michelozzo, his favorite architect, build.

6. For the "Committee of Eight," see Dati's description of the Florentine magistratures.

7. Sen., *Epist.,* 107.11.

8. Stefano da Bagnone, a priest, who was also Jacopo Pazzi's secretary.

9. Guglielmo was Lorenzo's brother-in-law through marriage to his sister Bianca. He did not take part in the conspiracy.

10. Virg., *Geo.,* 1.500. By drawing on Virgil's famous passage, Poliziano replaces the pair Octavian–Julius Caesar with the pair Giuliano–Lorenzo de' Medici.

19

A Condemnation of Lorenzo's Regime

ALAMANNO RINUCCINI

Born into a renowned family of merchants, Alamanno Rinuccini (1426–1499) rejected the mercantile career pursued by his brothers and chose to study the liberal arts, and philosophy in particular. Rinuccini was a pupil of the Byzantine scholar Johannes Argyropoulos, and a member of a philosophical academy that became the model for Ficino's later and more famous Neoplatonic group. Rinuccini was, moreover, the author of political speeches, religious sermons, and a famous funeral oration for the humanist Matteo Palmieri. He also translated Plutarch, Isocrates, and Apollonius into Latin and held many important offices in the Florentine government. He was elected prior in 1460 and a member of the Dodici two years later. In 1466, he participated in the balìa created by Piero de' Medici to exile his opponents after the conspiracy of Luca Pitti. In 1472, Rinuccini became one of the trustees of the University of Florence, and three years later, when the relations between Florence and the papacy were particularly tense, he was appointed ambassador to Pope Sixtus IV.

Rinuccini's most famous work is his dialogue On Liberty, *written in 1479, one year after the Pazzi conspiracy.* On Liberty *bears witness not only to the deterioration of the author's relationship with Lorenzo de' Medici but, more generally, to the crisis of Florentine civic humanism as a whole. The three interlocutors in this work—Alitheus, Eleutherius, and Microtoxus—discuss the nature of liberty by commenting on the last few decades of Florentine history. They complain about the present tyranny of Lorenzo de' Medici and praise the ideals and achievements of the previous generations of Florentines.*

Florence—as Alitheus explains—extended its just rule over Tuscany and the neighboring regions, inspiring the Italian people with the principle of liberty and the necessity to do battle against tyranny. This is why, Rinuccini believes, the Pazzi conspiracy should be deemed "a glorious act, worthy of the highest praise," undertaken by the members of that distinguished family "to restore their own liberty and that of the state." The work ends by condemning Lorenzo de' Medici as "the tyrant of Florence" who has usurped the liberty of his fellow citizens.

Source: Alamanno Rinuccini, *Dialogus de libertate,* ed. Francesco Adorno, in *Atti e Memorie dell'Accademia Toscana di scienze e lettere La Colombaria,* n.s., 8 (1957), pp. 270–271, 281–290.

PREFATORY LETTER TO ALESSANDRO RINUCCINI

I know full well, my dear brother, that when I took up this lifestyle—which, after all, is not so different from yours—some men, out of either envy or lack of wisdom, criticized my choice, despite the fact that you and several friends support it. I have resolved, in fact, to abandon all civic affairs and retire to this small house in the country. Here I shall care for the little estate as if I were in exile from the city, detached from political life and the company of my fellow citizens. Although I could easily confute this criticism by bringing forth examples of famous men, you alone suffice to prove my case. You work in the immense English city of London as a representative of the greatest trading company that can be found in that market. Your superiors hold you in the highest esteem and truly appreciate you. You have not amassed an incredible fortune through your work, simply because that was not your intention. You have preferred to lead a quiet life of honest leisure, disregarding all luxury, and, what is more, giving up a vast portion of your inheritance. As a married man and a father, I could not choose to do the same, and I thus resolved to come as close to it as possible by detaching myself from city life and its innumerable anxieties caused by greed and ambition.

I cannot avoid, however, my friends' kind reproaches, which I have answered at length. My reply, as you shall see, was such that, far from changing my way of living, I almost convinced them to take up this way of life themselves. After my only son's most tragic death, I withdrew for a while to the same villa where he himself had often spent time; I avoided company and lived alone with my deep sorrow. There, one day, two members of our academy[1] came to visit me and express their sympathy. I prefer not to say who they were in case anything said in that friendly conversation [which I shall be recounting here] would offend someone. [For this dialogue of mine], therefore, I have invented names in keeping with their characters and their thoughts, I believe, and if you happen to know them, I look forward to hearing what you think.[2] Even if you have nothing to say regarding my choice of names, I would still like to hear whether or not you agree with the ideas expressed in the dialogue.

This is how things went: [the two men] were returning from Casentino and decided to make a little detour to pay me a visit. They found me at home reading, and having exchanged those words which are customary when friends meet again, they offered me their condolences and spoke at length to comfort me. To distract me from my intense grief, Alitheus urged Microtoxus to report what they had been saying about me during their trip. He thus began as follows.[3]

BOOK ONE

. . . *Alitheus:* I became acquainted long ago with this attitude of yours, Micro-toxus; nothing seems to frighten you more than learning something new. Nonetheless, listen to what I have to say. I do not hold that a man forced to obey the laws of his country is deprived of his liberty, since, as Cicero wrote,[4] we obey laws in order to be free, and many things can be prohibited in a man's life without his being deprived of his liberty. Likewise, I do not think that a man should be said to be deprived of his liberty if he is forbidden to hurt a fellow citizen, take away other people's property by force, or rape somebody's wife. Well-governed cities prevent the committing of such acts through the promulgation of laws and the enforcement of severe punishments. There are also many things which, although not prohibited by law, are not permitted by either tradition or civil custom, as they appear to be acts of insanity. These things, in my opinion, do not limit liberty either. I would not say, for instance, that a person who dwells in Florence is less free because he is not allowed, if he wants to be considered sane, to speak in public in a pair of riding boots and a raincoat. If he is a newly arrived traveler, however, he may do so.[5] Our customs also prevent a man of quality from dancing and singing in the market square, although there is no law prohibiting it. And I think you will agree with me when I say that a man is no less free because, in order to maintain his reputation, he restrains himself from doing such things.

Microtoxus: I certainly agree, and I even admit that nothing can be truer than what you have just said. I now see how wrong I was in not realizing that the last points of your definition were as important as all the others.[6] Since you have clearly explained the first part of the topic of our discussion and carefully illustrated your stance, I am ready to hear you discuss the other part of the subject. Now that the sun is not blazing, this shade and pleasant breeze seem somehow to invite you to speak. I would thus like you to continue by telling us how our way of living differs from the liberty you have previously described, for I believe that it will be difficult for you to prove this point.

Alitheus: You invite me, distinguished friends, to discuss an important question, the very thought of which, not to mention actually speaking about it, causes me great sorrow. I cannot think about this topic without bursting into tears, for I am ashamed to see the people who once dominated not only most of Tuscany but also the neighboring regions ruled now according to the whim of a single young man. In this city today, so many men—estimable for their great intellect, their age, and their wisdom—are so oppressed by the yoke of servitude that they are hardly aware of their present situation, nor do they dare free themselves; worst of all, they unwillingly oppose those who try to liberate them. Our way of living has degenerated so much since the time of our virtuous ancestors that if they were to come back to life they would not acknowledge us as their descendants. They founded, maintained, and developed this republic through their customs, sacred laws, and institutions, created to promote upright living. Who, in fact, would deny that the old laws of our city were equal, if not superior, to the constitutions that Lycurgus, Solon, Numa, and all the other legislators wrote to protect the liberty of their people? The facts prove this to be so. When our city lived according to its laws, its wealth, dignity, and authority increased as well, so much so that it surpassed all other Tuscan cities and became an example of power and virtuous living.

I see that today all despise these very laws, and that it is the whim of a small group of unscrupulous citizens that has gained the force of law. Please tell me, who believes that liberty rests upon anything but civic equality? Equality is the first thing for which we must strive in order to prevent the rich from oppressing the poor and the poor from attacking the rich, and everyone can feel secure about the safety of his own property. Judge for yourselves how these things are now managed in our city. What can I say about the corruption of justice? It is shocking to recall how just our city's juridical system was at the time when Florence enjoyed freedom, by contrast with how corrupt it is today. I cannot relate without displeasure how no one dares to contest, by either word or vote, charges (usually supported by false denunciations) that are made in favor of a powerful citizen. It seems a great gift of Fortune to have an honest excuse for why you cannot be involved in judging a given case.

Florence was once so renowned for its justice that people from distant lands wanted to have their cases tried here. Today, by contrast, even for cases within Florence, a verdict is reached only after a long time, immense expense, all sorts of fraud, bribes, and plots by powerful men. It is now the richest man, not he who is right, who often prevails. This corruption is what has led many to complain about losing their houses and property or about having been dispossessed of the palaces in which their families have lived for generations or about being despoiled by force and fraud of their possessions and wealth. How can I compare the past freedom of speech in the senate and in public meetings with today's silence? In the past, the intelligence, the eloquence, and the intense patriotism of every single citizen was evident. Wise men debated decisions by weighing the pros and cons in such a way as to easily discern the truth in each proposal. Consequently, they were seldom wrong in their decrees, and once they reached a decision, they did not immediately reverse it through a sudden change of mind. Today, on the contrary, our Catos[7] invite only a few select people to join their discussions on important matters, and we often see them reversing their decisions, perhaps following someone's advice the very day after they have rejected it.

Our city, therefore, lacks what Aristotle said was characteristic of a free state—namely, its unity: a single body with many heads, hands, and feet.[8] Lacking something is just as bad as having something but being unwilling to use it. At present, because of both the arrogance of a few shameless men and the indolence of other citizens, these few men have taken possession of what belongs to the people. Their blind greed and their ambition are so powerful that they have repressed the authority of the councils and the voice of the people. It is very seldom that in the assemblies one hears the voice of the herald—so praised by Demosthenes—inviting all citizens to participate in the debate after the government's ruling.[9] On the rare occasions when, for the sake of tradition, the herald summons them, everyone knows that it is a sound made in vain, for fear obstructs the citizens from participating.

Who does not know how important it is for a state to have the authority to punish criminals? The fear of being convicted and disciplined, in fact, deters wicked and nefarious men, whom neither shame nor love of virtue and honor would prevent from breaking the law. Once these deterrents are removed, there is no monstrous crime that the greed of the wicked would fear to commit, for the lack of punishment is, for them, tantamount to the freedom to do wrong. Do criminals fear committing any crime these days? Why should they, since they enjoy protection and immunity for their crimes, thanks to bribery and the influence of corrupt citizens whose faction they support? Why should they be kept from doing whatever they want, since men who have been sentenced to exile or death do not hesitate to walk freely in the city streets before everybody's eyes, relying on the immunity which is granted them not by a judge, but by a single private citizen? Men sentenced to life imprisonment by the Committee of Eight[10] have been released from jail in compliance with the desire of a private citizen—or should I say, tyrant.

Why, then, should I complain about the elections to public offices? We know that in free cities officers are usually chosen by drawing lots, a practice that is fully in accordance with liberty and justice, for whoever privately supports the state through the payment of taxes also shares in its benefits and advantages. Now, however, we see that the main officials, or whoever holds a post of some responsibility and importance in the city government, is chosen not by lot but by appointment. As a consequence, it is not worthy men, notable for their wisdom and probity, who are elected, but associates of the powerful—those who indulge their whims and desires—whoever, in other words, is ready to serve them in the most humiliating ways. This is the reason officials have no authority whatsoever, or very little at best; for good men and all those who should take up posts in the government are justly irate and prefer not to be involved in the political life of the city. This gives a few wicked men even greater power to exploit and ruin the republic.

These facts incite such anger that I could continue to lament at length if grief, O God, and the atrocity of these crimes did not force me to end my speech. I cannot leave unmentioned, however, the most tremendous wrong of all, one so great that every citizen should flee it as one would death. What could be more outrageous than the things that have happened in our city in these last years? The payment of innumerable taxes has drained every man of all his wealth, while all Italy has been enjoying great peace. All the money thus collected, moreover, has been used to satisfy the whims of a single man, although it was said to have purchased extra wheat, or to have been spent on some other unlikely item. We need not wonder, then, where these wicked men get the money to construct numerous buildings both in the city and in the countryside, and to maintain the myriad horses, hounds, birds, actors, spies, and sycophants. To spend this much money in just a few months shows how false [Lorenzo de' Medici's] display of wealth is, and, as he openly asserts, how he is not obliged to pay his debts. Moreover, he has always extorted money on any pretext from people with whom he was acquainted as well as from strangers, thinking that his situation would never change and that he would always be in the position to use the property of others, either public or private, as his own.

Such things and others similar to them, Microtoxus, in my opinion greatly endanger liberty or, should I say, have already uprooted and destroyed it. Although these things are inherently wicked and despicable and should be avoided like the plague by any righteous man, they seem even worse and less tolerable when I am reminded (partly by listening to the accounts of elderly citizens, partly by reading the writings of historians) of how much effort our ancestors put into defending liberty, and how they devoted themselves to preserving civic equality. They used to hold assemblies, for example, to discuss the behavior of rebellious citizens or, to use legal terminology, citizens "who were involved in a scandal," eventually sending them into exile once they had been found guilty. This practice was employed by the Athenians and later by all free republics, since they understood that civic equality is the main way to preserve liberty. I think you know that Giorgio Scali, a knight noted for his noble birth and the offices he has held in the government of our city, was sentenced to death for having released one of his men, Scattizza, from the prefect's prison.[11] Vieri Cerchi, moreover, was sent into exile for acting as if he had more rights than the rest of the citizens.[12] Having married the daughter of Uguccione della Faggiuola and become a relative of the tyrant, Corso Donati was forced to leave the city by an angry mob that suspected him of tyrannical aims; he was eventually killed in battle. The people of Florence greatly valued liberty, since, as is proper, they were the real rulers and leaders of the republic. Today, however, they seem to have lost all hope; they tolerate the whims of strangers[13] and are at their mercy. Not by choice or out of mere ignorance, but as a result of violence and threats, the Florentines do not dare exercise their rights, although in former times they spared neither their own lives nor their wealth to defend themselves from the attacks of powerful states and tyrants. Who does not know how valorously and with what military power and strategic ability they fought their neighbors, resisting their attacks or waging war against them in order to take revenge for the wrongs they had suffered? They fought Volterra, Pisa, Arezzo, and Pistoia until all were under their complete dominion. They battled so fiercely against Siena, Perugia, and Bologna that these cities considered it a blessing when Florence accepted their peace proposals. It is true that to speak about the war with Lucca is somewhat embarrassing; we have repeatedly conquered this city but we have never managed to keep it under our control. I do not know how this city, despite its frequent subjugation, has always found a way to slip out of our hands—it could rightly be considered an abyss that has swallowed up Florentine money and blood. It would take me too long to name all the tyrants and princes whom the Florentines have fought in violent wars in order to maintain liberty, if only in name. To this end, they first fought Manfredi by the River Arbia, and again at Benevento, where he was defeated and killed.[14] It was this same love of liberty that spurred our ancestors, who were always devout Christians and pious members of the Church, to wage war without hesitation against unjust popes, such as Gregory X, who excommunicated our city for three years.[15] They then battled Emperor Henry, who encamped his army as close as the monastery of San Salvi.[16] They likewise opposed Uguccione della Faggiuola and Castruccio of Lucca, who, despite the heavy losses they inflicted on the city, never succeeded in taking away our liberty.[17] The same was the case in regard to the tyrant of Arezzo, Guido Tarlati; and Louis of Bavaria himself tried in vain to deprive the Florentines of their liberty when he was on his way to be crowned Emperor of the Romans.[18] Moreover, Mastino, that treacherous despot, not only occupied Lucca—which, according to the agreement, should have been given to Florence—and kept it against all law and custom, but also waged war on the Florentines, who valiantly managed to protect themselves from his fraud and his army.[19] Following his example, the archbishop of Milan, a member of the Visconti family, tried to subjugate the Florentines with both deception and force. After a long and wearisome war, however, he was glad to make peace with them.[20] There followed that great and extremely expensive war against the unjust rulers of the Church who, disregarding both human and divine law, attempted to take away our liberty. They tried first through famine and then, finding this ineffectual, by force. Since Pope Gregory XI was in Avignon at the time, the Florentines, through the action of the eight officials specifically elected to conduct this war, managed to incite many papal cities to revolt against the Church.[21] Soon after, they faced that tremendous war against the tyrant of Milan Gian Galeazzo Visconti. The amount of money that the Florentines had to spend on that war was colossal. Having managed to resist for many years, they finally decided to summon Duke Robert of Bavaria into Italy with the promise of four hundred thousand gold pieces. The truce they had made with Gian Galeazzo, however, did not hold, as the Milanese duke disregarded the peace. He was, in fact, lying in wait for the Florentines, ready to resume the war with larger forces. The Florentine so hated the tyrant and so loved liberty and their city, that in just one night they gathered the necessary sum of money (and probably even more) and brought it to the government officials. Likewise, they later showed great valor and might in their fight against the perfidious King Ladislas of Naples. Despite the heavy pecuniary losses caused by the conflict itself, and by the fact that the corrupt king had intercepted Florentine money, Florence managed to extend its dominion by purchasing the city of Cortona from Ladislas himself.[22] Afterward, the Florentines warred not only once but often with Filippo Visconti, duke of Milan, as this wicked man and sower of discord menaced our liberty with great force and every possible fraud. Our forebears opposed his attempts with such force that he was compelled to fear for the safety of his own state. Shall I also recall the struggles with King Alfonso of Sicily? Yielding to the requests of Pope Eugenius IV and the Sienese, he first waged a cruel war on the innocent Florentines, who had no reason whatsoever to expect such an attack. He then conspired with the Venetians in expelling our merchants from both states. Finally, he invaded our territory with his son Ferdinand at the head of an impressive army. Without having looted on either of the two fronts, he shamefully returned to his kingdom with a starved, exhausted army.

As for the present conflict with Pope Sixtus IV and King Ferdinand, I have nothing to say, for they both openly assert in speech and writing that they are not fighting in order to deprive the Florentine people of their liberty but on the contrary to give them back the liberty that they have lost. Moreover, they say that this war is not against the Florentines, but against Lorenzo de' Medici, whom they call tyrant, rather than citizen, and have branded with all kinds of ecclesiastical censures. I therefore do not know whether those who oppose them should be considered to be fighting for liberty or for servitude.

I merely wanted to review these facts to show you the great care our forebears have always put into maintaining and defending liberty, for they protected it first with their own blood, as long as they fought themselves, and then through the expenditure of vast sums of money, once they started making use of mercenary troops. They were not satisfied with Italian forces, and thus made numerous agreements with powers north of the Alps. These powers became their allies: they summoned foreign kings into Italy, such as Charles of Bohemia, whose aid they requested to oppose the army of the bishop of Milan. Likewise, in the war against King Ladislas of Sicily, they summoned Louis of Anjou from France, with whom they became allies and friends after stipulating an agreement also involving Pope Alexander V. With the promise of a large sum, moreover, they convinced the count of Armagnac to come to Italy and help resist the attacks of Gian Galeazzo Visconti. Although they did so in vain, they also sent Robert, duke of Bavaria and pretender to the title of Emperor of the Romans, to fight Visconti.[23] In our time we have seen former King René of Sicily summoned to Italy from the south of France to help Francesco Sforza—with whom we had formed a close alliance—carry out the campaign against the Venetians. King René decided to keep a presence in Italy as long as need be, and thus left behind his son, John, duke of Calabria (who spent a long time in Florence), to punish Alfonso and Ferdinand for having tried to deprive the innocent Florentines of their liberty.[24]

This is what I have to say regarding liberty, my excellent friends, and I hope that you have not found my speech too long. The subject, however, was such that I could not help pursuing it at length. Please forgive me if my discourse has been so wordy as to bore you. If instead it pleased you even slightly, you must thank liberty herself, whose name is a delight to hear.

1. One of them (Alitheus) is the humanist Donato Acciaiuoli. It is not known who the other interlocutor in the dialogue might be.
2. The characters' names are Alitheus (the Truthful), Microtoxus (the Simpleton), and Eleutherius (the Lover of Liberty). As in many humanist dialogues, the ideas of the author are not necessarily expressed by a single interlocutor. Although Eleutherius seems most to resemble Rinuccini, Alitheus also acts as his mouthpiece at various points throughout the text. This need not surprise us either, for Acciaiuoli and Rinuccini had similar political views.
3. We have left out the section in which Microtoxus reports the conversation with Alitheus that afternoon. We begin with the point at which Microtoxus and Alitheus are speaking with Eleutherius.
4. See Cic., *Par.*, 5.34.
5. Alitheus means to say that the expectation that people be properly attired for an official occasion is not a sign that a society sets limits on personal freedom.
6. Microtoxus is referring to the definition of liberty that Alitheus gave at the beginning of the dialogue, drawing on Cic., *Par.*, 5.34: "Liberty is a kind of potential for enjoying freedom within the limits set by law and custom." Alitheus has stressed that liberty is a kind of fortitude, for the wise man is not induced by bribes or threats to give up his liberty. Like any human faculty, he explains, liberty is a natural gift that each man has the potential to develop and bring to perfection through study and education. What Microtoxus has not clearly understood is the last part of Alitheus' definition, namely, that liberty must be enjoyed "within the limits of law and custom."
7. Here "Catos" is said ironically, to indicate the Florentine officials. Cato the Censor (234–149 B.C.) and Marcus Porcius Cato (94–46 B.C.), in fact, were two Roman senators renowned for their integrity.
8. Arist., *Pol.*, 3.1279a and 1281b.
9. Dem., *De cor.*, 169–170.

10. For the function of this council, the Otto di Guardia, see Dati's description of the Florentine magistratures (document 8).

11. Giorgio Scali, the descendant of an ancient Guelph house, became a leader of the popular party at the time of the Ciompi revolution. He was executed in January 1382 for having released Bartolomeo Scattizza from the city prison. The tragic collapse of Scali's political career became proverbial in Florence; it is memorialized by various authors, including Machiavelli in his *Istorie fiorentine*, 3.20–21, and *Principe*, 9.

12. Vieri Cerchi (ca. 1240–ca. 1313) was one of the main political figures in late thirteenth-century Florence. In 1295 he half-heartedly supported the nobles' revolt against the Ordinances of Justice of Giano della Bella. He was forced to flee the city in 1302, after the arrival of Charles of Valois and the return of numerous exiles of the Black Guelph faction.

13. The expression used by Rinuccini, *alienam libidinem,* is meant to underscore both the Medici's origin in the Mugello Valley and their estrangement from the Florentine people because of their tyrannical conduct.

14. At the battle of Montaperti, in the Arbia Valley, the Ghibellines of Florence and Siena defeated the Florentine Guelphs with the aid of Manfredi (September 4, 1260). Manfredi died in the Battle of Benevento (February 26, 1266).

15. From September 1273 to January 1276.

16. Henry VII besieged Florence from early September 1312 until the end of October of the same year. The monastery of San Salvi lay just outside the city walls.

17. Uguccione, the Ghibelline lord of Pisa, defeated the Florentines at Montecatini on August 29, 1315, but was overthrown by Castruccio Castracani the following year. Castruccio, lord of Lucca, waged war against Florence from 1320 until his death on September 3, 1328.

18. Guido Tarlati was bishop and lord of Arezzo from 1321 until his death in 1328. Having allied himself with other Ghibelline forces, he expanded his dominion in Tuscany, thanks to the help of Louis of Bavaria, whom he crowned emperor. Emperor Louis repeatedly threatened Florence with Castruccio Castracani in 1328. After the latter's death, Louis was forced to abandon his hope of helping the Tuscan Ghibellines and conquering Florence.

19. Contrary to Rinuccini's account, Florence bought Lucca from Mastino della Scala, lord of Verona, who had conquered it in 1335. In 1342, however, Florence lost it to Pisa, then allied with Viscontean Milan.

20. Rinuccini refers to the long struggle against Archbishop Giovanni Visconti in the 1350s.

21. The so-called War of the Eight Saints, named after the eight officials mentioned by Rinuccini in this passage, was fought between 1375 and 1378.

22. Ladislas took Cortona, the southernmost outpost of Tuscany, in 1409. Florence purchased it from him in 1411.

23. In the 1390–1392 war against Milan, the Florentines called on Jean, count of Armagnac, to invade Lombardy from the west while they attacked the Visconti state from east and southeast and Duke Stephen of Bavaria from the north. In his *Istoria,* Goro Dati narrates that, after an initial success, the plan failed because of the count's reckless behavior.

Against the same Gian Galeazzo Visconti, moreover, in the autumn of 1400 the Florentines summoned Robert of Bavaria, whose army, however, was quickly defeated by Milanese forces.

24. René of Anjou and his son John landed at Porto Pisano in 1438 on their way to fight Alfonso of Aragon for the kingdom of Naples. At the end of 1453 and for several months in 1454, John was in Florence to lead Florentine forces against Alfonso. He returned later in the autumn of 1459 on his way to fight Ferrante of Naples, a war that he ultimately lost in 1464. He died in 1470.

20

The Entry of Charles VIII, King of France, into Florence

LUCA LANDUCCI

Luca Landucci (1436–1516), a shy and devout shopkeeper who avoided any direct involvement in city politics, left us one of the most readable and informative diaries from the second half of the Florentine quattrocento. As Landucci himself asserts in his memoirs, in the midst of the dramatic changes that characterized the society of his time, he always strove to pursue the happy mean. He followed the Savonarolan movement at one point and later became a supporter of the Medici party once the powerful family regained control of the city government in 1512. The pages of Landucci's diary show how his genuinely republican spirit, like that of most of his fellow citizens, could be roused by political propaganda that proposed as its main goal the defense of the commune's liberty and the expansion of Florentine control.

In the convoluted yet fascinating prose peculiar to the memoirs of Florentine merchants, Landucci records all the crucial events he has witnessed, such as Cosimo de' Medici's rise to power, the Pazzi conspiracy, the expulsion of Lorenzo the Magnificent's son Piero, the entry of Charles VIII into the city, Savonarola's initial success and ultimate downfall, and the placing of Michelangelo's David in the Piazza della Signoria. A true patriot, proud of Florentine achievements in all fields, Landucci does not neglect to mention the fame attained by his fellow citizens beyond the borders of Tuscany. At the very beginning of his diary, he lists the most renowned Florentines of his time: humanists, scientists such as the mathematician Paolo dal Pozzo Toscanelli, artists, the Archbishop Antonino, and naturally Cosimo de' Medici, "known the world over as the great merchant."

In the pages we have selected to translate, Landucci gives his impressions of the stay of King Charles VIII of France in Florence (November 1494). His opinions are representative of those of the majority of the Florentine population at the time. The initial enthusiasm for the arrival of the long-awaited ally soon gave way to popular rage at having the king's soldiers billeted in town and fear of being plundered. In Landucci's eyes, both the determination with which the Florentines opposed the king's request to let the Medici return to the city and the efforts of the population to establish a more open political system testify to a genuine love of freedom and justice.

Source: Luca Landucci, *Diario fiorentino dal 1450 al 1516 continuato da un anonimo fino al 1542,* ed. Iodoco del Badia (Florence: Sansoni, 1883), pp. 80–89.

On November 17, 1494, at 4 P.M., the king of France entered Florence. He arrived at Porta San Frediano and approached the main piazza. The procession moved so slowly that it was 6 P.M. when they entered Santa Maria del Fiore. He dismounted from his horse before the church steps and went to the high altar, walking between two lines of people holding two-branched candelabra. His barons and the city authorities followed him to the high altar amid loud cries of "Long live France"—no one had ever heard such a great ovation. All the citizens of Florence were there, some inside the church, some outside it, and everyone was cheering: children, adults, the aged, and all with great sincerity. When the people saw him on foot, they were slightly disappointed, for he was rather short. Nevertheless, everyone truly loved him. If only we could have convinced him that everyone's heart was filled with lilies,[1] and that we were thrilled to have him in our city! [We believed that] he should have faith in us and love us more than anyone; for he would come to see how great the Florentines' trust in him actually is.

As he left the church, he remounted his horse and rode to Piero de' Medici's palace, while the crowd kept shouting, "Long live France." There had never been such joy, nor such celebration, for everyone hoped that he would bring peace and calm to the city. Things took a different turn, however, for he deprived us of Pisa and gave it to the Pisans, which he should not have done, since he gave away something that did not belong to him.

On Tuesday November 18, the king went to Mass at San Lorenzo; I, too, went to that Mass, and had the opportunity to see him up close inside the church. On Wednesday the 19th, he went to Mass again at San Lorenzo, then walked and rode about Florence. He also asked to see the lions,[2] and to have some men released from jail who had been imprisoned for political reasons, among whom were a certain Ser Lorenzo and someone called Andrea. He had wished to do this charitable act while in Florence, and he was granted his request.

On Thursday the 20th nothing notable happened, apart from the fact that rumors were spread concerning the king's intention to let Piero de' Medici come back to Florence. This seemed to worry the citizens.

On Friday the 21st, at about 3 P.M., the signori called a meeting of the most distinguished citizens. There they discussed the fact that the king seemed to be about to do something different from what he had previously promised, and they debated what to say to him regarding his intention to let Piero de' Medici come back to the city. They all agreed that to let Piero return was out of the question, no matter what the king's wishes might be. The assembly decided to tell the king that anything would be granted him except this. All the citizens, moreover, were resolved to take up arms and fight the king, if need be, or fight anyone opposed to their decision. "If the king has twenty thousand soldiers," they said, "we have fifty thousand within the city walls." They proved not to be afraid of the king, and they also showed how great the citizens' hatred of Piero de' Medici had become. God knows whence all this hatred had come.

As it was God's will, there was increasing turmoil in Piazza della Signoria. The entire population was suspicious at even the slightest rumor and ready to revolt. Everyone was waiting for something horrible to happen. People were seized with fear and did not know what to do. Even more, they could not stand having to host the French in their houses. Some rumors were spread that the king had promised to let his soldiers ransack Florence. The turmoil in the piazza caused many people to rush home and lock their shops; some had cloth and drapery sent to their homes, or wherever they thought the merchandise would be safer. Although this is how people acted, they did not express their fears in words. Many of the French, being no less afraid than we were, took up arms; they gained control of Porta San Frediano and of the bridges, in order to be able to leave the city at any time. Once the citizens who were attending the meeting called by the signoria to discuss the aforesaid issues came to know that all the Florentines were locking their shops, they started regarding Piero's return to Florence as an even more imminent danger. The signori then ordered the assembly and the most distinguished citizens to show the king how great the impending peril was and requested him not to invite Piero to return, for that would cause great harm to everyone, not only to the city. Having understood the citizens' feelings and realizing what risk he, too, was running, the king said, "I am not here to stir up hatred, but to bring peace. I proposed that option only because I thought that it would please the city and everyone else." He claimed that he wished only for the welfare of the people and that he would never again speak of Piero's return. Whereupon the citizens courteously replied to the king, "We are ready to support you in whatever way you may wish from this free city." He then asked to borrow 120,000 florins from Florence, 50,000 of which he would have immediately, 70,000 before the end of July, and 12,000 florins each year for the whole duration of the war. He promised that when the war was over, he would free our city from all his soldiers and everything else and that, likewise, if he died, the city would be totally freed. Regardless of the outcome of the war, whether positive or negative for him, he promised he would free the city from his army. He wanted only to keep the castles of the territory of Pisa and a few others he had seized near Sarzana, in order to be able to return to France whenever he wished. On this last point, he was not immediately given an answer. With regard to the florins, they said they would soon give him an answer.

On Saturday the 22nd people feared that the soldiers would plunder the city, and many said, "The king does not want to sign the agreement, and this is a bad sign." In the meantime, the king's soldiers were slowly taking over the city. They requisitioned weapons and did not allow the citizens to wear arms either by day or by night; in addition to this, they injured people with sticks and knives. No one dared speak or go out after dusk, for the French soldiers who served as guards walked about the city all night and stole everything from whomever they met. Everyone was distressed and afraid. As soon as the French soldiers saw someone carrying stones or pebbles, they would go crazy and start beating him up.

On Sunday the 23rd the king rode around Florence escorted by a large retinue. He passed through the district of San Lorenzo and in front of the Church of San Giovanni. Once he arrived at the steps of Santa Maria del Fiore, he turned left and took Via dei Servi. He then went on for a few steps before turning left, until he was once again in front of San Giovanni; then he took the narrow alley behind the church and passed under the Volta di San Giovanni, by the Cialdonai. Those who saw him found the whole scene truly laughable and said that such [indecisiveness] was certainly more detrimental to his reputation than beneficial. He then proceeded to the Mercato Vecchio and went as far as Piazza San Felice to attend the feast of San Felice, which had been arranged in his honor. Once he arrived in front of the church door, however, he did not want to go in. The pageant was performed several times, but he never entered. Many said that he was afraid and that he wanted to avoid being in an enclosed space. This proved that he was more afraid than we were. Woe to him if he had started to fight against us, although we, too, would have run a great risk. But God Almighty has always helped us by virtue of the prayers of His devout servants and of the many righteous and pious people who live in this city and invoke the Lord with pure hearts.

Around this time, two Venetian ambassadors came to speak with the king, as well as a few ambassadors from Genoa, who had come for Sarzana and other things.

On Monday the 24th rumor and suspicion spread among the populace, and many people were saying, "The king does not know what he wants, and he still has not signed the agreement." They said that some of the king's counselors were plotting against the city, such as a certain lord of Brè,[3] who was lodged at the house of Giovanni Tornabuoni. They said that he had promised to have Piero de' Medici reinstated in Florence and that he would urge the king to make sure this happened. Maybe this was not true, but many believed it to be so, hence the terror of the populace. The fear became even greater when news spread that the king was to have lunch with the signoria at the Palazzo [della Signoria] that morning, and that he had ordered the palace free from the communal guards, whereas, as it was reported, he actually wanted to go there with a large armed escort. This inspired suspicion in the entire population, and that morning everyone filled his house with bread, weapons, stones, and anything else that would be helpful in defending his family. All were ready to take up arms, die, and kill, if necessary, as they had done during the Sicilian Vespers.[4] The populace was so afraid that at lunchtime you could hear people shouting, "Lock up, lock up!" Everything in Florence was closed, and people kept running around without any reason other than suspicion and fear. Consequently, many of the French rushed to Porta San Frediano and seized the Ponte alla Carraia. At Ognissanti, Palazzuolo, and San Frediano people threw so many stones from their windows that the soldiers were prevented from taking those city gates. If one had asked what was going on, no one would have been able to answer. This situation kept the king from going to the Palazzo della Signoria for lunch. It was by God's grace that everyone became so suspicious; this, in fact, led the French to change their inimical attitude toward us—we who have always been amiable to them. God never abandons Florence, but we are not always grateful enough. News spread that the king's troops quartered in Romagna had started to march in the direction of Florence and Dicomano.

On Tuesday the 25th nothing notable happened, apart from the fact that the French were so scared that they were on guard day and night. They requisitioned all the weapons they could find and despoiled whomever they met at night of everything. And so it happened that a number of reckless Florentines, who had decided to murder French soldiers whenever they came across them after dark, actually did kill and injure a few. If the king's troops had stayed much longer, they would have killed many more, and this would certainly have had detrimental ramifications. Such rash persons always put a city in great danger, for they are not aware of the fires they start with their thoughtless actions. At times it happens that a person who is worth nothing makes a king angry by doing something ridiculous, the city having nothing to do with it and not being at fault.

On Wednesday the 26th the king went with the signoria to Mass in Santa Maria del Fiore. There he swore to observe the terms of the agreement that had been prepared, which were as follows: we were to lend him 120,000 florins: 50,000 immediately, the rest before the end of July 1495. He, in turn, was to give us back once and for all Pisa's castles and all our other possessions. Piero de' Medici had to remain in exile at least one hundred miles away from Florence; the 2,000-florin price set on his head and on those of his brothers was to be removed. He [the king] swore to observe all these terms and gave his word as king on the altar of Santa Maria del Fiore, before Jesus Christ.

On Thursday the 27th the king went to the Prato d'Ognissanti to see some pavilions which the duke of Ferrara had offered to him. One of those pavilions was particularly beautiful, truly worthy of a king, equipped with a hall, a bedroom, a chapel, and many beautiful things. He was to leave that morning, but he did not. The festive bells rang and there were fireworks in the evening. On that same morning, many of the king's men who had left Romagna arrived at Dicomano. They were quartered there, and even on my property there must have been about twenty horses. I left my young son Benedetto there, whose life was threatened several times, despite his having treated the soldiers well, as I had ordered him. They cost us a great deal of money indeed. They were quartered all over the Val di Sieve, even as far as Pontassieve and Le Sieci, and then moved on to Upper Valdarno.

On Friday the 28th the king left Florence after dinner and spent the night at the Certosa. Most of his men followed him, and only a few remained in the city. People said that Fra Girolamo da Ferrara, our famous preacher, went to meet the king and told him that remaining in the city was against God's will, and that he must leave. They also said that Fra Girolamo went again to the king upon seeing that he had not left, and told him that he was acting against God's will and that the harm that was to be done to others would fall on him instead. This was thought to be the reason for the king's early departure, for at that time Girolamo was considered a prophet and a saintly man, both in Florence and all over Italy. On that same day the captain of the king's troops in Romagna arrived in Florence. His name was Begnì,[5] and he told the king, in a rather rude manner, that it was time for him at last to leave the city, for the situation was auspicious. He seemed to disapprove of the king's long stay in Florence. In truth, the king left because he relied on the lord more than on anything else, and rightly so, for in the opinion of most people he was a very wise and good man. This, therefore, was the principal motivation behind the king's early departure.

On Saturday the 29th the rest of the king's army, which until then had remained in Romagna, passed the border, then San Godenzo, Dicomano, Pontassieve, and Upper Valdarno, wreaking havoc. In Corella they killed about eleven men, took prisoners, set a price on certain people's heads, plundered the whole village, and set fire to it. They broke down the wall of my house there, as well as the doors; they invaded my little farm, took my wine, fodder, and all the household goods they wanted. Those they killed were aged inhabitants of Corella, who were ready to host them, but this was misunderstood. It is true that some young men at first tried to drive them out of the town. Soon, however, the older folk tried to induce the French to come back, but those violent French soldiers struck them on their heads, and left many of them dead in the fields. They then took to committing all sorts of cruelties.

On November the 30th people did nothing but talk about the atrocities of the French, continuing to do so on Monday, December 1, 1494. On the 1st, the rest of the king's troops from Romagna passed through Valdisieve.

On Tuesday December 2, 1494, a meeting was called in the Piazza della Signoria, at about 3 P.M. All the gonfalons came in procession to the piazza, with the banner in the front line followed by a crowd of unarmed citizens. A multitude of armed guards were positioned throughout the piazza. They read forth a great number of written documents and statutes. First, however, the crowd was asked whether two thirds of the population was present in the piazza. When that was confirmed, they began to read forth the following decisions: all laws passed from 1434 on were abolished, as were the offices of the Settanta[6] the Dieci, and the Otto di Balìa. They also read decisions concerning the Consiglio del popolo and the Consiglio del comune. Other resolutions, furthermore, were that elections be performed by drawing lots, as was once customary in the commune,[7] and that a list of candidates be prepared.[8] For the time being, they decided to create a council of twenty men, chosen from the most distinguished and experienced citizens, which, together with the signoria in office and the collegi, had to select people who were to serve in a temporary signoria and in all the other official posts until the completion of the list of candidates. After the election the council would be dissolved. Ten of the twenty men were appointed to attend to the war against Pisa and other matters of primary importance.

1. The lily was the symbol of both Florence and the royal house of France.
2. The commune's lions; see document 14, n. 5.
3. Philip of Bresse, who later became duke of Savoy.
4. The popular revolt which in 1282 overthrew the Angevin monarchy in Sicily.
5. Robert Stuart, lord of Aubigny-sur-Nerre.
6. Established by Lorenzo the Magnificent in 1480, the Consiglio dei Settanta had the authority to appoint the signoria, the Otto di Pratica, and other important administrative bodies. Because of its great power, the supporters of the republican faction considered it a detestable symbol of the Medici regime.
7. He is referring to the intervention of the accoppiatori, through whom the Medici had managed to control the Florentine electoral system. The accoppiatori were entrusted to place the names of the eligible citizens inside bags from which they were to be drawn by lot. In practice, however, they had the power to decide to which offices the candidates were to be assigned. During the second half of the fifteenth century, the enemies of the Medici demanded their removal as a fundamental step towards the re-establishment of Florentine freedom. Rinuccini, for instance, presses for this measure in his dialogue *On Liberty.*
8. For a compilation of these deliberations, see the bibliography section on Landucci. The changes introduced into the Florentine political system by the 1494 resolutions, which eventually established the republican Consiglio Grande praised by Savonarola in his *Trattato* (document 41), are also cited by Francesco Guicciardini in his *Storie fiorentine.*

1. The Florentine coat of arms, an inlay of semiprecious stones. The Medici Chapels, interior of the Chapel of the Princes, Florence (S). Illustrations accompanied by the symbol (S) are reproduced courtesy of the Sovrintendenza per i Beni Artistici e Storici delle Province di Firenze e Pistoia.

2. *Marzocco,* by Donatello. Museo Nazionale del Bargello, Florence (S).

3. *Map of Florence,* by Piero del Massaio. This illumination is from a manuscript (ca. 1469) containing the Latin translation of Ptolemy's *Geography* by Jacopo Angeli da Scarperia. It highlights the city's main religious, public, and private buildings. MS. Lat. 4802, Bibliothèque Nationale, Paris (K). Illustrations accompanied by the symbol (K) are reproduced courtesy of the Kunsthistorisches Institut in Florence.

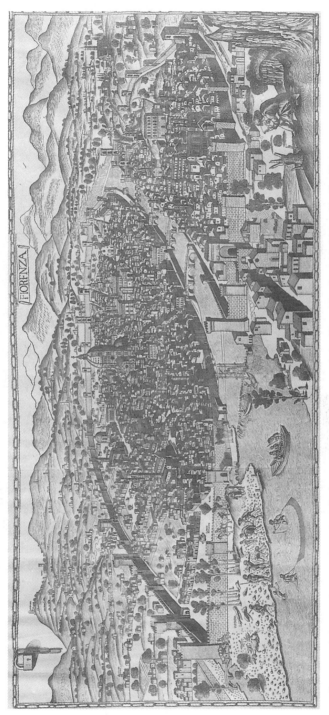

4. The view of Florence by Francesco Rosselli (ca. 1472) known as *Map with the Chain*. Kupferstichkabinett, Berlin (S).

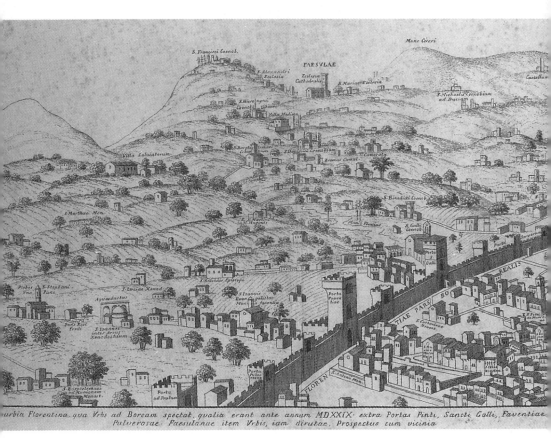

5. Detail of a copper engraving of Rosselli's *Map with the Chain*. It shows the main private villas and religious buildings in the countryside between Florence and Fiesole. Società Colombaria, Florence (K).

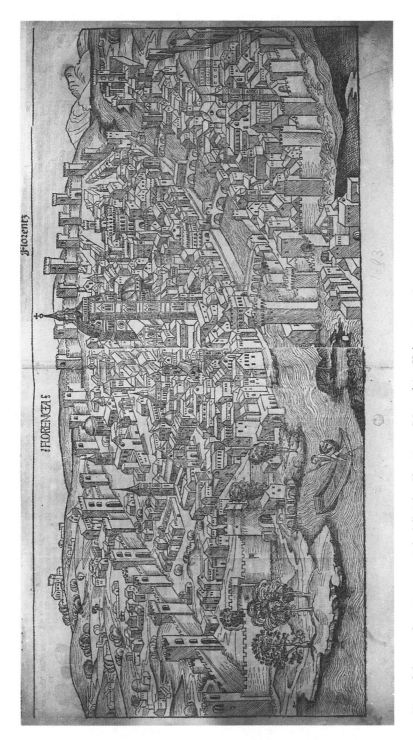

6. View of Florence from Hartmann Schedel's *Liber Chronicarum* (Nuremberg: Koberger, 1493).

7. The Palazzo della Signoria and the Loggia dei Lanzi (K).

8. The cathedral of Florence and Giotto's bell tower. The dome of the baptistery can be seen to the left of the bell tower (S).

9. Brunelleschi's dome for the cathedral of Florence (K).

PART THREE

Literature

21

The Lives of Dante and Petrarch

LEONARDO BRUNI

The rethinking of the contributions made by Dante and Petrarch is a fundamental aspect of Florentine humanism. This is particularly true in the case of Bruni, who in his Dialogi ad Petrum Paulum Histrum (1406) *evinced a somewhat equivocal opinion of the two Florentine writers. Later, however, he was to praise them highly. The structure of Bruni's biographies of Dante and Petrarch is modeled on Plutarch's famous portraits of Greek and Roman personalities.*

Bruni wrote The Lives of Dante and Petrarch *at a crucial moment in the history of Florence: Milan was once again threatening the security of its rival. In 1436, Florence, Venice, and Genoa formed an alliance to resist the re-emergent power of the Visconti. Once again, Filippo Maria Visconti, lord of Milan, decided that literary works of political propaganda were needed to reinforce his military enterprise. The Milanese chancellor Pier Candido Decembrio composed a panegyric of the Lombard state in reply to Bruni's* Laudatio florentinae urbis, *which the chancellor of the Florentine Republic had recently circulated again, some thirty years after its original composition.*

It was in such circumstances that Bruni, probably yielding to a request from the Florentine government, composed his biographies of Dante and Petrarch. The context in which the work was written partially accounts for the fervent civic spirit pervading Bruni's view of Dante, whose activity in the government of the city Bruni repeatedly emphasized, together with his participation in the Battle of Campaldino. Petrarch, by contrast, embodied, in Bruni's view, a scholar dedicated to a life of contemplation and study.

Source: Leonardo Bruni, *Le vite di Dante e del Petrarca,* ed. Antonio Lanza (Rome: Archivio Guido Izzi, 1987).

PREFACE

Having recently completed a lengthy work, I felt like refreshing my spirits by reading something in the vernacular. Just like eating the same food day after day, reading the same work again and again becomes unpleasant. While I was thus carrying out my search for a book in the vernacular, I came across a small work by Boccaccio called *On the Life, Customs, and Studies of the Most Illustrious Poet Dante.*[1] Although I already was well acquainted with the text, this second reading gave me the impression that Boccaccio, a most agreeable and refined man, had written on the life and customs of so excellent a poet as if he had been writing either the *Filocolo* or the *Filostrato* or the *Fiammetta.* His work is filled with amorous thoughts, sighs, and burning tears, as if man were born into this world only to experience those ten days of love narrated in the *Hundred Tales*[2] by enamored maidens and delightful young men. Boccaccio was so inflamed while discussing matters regarding love that he omitted the most important aspects of Dante's life, concentrating instead on things of lesser significance.

I have therefore decided to write a new life of Dante in which particular attention will be paid to weightier topics. I do not mean to criticize Boccaccio; I write this work only so that it may supplement his. I shall also add a life of Petrarch, for I believe that the knowledge of these two poets and their fame brings much glory to our city.

Let us start with the life of Dante.

LIFE OF DANTE

Dante's ancestors descended from an ancient Florentine family and, as he seems to imply in one of his texts,[3] they were among those Romans who founded Florence. This is an unattested fact; in my opinion, it is a matter of conjecture. As regards, on the other hand, those ancestors of whom we have certain knowledge, his great-great-grandfather was Cacciaguida, a Florentine knight who fought under Emperor Conrad.

Cacciaguida had two brothers, one named Moronto, the other Eliseo. No written document mentions any descendant of Moronto, whereas from Eliseo came the family called Elisei, which had possibly had this name from an even earlier time. From Cacciaguida descended the Alleghieri, whose name derived from a son of his, called Aldighieri after his mother's family.[4] Cacciaguida and his brothers lived, as had their ancestors, near Porta San Piero, at the entrance to the Mercato Vecchio, which is close to the houses still called delli Elisei,[5] so named for the Elisei who had lived there since ancient times. The descendants of Cacciaguida, the Alleghieri, lived in the piazza just behind the Church of San Martino al Vescovo, opposite the street leading to the house of the Sacchetti; on the other side of their house were the residences of the de' Donati and de' Giuochi.

Dante was born in the year 1265, shortly after the Guelphs, who had been exiled following their defeat at Montaperti, had returned to Florence. He was well instructed in the humanities and entrusted to teachers of literature. He immediately showed an outstanding genius and a remarkable capacity for great success. He lost his father Aldighieri when he was still a child but was comforted by the members of his family and by Brunetto Latini, a man valued in the culture of that time. He gave himself not only to literature but to all liberal studies, neglecting nothing that makes a man great. All this, however, did not compel him to retire to a life of scholarly leisure and flee the company of people; on the contrary, he frequented his contemporaries and was known to be polite, well mannered, and capable in all the activities typical of youth. He participated as a young, well-respected man in the memorable Battle of Campaldino, in which he fought gallantly on horseback in the first rank—risky indeed, as the knights of the two armies were the first to clash. In this initial attack, the knights of Arezzo defeated and routed the Florentines, forcing them to return to their foot soldiers in complete disarray. This retreat eventually cost the army of Arezzo the battle, for its knights chased the fleeing enemies for a great distance and left behind their own foot soldiers. From then on, the two parts of the army of Arezzo were unable to fight the battle together, the knights lacking help from the foot soldiers, and the latter lacking help from the former. On the Florentine side, meanwhile, the exact opposite happened, for once the routed knights had joined the foot soldiers, the whole army was reunited, so that they were able first to defeat the enemy knights and then the foot soldiers.

In one of his letters, Dante recounts this battle. He describes it and claims to have participated in it.[6] We should keep in mind that the Uberti, the Lamberti, the Abati, and all the other Florentine exiles were fighting with the army of

Arezzo, whereas all those who had left Arezzo—Guelph nobles and common people who during that time had been banished—sided with the Florentines. This is the reason that an inscription in the government palace reads "When the Ghibellines were defeated at Certomondo," rather than "When the people of Arezzo," in order not to offend those people of Arezzo who won with the commune.

Returning now to our subject at hand, I would like to state that Dante fought bravely for his city, and I wish our Boccaccio had mentioned this, instead of recounting the nine years of love and similar light, trivial matters. But why harp on this? The tongue always goes where the tooth hurts, and he who likes drinking always speaks about wine.

After this battle, Dante returned home and dedicated himself to his studies with even greater intensity. He did not, however, abandon urbane and civic activities. Despite his perpetual absorption in study, no one would have ever had the impression that he was a scholar, as he had a most agreeable character and willingly engaged in juvenile chatter. Noting this, I intend to criticize many ignorant people who hold that no one is studying unless he hides himself away in solitude and leisure. Personally, all those I have known who remove themselves from conversation never possessed great knowledge. The mighty and great intellect does not need such torments. It is an undoubtedly true and most certain maxim that he who does not learn soon will never learn. Therefore, to distance and remove oneself from conversation is typical of those whose poor intellect makes them unfit to learn anything.

Dante not only interacted civilly with his fellow citizens but also married, in his youth, a gentlewoman of the Donati family. Her name was Gemma and she bore him several children, as we shall discuss later. Here Boccaccio does not wish to deal with such matters and says that wives are contrary to a life of study. He does not remember that Socrates, the greatest philosopher of all time, married, had children, and also held offices in his republic; Aristotle, whose wisdom and doctrine are unparalleled, married twice and had many children and possessions; Marcus Tullius, Cato, Seneca, and Varro, those great Latin philosophers, also had wives and children, held offices and participated in the government of their republic. Boccaccio's opinions in this respect, if I may say, are highly superficial and far from the truth. Man is a social animal, as all philosophers hold: the first union, from which the city multiplies, is husband and wife. Wherever this is lacking, there is imperfection, for this is the only natural, legitimate, and permissible love.

Bruni then goes on to address the civil strife in Florence at the end of the thirteenth century and touches on the cause of Dante's banishment in 1300. He briefly illustrates the years Dante spent in exile: his vain attempts to return to Florence, the hopes he had regarding Henry VII's arrival in Italy, and Dante's last years and death in Ravenna. This summary is followed by a description of Dante's character and studies in which Bruni speaks of the poet's ability as a draftsman and the elegance of his handwriting. Before entering into a discussion of Dante's works, Bruni engages in a digression on the two ways of writing poetry: 1) possessed or inspired by divine madness (as were Orpheus and St. Francis), and 2) dispensing knowledge acquired through discipline. Homer, Virgil, and Dante were all poets of this second sort.

Having discussed the character of poets, we shall now discuss their title, "poet," which will lead us to understand the nature of their art. Although it is difficult to discuss these subjects in the vernacular, I shall strive to explain them as best I can, for I believe that the poets of our time have not understood them properly—which should not be surprising, since they are ignorant of Greek.

The term "poet" comes from the Greek and means "maker." Since this alone does not suffice as an explanation [of what a poet is], it is necessary to consider the issue in greater detail. Most people are merely readers of works written by others and write nothing themselves. Some, however, are makers of such works—for example, Virgil, who "made" the book of *The Aeneid,* Statius the book of *The Thebaid,* Ovid that of *The Metamorphoses,* and Homer those of *The Odyssey* and *The Iliad.* They who "made" these works, therefore, were poets—that is, makers of the works we read. We are the readers; they were the makers. And when we hear a great man of learning being praised, we usually ask, "What has he written? Will he leave behind any work that he himself has composed?"

The poet, thus, is he who makes a work; he is the author and composer of what is read by others. Someone might object that, according to what I have said, a merchant who puts down his accounts and makes a book of them should be considered a poet, and Livy and Sallust would be poets, since they both wrote books and works intended to be read. I reply to this by saying that the expression "to make works" refers only to poems. This is owing to the merits of the style, for syllables, meter, and sound are proper only to those who compose in verse. We usually say in the vernacular, "He makes ballads and sonnets," but we would never say that one has "made a work" when he has written a letter to his friends. The word "poet" implies a superior and admirable style in verse, covered and concealed by enchanting, subtle fiction. Furthermore, as every leader commands and rules, but only the one who rules all is called emperor, so he who writes in verse and proves to be excellent in writing such works is called a poet. This is the certain truth regarding the name and the qualities of poets. Writing in the rhetorical as opposed to the common style does not have anything to do with it, nor does writing in Greek or Latin.

Each language has its own perfection, its peculiar sound, and its own refined and scientific way of speaking. If someone asked me why Dante chose to write in the vernacular rather than in Latin and in a rhetorical style, I would answer truthfully—to wit, that Dante was aware of being more adept in the vernacular and in rhyme than in the rhetorical style of Latin. He gracefully expressed in vernacular rhyme many things that he could not have said in Latin and in epic verse. The evidence of this lies in the *Eclogues* he composed in hexameter, which, although beautiful, is nonetheless greatly inferior to many other verses by him we have seen. To put it bluntly, our poet's greatest talent was vernacular verse, in which he is superior to all others. In Latin and in prose, instead, he hardly reaches the level of ordinary authors. The reason for this is that his century was primarily interested in composing rhymes, and the men of that epoch did not understand anything about refined prose and Latin poetry, for they were uncouth, rude, and devoid of all knowledge of letters; they were cursorily, scholastically educated in these subjects.

The first works in vernacular verse, as Dante relates, were written one hundred fifty years before his lifetime. The first poets in Italy were the Bolognese Guido Guinizzelli, the knight of our Lady Guittone of Arezzo, Buonagiunta of Lucca, and Guido of Messina. Dante surpassed them all in the clarity, elegance, and grace of his works; so much so that experts in this field believe that no one will ever outdo Dante in rhymed poetry. The greatness and sweetness of his language are truly admirable; it is virtuous, rich in moral teachings, dignified, and extraordinarily varied. It shows philosophical learning, acquaintance with ancient history, and such a knowledge of modern things that he seems to have been witnessing each event of his time. Such fine things admirably expressed in rhyme could capture the mind of any reader, and particularly of the reader who understands the meanings more keenly. Dante's fiction is astounding, and invented with great genius. It embraces descriptions of the world, heaven and the planets, mankind, the rewards and punishments of human life, happiness, misery, and the middle ground between the two extremes. I do not believe that anyone before Dante ever undertook a larger or richer subject, or elucidated the meaning of his every thought by means of spirits—

spirits that talk about the reasons and causes for things, about different countries, and about the vagaries of fortune.

Dante started his main work before he was banished and finished it in exile, as one can clearly assess from the work itself. He also wrote moral *canzoni* and sonnets. His canzoni are polished, delightful, filled with subtle thoughts, and they all begin with exquisite verses, such as the following:

> *Amor che muovi tua virtù dal cielo,*
> *come il sol lo splendore,*[7]

in which he draws a philosophical and subtle comparison between the effects of the sun and the effects of love; and

> *Tre donne intorno al cor mi son venute;*[8]

and:

> *Donne, che avete intelletto d'amore.*[9]

He likewise demonstrates refinement and skill in other canzoni, whereas his sonnets do not always reveal his talent. Such are his vernacular works.

In Latin he wrote both in prose and in verse. He wrote the *Monarchia* in a rough prose, completely devoid of eloquence. He also composed another book, entitled *De vulgari eloquentia*. He wrote, moreover, numerous letters. He composed several eclogues and he began his main work in epic verse, which he abandoned, when he found that style difficult.

Dante died in Ravenna in 1321. One of his sons, Piero,[10] studied law and became a man of note. Thanks to both his virtue and that of his father, he became an important personality and amassed a fortune, finally settling in Verona with a significant patrimony. Piero had a son named Dante, from whom Leonardo was descended—who is alive today and is the father of several children. Not long ago Leonardo traveled to Florence with other young men of Verona to meet me and inquire about his forebear Dante. I showed him the houses in which Dante and his relatives once lived, and told him about many things that he had not known, as he and his family had moved away from the city some time ago. And so Fortune spins this world and changes its inhabitants by turning her wheel.

LIFE OF PETRARCH

Francesco Petrarch, a man of great intellect and no less virtue, was born in Arezzo in the Borgo dell'Orto on July 21, 1304, shortly before dawn. His father was Petracolo, his grandfather Parenzo; and they were originally from Ancisa. His father lived in Florence and held various offices within the republic: he was often appointed the city's ambassador on very difficult occasions, was frequently entrusted with important tasks as a member of different commissions, and served as a scribe of the Riformagioni in the government palace. He was a valuable, active, and respected man.

In the unfortunate partition of Florence between Blacks and Whites,[11] he belonged to the White faction and was thus banished from Florence, together with other citizens. He then found shelter in Arezzo and settled there, continuing to support his faction with all his might as long as the hope of returning home lasted. Afterward, having lost hope, he left Arezzo and went to the papal court, which had been transferred to Avignon for the first time. There he was well employed in an honorable and remunerative post at court. It was in Avignon that he raised his two sons, whose names were Gherardo and Checco, the latter being the one who was later called Petrarch, as I shall explain in this description of his life.

As Petrarch grew up, people noticed that he possessed dignity and a high intellect. He was handsome, a characteristic he maintained throughout his life. As soon as he learned to read and write and had completed his initial studies, he complied with his father's command and gave himself over to the study of civil law, which he continued to pursue for several years. By nature, however, he was inclined toward higher things, holding jurisprudence and lawsuits in low esteem and considering those subjects to be beneath his intellect. He secretly devoted all his studies to Cicero, Virgil, Seneca, Lactantius, and other philosophers, poets, and historians. Because he had elegant and refined speech and was skilled at composing prose, sonnets, and moral canzoni, he held laws, together with their tedious and uncouth commentaries, in contempt. Had it not been for the reverence he had for his father, he would not have pursued the law, and even if the law had pursued him, he would have fled from it.

Having become his own master after his father's death, he openly dedicated himself to those disciplines which, out of fear of his father, he had previously studied in secret. His fame immediately spread, and he began to be called Petrarca, rather than Petracchi—the form of his name being made more noble out of reverence for his virtues.[12] He was endowed with such great intellect that he revived certain studies which, after having been long ignored, finally have attained the high status and respect they enjoy today. To elucidate this point, let us move back a number of years.

The Latin language attained its perfection and greatness in Cicero's time. Before then, it was neither clear nor polished nor precise. Gradually improving, however, it reached its acme, but after a while, it started to decline, exactly as it had previously risen, so that within a few years it had suffered a considerable deterioration. We can legitimately assert that literature and the study of the Latin tongue went hand in hand with the Roman Republic, for before Cicero they augmented, whereas after the Roman people were deprived of their liberty by the tyranny of the emperors, who had no qualms about murdering and ruining worthy men, both the good state of Rome and the good condition of studies perished. Octavian, who was the least wicked of all emperors, sentenced thousands of Roman citizens to death. Tiberius, Caligula, Claudius, and Nero spared no one. Then Galba, Otho, and Vitellius followed, who within a few months killed one another. None of their successors were of Roman blood, for the country had been completely bereft of its worthy men by the previous emperors. Vespasian, who became emperor after Vitellius, was from Rieti, as were Titus and Domitian, his sons; Nerva was from Narni; Trajan, who was adopted by Nerva, was from Spain, like Adrian; Severus came from Africa, Alexander from Asia, Probus from Hungary, Diocletian from Slavonia, and Constantine from England. Why am I bothering to list these names? Merely to show that as the city of Rome was wrecked by these emperors and perverse tyrants, so Latin studies and letters suffered a similar decadence. It became almost impossible to find anyone who spoke Latin with a modicum of elegance. Italy was invaded by the Goths and the Lombards, barbarous and foreign peoples, who almost extinguished all knowledge of letters, as we can see in the documents of those times, which were written in an utterly uncouth and coarse style.

After the peoples of Italy regained their liberty by forcing the Lombards to flee the country they had occupied for two hundred and four years, the Tuscan cities and other cities started to recover. They then resumed studying and put great efforts into refining their style. They gradually regained their vigor, although without any sound understanding of literary elegance, and devoted themselves almost exclusively to the composition of vernacular verse. Until Dante's time, very few had any knowledge of rhetoric, and those who did were only very superficially acquainted with it, as we said in the "Life of Dante."

Petrarch was the first to possess an intellect that could reinstate the ancient elegance of the lost style. Although he himself did not master it, he was able to see and open the way to this perfection, for he not only rediscovered the works of Cicero,[13] but also appreciated and understood them, using their superior eloquence as a model. There is no doubt that his paving the way for posterity is, in itself, a great deed.

Having devoted himself to such studies and showing such virtue, Petrarch was honored and praised from the time of his youth. The pope [Urbanus V] repeatedly invited him in vain to be his court secretary.[14] Petrarch did not value money, but in order to lead a honorable and leisurely life he accepted benefices and became a regular cleric. He did not do this of his own accord, but out of necessity, for he had inherited little or nothing from his father, and whatever his father bequeathed him was spent on marrying off one of his sisters. His brother Gherardo become a Carthusian monk and was for his whole life a member of that order.

Petrarch received more honors than any other man of his age, not only in Italy, but also beyond the Alps, and was solemnly crowned poet in Rome. He himself writes in one of his epistles that in 1350 he went to Rome for the jubilee and on his way back he stopped in Arezzo to see his birthplace.[15] Having heard of his arrival, all the citizens came out to meet him, as if a king were approaching. In summary, his fame throughout Italy, in every town, land, and people was incredible. He received invitations and honors not only from common folk and the middle classes but also from renowned princes, who lavishly entertained him at their courts. He resided for a long time at the court of Galeazzo Visconti, who had most graciously asked him to condescend to stay with him. He was likewise honored by the lord of Padua [Francesco da Carrara]. His repute among these men and the reverence they had for him were such that they often debated whether it was proper to have him walk in front of them—thereby granting him the highest honor—when they approached a city and entered it. Petrarch spent his whole life with such satisfactions, honors, and fame.

In his studies, Petrarch was endowed with a peculiar gift: he was very adept at both prose and verse and composed numerous works in both forms. His prose is agreeable and ornate, his verse refined and subtle. Other than in Petrarch, such an ability in both styles can be found in few authors if any at all, for nature seems to endow men with either one or the other, and man usually pursues that activity at which he knows he is more likely to succeed. That is why Virgil, who excelled at writing verse, was not able to write exceptional prose; and Cicero, the greatest master of prose, was useless at verse. The same happens with other poets and orators who are praised for their excellence in either one of these two forms of writing. I do not recall having read about anyone who was praised for both. By virtue of his unique gift, Petrarch is the only one to have excelled at both forms; his myriad works in prose and verse need no mention here, as they are all well known.

Petrarch died in the year 1374 in Arquà, a village near Padua, where he had retired in his old age for a quiet life of leisure, free from worry. Petrarch was bound by a close friendship to Giovanni Boccaccio, who was also a renowned scholar and author. After Petrarch's death, the Florentine Muses became, so to speak, the inheritance of Boccaccio, in whom the fame of literary scholarship resided. It was also a natural progression, for when Dante died, Petrarch was seventeen, and when Petrarch died, Boccaccio was nine years his junior. This is how the Muses were handed down.

AN ACCOUNT OF BOCCACCIO AND A COMPARISON BETWEEN DANTE AND PETRARCH

I shall not on the present occasion write a life of Boccaccio, not because he does not deserve great praise, but because I know neither the details of his birth nor his private condition and life, and without the knowledge of such things one should not write at all.[16] I am very well acquainted, however, with his writing, and I see he was a man of great intellect, scholarly and industrious, with an extraordinary number of works to his name. He learned Latin only in adulthood, and this is the reason he never managed to master the language. His works in the vernacular, however, show that he was naturally eloquent and a gifted orator. Among his Latin works, the *Genealogia deorum gentilium* is the most important.[17] As he was burdened by poverty and never satisfied with his lot, in his writings he always lamented and deplored his state. His weak and disdainful personality caused him many problems, since he could not bear either to lead an independent life or to stay at the courts of princes and lords.

Leaving Boccaccio aside, therefore, and saving a discussion of his life for another time, I shall return to Dante and Petrarch, of whom I wish to say the following: if I had to compare these most worthy men about whose lives I have written, I would say that they both were extremely clever and deserving of the highest commendation. If, however, I wanted to examine them closely to compare their virtues and merits and ascertain which writer is superior, my opinion is that I would have to enter into no small dispute, for their glory and fame are almost equal. We can, however, speak of them in the following manner: in the active and civic life Dante was worthier than Petrarch, for he nobly helped his country both in war and by holding office in the government. Petrarch did not live in a free city ruled by a civil government, nor did he fight for his country, which, as we know, is a highly virtuous act. Moreover, although constrained by exile and poverty, Dante never abandoned his studies, and he managed to complete his beautiful work amid many difficulties. Petrarch composed his works while leading a tranquil and distinguished life, troubled by few concerns. Although tranquillity is certainly more desirable, it is nevertheless more virtuous to succeed in keeping one's mind on studies amid the adversities of fortune, especially when falling from prosperity to a miserable state. Dante devoted much time to the study of philosophy and mathematics, and he thus had a deeper knowledge of these subjects; in this regard Petrarch is inferior to him. For all these reasons, it looks as though Dante should be considered superior.

Conversely, through an examination of Petrarch's merits, one could confute the first point, the one concerning the active and the civic life. One could object that Petrarch was wiser and more prudent in choosing a peaceful and leisurely life, rather than involving himself in the government of the republic and in the city's struggles and factions—which owing to [others'] wickedness and ingratitude often result in banishment and ruin, as befell Dante. Dante's contemporary, Giano della Bella, from whom the people of Florence had received many benefits before they condemned him to the exile in which he died,[18] should have certainly offered an example sufficient to persuade Dante not to become involved in the government of the republic. Regarding the active life, one could make the further claim that Petrarch was more consistent in maintaining the friendship of princes, for he did not continuously alternate between them, as Dante did. Undoubtedly, Petrarch had to demonstrate his virtue, wisdom, and resolution in order to maintain his fame and lead a life acclaimed by all the lords and the people.

As regards the fact that Dante kept his mind on his studies amid the adversities of fortune, one can retort that it is no less virtuous to keep the mind on one's studies in a happy life of prosperity and tranquillity than in adversity, for prosperous things corrupt the mind of men more than adversity does. "Gluttony, sleep, and soft feathers" are mortal enemies of study.[19] Just as Dante was more learned in philosophy, in astrology, and in the other mathematical sciences, it is true that in many other disciplines Petrarch was more learned than Dante, for Dante's knowledge of letters and Latin was much inferior to Petrarch's. The Latin language consists of two branches: prose and verse. Petrarch is superior in both, for his excellence in prose is decidedly greater, and his verse is more sublime and refined than Dante's. It follows that in every aspect of the Latin language, Dante is not Petrarch's equal. In the vernacular, Petrarch is on par with Dante in writing canzoni, whereas in the writing of sonnets he exceeds him. I must admit, however, that Dante's main work is superior to all those of Petrarch put together.

And so, in conclusion, each one holds the primacy in part and is in part defeated. The fact that Petrarch was crowned poet laureate and Dante was not has no importance for this comparison, for it is more estimable to deserve the crown than to receive it, especially since virtue is certain, whereas at times, owing to a superficial judgment, the crown can as easily be bestowed upon those who do not deserve it as upon those who do.

1. The title most commonly assigned to Boccaccio's work is *Trattatello in laude di Dante* (*Short Treatise in Praise of Dante*).
2. *The Decameron.* The other works by Boccaccio that Bruni mentions here were strongly influenced by Breton-French medieval literature.
3. See *Inf.,* 15.73–78.
4. See Cacciaguida's account on Dante's ancestors in *Par.,* 15.88–96, 136–141, and 16.40–42.
5. "Those of the Elisei."
6. Bruni is the only author who mentions this letter, which is not to be found among Dante's extant letters.
7. "Love, you who take your virtue from heaven, / Like the sun its splendor."
8. "Three ladies have encircled my heart."
9. "Ladies, who possess knowledge of love" (*Vita nuova,* bk. 19).
10. Dante also had another son, Jacopo, and one daughter, Antonia.
11. The Florentine Guelphs were divided into Whites and Blacks. The Whites were in favor of a policy of not maintaining alliances with outside powers; the Blacks, by contrast, sought the support of Pope Boniface VIII. Having obtained it, the Blacks managed to drive the Whites out of Florence and gain control of the city toward the end of 1301.
12. Probably out of similarity with such words as *patriarca* ("patriarch"), *monarca* ("monarch"), and the like, the form *Petrarca* (Petrarch, in English) was deemed more distinguished than Petracchi. The same explanation for the change in name is given by Manetti in his Latin *Life of Petrarch;* see document 22.
13. Petrarch rediscovered Cicero's letters *Ad Atticum, Ad Quintum fratrem,* and *Ad M. Brutum.* Cicero's other collection of letters, the so-called *Familiares,* was rediscovered by Salutati in 1392.
14. See Pet., *Sen.,* 2.2 concerning Pope Urban V's offer in 1362.

15. Ibid., 13.3.

16. Much more likely, Bruni preferred not to insert a biographical sketch of Boccaccio, to avoid disrupting the pattern of Plutarch's *Parallel Lives,* which he follows in this work.

17. The *Genealogy of the Pagan Gods,* an encyclopedic study on ancient mythology.

18. An important figure of late thirteenth-century Florentine politics, Giano della Bella, during his priorate, wrote the Ordinances of Justice (1293–1295), which aimed to exclude numerous noble and particularly influential families from city government, thus granting more political power to the lower classes. He was forced to flee Florence in 1295.

19. The first verse of a famous Petrarchan sonnet in which the poet urges a friend to study letters and philosophy; see *Canzoniere,* 7.

22

Lives of the Illustrious Florentine Poets Dante, Petrarch, and Boccaccio

GIANNOZZO MANETTI

Like many humanists, Giannozzo Manetti (1396–1459) was a versatile writer. Born into a family of wealthy Florentine merchants, he became a successful businessman himself. Manetti belonged to the second generation of humanists, for which values and ideas fostered by such intellectuals as Salutati, Bruni, and Bracciolini had become paramount and were providing the foundation for the growth of new tenets. The diversity of Manetti's works and interests bear witness to this trend. He was one of the first scholars of Hebrew: he translated the Psalms and, in Book 5 of his Apologeticus, *wrote a short treatise on the art of translating (1456). His study of Hebrew and his philological approach to the different versions of the Bible were components in his defense of the Christian religion in the twenty-volume work* Adversus Judaeos et gentiles pro catholica fide. *In his best-known treatise,* De dignitate et excellentia hominis *(1451–1452), Manetti celebrates the virtues he sees in man, by contrast with those considered by Pope Innocent III in his* De contemptu mundi. *Deserving of mention among Manetti's other works are the translations of Aristotle's moral texts, the parallel lives of Socrates and Seneca, and a biography of Pope Nicholas V, at whose court Manetti served as a secretary. His indebtedness to Boccaccio, Filippo Villani, and especially Leonardo Bruni, whom he openly acknowledged as his master, is evident in the biographical sketches he composed of the so-called three crowns of Florence. The main importance of Manetti's* Lives of Dante, Petrarch, and Boccaccio, *however, lies in the evidence it provides that by the middle of the quattrocento, the self-awareness of Florentine intellectuals had brought in a new periodization of the history of literature, one in which Manuel Chrysoloras' arrival in Florence to teach Greek was regarded as a crucial event. Like all humanists, moreover, Manetti considered Chrysoloras' presence to be the fruit of Petrarch's and Boccaccio's pioneering efforts in promoting the study of Greek in the fourteenth century.*

Source: Giannozzo Manetti, "De vita et moribus trium illustrium poetarum Florentinorum," in *Le vite di Dante, Petrarca e Boccaccio scritte fino al secolo decimosesto,* ed. Angelo Solerti (Milan: Vallardi, 1904), pp. 108–112, 136–151, 306–311, 318–319, 684–693.

PREFACE TO THE LIVES AND HABITS OF THE THREE ILLUSTRIOUS FLORENTINE POETS.

Having recently completed a laborious and lengthy work in six books about great men who reached a ripe old age,[1] I have decided to do something different and enjoyable by composing a Latin text on the lives of the three illustrious poets. In the *De longevibus claris* I briefly summarized the most important deeds of the men of every country who, for more than five thousand years after the beginning of the world, distinguished themselves for the piousness of their habits, the excellence of their doctrine, and their military glory. Regarding this present collection, however, I do not think I am ill suited to describe the public and private lives of our poets. [To do so] is utterly appropriate for a person who has recently revived, collected, and illustrated not only the lives of our fellow citizens, but also those of Romans, Greeks, and distinguished foreigners. Partly because of the paucity of writers and partly because of the decadence of the times, these lives have fallen into partial oblivion and undue neglect, and [the accounts of them] dispersed in diverse manuscripts. Someone may argue that numerous learned and eloquent men have already discussed the topic I have chosen. Far from denying it, I admit that Giovanni Boccaccio, a most erudite author, wrote a book in the vernacular on the life of Dante. Leonardo Bruni, the most eloquent man of our time, later composed another life of Dante in the vernacular, which is not only more elegant than the previous one but is also followed by a life of Petrarch. Furthermore, Filippo Villani, who wrote after Boccaccio and before Bruni, collected information on renowned Florentines and compiled it into a booklet.[2] The work I am about to commence, therefore, might seem redundant, given that various and worthy authors have already treated the same subject. I shall thus touch first upon the reasons for undertaking this project.

The masses have praised Dante, Petrarch, and Boccaccio—our three il-

lustrious poets whose lives I have concisely described in my latest work—more
than any other famous poet since the beginning of time. They were, in fact,
superior to all others in prose and vernacular poetry, although in Latin they are
inferior not only to many ancient authors but even to authors of our own time.
Common folk, despite their complete ignorance of literature and any kind of
doctrine, highly admire these illustrious men for their intellect and their erudition. The learned, on the other hand, disregard their vernacular works, in
which they showed themselves to be real masters, and look down upon such
writing. Frequently, these poets are praised by the ignorant, while erudite men
read their verses, their stories, or any other of their works only for entertainment. This certainly is not befitting either the worth of these authors or the
praise they deserve. I also doubt that this is the fate they hoped for in their lives,
nor do I believe they would long for it now that they are dead; that is, if they
happened to be interested at all in the present happenings of this world. The
learned of any age want to be praised by honorable and renowned men, despising, meanwhile, all other commendations, just like Hector, the character in
Nevius, who longed for the praises only of persons of good repute.[3] I have read
this in Nevius, and it is likely that he, not Hector, is the real author of this
opinion. If the learned wanted to receive the praise solely of erudite men, then
our poets, if they were still interested in the things of this world, would certainly care little for the encomiums of the ignorant and the unknown, or, at
least, they would not be satisfied with the commendations they receive from
these vernacular writers.

We must also note that while Boccaccio wrote only the life of Dante, Bruni
composed the lives of Dante and Petrarch and completely disregarded Boccaccio. My previous comments on these two most learned scholars will suffice.
Things are different, however, regarding Villani, who, unlike those notable
men [Boccaccio and Bruni], used Latin rather than the vernacular to write the
lives of our poets. I have read his *Liber de civitatis Florentiae famosis civibus,* in
which he collected the lives of all the men who were notable either in the
military sphere, the sciences, the arts, or in any other worthy endeavor. He
then appended the praise of various rulers, doctors, theologians, judges, poets,
and painters, and a succinct tribute to our poets, practically cramming them
into the corner of his book, without developing them at length as such an
important topic merits.

Such are the reasons which have inspired me to help, as much as I could,
our three illustrious citizens and excellent poets by writing their lives in Latin.
Above all, I was moved by the desire to have their worth, hitherto recognized

only by common folk, finally brought to the attention of those learned and erudite men who have always scorned and derided the vernacular literature of which our poets have offered many outstanding examples.

Manetti mentions the Roman origin of Dante's family, noting that one of Dante's ancestors, a certain Eliseo, is said to have been among the Roman settlers from Sulla's army who founded Florence. He then cites Dante's other distinguished ancestors, such as his great-great-grandfather Cacciaguida. Drawing on Boccaccio's Trattatello, *Manetti relates a dream that Dante's mother had shortly before his birth in which a child in a green meadow was drinking from a fountain and picked berries from a laurel. The symbols in this dream presaged a future, according to his mother's interpretation, in which Dante would attain great fame as a poet. Manetti then summarizes the main events of Dante's youth in Florence: his encounter with Beatrice, his studies, his involvement in city politics, his valiant participation in the Battle of Campaldino, and his marriage to Gemma Donati.*

After relating the internal conflicts among the Florentine Guelphs that led to Dante's banishment, Manetti launches into a biting invective against Florence for having exiled such a worthy citizen, and for not having asked to bring home his remains after his death and subsequent burial in Ravenna. The author stresses that poets were held in great esteem by the Ancients for bringing glory to their homeland. Manetti urges Florence to obtain Dante's remains and rebury them in the poet's native city. He then goes on to describe Dante's fruitless attempts during his exile to return to Florence, a hope he abandoned on the death of Henry VII of Luxembourg.

LIFE OF DANTE

Having passed the Apennines, Dante headed for Romagna. At the time, Ravenna, the most ancient city of that region, was ruled by Guido Novello, who was the best-read and most knowledgeable prince of Italy. He used to favor the learned and showed a particular benevolence toward scholars. As soon as he found out that such an illustrious poet, famous not only in Italy but nearly the world over, was approaching Romagna, he decided to invite him to stay with him as a member of his court. Novello sent letters and messengers to Dante to communicate his fervent wish. Since it was impossible for Dante to live in his native town, Novello invited him to be his guest and offered him mountains of gold, as a famous verse of Terentius goes,[4] to convince him. When Dante was informed of all this, he was seized with a genuine admiration for the generosity of such a noble man and immediately went to Ravenna to honor the distinguished prince and spend the rest of his life as a member of his court, having lost all hope of returning to his native city.

Novello thus benevolently welcomed Dante to Ravenna, where Dante spent a number of years and then passed away. During his stay in Ravenna, Dante once again befriended books,[5] in part through reading, in part through teaching, and in part through writing. Until the last day of his life, he diligently continued his studies, despite his being burdened with diverse concerns. We can only imagine what an extraordinary man this divine poet could have been if he had had the opportunity to pursue his studies with greater calm and tranquillity, rather than in such uncertain and difficult conditions. His most renowned works, in fact, clearly testify to the outstanding level of erudition he attained, even being hampered by so many grave concerns. In Ravenna, during the last years of his life, Dante taught writing in the vernacular to several men of distinguished intellect, some of whose poetry in the vernacular is not considered vulgar at all.[6] The art of writing poetry in the vernacular, which began in Italy only a few years before Dante, was first ennobled by this poet— similar to what Homer did among the Greeks, Virgil among the Romans, and other great authors throughout history in their own countries. Because he was the first to express a vast knowledge of things human and divine in the Florentine tongue, people generally consider Dante the one who ennobled this language more than anyone else before him. Previous authors who wrote in the vernacular avoided debates on important subjects in their poems, choosing as their topics only matters of little importance. In his divine poem Dante, by contrast, was able to discuss with particular and remarkable elegance many weighty matters. When, regrettably, he departed this life, he was still working and meditating on such things. Before speaking of his death, however, I think it is fitting to report all I know about his appearance, his habits, his studies, and his style of life.

It is said that this renowned poet was of middle height, with a particularly long and narrow face, rather large eyes, a hooked nose, large and flabby cheeks, a slightly protruding lower lip, dark skin, a black beard, and long, black, slightly curly hair. To show that these things, although mere details, are true, I shall report an episode concerning Dante's dark skin and hair, which is said to have taken place while he lived in Verona. One day, as he was walking through the streets, he stopped in front of a house where a group of women were sitting and chattering, a common sight in that city. After Dante passed by, one of the women said to the one next to her, "Look, look at the man who came back from Hell to report to the living the things he saw there among the shadows." Clearly, the first part of his *Commedia* was already quite famous. The other woman, spurred by her friend's remark, replied in a foolish manner, as is typical of women, "You speak the truth, my friend; his curly beard and his skin blackened by the dense smoke of Hell clearly prove that your words are true."

Dante was a man of noble and lofty bearing, often pensive and absorbed in his thoughts. In his old age he walked hunched over. Some believe that he was actually more handsome than this; at any rate, a faithful portrait of him, by an outstanding painter of his time, can be seen on the walls of the Church of Santa Croce [in Florence]. What is more, before his banishment he dressed elegantly, though not ostentatiously, as befits the serious demeanor of such a distinguished man. His patrimony was not meager, for he possessed substantial properties in Florence and near the city walls. He was temperate in eating and drinking: he praised delicious food but usually ate frugal meals, sneering at those who are obsessed with eating—the *gastrimargos,* as the Greeks called them. He used to say, following the maxim of an ancient sage, that these men do not eat to live, but live to eat.[7]

In his youth he was fond of music and singing, and he became friends with the most famous musicians of his time. He was so attracted to their art that he composed numerous poems and prose works in the Florentine vernacular, a genre in which he proved to be utterly superior—may I say without offending anyone—to all his predecessors. He also made the distinguished men of future generations who were endowed with an outstanding elegance of speech and eloquence eager to imitate his refined style.

He seemed to have yielded to lustful passions more than would befit so great a philosophical spirit, a fact which I think should be attributed more to his amiable nature than to any intentional levity on his part. Something similar, after all, is said about Socrates, the most austere of all philosophers, who, as some wrote, had the reputation of being rather inclined toward lechery. This tendency in Socrates was noticed by a famous physiognomist of that time who claimed to be able to tell the nature and the inclinations of a person by looking at his physical appearance. While everyone was surprised and laughed at the physiognomist, Socrates confessed that his opinion was right, for he was inclined toward lechery by nature but had managed to control this tendency and had eventually overcome it completely.[8]

Dante seldom spoke unless he was asked a question, and he never said anything superficial; his words seemed to come, so to speak, from the heart, and after deep thought. He was so absorbed in his studies that he continued to read even in the middle of the street—he might have been rightly called "a glutton for books," as Cicero writes about Cato.[9] Cicero narrates how Cato, despite his most serious and wise nature, used to read at times in the Senate while waiting for the sessions to begin, just as this most commendable man, Dante, they say, did in the streets. Once, for instance, near an artist's workshop in Siena, Dante was offered a little book he had never seen before. He started reading it with such attention and intensity that the pleasant music being played around him at that moment did not distract him even for a second. He managed to read the whole book, in spite of the fact that the entire community of citizens was celebrating a traditional feast, to the accompaniment of all sorts of musical instruments. Even more astonishing is that when he was asked why the noisy festivities all around him did not make him turn his head even for a moment, he replied that he had not heard a thing.

Some say that he was an excellent orator, as we can assess from the number of times he was sent as an ambassador to illustrious princes and popes. They also say that by virtue of his unparalleled eloquence, he ruled as a sort of prince in the republic. He possessed, moreover, a sharp mind and an excellent memory. I could set forth evidence to prove this last point, but not wishing to be prolix, I shall restrict myself to just one anecdote. Soon after the death of Frederick Augustus, Dante went to Paris. One day, Dante was responding to the objections of a large group of distinguished men, discussing the theological issues in question with great acumen. After each interlocutor had expressed his opinion on the fourteen difficult problems being considered, Dante accurately repeated all the fourteen problems in the exact order in which they had been formulated, and then solved them in a most exceptional way, arousing the admiration of all present.

Throughout his life he was more eager for honor and glory than might seem appropriate to such a noble philosopher. The desire for glory is a natural thing, and it is a virtue that has attracted even renowned philosophers and austere theologians, regardless of their having written many a book filled with considerations on the fundamental importance of despising it. I believe, therefore, that our poet was led to such an unparalleled love for poetry by this natural desire for glory. At the time, in fact, there were very few good poets, or even philosophers, mathematicians, and theologians. It has always been like this since the world's inception; in all ages, in fact, good poets and orators have been very rare. In Dante's time, it was still common to give a crown of laurel to poets and emperors, following the ancient custom of the Greeks and the

Romans. Dante never denied his eagerness to obtain such an award but even openly confessed it in his works. His head would certainly have been graced with the well-deserved laurel crown if he had ever returned from exile, but his being away from his native town prevented him, in my opinion, from obtaining what he had long desired.

I think that Dante's poetic genius can be more easily recognized than expressed in words. This exceptional poet was the first to bring poetry back to life after a nine-hundred-year sleep. He was the one who raised poetry from the ground, where it was lying prostrate. It seemed as if he had brought it back to its native country from exile, or rescued it from oblivion. Not only did he do this, but he proved it to be perfectly consistent with our Christian doctrine, as if the ancient poets had somehow been divinely inspired to sing the teachings of true religion. Furthermore, this divine poet managed to render poetry attractive not only to the learned but even to the many who lack Latin—giving them the opportunity to know poetry as well.

Dante was also a proud and noble-minded man, as we can see by the fact that despite his intense desire to return to his native town, he decided not to, for his loftiness of spirit abhorred the only possible means of doing it. Some friends of his, moved both by their genuine friendship and by their desire to satisfy his continual requests to return from exile, truly wanted to help him. Thus they carefully discussed this matter with important fellow citizens, but all their efforts were destined to be ineffective unless Dante agreed to submit to a most dishonorable procedure. He first had to abandon all his pride, plead with his enemies for mercy, and spend some time in the city prison. In addition to [submitting to] such humiliations, he also had to go to the cathedral in Florence after he had been released from prison and be offered to God, as they used to do with the criminals during feast days. As soon as he was informed of this, Dante refused to submit to such injurious and ignominious requests; he actually was so offended at the proposal that he immediately made up his mind to spend the rest of his life in exile rather than return to his native town in such a disgraceful way.

They say he was very arrogant, as he proved to be especially on the day when Pope Boniface decided to fulfill the Ghibellines' requests by sending Charles, a relative, if not a brother, of King Philip of France, to bring peace to Florence. The Guelph leaders, who strongly opposed this decision and were then in power, gathered to discuss it. They finally decided to send ambassadors to the pontiff and unanimously elected Dante as the head of the mission on account of his extraordinary intelligence and eloquence. They say that as soon as he was informed of this decision, he asked, "If I obey your order, as I must, and leave to carry out my duty, who will stay to govern the republic? If, on the other hand, I stay, who will be a good head of this mission?" It is said, however, that his words, which he uttered in the vernacular, were more elegant than this. People tend to ascribe these and other, similar phrases to Dante's peculiar arrogance, but if you were attentive, as you should be, to the context in which Dante uttered these words, you would realize that this episode should more likely be ascribed to Dante's love for the republic and a kind of noble-mindedness. Just recall how many evils Florence had already suffered in Dante's time owing to the enduring civil struggles. Remember also that during his priorate, Dante had sent various citizens into exile, to punish them for having sought help from a foreign prince. If, finally, we consider that the aim of the pope's decision was to call back Dante's enemies from exile, his aforementioned words will cease to surprise us. We shall instead find them fitting, contrary to the opinion of those who deem them arrogant, simply because they do not take into due consideration the time in which they were uttered.

Dante wrote some of his works in the vernacular, others in Latin. He composed texts in the vernacular both during his youth and in his later years. Besides sonnets and ballads, he wrote two excellent works when he was young: the *Vita nuova* and the *Convivio,* both containing poems accompanied by detailed commentary. In his maturity he composed his more-divine-than-human poem, the *Commedia*. He started to write it in Latin, the first verse running as follows, "Ultima regna canam fluido contermina mundo."[10] He would have certainly continued it in Latin verse with great elegance, but he decided to start it all over, using his native language and a different style, as he thought that the first part of the poem and the rest would not match otherwise.

Through this divine work, as I said, Dante was able to provide us not only with all the things proper to poetry, but also with a knowledge of moral philosophy, science, and theology, thus inspiring great admiration in his readers. He worked on it for more than twenty-five years, composing verses and then polishing them. He completed seven cantos, which the Greeks call odes, before being sent into exile. Although Dante's house was looted after he was banished, they say that these cantos remained hidden in a well-concealed spot, together with many books and notarized documents. One day his wife asked a notary to look for her dowry document. The notary happened to be searching through a great pile of books and documents in a corner of the house when he came upon a small manuscript containing seven cantos. He started reading them and was so impressed that he decided to take them home with him. He kept on reading and rereading them, as he was stirred by their eloquence, until he finally decided to send them to their author, who was beside himself with joy. The verse "Io dico seguitando . . . "[11] clearly attests that Dante resumed the composition of his poem from this point, eventually completing it only a few days before he died. Evidence of the divine nature of his poem can also be assessed through considering the miraculous episodes that took place after his death. Dante had sequestered some sheets containing the last cantos in a cranny of his house. He had not inserted them into the poem yet, probably waiting for the proper time to polish them. The work thus seemed incomplete. They say, however, that the shadow of the dead poet appeared in a dream to Jacopo, his eldest son, who was most eager to see the poem finished. In this vision, so the story goes, the son was informed of where the last cantos of the *Paradiso* had been put. Immediately after dawn, Jacopo started looking for them and found them in the place his father had indicated to him in the dream. Some may ask why I speak so much of such dreams and visions. I do so in order to prove the authenticity of what I have just been saying—namely, that it took Dante twenty-five years to complete his divine poem. In fact, if the poet had finished seven cantos before his banishment and managed to complete the whole work in the year of his death, and if, moreover, he was sent into exile at thirty-five and died at fifty-six, it took him precisely that number of years to finish it. It is very likely, also, that he spent time polishing his first seven cantos.

Dante is also the author of many a work in Latin, among which are numerous epistles and a bucolic poem. He composed, moreover, a famous prose work entitled *Monarchia,* which is divided into three books, each one astutely discussing a particular issue. In the first book he follows the dialectical method to consider whether the rule of one, which the Greeks call monarchy, is necessary for the good of the whole world. In the second book he considers whether the Roman people justly obtained this universal rule. In the third and final book he examines whether this rule was ordained by God alone, or by one of His ministers. This notable work caused him to be sentenced for heresy, as a famous jurist records, for it was considered a text written against the popes of the Roman Church.

Having accomplished these things, he died at the age of fifty-six in Ravenna in the year of our Lord 1321. Some hold that the cause of his death was as follows: the Venetians were waging war on the aforementioned Novello, ruler of Ravenna, who decided to send Dante on an ambassadorial mission to Venice because of his remarkable eloquence. Upon his arrival, Dante, eager to perform the task with which he had been entrusted, immediately requested a public audience. Having repeatedly tried in vain to gain a reception, he finally realized that the Venetians would never grant his plea, on account of their implacable hatred for Novello. He thus acknowledged the failure of his mission and decided to return to Ravenna by land, as he heard that the expanse of sea between the two cities was carefully controlled by the fleet of the Venetian admiral. On his return he was obviously distressed regarding the negative outcome of his mission, and also weakened by the discomforts he had suffered during the trip. Before he reached Ravenna, he fell sick with a violent fever and died within a few days of his return. Such was the death of our illustrious poet.

He was buried in Ravenna in the church of the Franciscans. A tall, square gravestone was made in his honor, a nicely decorated work. An epitaph was carved on the square gravestone, with the following first lines:

> Theologus Dantes nullius dogmatis expers
> quod foveat claro philosophia sinu.[12]

These were later replaced by six verses, composed by a most learned author and much more elegant than the previous ones:

> Jura monarchiae, superos, Phlegetonta lacusque
> lustrando cecini, voluerunt fata quosque.
> Sed quia pars cessit melioribus hospita castris
> auctoremque suum petiit felicior astris,
> hic claudor Dantes patriis extorris ab oris
> quem genuit parvi Florentia mater amoris.[13]

LIFE OF PETRARCH

Having briefly discussed Petrarch's birth, Manetti depicts the personality of the poet's father, whose life he sketches from the time of his banishment from Florence in 1301 together with Dante, until his arrival in the papal court of Avignon, where Petrarch spent his youth. Despite his intense desire to study classical Latin authors, his father forced him into a career in law. When his father died, Petrarch gave up jurisprudence and devoted himself completely to literature.

Thanks to an uncommon and almost divine excellence of intellect, Petrarch progressed so far in his study of things human and divine that it was he who revived the art of eloquence, which had long been lacking. Eloquence had been dead for more than a thousand years, first because of the inhuman ferocity of the Roman emperors, who had oppressed their people with every sort of cruelty, murdering righteous and learned men, and then because of the violent rule of the Lombards, who sacked all of Italy during their two-hundred-year occupation. Because of his incomparable diligence, Petrarch was the first to revive many of the works of Cicero hidden from the Italians for centuries. He collected Cicero's scattered epistles and organized them into the format in which we now read them. His eloquence rendered him a model for future writers of poetry and prose. I do not know of anyone who, before Petrarch's time, was as expert in both forms of writing. If we note that among both the Romans and the Greeks their two greatest geniuses were that in just one form of writing, what should we think of the others? We know for sure that the immortal minds of Demosthenes and Cicero excelled at prose but were weak at verse. Homer and Virgil wrote venerable and majestic verses, but their prose is comparatively so feeble that one would hardly believe them to be the authors of the prose works that they have left us. The same is the case in other disciplines, since no one can excel in all fields. It is said that nature is the cause of this, for if, like a mother, she bestowed all or most gifts upon a single person, nothing would be left for the others.

Being the only one, therefore, to possess this rare and almost divine blessing, Petrarch excelled at both forms of writing. He became so renowned that his name was lengthened from Petraca to Petrarca.[14] All people, even if only minimally educated, seemed to venerate him. The people of Arezzo, for instance, as soon as they found out that he was approaching their city on his way back from Rome, where he had been for the jubilee, to visit the house where he was born, ran toward him and crowded in front of the city walls with so much joy that even a king or a great prince could not have been better received, as he himself recounts in a letter.[15] Even the Florentines, who had exiled his father, revoked the banishment and pardoned him, so great and renowned a man. To express his gratitude to the Florentine people for such a significant and uncommon event, he wrote a letter filled with praise and thanks.[16]

Illustrious princes were moved by the incredible fame of his virtues and competed with one another to have him at their courts. Even the sovereign pontiff invited him to the papal Curia promising to appoint him to high office. Although constrained by the meagerness of his patrimony, Petrarch received the so-called first tonsure, which would help fulfill his desire to lead a leisurely life, but he firmly turned down the pope's grander offers, fearing that they would disturb his tranquil studies. The most powerful ruler of Milan and the illustrious lord of Padua also offered him high position and promised him immense gifts if he would join their courts.

He did spend some time, however, with several renowned princes. In his youth, he also stayed for a while at the papal Curia. He left it, however, so disgusted by that sort of life that he decided never to return there, even though he was frequently invited by the pope himself. He spent several years with Galeazzo Visconti, lord of Milan, and with other distinguished princes, for whom he served as an ambassador on three important occasions. He was sent to Venice to negotiate a peace agreement between the Venetians and the Genoese; he was also sent to His Most Serene Highness, Emperor of the Romans, who was then dwelling in a distant barbarous country, to discuss the Ligurian peace, as he himself calls it.[17] Finally, he gave an oration congratulating King John of France on his release from the captivity of the English, as we know from a letter he [Petrarch] wrote to Boccaccio.[18] These princes held him in such high esteem that they often debated whether he should walk ahead of them when they were out together, as often happened. Being an extremely prudent man, and no less modest, however, he never agreed to be accorded this honor.

What more can I say regarding his honors, as there are innumerable things of a similar nature that show his outstanding glory? Leaving them aside for brevity's sake, I shall recount just one wondrous episode which, in my opinion, cannot be left out, since something similar is reported by ancient authors who considered it a miracle. When he was still a youth in the Po Valley, as he writes in a letter, noble and learned men came to visit him not only from other parts of Italy, but also from France.[19] What he adds in that same letter is even more prodigious and it would be hard to believe were it not reported by such a trustworthy man. He writes, in fact, that a blind teacher finally succeeded in meeting him after having searched for him all over Italy; he also describes how the old man, whose son and a student were supporting him with their arms, was so seized with the desire to meet him that he repeatedly kissed his forehead and his right hand as if that could satisfy his eagerness, as he was unable to see him. He narrates this in a letter to a teacher, Donino of Piacenza. This is why he says not to be surprised that noble men went to Rome from the most remote regions of Spain and Gaul just to see Livy, as Jerome recounts, for greater things had befallen him.[20]

The only emblem that seemed to be lacking to complete the glory of this man was the laurel crown, which among the ancient Greeks and Romans was granted to emperors and the greatest poets, but he did eventually receive it in Rome after a most memorable and solemn ceremony. He was deservingly elected poet laureate, a title that had not been granted to anyone for more than nine hundred and fifty years, from the time of Claudianus, who wrote during Theodosius' rule. It happened, therefore, that a Florentine poet and new seer received in the same manner what had last been obtained so long before, in ancient times, by another Florentine poet.[21]

Following the example of the most illustrious philosophers, Petrarch chose to spend the rest of his life in Arquà secluded with his books. After a physical description of the poet, Manetti records his numerous works of renown and gives an allegorical interpretation of the "Canzoniere," to defend Petrarch from those who charge him with having written erotic poems. The author also underscores the importance of Petrarch's attempts to learn Greek, a language utterly unknown in Italy at the time.

Having thus led such a glorious and happy life devoted to the study of various important subjects, at the age of seventy he died in Arquà, where he had retired, as I have previously mentioned. It is said that the last part of his life was quite consonant with his earlier years; from youth until about middle age his integrity and his learning brought him great honors, and from then until the very end of his life, he gladly gave himself over as to a blessed retreat to the constant contemplation of the holy mysteries and an incessant meditation on eternal life. We can, therefore, legitimately hope—also on account of what they say occurred at his death—that he passed away in God's grace, leaving behind this dark prison and returning to the heavenly home.

They say that a distinguished student of his, Lombardo, whom Petrarch held particularly dear and in whose arms he died, reported that at the moment of his death, when Petrarch breathed his last sigh, he exhaled something like a surpassingly white cloud that, similar to incense, went up to the ceiling and stayed there for a short time before vanishing in the limpid air. This extraordinary event, whose authenticity is proved by the authority of the aforementioned student and by the testimony of others who were present, is considered a miracle, clearly confirming that the soul of the divine poet returned to God. I have never read, in effect, that anything of this sort happened upon the death of an ordinary person who had led a normal life.

Having departed this life in such a glorious manner, our poet was buried in

Arquà in a marble tomb upon which the following simple verses of his were engraved:

Frigida Francisci lapis hic tegit ossa Petrarchae.
Suscipe virgo parens animam, sate virgine parce,
fessaque iam terris coeli requiescat in arce.[22]

Coluccio Salutati, a notable poet of our time, wrote of Petrarch's unusual death.[23]

LIFE OF BOCCACCIO

Drawing on Bruni, Manetti opens this last biographical sketch by emphasizing that Petrarch succeeded Dante as the best poet of his time, and that Boccaccio, in turn, replaced Petrarch after his death. He then focuses on Boccaccio's birth and early studies, which were initially carried out under the guidance of Zanobi da Strada, a well-known Florentine poet and a friend of Petrarch. Soon, however, in deference to his father's stated wish and against his own will, Boccaccio abandoned literature to study arithmetic, before apprenticing to a merchant for six years. As soon as he reached maturity, however, he enthusiastically returned to the study of literature, just as Petrarch had done before him, and in a very short time he managed to attain a thorough knowledge of classical authors by diligently transcribing their books, and in particular their poetry.

Having come thus late to the knowledge of the seers,[24] it is hard to believe how quickly Boccaccio managed to acquaint himself with their mysteries by devoting all his efforts to the constant perusal of ancient poems and the transcription of numerous Latin texts. Since he did not own any books, and his scanty finances prevented him from purchasing them, he decided to supply his need by copying not only a great number of volumes by the ancient poets but also all those by the Latin orators and historians and as many ancient Latin works as could be found. Anyone who takes into account the great number of his transcriptions would find it hard to believe that a rather fat man such as he could succeed in copying so many volumes on his own. Such an accomplishment, in fact, would have been difficult for an untiring scribe who devoted his whole life to such a project, let alone a man intensely involved in the study of things human and divine, who later committed his thought to writing, which, as we shall see, he did most successfully. Moreover, being dissatisfied with the number, or rather the scarcity, of Latin books available to Italians at the time, he grew eager to learn Greek in order to compensate for the lack of texts in Latin. I believe that in doing so he followed Petrarch's example and eventually learned Greek better than he. Petrarch resolved to learn the language from the Basilian monk Barlaam, a man who possessed an excellent knowledge of Greek letters. He sought to satisfy thereby his insatiable desire for books through the reading of the Greek authors, since the Latin ones had not sufficed. For three years, accordingly, Boccaccio attended both the public and the private Greek lessons of a certain Leontius Pilatus of Thessalonica. He was a very good student of this monk and eventually became an expert in Greek studies himself. Leontius Pilatus had already made up his mind to leave Venice and move to some distant country when Boccaccio's offers persuaded him to come to Florence, where Boccaccio was then residing. Boccaccio hosted him in his own home for quite a long time and managed to have him appointed a lecturer in Greek with a public stipend. Pilatus was the first to have such a position in our city. They say that soon afterward, Boccaccio, still motivated by his increasing desire to study Greek literature, brought back from the center of Greece to his native land of Tuscany not only Homer's works but also various other Greek manuscripts, at his own expense and despite his onerous poverty. These Greek texts brought in by the two renowned poets Petrarch and Boccaccio seem to have been like seeds which, planted in particularly fertile ground, grew day after day until they finally flourished and bore in our times the richest of fruits. To make this point clearer, I shall seize the present opportunity to illustrate briefly the progress of Greek studies from the beginning.

Before Petrarch's age, after the Latin language had gradually begun to lose its original vigor, there had been almost no mention whatsoever of Greek literature for centuries, and the men of those times, being satisfied with their own disciplines, were not eager to become acquainted with foreign ones. Petrarch was the first among us, as we said, to try to learn foreign letters by becoming a student of the monk Barlaam, the most erudite Greek of the time. If the unfortunate death of his teacher had not hampered him as he was just starting to learn, he would doubtless (not "perhaps," as he modestly says of himself) have made great progress, thanks to his intelligence and his outstanding memory. Taking him as an example, Boccaccio managed to attain a fairly good knowledge of the language after three years of study under the guidance of the Greek scholar Leontius of Thessalonica. He would have learned much more, as he says, had the teacher, fickle as is typical of his race, continued his task. The education he had received, however, provided him with sufficient knowledge to understand Homer's renowned poems, the *Iliad* and the *Odyssey*, as well as other texts. Moreover, his teacher's lessons acquainted him with the writings of many other poets, which he later used in the production of that excellent work of his, *Genealogiae deorum gentilium*. Shortly after Boccaccio's death, many youths appeared, who, following the example of Boccaccio and Petrarch, explored the whole field of Latin language and devoted themselves to the study of Greek. Moved by an intense desire to learn, and not without [making] great promises, they invited a certain learned man named Manuel from Constantinople to Florence.[25] Upon his arrival, they provided him with both a public and a private stipend to teach and retained him in the city for several years until many of his students had acquired an adequate knowledge of Greek. What can I add concerning Greek studies, since I believe I have said more about their origin and their progress than I first intended? This erudite teacher is none other than the famous Manuel Chrysoloras, the teacher of so many students who have disseminated the Greek language, as if it were a new seed of letters, not only all through Tuscany but throughout other Italian regions. These studies have grown and are flourishing, as we see, in our time. One might ask why I have spent so much time discussing Greek. Why? To show that we owe all our present knowledge of Greek letters to Boccaccio, who first brought to Tuscany, at his own expense, a teacher and Greek texts that had previously lain far away, over land and sea.

Being thus dedicated to the study of humanities until the end of his life, Boccaccio left many monuments of his literary activity—some in the vernacular, some in Latin—all of which we have among us. He composed his vernacular works partly in verse, partly in prose. Although written in his youth, the charm and the elegance of the language gracing these texts are such that they fascinate even readers who do not know Latin but are of average intelligence. It also happens that, by imitating his graceful style, they manage to write with some elegance. Boccaccio's Latin works are also of two kinds: prose and verse. He divided his *Bucolicum Carmen* into sixteen eclogues, and he also composed a number of epistles in verse. All the rest of his Latin work is in prose, namely *De casibus illustrium virorum,* in nine books, dedicated to Carlo Cavalcante, a knight and prefect of the Kingdom of Sicily; the volume entitled *De mulieribus claris,* to Lady Andreina Acciaiuoli, countess of Altavilla; and finally what is generally considered his main work, the renowned fifteen books of the *Genealogiae,* addressed to Hugo, king of Jerusalem and Cyprus.

Having thus far discussed the beginning and the progress of his studies, there remains the description of his physical appearance and his style of life. He is known to have been tall and fat and to have had a round, cheerful face. He was so sharp-witted and amiable that his great cleverness was apparent in his every word. Almost until maturity, he was exceedingly attracted to sensuality. He was often preoccupied by his poverty, for he saw it as obstructing the smooth course of the studies in which he desired to excel, as he did regardless. He knew well, from personal experience, [the truth of] that famous saying by Juvenal:

Haud facile emergunt quorum virtutibus obstat
res angusta domi.[26]

Being unable to overcome all the obstacles placed in his way by poverty, and to flee poverty itself, he strove with all his might, night and day, to reduce it, if not somehow remove himself from it entirely. He therefore copied numerous manuscripts, so that in carrying out this incessant task, he partially satisfied his intense desire to read. The precious library that the erudite Niccolò Niccoli built at his own expense, as people say, inside the basilica of St. Augustine many years after Boccaccio's death, bears witness to the great number of texts he copied. There are all the works of poets Boccaccio copied, together with the excellent Latin texts he edited, preserved as an everlasting testimony to his great and incredible diligence in copying manuscripts. By nature he was so proud that, despite his vexation over the meagerness of his patrimony, he never agreed to live at princes' courts. I believe that this pride lay at the root of his constant complaining about his financial state, which we often find in his writings.

He died at the age of sixty-two, after having led a life devoted to study. He was buried solemnly in Certaldo inside the basilica of St. James, in a tomb upon which is carved the following epitaph he wrote:

Hac sub mole iacent cineres atque ossa Joannis,
mens sedet ante Deum meritis ornata laborum
mortalis vitae. Genitor Boccaccius illi,
patria Certaldum, studium fuit alma poesis.[27]

Finding these verses too modest for the unique excellence of such a poet, the great and learned Coluccio Salutati added to them twelve of his own:

Inclite cur vates, humili sermone locutus
de te pertransit? Tu pascua carmine claro
in sublime vehis, tu montium nomina, tuque
silvas et fontes, fluvios ac stagna lacusque
cum maribus multo digesta labore relinquis;
illustresque viros infestis casibus actos
in nostrum aevum a primo colligis Adam.
Tu celebras claras alto dictamine matres,
tu divos omnes ignota ab origine ducens
per ter quina refers divina volumina nulli
cessurus veterum: te vulgo mille labores
percelebrem faciunt, aetas te nulla silebit.[28]

COMPARISON BETWEEN DANTE, PETRARCH, AND BOCCACCIO

Having now described as well as I could the lives of these three excellent poets, a concise comparison between them remains to be made. Wishing to compare the outstanding qualities of these men, I find it fitting to offer as a preliminary remark a given: our life is twofold—namely, active and contemplative. This being an incontestable assumption of our comparison, we do not deem it rash to hold that in almost every aspect of both types of life, Dante should be preferred to the other two. First of all, he did not hesitate to take up arms and gallantly fight for his homeland. Secondly, he acted nobly while holding office in the government of his republic. All this obviously pertains to the active life, and it cannot be said to pertain to either Petrarch or Boccaccio, since they spent almost all their lives in solitary leisure studying literature, which is precisely what is generally called the contemplative life. Having set everything else aside, they devoted themselves exclusively to this type of life; they should therefore have surpassed Dante, since they led longer and more peaceful lives. But this is not true at all: for although Dante did not reach old age and never enjoyed much tranquillity in his life, he devoted much of his life to concerns of the republic. This distracted him from his studies, and though he was vexed by the torments of the exile, he rapidly succeeded in attaining a vast knowledge of things human and divine, thanks to the almost divine excellence of his intellect. As a matter of fact, in mathematics—the science that studies numbers, dimensions, and harmonics, together with the movements and the revolutions of the stars—in moral and natural philosophy, and finally in the Holy Scriptures, which embrace all matters divine, Dante excelled to such a degree that he is certainly superior to the other two poets. Dante, as has been said, does seem superior to Petrarch and Boccaccio in almost all respects. Petrarch, however, exceeds Dante in the exhaustive knowledge of both Latin literature and ancient history, as he possessed a greater and more precise erudition in both fields. Dante is also surpassed by him in the writing of rhymes and prose. Petrarch's verses are more polished and sublime, and his prose is more elegant. In the vernacular, Petrarch and Dante are considered to be just about equal, for Dante exceeds Petrarch in his *canzoni,* while his sonnets are inferior to those of Petrarch. It seems proper, thus, to judge them equal in their native tongue. Finally, Dante is superior to Boccaccio in almost everything, except for a few things of minor importance, such as the knowledge of Greek letters, which Dante lacked completely, and the writing of prose works in the vernacular, which he did not practice often. These two areas are also the only things in which Boccaccio exceeded Petrarch, whereas in everything else he was surpassed by him, as by his teacher.

1. He is referring to his *De longevibus claris* (1440), a collection of biographies of illustrious men who lived well into old age.
2. *De origine civitatis Florentie et de eiusdem famosis civibus.* See document 27.
3. Nevius' verse is quoted in Cic., *Tusc.,* 4.31.67.
4. Ter., *Pho.,* 68.
5. This expression is taken from Cic., *Fam.,* 9.1.2.
6. A pun on the double meaning of "vulgar" as "uncouth" and "vernacular."
7. Manetti also mentions this famous saying of Socrates in his *Vita Socratis et Senecae,* ed. Alfonso De Petris (Florence: Olschki, 1979), paragraph 22, pp. 146–147. Classical sources reporting this maxim are Au. Gell., 19.2.7 and Diog. Laert., 2.34.
8. Manetti recounts this famous anecdote also in his *Vita Socratis et Senecae,* cit., paragraphs 31–32, p. 151. He probably read it in Cic., *De fato,* 5.10 or *Tusc.,* 4.37.80.
9. Cic., *De fin.,* 3.2.7.
10. "I will describe the kingdoms of the beyond that encircle the fluid world."
11. "To go on with my story" (*Inf.,* 8.1).
12. "Dante, theologian, whose knowledge embraces every principle / Nursed by philosophy at her noble bosom."
13. "The kings' rights, the gods, the River Phlegethon / In song I did describe till fate allowed me. / But part of me to better realms went / More happily his creator to behold amid the stars. / Here Dante rests, from his native land exiled, / Born of Florence, a hardly loving mother."
14. See Bruni's *Life of Petrarch.*

15. Sen., 13.3.
16. See *Fam.*, 11.5.
17. Manetti refers to the ambassadorial mission of Petrarch to Charles IV of Bohemia in Prague in the summer of 1356 *pro ligustica pace*. In several letters, Petrarch mentions this embassy, which he was sent on by the Visconti; see especially *Fam.*, 21.1–2, 5–8.
18. Petrarch mentions his embassy to John II of France in various letters, but none of them is addressed to Boccaccio.
19. Pet., *Sen.*, 16.7.
20. See Jer., *Epist.*, 53 "Ad Paulinum" (*PL*, 22.541). Manetti reports this anecdote also in his *Vita Socratis et Senecae*, cit., par. 17, p. 116.
21. Many Florentine authors believed that the Latin poet Claudianus (d. 408) was born in Florence; Filippo Villani, for instance, included a biographical sketch of Claudianus in his collection of lives of illustrious Florentines.
22. "This cold stone covers Petrarch's remains. / Virgin mother, receive his soul; son of the Virgin have mercy upon it, / And let it rest, weary of the world, in the highest heaven."
23. This work by Salutati is now lost. Salutati mentions it in a letter of March 24, 1375, to Benvenuto da Imola and in a later one to Francescuolo da Brossano.
24. The classical poets, *vates* in the Latin text.
25. Manuel Chrysoloras arrived in Florence in 1397 at the invitation of Palla Strozzi and Coluccio Salutati.
26. "Success is difficult to achieve for those whose accomplishments are impeded by scanty possessions" (Juv., *Sat.*, 3.164–165).
27. "The ashes and the bones of Giovanni lie under this mass, / While his mind sits before God, honored for the labors / Of his mortal life. Boccaccio his father, / Certaldo his homeland, sacred poetry his study."
28. "Renowned poet, why do you utter such humble words / To describe yourself? In fine verses / You celebrate the pastures. You describe in order and with great effort the name of mountains, / Of woods and fountains, rivers, swamps and lakes, / And of the oceans. / You bring together the illustrious men and their exceedingly great misfortunes / From Adam to our own age. / You celebrate mothers of repute in solemn style, / You depict the gods revealing their unknown origin / In fifteen divine volumes not inferior / To any ancient author's. Among the people, your many labors / Have brought you immense fame; no future age will remain silent about you."

23

A Heavenly Vision After the Battle of Campaldino

MATTEO PALMIERI

The congruence between Matteo Palmieri's (1406–1475) dynamic public career and the ideals animating his literary works makes the writing of this pious and erudite apothecary one of the most valuable examples of what scholars of the Italian Renaissance have defined as Florentine civic humanism. Palmieri remained faithful to the Medici party throughout his whole life, a loyalty which certainly contributed to his success in the political sphere. He figured among the members of the 1434 balìa, which called Cosimo back from exile, and was later elected to important posts within the Florentine government, such as gonfaloniere di compagnia, ufficiale del Monte, and prior. Palmieri was a pupil of the humanists Giovanni Sozomeno da Pistoia, Carlo Marsuppini, and Ambrogio Traversari; he was also a close friend of Leonardo Bruni and Poggio Bracciolini. His cultural interests focused on ethical theory in classical texts and on the works of the "three crowns" of Florence, especially Dante (as we can see in his theological poem La città di vita, *whose commentary and preface were composed by his Dominican friend Leonardo Dati, as well as in his most famous work, the* Vita civile*). Palmieri also tried his hand at historiography—he wrote successively an account of the Florentine conquest of Pisa in 1406 (*De captivitate Pisarum*), a universal history from the creation of the world to his time (*Liber de temporibus, 1449*), and a record of the main events in Italy from 1429 to 1434 (*Annales*). He also wrote a biography of Niccolò Acciaiuoli which, like Vespasiano da Bisticci's* Life of Cosimo de' Medici, *celebrates the ideal of the successful Florentine merchant who also distinguishes himself as an astute politician* *and a patron of the arts. When Palmieri died in 1475, he was renowned even outside Florence. The humanist Alamanno Rinuccini composed a magnificent funeral oration for him.*

Palmieri is most famous for his Vita civile, *a treatise he wrote between 1438 and 1439. The author imagines he is with three friends in a Florentine villa during the plague of 1430. Their discussion focuses on the value of culture and the importance of moral probity. Book 1 treats the topic of educating children; Books 2 and 3 are devoted to the practice of justice, prudence, temperance, and fortitude by citizens in both private and public life. Book 4 celebrates civic industry and closes with an account of a vision that one of Dante's friends had after the Florentine army defeated the Ghibellines of Arezzo at Campaldino (March 2, 1289). In this vision, Dante's friend, who has just died in battle, miraculously reveals to the poet the heavenly rewards awaiting those who act for the good of their country. Dante listens to his friend's astonishing recital, which strengthens his resolution to pursue a virtuous civic life. The final pages of the* Vita civile *are a true celebration of both Dante and the tenets promoted by Florentine civic humanism. Like Socrates at Potidaea, Dante personifies the ideal of the wise and learned citizen who does not refrain from putting his own life at risk to defend the liberty of his country.*

Source: Matteo Palmieri, *Vita civile,* ed. Gino Belloni (Florence: Sansoni, 1982), pp. 198–208.

BOOK 4

. . . Nature itself calls us to act according to justice, and to this same end we are impelled by divine and human laws, motivated by the common utility of all men, and prompted by religious and philosophical texts. This virtue [of acting justly] helps us in private affairs; in politics it is not only the most useful virtue but [one that is] utterly necessary. This is why, in discussing civic life, we have spoken more about justice than about any other virtue. He who leads a just life, especially if he happens to participate in the governing of a republic, will have prudence, steadfastness, temperance, and modesty. He will righteously rule the people who live together according to civil laws. Nothing on earth pleases God more than this.

I cannot expound on this topic any further owing to my numerous respon- sibilities and preoccupations. Everyone must firmly believe, however, that whoever lives both in private and in public according to the ideals we have described above will be rewarded in heaven with eternal beatitude. The latter will be commensurate with the benefit that just rulers of republics duly receive in preserving society. The good done by him who preserves the life of many, in fact, is greater than that of him who is only concerned with his own preservation.

Throughout human history, men of great intellect have always asserted that all just rulers of republics come from heaven and return there. Near the end of his divine *Republic,* Plato writes that once freed of their mortal bodies, the souls of great rulers are granted a place among the stars, where they live in eternal beatitude.[1] Likewise, our Cicero, at the end of his *Republic,*[2] introduces the character of Scipio to demonstrate that there is a specific place in heaven where the souls of rulers of republics are received. Cicero narrates how, after his death, Scipio the Elder returns to such a place. He later appears to Scipio the Younger and spurs him to act justly for the good of the republic so that he, too, will be accepted into that most desirable dwelling. He shows Scipio the Younger how his ancestors dwell together with other fellow citizens who dedicated themselves to protecting and nurturing the republic.

These things remind me of an episode that I have been told happened to our poet Dante upon Florence's victory at Campaldino. I shall report what I have often heard about this event for the benefit of all those who hold public office, so that before this work of mine comes to its conclusion, readers may see and understand what a magnificent destiny awaits good rulers of republics.

Shortly before the great Battle of Campaldino, in which Florence fought Arezzo, Dante—who was a young poet then and eager for glory—went to the Florentine camp with a close friend, a scholar of philosophy and one of the period's most learned men in literature and the liberal arts. They stayed there for quite a while, giving advice to the captains of the army. When the day of the battle came, both armies bravely arranged their ranks and fought for hours, neither of the two prevailing. Fortune, however, eventually favored the Florentines, who, despite suffering many injuries and losses, vanquished their enemy and put him to flight.

Dante fought in that battle with great courage. The Florentines chased the disbanded foe, only a few of whom managed to escape them. In the next two days they also seized Bibbiena and many other villages in the territory of Arezzo, a series of events, however, that took them far from the original site of the battle. On the third day they finally returned to the field where the tremendous battle had taken place, finding the corpses of many of their comrades next to those of the enemies. The joy of victory was thereupon immediately mingled with the sorrow for those dead. They tried to comfort one another on the loss of a relative or a friend, and the tragic fate of those who died. Having vented their grief for quite some time and relieved their sorrow by thinking about the glorious nature of those deaths and the victory that ensued, they took to burying their fellow citizens, starting with those noblest and most distinguished. Like all Florentines, Dante spent a long time looking for his comrades' bodies, and especially that of his dear friend, who had died of multiple wounds. I do not know whether his friend came back to life or had never actually died, but I do know for sure, for I have been told, that when Dante finally found his friend's lacerated and bloodstained body, his friend stood up before him as would a living person.

Dante was beside himself with joy when he saw his friend standing upright. [Dante] was filled with wonder, his whole body trembled, and he was, at first, unable to speak. The wounded man finally began, "Be calm and do not fear, for it is by special grace and not without reason that I have been sent from a star[3] to report to you what I have seen in the last three days in which I passed from my mortal life to the present one. Listen carefully and try to remember what I am about to tell you, for it has been ordained that you will reveal to mankind the secrets I have seen."

Having heard this, Dante collected himself, overcame his fear, and said, "I shall be glad to listen to your words, whatever they may be. First, though, I beg you to tell me about your condition, if you can, in order to help me understand by what grace you have remained alive and intact despite your numerous wounds and lack of food or aid of any kind."

He answered, "I am deeply sorry that I cannot satisfy your request; if it were possible, I would gladly tell you everything. But take from me what I can give you, for I am not permitted to grant you more."

"While we were arranging our ranks for the battle," the vision began, "my heart was seized with so great a terror at seeing our enemies strong and organized in the field that, out of fear, I nearly ran away from our camp. I intended to do this until Vieri de' Cerchi—the one who truly saved our army that day[4]—prompted us to attack our enemies, who outnumbered us, by shouting, 'Whoever wants to save our country, follow me!' As soon as I heard these words uttered by our wealthiest and most distinguished citizen and saw him, out of love for his country, rushing with his nephew and his son toward great danger and certain death, I bitterly regretted my terrible error. I then gathered my courage, ready at last to fight valorously and put the safety of my country above my life and private possessions. Thus animated, I and many others strove to imitate Vieri's courage and boldness, gallantly fighting our enemies, who bravely defended themselves from our attacks. During the fight we both caused and suffered wounds and losses, until finally we succeeded in overcoming their first two ranks. We were already weary when Guglielmino,[5] their leader, joined the battle with a new division of specially trained soldiers and started massacring our comrades. It seemed that they [the enemy] were about to win the battle. Distressed at so many losses, I asked God to forgive my sins and then hurled myself at the enemy, straight at Guglielmino, the head of the army, whom, by God's will, I dealt a mortal blow. Afterward, I managed to ward off the blows of Guglielmino's soldiers who surrounded me, until my limbs finally lost their strength and I suffered the injuries you see. Our forces eventually overcame the enemy, with much bloodshed, and they fully avenged my death with the victory.

"From this point onward my memory is hazy and I cannot answer your question, for I do not know whether I was still within my body or detached from it, but I was certainly alive, and, like one who dreams about being in danger and is unable to do anything to protect himself, I felt my limbs restrained from movement. Without knowing how, I suddenly found myself before a shining globe, greater than anything I had ever seen before, which appeared to reflect a splendor from a source of light and to illuminate the whole earth. My eagerness to approach it was of no avail, for I was unable to move. Right at that moment, a venerable old man appeared, resembling the figure of an emperor whom I had often seen in paintings. When I looked at him, my whole body started to tremble. He took my right hand and said, 'Do not be afraid. Remain calm and remember the things that I am about to tell you.'

"Being partly reassured by his words of comfort, with trembling voice I dared to speak thus: 'Most excellent father, before you proceed with your speech, please reveal to me who you are, if this is something you can grant me, and if I am worthy of such an honor.'

"He benevolently replied, 'Charlemagne was my name on earth.'

" 'O holy Emperor,' I said, 'too great a blessing it is for me to see you,' and bowed to kiss his feet with great devotion. I then stood up and said, 'Charles, you are rightly called "the Great," not only on account of the excellence and the glory of your noble deeds, but also for your many outstanding virtues, your temperance, mercifulness, surpassing justice, and prudent words and actions, qualities which, moreover, are accompanied and embellished by doctrine and the study of both divine and human letters. Your immense glory and repute still rightly endure in the world, and will endure as long as the world itself shall last.[6] In the name of the Christian faith, you fought many nations, subduing and converting Spain, Flanders, Gaul, and even the most distant lands, Britain and Ireland. You then turned to redress the miseries of Italy, which for the last five hundred years had been enslaved by the barbarians. You succeeded in freeing it from the hands of the tyrant Desiderius, thus bridling the violence and the rage of the destructive Lombards. You were the one to restore the sovereign pontiff, who had been insulted and deprived of his authority for many a year, to his honor and previous estate by returning him to the apostolic throne. You managed to restore to the empire its ancient dignity, which had been in complete disarray for a long time. You alone saved Christendom, as well as freed and repaired many cities of the world.'

"The blessed patriarch then interjected, 'Your words are superfluous to me and simply delay the things at which you will rejoice. Listen, then, and pay attention: you are now at the midpoint of the universe. All those immense stars diffusing so much light above you are able to think by virtue of their lofty intellect; they are eternal and first causes, everlasting and unchanging. That which lies beneath you is mutable, however, and varies constantly because of the action of the eternal bodies up above. All these things within the universe, created by the first causes, are related to one another, and by virtue of the single force that animates them, they will continue to operate together forever. Because of this, all the animals on earth exist: those which fly through the air, and all the marvels that the vast ocean hides beneath its waves. An ardent vitality, equally distributed in all beings, pervades and sustains the weak limbs of the mortal bodies living in this mutable lower part that I have just shown you. Human creatures alone are endowed with the soul of those luminous bodies that live eternally animated by divine light. In the lower realm, by contrast, whatever pertains to our corruptible bodies is base, subject to death, and, as such, common to all beasts as well. Were it not for our divine soul—which, being stable, obeys God's order to control our instincts—we would be completely blinded, overruled, and vanquished by worldly passions; disregarding all honesty, we would give ourselves over to pleasures and act like beasts. He who chooses not to abide by these laws and acts only according to his own desires disobeys the commandment of God who created this firmament and all that you see. This is why He treats such a man like an unfaithful servant and a rebel against His law and does not allow him to enter these doors through which I passed to come to meet you. Nor does He permit him to return to his homeland on earth, but relegates him forever to a specific place, according to the vice in which he indulged most. Both we in heaven and you on earth call this place Hell. All souls imprisoned within the borders of Hell are dead, for they are separated from their only source of life. This is the reason that what we define as "life" on earth is nothing other than sure death, for the only ones who are alive are those who obey God and who upon abandoning their mortal remains are admitted to these heavenly realms. This luminous globe to which you have come is the moon, which, as you say on earth, is embellished with the light it receives from another planet.'

"As he finished his speech, I can assure you that I was astonished. Had he not told me, I would have never realized that I was on the moon, for it looked so different from the earth, and it was larger than I could have ever imagined. Out of respect, I did not wish to interrupt his speech.

" 'This,' he said, 'is the border between life and death. Beyond this point, everything is eternal joy and never-ending beatitude. Beneath, by contrast, lie all sorts of evils, torments, and unbearable punishments. This is the world devoid of light where Lethe,[7] Acheron, Styx, Cocytus, and Phlegethon are to be found. Everything is subject to the laws of Rhadamanthus and Minos, who judge and condemn the guilty. There one finds vultures feeding on imperishable hearts. There famine rages in the midst of appealing and bounteous food; there the wheel that tortures turns with its sharp, curved teeth. Some souls can be seen rolling heavy weights forward with their chests; others are constantly seized with fear that the heavy rocks looming above their heads might fall and crush them. In brief, Hell is the center of all tortures. Charon takes the guilty there to be devoured by Pluto and Cerberus. The soul subjugated by worldly passions easily falls into this abyss through a wide gate, but it is extremely laborious then to climb back up to the stars above, for the steep incline of the path forces one to cling to the shining cliffs he happens to find. The first way to attain salvation is to keep desires under the control of the mind, not to disregard reason, which God gave us as a means of salvation. No other act on earth can please God more than to love justice, mercy, and piety—virtues which, although great by themselves, nevertheless deserve the highest praise when practiced for the good of one's own country. The path to heaven and the eternal places you now see are wide open for those who by their rule preserve their country.'

"As I heard this, with fear and reverence I asked him whether I would be allowed to have a closer look at those eternal lights. He answered, 'Only the intense love for your country that caused you to fight most gallantly at Campaldino renders you worthy of having your desire fulfilled. To no one else does God so easily grant permission to pass through these gates as to the rulers of republics who keep society united by its common obedience to just laws. Such an intense love for the well-being of the entire world was my guiding principle during my mortal life. Now in heaven I experience a much greater joy with the other blessed souls. My love for this virtue, however, is still so profound that I hold dear whoever practices it on earth, as we pursue the same goal. This, therefore, and my seeing that you gave your life out of love for my dear Florence, a city I once rebuilt, induced me to come down to you to show you the glory destined for all those who have devoted their lives to such a purpose.'

"This said, he surrounded me with light, as if he had taken out a bright lantern, and I suddenly felt liberated from the weight of my body. He then started to move, and I followed him, being led to the first, eternal light. Once we arrived there, he told me, 'Pay attention during our trip and notice that the whole universe is held together by nine spheres. You should already be familiar with the lowest one, which is stable and placed in the middle; all bodies are drawn to it, on account of their weight. See how small the earth looks already, and as you ascend to the succeeding heavenly sphere, it will appear no greater than a speck. We are now on the smallest of the blessed stars, the one closest to earth and farthest away from the highest heaven. See how it is illuminated and enhanced by the rays of the sun. Mercury is next, revolving with incredible speed, and splendid Venus comes third, whose beauty shines closest to the sun. Here now is the sun, placed at the center, as it is the guide and the chief of all stars; its all-pervasive light illuminates everything, and its name on the earth is "Sol," for it is the sole planet among the celestial lights that can be seen. This reddish and menacing-looking one is Mars. Now we climb to Jupiter, splendid and benevolent; Saturn is last, the closest to the starry sky.'

"As I arrived there I was seized with great admiration, for I saw innumerable stars which I had never been able to see from the earth and whose magnitude far exceeded one's imaginings. I could see the sky adorned with so many and such diverse stars that it looked like a masterpiece by an extraordinary artist. The sky was divided into ten sections, each marked by a constellation, one of which seemed to be particularly bright and luminous, shining with a reddish glare and surrounded by darting flames. Two gates could be seen in the sky, one bearing the sign of Cancer, the other of Capricorn. The sun marked his footprints as he climbed upward. 'The blessed,' said my guide, 'live beyond those gates.' Having warned me that a living being cannot pass through the main gate, he let me in through the gate of Cancer. In vain would I, even if I could, mention all the innumerable souls and the holy deeds of those immortal creatures who dwell there in eternal beatitude. I would not be far from the truth, however, if I said that for each man who ever lived on earth, one finds there thousands of heavenly souls. I saw the souls of all those citizens who in their lives had justly ruled their republics, such as Fabricius, Curius, Fabius, Scipio, Metellus, and many others who put their own lives and their possessions second, after the safety of their country. Filled with joy, Charles turned to me and said, 'Now you can see that men are not mortal creatures, but it is only their flesh that dies. A man's appearance is not his true nature. A man's worth depends upon his mind; if he nourishes it properly, he will eventually join God and live forever as an eternal being. Nothing on earth is nobler than exercising our minds through arts and excellent deeds. No action among men can be said to be worthier than taking care of one's own country, protecting one's city, and preserving well-organized societies in unity and peace. Whoever practices these things will be the first, before anyone else, to inhabit this heavenly abode as his own home in eternal joy with the other blessed, for this is the place whence all the souls of statesmen left to descend to earth, and whither they all must return after death and remain for eternity.' "

Having listened with great astonishment, Dante wanted to reply and say, "Since you have revealed to me the existence of such a noble reward, I shall strive with all my might to attain it." He had just begun to speak, however, when his friend fell down dead. He waited in vain for him to recover, then finally buried him and rejoined his army.

1. Pla., *Rep.*, 10.614–621.
2. Cic., *Rep.*, 6.9–26.
3. See Dante, *Par.*, 4.49–60 in which Beatrice explains Plato's theory in the *Timaeus* that souls descend from the stars, and return to them through a process of reincarnation.
4. On Vieri de' Cerchi, see document 19, n. 12.
5. Guglielmino degli Ubertini, bishop of Arezzo and leader of the Ghibelline forces.
6. See Dante, *Inf.*, 2.59–60, where these words of praise refer to Virgil.
7. Unlike Dante, Palmieri follows the classic tradition that situates the River Lethe in Hell. From this point on, Charlemagne's speech is drawn mainly from Dante's *Commedia;* in a few cases, though, on the episode of Aeneas' descent into Hades in Virgil's *Aeneid,* bk. 6.

24

The First Anthology of Vernacular Poetry

ANGELO POLIZIANO

In 1476 Lorenzo de' Medici commissioned Angelo Poliziano, a distinguished humanist and his faithful secretary, to put together an anthology of vernacular poems for Frederick of Aragon, son of King Ferdinand of Naples, whom the Florentine ruler had met in Pisa earlier that year. Poliziano completed the work by 1477, and Lorenzo sent the Neapolitan prince a manuscript. The anthology collected the main works written in the vernacular from the earliest Sicilian poets onward and ended with a sample of Lorenzo's poetry: nine sonnets, two canzoni, and five ballads. The aim of this cultural enterprise was manifold. On the one hand, Lorenzo hoped to gain the support of the Aragonese court at a time when his relations with Pope Sixtus IV, Ferdinand's most powerful ally on the peninsula, were particularly strained. On the other hand, Lorenzo once again sought to influence the realm of Florentine literature through political propaganda. The abundance of Tuscan authors included in the anthology was evidence that the cultural vitality of that region was a consequence of its enlightened political leadership.

In writing the dedicatory letter for the volume, Poliziano seized the opportunity to demonstrate his rhetorical ability once again. In the preface, Poliziano depicts Frederick of Aragon as a new Pisistratus: the latter had rediscovered and collected Homer's verse, whereas Frederick had inspired an unprecedented anthology of the main Italian vernacular poets, thus marking the beginning of a new period in the history of Italian culture. Beneath the rhetorical veneer of the dedicatory letter to Frederick, however, the true object of Poliziano's praise is Lorenzo the Magnificent. In this respect, the preface to the

Raccolta Aragonese offers a significant example of a literary comparison between classical Athens and fifteenth-century Florence that proposes to establish a political and cultural parallel between the two cities. According to Poliziano, moreover, Lorenzo's patronage also coincided with an improvement in vernacular literature over any written previously. In paying homage to the genius of Dante, Poliziano asserts that his most outstanding contribution was to have brought the vernacular into the literary realm. Poliziano then goes on to claim that more recent poems (especially Lorenzo's, obviously) reveal even greater stylistic refinement than the works of Dante, thus attesting to the admirable progress made by Florentine culture during the decades of Medicean leadership.

Source: *Prosatori volgari del Quattrocento,* ed. Claudio Varese (Milan: Ricciardi, 1957), pp. 985–990.

TO THE MOST ILLUSTRIOUS LORD FREDERICK OF ARAGON, SON OF THE KING OF NAPLES

My most illustrious Lord Frederick, I have often debated with myself which among the many and innumerable good customs of ancient times was most excellent. I finally chose one that I believe should be considered the most glorious of all: that in those times, no illustrious and virtuous work produced by either hands or intellect lacked for rewards and grand tributes, both in private and in public. Consequently, as all rivers and springs are said to origi- nate in the Ocean, so all famous deeds and wondrous works of the Ancients are held to have derived from this worthy custom.

The granting of honor is what truly nourishes all the arts—it is nothing other than glory that inspires the human mind to accomplish noble deeds. For this purpose, the Ancients enthusiastically celebrated magnificent triumphs in Rome, the famous Olympic games in Greece, and in both places, contests of poetry and rhetoric. Consequently, they honored the winners with chariots and triumphal arches, marble trophies, lavishly decorated theaters, statues, palm leaves, crowns, funeral orations, and all the other innumerable and admi- rable adornments. This, furthermore, was the true origin of the Ancients' worthy and noble accomplishments of sword and pen, and of many other excellent enterprises. They will exult in glory, as our Tuscan poet says, "until the universe dissolves."[1]

These were admirable and truly divine men, intensely eager both to be immortalized by praise and to be animated by a profound love for those able to render immortal the noble deeds of great men through poetry. This very desire inflamed Alexander the Great when, upon arrival at the famous tomb of Achilles in Sigeum, he uttered that eternally memorable, regal phrase, "O fortunate man, whom such a noble poet / Did find to sing such sublime verses of."[2] He certainly was fortunate, as, had it not been for Homer, that divine poet, the tomb would have enclosed both the body and the fame of Achilles. Homer, in turn, would not have attained such honor and renown if a most noble Athenian had not brought him back to life. After his death, the sacred works of this extraordinary poet were dispersed throughout Greece. The lord of Athens, Pisistratus, a splendid man of numerous virtues—both physical and intellectual—promised great rewards to whoever could bring him Homer's verses.[3] With the greatest diligence and care, therefore, he managed to gather all the works of this most hallowed poet, and as he gave Homer endless life, so he obtained immortal glory and outstanding repute. This is the reason for which he wanted to have no other inscription carved on the base of his statue than the following, "To the one who collected the glorious verses of Homer." O truly divine beings, born into this world for the benefit of mankind!

This worthy prince knew that all his other noble deeds, although plentiful and admirable, were nevertheless inferior to this single accomplishment, through which he endowed both himself and the poet with eternal life and glory. Such were those ancient men, whose virtuous deeds are now difficult not only to imitate, but also to believe. The reason for this is that the rewards granted to those virtuous men no longer exist, which in turn has caused any benign light of virtue to disappear. Moreover, since men no longer do anything worthy of praise, they have come to despise such blessed praise as well. Had this not happened in the centuries immediately before ours, the grievous and unfortunate loss of so many worthy works of Greek and Latin authors would not have taken place. During that tragic time of loss and destruction, many poets began to cultivate the previously deserted field of the Tuscan language, and today it blossoms with copious flowers.

Your benign hand, most illustrious Frederick, which you have deigned to give to these poets after their many and lengthy labors, has finally guided them into port. Last year, during that discussion we had in the old town of Pisa concerning the poets who wrote in the Tuscan tongue, Your Lordship did not conceal his laudable desire to have me collect all these authors in one volume. Therefore, since in this, as in anything else, I am eager to satisfy your most heartfelt wishes, I have managed, not without great toil, to find the original texts. I then selected the least coarse pieces and gathered them in this volume that I now send to Your Lordship in the hope that you will enjoy this work of mine, whatever its worth may be, and that you will accept it as a token of my profound respect for you.

No one should scorn the Tuscan language for inelegance and inadequacy, for if its riches and adornments are properly considered, this language is one that will be judged bounteous and highly refined. It is impossible to imagine anything worthy, lavish, delightful, or elegant; anything acute, distinguished, clever, or subtle; anything sublime, magnificent, or melodious; and finally, anything passionate, intense, or agitated of which numberless and most notable examples do not shine in those two most sublime authors, Dante and Petrarch, as well as in these others, whom you, O Lord, have returned to a place of glory.[4]

The use of verse, as Petrarch writes in a Latin epistle, was held in high esteem by the ancient Romans.[5] After having been abandoned for a long time, it began to flourish again in Sicily, just a few centuries ago. It then reached France, and finally Italy, as if that place were its home. The first among our authors to outline the fair new style was Guittone d'Arezzo, followed by his famous Bolognese contemporary, Guido Guinizzelli. They both were learned in philosophy, had grave countenances, and were profoundly concerned with questions of morality. The former, however, was definitely coarse and uncouth, and he lacked any spark of eloquence. The latter was much more refined, melodious, and elegant, so much so that our honored Dante does not hesitate to call him his own master, and master "of men better than I, / Whose love poems were always sweet and agreeable."[6] Guinizzelli was certainly the first to embellish the beautiful form of our native idiom with a graceful color, after it had been barely outlined by that uncouth poet of Arezzo. Following these two poets shines forth the delicate work of Guido Cavalcanti of Florence, an exceedingly subtle dialectician and one of the most renowned philosophers of his time. As he was handsome, charming, and of noble birth, in his works he seems to be somewhat more beautiful than the others, more refined and original, subtle in his invention, pre-eminent, admirable, and solemn in his moral teachings, unstinting and careful in the composition of his poems, orderly, wise, and clever. All these virtues array him in a delightful, sweet, and peculiar style, as in costly attire. Had he tried his hand at other forms of writing, he would have certainly obtained the greatest honors. Of all his works, the most noteworthy is a canzone in which this remarkable poet skillfully discusses all the qualities, properties, and accidents of love.[7] This canzone received so much praise at the time that three notable philosophers, who were contemporaries of his and among whom was the Roman Egidio Colonna, wrote very learned commentaries on it.[8] Nor can we forget to mention Bonagiunta da Lucca and the notary Jacopo da Lentini. They are both solemn and principled in their teaching, but so deprived of every bit of elegance that they should rejoice at being included in this group with such honored men. Along with them, at the time of Guittone, was Pier delle Vigne. He, too, wrote a number of serious and erudite—although brief—works. He is the one who, as Dante says, "held both the keys / To Frederick's heart, and turned them, / Locking and unlocking so gently."[9] After them radiate those two wondrous suns which have illumined this language: Dante, and not far behind him, Francesco Petrarch. I would rather not praise these poets, as Sallust says of Carthage, than say something in passing.[10]

The Bolognese Onesto and the Sicilians, who were the first poets to write in the vernacular, came before Dante and Petrarch and could have benefited from some refining, although they did not lack either talent or motivation. Cino da Pistoia's work certainly lives up to its reputation. He was a delightful poet and superb author of love poems, the first, in my opinion, who truly detached himself from that old coarseness that not even the divine Dante, despite his excellence, completely avoided. Numerous young poets imitated Dante and Cino, although they never came even close to comparing with them.

Together with a number of our current poets, O Prince, these poets come to give you eternal thanks, as you have infused them with life, immortal light, and form. You thus become much more deserving of glory than that aforementioned ancient Athenian. He, in fact, revived only a single poet, although the greatest, whereas you revived many. In the hope of pleasing you, I have also appended a few of my sonnets and canzoni to the end of this volume, so that by reading them you may once again be reminded of my loyalty and profound respect for Your Lordship. These poems of mine do not deserve to be included among such marvelous verses of other poets. I have inserted them in the collection, however, to serve as a contrast to the others, thereby making the latter appear more elegant.

Welcome these poems and me not only into your house, my most illustrious Lordship, but also into your heart and mind, just as it is with great joy that I always keep you in my heart and in my mind.

1. Petrarch, *Canz.*, 53.34.
2. Petrarch, *Canz.*, 187.3–4. See also Cic., *Pro Arc.*, 10.24.

3. For this episode, see Cic., *De orat.*, 3.137.
4. That is, by occasioning this anthology of their poetic works.
5. Pet., *Fam.*, 1.1.
6. Purg., 26.98–99.
7. The famous poem "Donna me priega." Note that because of the philosophical nature of this canzone, the expression "accidents of love" should be understood in an Aristotelian sense.
8. Scholars no longer believe Egidio Colonna to be one of the commentators. Dino del Garbo composed a renowned commentary on Cavalcanti's canzone, but it is not known who the third commentator might have been.
9. *Inf.*, 13.58–60.
10. Sall., *Bel. Iug.*, 19.

25

Proem to the First Edition of Dante's *Divine Comedy*

CRISTOFORO LANDINO

A university professor, Cristoforo Landino distinguished himself primarily in the writing of commentaries on classical authors. His commentaries on Horace (1482) and Virgil (1488) were widely disseminated and hold a prominent place in Italian literature. He was an ardent advocate of literature in the vernacular, and devoted some of his best scholarship to the "three crowns" of Florence. Landino's inaugural lecture on Petrarch at the University of Florence in 1467, for instance, is justly regarded as a turning point in the history of Petrarchan studies. Even more important, however, is his Commento sopra la Comedia, *which he composed for the first Florentine edition of Dante's poem in 1481. This Neoplatonic commentary—which attests to the new and singular climate of Florentine culture of those years and to the spread of Ficino's teaching—is not the only element that contributed to the deserved celebrity of this incunabulum. The 1481 edition of the* Commedia *by Niccolò della Magna, in fact, included twenty drawings by Botticelli and was an outstanding success—indeed, it was reprinted six times before the end of the century.*

Landino's commentary is certainly the most important humanist study of Dante's Commedia; *it presents the poet as a philosopher whose teachings, cloaked in elegant rhyme, disclose scientific, moral, and theological knowledge in unusual profusion. Landino's firm reply to Poliziano's thesis on the alleged "obsolete coarseness" of Dante's style, his praise of the fellow citizens who have attained fame in various fields, and his appeal to the most eminent intellectuals of the city in order to emphasize the role of Dante as a peculiarly Florentine poet are among the features that render Landino's proem a true celebration, not only of the poet's genius but of his native language, his homeland, and the culture of his city. For brevity's sake, we have included only the translation of the first section of the proem.*

Source: Cristoforo Landino, "Proem," *Commento di Cristoforo Landino fiorentino sopra la Comedia di Dante Alighieri poeta fiorentino,* in *Scritti critici e teorici,* ed. Roberto Cardini (Rome: Bulzoni, 1974), vol. 1, pp. 100–102.

There is no class of learned writers, most distinguished lords of our state,[1] which does not deserve to receive the highest and most enduring gratitude from mankind. This is just, for the aim of all their efforts, all their most attentive scholarship and laborious logic is to benefit not only themselves and their contemporaries but also all posterity for centuries to come. Although I have read many authors who have, either in Latin or in Greek, written their own memoirs, I have not found anyone who can rightly be compared with Dante or be considered on a par with him. I have not found anyone, in fact, who, with a profound and vast learning, with elegant, rich, and elevated style could not only show us important things fundamental to our life and to our salvation but also veil them in a magnificent apparel. Besides the immense usefulness that such vast and varied knowledge offers us, the soul and the senses, when properly educated and refined, delight in such a poem. I shall soon speak of the extraordinary poetic qualities of this work. For the moment, however, I wish to speak of something else. From the time of my earliest adolescence, I have been convinced by the authority of many learned men of different nations and languages—who have always considered poets to be worthier than all other writers—to study the poets, and I have spent no small part of my life doing just that. Now, since I have written a new commentary in Latin on Virgil's *Aeneid* in which I focus on the allegorical meaning of this work,[2] I thought it would be rather useful and pleasing to my fellow citizens to investigate, as much as my culture and zeal allow me to, the secret, occult but entirely divine meanings of the *Commedia* by the Florentine poet, Dante Alighieri. As I wrote about the Latin poet Virgil in Latin, so I shall comment on the Tuscan in Tuscan. Because of its magnitude, the vast number of subjects to be treated, and especially its novelty, this task would certainly bring honor to any scholar. As I am not gifted with either erudition or eloquence, [this task] has been a most laborious enterprise, which, perhaps, I undertook a bit naively. My intense love for this kind of muse,[3] however, has lightened the burden, and, as the sages say, "Nothing is difficult for the lover."[4]

Some, however, may deem my undertaking idle if I do not properly complete what I set out to do. Or perhaps they may consider my work superfluous, as there have already been many commentators on the *Commedia* who, as contemporaries or near-contemporaries of the poet, seem to have been in a better position to understand the meaning of his work. Such commentators, moreover, were expert theologians, and appear to be able to comprehend more easily the profound theological notions he has hidden in the poem. Much to the reader's amazement, Dante miraculously drew these notions from the innermost recesses of theology. The poet's two sons, Francesco and Piero, wrote commentaries in Latin on his work, as did Benvenuto of Imola.[5] Jacopo Bolognese, by contrast, commented on Dante in the vernacular, as did Andrea—from Naples, I believe—and Guiniforte, a jurisconsult from Bergamo. Giovanni Boccaccio, too, started a commentary on Dante's work, but he did not get more than halfway through the first canticle. I praise them all, for they wrote many a thing worthy of their learning and quite useful to the reader. Francesco da Buti commented upon Dante in the Pisan language, and except for Boccaccio, he is the only one who strove to reveal the allegorical meaning of the poem, although not in all its parts.

I, however, have decided to interpret the meaning and aim of Dante's work according to a higher principle and, remaining faithful to this perspective throughout the poem, to investigate its most recondite teaching. Whenever I reflect upon this topic, I immediately fall into a stupor and become like a little bat in front of a blazing light. As those who live near the falls of the Nile are made deaf by the excessive noise, so my mind loses all its acuity and strength, for it is overwhelmed by both the subject and the invention, for which it is impossible to find a close second that is not considerably inferior, let alone an equal. Yet thanks to God's grace in fueling my desire to accomplish this task, I have discovered some barely noted traces of this divine poet. First, I followed them down the steep precipices to a profound abyss; then, led along by Dante's help, I moved up to the arduous mountain ridge of Purgatory. Upon his wings, I easily moved along the path until I finally arrived at the end of a long pilgrimage. I shall leave to men of greater erudition than my own to judge how much I have gained from this enterprise. I wish to assert only one thing: [by writing this commentary in the Florentine vernacular] I have set our citizen free from the barbarism of the foreign languages in which commentators have corrupted him. I have considered it my duty, therefore, most distinguished lords, to present him to you in such a way that, by the hands of the most important magistracy of the Florentine Republic, he may be returned to his homeland after a long exile and recognized as being neither from Romagna nor from Lombardy, and as speaking none of the other languages in which his commentators wrote, but pure Florentine. The extent to which this language exceeds all other Italian idioms is clearly shown by the fact that anyone who possesses either intellect or learning has always tried to use Florentine for verse or prose; but I shall speak about this later.

Therefore, most distinguished lords, you will applaud your country for having received so great a gift from Almighty God. In this work of mine, in fact, you will recognize the divinity of Dante's intellect, which is considered to be one of the rarest by anyone who looks at centuries of history and the memories of all nations. You will also notice that the wondrous abundance of his varied, complex, and recondite erudition is such that whoever possesses great knowledge knows only the slightest amount of what he does. You will read your poet often, since by imitating him—the greatest glory of Florence, and rare model of both eloquence and learning—you will adorn your speech with eloquence and dignity, your life and habits with wisdom and integrity, and your mind with knowledge and concern for humanity.

1. The edition was dedicated to the members of the Florentine signoria.
2. That is, in the last two books of the *Disputationes Camaldulenses.*
3. Vernacular literature.
4. See Virg., *Ecl.,* 10.69.
5. As Cardini pointed out in the notes to his critical edition of this text, Landino's mistakes are due to his relying on the preface by Martino Paolo Nidobeato to the edition of the commentary by Jacopo della Lana. Dante never had a son named Francesco, nor are Jacopo's glosses on the poem in Latin, but rather in the vernacular. Other, similar mistakes punctuate the section that Landino devotes to the early commentators of Dante.

26

Florence Welcomes Dante upon
His Return from Exile

MARSILIO FICINO

Inserted by Cristoforo Landino in his proem to the 1481 edition of Dante's Divina
Commedia, *the importance of this brief passage in Latin is twofold. On the one hand,
it bears witness to the beliefs Landino shared with Ficino regarding the Neoplatonic
interpretation of Dante's masterpiece; on the other hand, it is a tribute to the Florentine
philosopher and a means of celebrating the Tuscan city in which Ficino's school was
flourishing. Moreover, the passage emphasizes the high regard both scholars had for
Dante's literary style and education. More than forty years after Bruni's* Lives of Dante
and Petrarch, *the debate over the two most important Italian writers had not come to an
end, and presentation of Dante's work still called for a eulogistic introduction. It was
Ficino who, in 1481, carried out this task, just as he had done in 1468 in the preface to his
Italian translation of Dante's* Monarchia. *Furthermore, the numerous attempts made
by notable fifteenth-century Florentines—such as Matteo Palmieri, Antonio Manetti,
and Landino—to bring Dante's remains back to his birthplace were unsuccessful. In the
eyes of Ficino, the first printed edition of the* Commedia *was tantamount, as this
passage reveals, to a symbolic return by Dante to Florence.*

Source: Cristoforo Landino, *Scritti critici e teorici*, ed. Roberto Cardini (Rome: Bulzoni,
1974), vol. I, pp. 153–154.

Florence, long sad but joyful at last, warmly congratulates its poet Dante, who has come back to life and to his homeland for a glorious crowning after an absence of two centuries. O my Dante, during your exile you predicted that one day piety would overcome cruelty and that you would gladly return to your homeland and receive Apollo's crown in the marvelous temple of St. John the Baptist.[1] Your parents did not tell you of the omen in vain,[2] for recently, Apollo—filled with pity from my long weeping and your eternal exile—ordered Mercury to enter the devout mind of the divine poet Cristoforo Landino, assume Landino's appearance, awaken you from sleep with his sacred wand, take you upon his wings, bring you inside the walls of Florence, and finally crown your temples with Apollo's laurel. Today at last, Apollo's divine order has been carried out, Mercury's and Landino's devout tasks accomplished, Dante's prophecy come to pass, and Florence's wish be fulfilled. You have finally returned home, accompanied by the noble assembly of all the poets. Minerva showed you the way, and Mercury was your guide. The Graces joyfully welcomed your arrival, and the Muses and the nymphs embraced and kissed you.

> Have you come at last? Has the love your father awaited
> Finally overcome the toilsome journey? May I see your face,
> Dear son, and hear our voices utter familiar tones?
> I truly felt within my soul that this would come to pass;
> Thus did I foresee it as I counted the days, and see now
> that my yearning has not failed me.[3]

O dear son, how much more distinguished and blessed you are now than when I lost you! Your countenance, which was once mortal, has now become immortal and divine. The night of your Florence has become the day; your Florentines' grief has become joy. Rejoice and exult, most blessed citizens, for whom two suns rise in the place of one and are double not in flames, but in rays.[4] Can you not see that today the heavens themselves revel in your happiness? Lift up your eyes to the heavens, O citizens, glance up just for a moment. Watch as they crown our Dante, and how "the abode of omnipotent Olympus is thrown open."[5] The flames of the empyrean have never been more visible than they are today, shining brightly for us as we congratulate Dante upon his crowning. What do you think this sweet new sound is that our ears descry? Yes, it is the sound of the spheres and the nine Muses, which has not been heard for centuries and today openly applauds Dante's ceremony. O hear the sweet melody of the archangels singing within the sphere of Apollo and the exquisite hymns of the archangels in Mercury's sphere: "Glory on high to great Apollo! Glory to the Muses forever! Glory to the Graces! Peace, bliss, and joy to the Florentines now rejoicing in their double sun!"

1. *Par.*, 25.1–9.
2. This refers to the famous dream that Dante's mother had concerning her son's future glory. Boccaccio reports it in his *Trattatello*, as does Manetti in his biography of the poet. See document 22.
3. The meeting of Anchises and Aeneas in Virg., *Aen.*, 6.687–691.
4. Ficino views Dante and the first edition of his masterpiece as two suns rising over Florence.
5. Virg., *Aen.*, 10.1.

PART FOUR

Art

27

Giotto's Revival of Ancient Art

FILIPPO VILLANI

Filippo Villani (1325–1405), son of Matteo and nephew of the famous Giovanni Villani, is an especially interesting figure in that, although involved in the humanist movement of the quattrocento, he retained the fourteenth-century outlook regarding the writing of history. He continued his uncle and his father's Chronicle, *the monument of Florentine trecento historiography, taking the narration as far as 1364. As a scholar of Dante, moreover, he was appointed by the Florentine commune to hold public readings of the* Commedia, *as Boccaccio had done before him. Filippo was strongly influenced by Coluccio Salutati, whom he revered as a master and whose advice he sought. He also upheld the patriotic tenets fostered by nascent Florentine humanism, as we can see in his most renowned work,* On the Origins of the City of Florence and Her Famous Citizens. *His civic spirit inspired him to add to this text an innovative section on the illustrious citizens of Florence. In his gallery of famous Florentines, Villani describes the achievements and the personalities of writers, jurists, doctors, military men, artists, and musicians. The following passage offers us the first example in Florence of epideictic literature devoted to artists, a new genre that would become extremely popular in the quattrocento.*

Source: Filippo Villani, *De origine civitatis Florentie et de eiusdem famosis civibus,* ed. Giuliano Tanturli (Padua: Antenore, 1997), pp. 411–413.

CONCERNING MANY FAMOUS FLORENTINE PAINTERS, AND IN PARTICULAR GIOTTO, WHO REDISCOVERED THE DEFUNCT ART OF PAINTING

The ancient authors included in their written histories discussions of excellent painters and sculptors, along with other famous men. The ancient poets, moreover, struck by Prometheus' brilliant and generous deed, imagined that he had created man by using the mud of the earth. These wise men thought that those who imitate nature in striving to make human figures with bronze and marble, could not have accomplished so much without a magnificent intellect, an outstanding memory, and a particularly sensitive hand. Among the illustrious men mentioned in their historical works are Zeuxis, Polycleitos, Chares, Phidias, Praxiteles, Myron, Apelles, Conon, Volarius, and many other such exponents of this noble art.

Following the example [of the ancient historians] and disregarding those who may deride me for my decision, I deem it proper to mention the famous Florentine painters who revived art from quasi extinction. The first among them was Giovanni, called Cimabue. Through his skill and genius he restored the capacity of art to imitate nature, a capacity that, because of the childish ineptitude of the painters [of the time], was at its nadir and on the verge of disappearing. It is well known that before him both Latin and Greek painting had been at the mercy of crude rendering for centuries, as we can see in those figures and images that decorate the panels and the walls of the churches.

After Cimabue came Giotto. Since [Cimabue] had already blazed the trail, Giotto—who should not only be considered equal to the ancient painters on account of his great fame but should be considered superior to them because of his skill and genius—restored the dignity of painting and its distinguished standing. The figures that he portrayed so closely resemble those of nature that viewers believe them to be alive and breathing; their gestures and their looks are so well depicted that they seem to talk, laugh, rejoice, and other such things. Those who view his works are so delighted that they praise this artist's genius and skill. Many rightly hold that these painters [Giotto and Cimabue] are not inferior to the masters of the liberal arts, since the latter acquire through study and learning the teachings passed on in books, whereas the former use their intellect and tenacious memory to bring to perfection what their talent has inspired in them.

Giotto was knowledgeable in many things other than painting. He was well versed in history and was so fond of poetry that whoever looks carefully at his works will notice that he painted the fictions of the poets. He was, as befits most sagacious men, more eager for glory than for money. Moved by the desire to increase his fame, he painted in the most eminent places of Italy's greatest cities. In Rome, he assembled a mosaic by the door of the Basilica of St. Peter depicting the apostles in danger on a boat. To those who flock to Rome from all over the world, this work shows such talent that it illuminates both Giotto's art and his city. With the aid of mirrors, he also painted himself and his contemporary Dante Alighieri, the poet, on the wall of a room in the Palazzo del Podestà.[1]

From this most honorable man, as from a pure and plentiful source, many limpid streams of painters have surged—disciples who rendered art (which had just then re-commenced its imitation of nature) both exquisite and enjoyable. Maso [di Banco] is one of these disciples; he painted with a wondrous elegance and extraordinary delicacy. Then there was Stefano,[2] called the ape of nature, who was so skilled at imitating whatever object [he selected to paint] that doctors learned of the exact position of arteries, veins, nerves, and even the smallest parts of the human body by looking at his works. They were so lifelike that, as Giotto said, they seemed to lack only the power to breathe. Taddeo, finally, painted so magnificently throughout Italy that he seemed to be a new Dynocrates, or a new Vitruvius, the author of the treatise on architecture. To mention all the others who, following these men, ennobled the art of painting in Florence would be an idle task proper to someone who wants to dwell too much upon this subject. Satisfied with having mentioned these artists for the topic at hand, I shall therefore pass on to discuss another category of citizens.

1. The Bargello Palace in Florence.
2. Giotto's son-in-law.

28

Giotto Brings Art out of the Dark Ages

LORENZO GHIBERTI

One of the greatest artists of the Florentine quattrocento, "a holy light of inspiration for many fellow citizens," as Vasari wrote, Lorenzo di Cione Ghiberti was born in Florence in 1378. After spending time in Rome, where he admired the works of Giotto and Cavallini, and then in some small northern Italian cities, Ghiberti returned to his birthplace. It was there that he defeated Jacopo della Quercia and Filippo Brunelleschi in the famous contest for the baptistery doors. In 1403 he started working on the first door, which he completed in 1424. In 1452, after twenty-seven years of work, he finished his renowned masterpiece, the so-called Porta del Paradiso, with the help of his son Vittorio. Among his numerous other pieces are the statue of St. Matthew for the Church of Orsanmichele, the tomb of St. Zenobius in the cathedral of Florence, and the bas-reliefs of the baptismal font in Siena. He died in Florence in 1455.

During the last years of his life, probably between 1447 and 1448, Ghiberti wrote the three books of his innovative Commentari. The first book, filled with citations and borrowings from Pliny and Vitruvius, focuses on ancient art; Book 2 discusses works of art from the late Middle Ages to the quattrocento. These first two chapters set the stage for Ghiberti to introduce a large section on his own artistic production, a sort of autobiography—the first, as far as we know, by an artist published in any language, ever. Book 3 is a sketch of auxiliary sciences, such as optics and anatomy, that the author considered prerequisites to artistic training; for this part of the Commentary, Ghiberti relies heavily on such medieval scholars such as Averroës, John Peckham, and Roger Bacon.

*One can assert with confidence that by reorganizing the numerous notes h
collected over the course of some twenty years and by commenting on them in the
nology successfully introduced by Alberti in* De pictura *and* De statua, *Ghiberti
posed the first survey of the history of art from antiquity to his own time. In so doing he
revealed the cultural self-awareness and the typically humanistic sense of history that will
characterize later Florentine surveys of art. We can see these features in the following
passage from the beginning of Book 2, in which Ghiberti, by resorting to an expertise
obviously much greater than that of the historian Filippo Villani, praises Giotto for
reviving classical art, whose long period of decadence was marked by the Byzantine and
the Carolingian styles.*

Source: Lorenzo Ghiberti, *I Commentari,* ed. Ottavio Morisani (Naples: Ricciardi, 1947),
pp. 32–34.

SECOND COMMENTARY

At the time of the Emperor Constantine and Pope Sylvester, the Christian
religion had grown. Idolatry was persecuted so violently that all statues and
paintings were destroyed, their ancient and exquisite beauty ruined. Likewise,
the volumes, commentaries, outlines, and rules that had instructed such an
excellent and noble art were lost. Finally, in order to delete every possible form
of idolatry, the Church proclaimed that all temples were to be white [inside and
out]. At that time, terrible punishments were inflicted on those who dared
produce any sort of statue or painting; this marked the end of the arts of sculpture and painting, and of any type of doctrine related to them.

After art was extinguished, temples remained white for about six hundred
years. The Greeks[1] had devoted themselves to the art of painting with utterly
unsatisfactory results, and so, too, the men of this age lacked in refinement and
expertise. This was 382 olympiads[2] after the founding of Rome.

The art of painting started its reascent in Etruria. In a village called Vespig-
nano, near the city of Florence, an extraordinary genius was born. One day,
when the painter Cimabue happened to pass through the village on his way to
Bologna, he saw a boy sitting on the ground bent over a flat rock, drawing a
sheep. Cimabue was seized with admiration for the boy, since the latter was so
young and yet capable of drawing so well. Seeing that the boy had talent, he
asked him his name. The boy answered, "My name is Giotto; my father's name
is Bondone and he lives in that house over there." Cimabue went with Giotto

to his father. Cimabue, a rather distinguished-looking man, asked the father to let the boy go with him. As the father was very poor, he gave Cimabue his boy, and Cimabue took Giotto with him to make him one of his pupils. Cimabue worked in the Greek style and obtained fame throughout Etruria. It was thus that Giotto became great in the art of painting.

Giotto championed this new art, abandoning the uncouth style of the recent painters, and became the most renowned artist in all Etruria. He produced excellent works, not only in Florence but throughout Italy as well. He had numerous pupils, all of whom he taught so well that they, too, became as good as the ancient Greeks. Giotto saw in art what others failed to grasp. He invented a natural style and grace without losing sight of proportion. He mastered all the arts, and he uncovered all those things which had been buried for nearly six hundred years. When Nature wants to bestow something, she lavishes it unstintingly. Giotto produced myriad, diverse works; he painted on walls, on canvas, on panels. At St. Peter's in Rome he made the mosaic with the boat and painted with his own hand the chapel and the altarpiece of St. Peter. In Naples, he brilliantly decorated King Robert's Hall of Famous Men and painted in the Castel dell'Ovo. He painted all the works in Padua's Arena Chapel. There is a *Worldly Glory* by his hand. At the headquarters of the Guelph party is his cycle of the Christian faith, and, at one time, there were many other works as well. In the church of the Friars Minor in Assisi, he painted most of the lower part. He also painted in Assisi's Santa Maria degli Angeli. In Santa Maria della Minerva in Rome, one can see two of his works: a crucifix and a panel.

In Florence, Giotto painted numerous works. In the Badia, on an arch over the main entrance, he painted a wonderful half-length Our Lady flanked by two figures. Here, he also painted the main chapel and its altarpiece. At the Friars Minor, he painted four chapels and four panels. He did excellent paintings for Padua's Friars Minor. One can still see his pieces in the Humiliate Friars in Florence—the chapel he painted is no longer there, but there are still a large crucifix and four panels: one which depicts the death of Our Lady with the angels, the twelve apostles, and our Lord around her; it is an extremely well-executed piece. There is a very large panel with Our Lady on a chair surrounded by angels. Over the door leading to the cloister is a half-length Our Lady holding the infant Jesus in her arms. In San Giorgio one can see a panel and a crucifix by him [Giotto]. At the Friars Preachers there are a crucifix and a sublime panel, along with many other things. He painted for many lords. He painted in the Palazzo del Podestà in Florence, where he depicted the city being robbed, and painted the chapel of St. Mary Magdalene.

Giotto deserves the greatest praise. He mastered all the arts, even the art of sculpture. The first figures on the building he erected, the bell tower of Santa Reparata, were all carved by his own hand to his own design. I once saw the marvelous preparatory sketches of these figures, which he himself had done. He was an expert in drawing as well as sculpting. Having inspired the diffusion of so much knowledge, he deserves the greatest praise. It is clear that nature endowed him with all the talent possible, thanks to which he managed to cultivate perfection in the arts. He had many pupils who later attained great fame.

1. By "Greeks" Ghiberti is referring here not to ancient Greek artists, but rather to the Byzantines.
2. On Ghiberti's puzzling method of dating by olympiads, see Krautheimer (1956), mentioned in the "Lorenzo Ghiberti" section of our bibliography.

29

The Marvel of Brunelleschi's Dome
for the Cathedral of Florence

LEON BATTISTA ALBERTI

Battista Alberti, born in Genoa in 1404, was the illegitimate son of Lorenzo Alberti, a member of the distinguished family banished from Florence at the end of the fourteenth century. Battista added "Leon" to his name later in life. After studying in Venice and with the humanist Gasparino Barzizza in Padua, he received his degree in canon law at the University of Bologna in 1428, the year in which he completed his first treatise, De commodis litterarum atque incommodis *(On the advantages and disadvantages of scholarship). The pessimism apparent in this text and others he wrote is rooted in the insecurities he felt over being an illegitimate son and an exile. While the* De commodis *clearly displays this pessimism, it also reveals his faith in the human intellect, which, along with the theme of virtue prevailing over fortune, appears in all his philosophical writings. We can find valuable examples of his thoughts on virtue in his* Intercoenales *(1440) and in his* Momus *(1443–1450). Drawing inspiration from Vitruvius'* Ten Books on Architecture, *Alberti wrote his own ten-part treatise entitled* De re aedificatoria *(1452). In the last years of his life, he devoted himself more and more to architecture, putting into practice the theories he had illustrated in his treatises. Among his most renowned architectural works are the "Tempio Malatestiano" in Rimini and the façade of Santa Maria Novella in Florence. He died in Rome in 1472.*

In 1434 Alberti was finally granted the opportunity to return to Florence, a city dear to him because of his family's history, and a city that he admired for the achievements of the Florentine artists and humanists of the early quattrocento. Understandably, Alberti tried to earn the respect of the local intellectuals and to be recognized as a genuine Florentine. To this end, he soon started working on his best-known text in the vernacular, the Libri della famiglia—*in which various interlocutors review the pros and cons of contemplative and active lives. In 1441 he organized the famous literary contest known as the Certame Coronario, with the help of Piero de' Medici.*

Alberti's acquaintance with Donatello and Brunelleschi, moreover, inspired him to write De pictura *(On painting). It was in fact to Brunelleschi that Alberti dedicated his Italian version of* De pictura, *which he finished in 1436, one year after the completion of the original Latin text. The importance of this treatise can hardly be exaggerated, and its innovative nature is explicitly pointed out by the author himself. As Alberti wrote, it gave him "a great satisfaction to have engaged in this subject," since, as he says, he was "the first to write about this most refined art." Needless to say, the artistic principles presented in this work, the first of its kind since antiquity, exerted an immediate and significant influence on artists of the Italian Renaissance.*

Apart from the technical importance of De pictura, *it is crucial to note that this relatively early text shows typically Albertian concerns found throughout his later writings. In reading Alberti's works, one should always remember that, in the eyes of this remarkable author, architecture is also a metaphor for the social, moral, philosophical, and political order. The human endeavor to reconstruct the harmony of nature goes hand in hand with an attempt to establish a universal harmony of which beauty is a fundamental feature.*

Source: Leon Battista Alberti, *Della pittura*, ed. Luigi Mallè (Florence: Sansoni, 1950), pp. 53–54.

LEON BATTISTA ALBERTI TO
FILIPPO DI SER BRUNELLESCO

I once used both to marvel and to regret that so many of the excellent and divine arts and sciences—which, as the artists' works themselves and the books of historians attest, were abundantly cultivated among those most noble men of antiquity—have now almost completely disappeared. Painters, sculptors, architects, musicians, geometers, rhetoricians, augurs, and other such noble and excellent intellects are today rare and scarcely deserving of praise. I was thus led to believe what many people were saying, namely that Nature, the teacher of all things, having grown old and tired, had stopped producing those scores of giants and wonderful intellects that she had brought forth in her youthful and more glorious days.

But after returning to our homeland, this most illustrious of cities, from the exile in which we Albertis have passed so many years, I recognized in many, but especially in you, Filippo, and in our dear friends, Donatello the sculptor, Nencio, Luca,[1] and Masaccio, a genius equal to any of those Ancients who gained fame in these arts. I thus came to realize that it was not only thanks to the gifts we have received from Nature but also to our ability and diligence that we have the capacity to achieve great distinction in any field. Because the Ancients had an abundance of models to imitate and from which to learn, it was easier for them to master those supreme arts which are so challenging for us today. Consequently, we deserve greater acclaim, in view of our lack of tutors and models, for we manage to discover arts and sciences hitherto unheard of and unseen. Who could be so dense, or so envious, as not to praise the architect Filippo after seeing such a grand structure, towering into the skies, large enough to cover all the Tuscan people with its shadow, built without the support of beams or scaffolding?[2] I believe that such an accomplishment, so great that the people of our times imagined it impossible, was equally unknown and unheard of in antiquity. But I shall sing both your praises, Filippo, and the virtues of our Donatello elsewhere, as well as those of all the others whose qualities I find most admirable.

For the time being, please continue discovering, as you do day after day, things that will bring eternal fame and repute to your outstanding intellect; and if you happen to have a free moment, I would be grateful if you would look over this little work of mine on painting, whose translation into the Tuscan tongue I dedicate to you. It consists, as you will see, of three books. The first is devoted to mathematics and reveals how this delightful and most noble art emerges from Nature's own roots. The second book puts the art into the hands of the artist, distinguishing and explaining art in all its parts. The third teaches the artist how he can and should master the knowledge of the art of painting.

Please read my work carefully and adjust it as you see fit. There is no writer who was ever so learned as not to need the help of erudite friends. Above all, I wish for your sage corrections where necessary, in order not to fall prey readily to the criticism of slanderers.

1. Nencio and Luca are, respectively, Lorenzo Ghiberti and Luca della Robbia.
2. The machines and scaffolding that Brunelleschi invented to erect the dome elicited an admiration almost as great as did the completion of the project itself; see the praise voiced by the anonymous author of *Notable Men in Florence Since 1400,* document 31.

30

Brunelleschi and Donatello Discover
Ancient Roman Treasures

ANTONIO MANETTI

One of those incredibly versatile figures characteristic of quattrocento Florence, Antonio Manetti (1423–1497) was a distinguished mathematician, astronomer, architect, scholar, scribe, and writer. Like many humanists, Manetti's cultural interests did not prevent him from participating actively in city politics. He was appointed to numerous offices, and, in 1495, he was even elected to the post of standard-bearer of justice. Manetti was acquainted with many Florentine intellectuals, and his studies on Dante were highly praised by the members of the Platonic Academy. Manetti's notes on the Commedia, *for instance, were repeatedly employed by Landino in his* Commentary, *and it was Manetti who urged Marsilio Ficino to translate Dante's* Monarchia *into the vernacular. Manetti's interest and pride in the cultural tradition of his city induced him to translate into the vernacular Filippo Villani's biographies of illustrious Florentines. He was, moreover, a talented writer, whose lively prose and inventiveness can be readily seen in his famous* Novella del Grasso legnaiuolo, *the account of a trick played by Brunelleschi and friends on a Florentine carpenter. This long and complicated tale of the "Grasso" lends itself to a wide spectrum of readings. Among the soundest interpretations, however, is that the tale represents one of the numerous tributes that Manetti paid to the genius of his favorite artist, Filippo Brunelleschi.*

In Manetti's most renowned text, the Vita di Filippo Brunelleschi, *Brunelleschi is presented as the greatest architect of all time. A polemical note, however, creeps into Manetti's discussion of Brunelleschi's Florentine successors. Various scholars, espe-*

ANTONIO MANETTI

cially Howard Saalman, have pointed out the "anti-Albertian" features of the Vita di
Filippo Brunelleschi, *an aspect that would certainly be in line with the conservative
trend in Florentine art in the 1480s, when this text was composed. At the same time,
however, another element of the* Vita *is worthy of particular attention. Despite its polemical spirit and simplistic criticism, Manetti's biography of Brunelleschi exerted a
lasting influence on all future appreciations of this artist. One finds evidence of this
in Vasari's portrait of Brunelleschi in his* Vite, *which quotes from Manetti's lively
description of Brunelleschi and Donatello's search for works of ancient Roman art.
One wonders whether the account is not significantly distorted by the narrator's fantasy
and laudatory purpose. Nonetheless, it is essential to recall that Vasari's life of Brunelleschi, patterned after the one by Manetti we have translated here, will, in turn,
become the basis of all subsequent studies on this Florentine architect well into the
nineteenth century.*

Source: Antonio Manetti, *"Vita di Filippo Brunelleschi" preceduta da "La Novella del Grasso,"*
ed. Domenico De Robertis and Giuliano Tanturli (Milan: Il Polifilo, 1976), pp. 64–70.

FROM THE ``LIFE OF FILIPPO BRUNELLESCHI''

Having thus resolved to bow out of the contest,[1] Filippo seemed to say, "I was
not apparently good enough for them to entrust me with the whole project. I
shall go, then, to [a place] where I can observe and learn from good sculptures."
And so he went to Rome, where, at that time, one could see excellent works of
art in public places. Some of these works can still be seen today, although not
many, as several popes and cardinals, from both Rome and elsewhere, have
taken them away. Since he had a sharp eye and happened to be intelligent and
quick to learn, Filippo came to understand both the way of building peculiar to
the Ancients and their use of symmetry, through studying their statues. He also
seemed to discern a precise arrangement of a man's limbs and bones, as if the
ancient artists had been enlightened by God in their knowledge of those
things. He paid close attention to this, for he found it to be in contrast with the
methods of his time. While carefully looking at the ancient statues, he also gave
equal attention to the arrangement and method proper to the various supporting frameworks, masses, lines, and structures of the buildings—all of which had
been shaped according to the purpose they were to fulfill—as well as those that
served as mere ornaments. He thus happened upon many astonishing and
beautiful pieces, whose excellence was due to the fact that most of them had

been done in different ages by masters who had become skilled through their practical experience and the opportunity to study vouchsafed them by the lavish patronage of princes. It must also be added that these artists were not ordinary men at all.

He thus decided to explore the Ancients' highly refined method of building and their use of harmonious proportions in order to find out how all these things could be properly executed without great difficulty and expense. Seeing that these works, despite their tremendous complexity, had been undertaken and completed, he wished to understand how they had been built and what sort of instruments the Ancients had employed. As he used to dabble in clockmaking and bells, with their many types of springs set in motion by a variety of mechanisms, he was familiar with contrivances that could help him conceive of machines for carrying, lifting, and pulling weights, according to the requirements of the art of building, with which he was quite familiar. He committed some of those mechanisms to memory, others not, as he thought best, according to the functions they fulfilled. He went to see ancient buildings—some in ruins and some still intact—which had different types of vaults, and studied the methods for centering the vaults and the other systems of support. He also tried to understand in which cases one could do away with these supports in order to save money and make the work easier, and what other methods to adopt instead. He strove to determine when armatures would be useless, either because of the size of the vault or for other reasons. He saw and meditated on many beautiful works that, as far as I know, had not been studied since the time of those ancient masters. His genius was such that his experiments and the time and effort he devoted to the study of these things finally rendered him an accomplished master of them all, as we can see in our city and elsewhere, and as this account, too, will reveal in part.

During his [Brunelleschi's] stay in Rome, the sculptor Donatello was constantly by his side. They had originally agreed to devote themselves to strictly sculptural matters. Donatello never showed any interest in architecture, and Filippo, in turn, never discussed with him his opinions on that subject, either because he did not find Donatello fit for such things, or because, realizing more and more how difficult they actually were, he was not sure about the possibility of carrying out his projects. Nevertheless, together they sketched almost all the buildings in Rome and in most of the surrounding countryside, recording what they could assess in a glance to be their approximate widths, heights, lengths, and so forth. They excavated different areas in order to see the buildings' joints and study their shape, that is, to see whether they were square, how many angles they had, or if they were perfectly round, oval, or otherwise. When possible, they measured the height of the buildings by calculating the distance from base to base; likewise, they estimated the distance between the entablatures and roofs and the foundations. They recorded these things on strips of parchment graphs by using numbers and symbols invented by Filippo.

They earned their living as goldsmiths—a craft at which they both excelled. As the days passed, they were given increasingly more work to do, more than they could handle, and Filippo cut many precious stones. Neither of them was burdened by family, since they had neither wife nor children. Neither of them gave much thought to what they ate and drank, to their health, or to their appearance; they worried only about whether they were satisfied with the study and the measurement of those buildings. Since they excavated in zones in which there were traces of ancient edifices, they were able to study the buildings' joints and uncover objects and other structures. To do their excavation, they had to hire porters and other laborers at great expense. No one else, in fact, did such work, nor was there anyone who understood why they were doing what they were. Such a lack of understanding was due to the fact that back then, just as in previous centuries, no one was interested in ancient building techniques. If any pagan author has ever explained the principles of this method, as Battista Alberti has done in our times, he has touched on little more than the mere basics. The real secrets of the art, which are peculiar to the master, must be the result either of practical investigation or of personal effort.

Returning to Filippo and Donato's excavations, people used to call them "treasure-hunters," for they thought they were spending their money and doing research in the hope of finding treasures. The people would say things like, "The treasure-hunters will dig in such and such a place today, and in such and such a place tomorrow." It is true that sometimes, although rarely, they found silver medals, and even gold ones, together with carved stones, chalcedonies, carnelians, cameos, and the like. This led people to believe them to be looking for treasures. Filippo dedicated himself to these excavations for many years. He noticed considerable differences among the beautiful and complex elements of the buildings: in the masonry, as well as in the different types of columns, bases, capitals, architraves, friezes, cornices, and pediments; in the masses of the temples, and in the diameters of the columns. Thus, by virtue of his careful observation, he finally became fully acquainted with the peculiarities of each style of ancient architecture: Ionic, Doric, Tuscan, Corinthian, and Attic. As one can still see today in looking at his buildings, he employed almost every style, and he did so according to the time and place he thought best.

1. The competition to choose the artist for the doors of the Florence baptistery.

31

Eminent Florentine Artists of the Quattrocento

The Biblioteca Nazionale in Florence possesses a miscellaneous codex that contains fourteen brief sketches of famous Florentines immediately following Filippo Villani's De origine civitatis Florentie et de eiusdem famosis civibus. *Despite its having been conceived as a sequel to Villani's work, this anonymous text, entitled* Huomini singhularii in Firenze dal MCCCC innanzi *(Notable Men in Florence Since 1400), focuses on artists rather than on men of letters, soldiers, jurists, prelates, and statesmen. Sixty-nine out of seventy-nine lines in this part of the manuscript concern famous artists who worked in Florence during the fifteenth century; the remaining ten lines merely mention Florentine humanists (Leonardo Bruni, Jacopo Angeli of Scarperia, Giannozzo Manetti, Poggio Bracciolini) and theologians (Luigi Marsili and Bartolomeo Lapacci).*

Since the manuscript seems to be in Antonio Manetti's handwriting, various scholars have considered him the author; the attribution of this work, however, is probably destined to remain unresolved. As regards the dating, we know that the work was composed later than 1472. On account of the reference to the Serragli Chapel in the sketch devoted to Masaccio, Peter Murray suggests a dating between December 1494 and the death of Manetti in 1497. Taking the year 1474 as the earliest possible date for Filippino Lippi's participation in the decoration of the Brancacci Chapel—a fact recorded in the life of that painter— we prefer to date the text more loosely between that year and the death of Manetti.

The importance of Notable Men in Florence Since 1400 *is that it provides further evidence of the civic pride that Florentines felt for their prominent artists. It also shows how aware they were of the significance of their artists' works to the history of art. Despite its extremely concise prose and lack of stylistic refinement, this brief series of portraits is another document bearing witness to the spirit and cultural milieu of Florentine artists of the quattrocento.*

Source: "Huomini singhularii in Firenze dal MCCCC innanzi," in *Letteratura artistica dell'età dell'Umanesimo: Antologia di testi 1400–1520,* ed. Gianni Carlo Sciolla (Turin: Giappichelli, 1982), pp. 81–83.

Filippo, son of Brunellesco, was an architect and man of outstanding genius. He built the dome of Santa Maria del Fiore from the round windows up, and built a vault for the tribune without any centering. He also made the lantern on top [of the church], using a remarkable kind of scaffolding and other building machines. He worked without ruining the materials or posing any risk to the masons. In Florence, he built the Sacristy of San Lorenzo and the transept of that same church; its bulk is the work of other masters who did not always follow his project. He built a chapel for the Barbadori family in Santa Felicita—the first one on the right-hand side as one enters that church—and the Pazzi Chapel in the first cloister of Santa Croce in Florence. He built part of the Palazzo della Parte Guelfa, the unfurnished room, and other beautiful things there. He laid the foundations and built all that has been constructed so far—that is, up to the chapel vaults—of the Tempio degli Angeli (Temple of Angels), and most of the arcade of the Spedale degli Innocenti. As regards this last building, some arrogant people have spoiled much of its façade and interior. He built Santo Spirito in Florence and left a detailed plan [for its completion]. After his death, however, the church was damaged by some haughty people. He built the fortress, or stronghold, of Vico Pisano, as well as two towers near the first bridge in Pisa, that is, at the new citadel. He built a magnificent castle to serve as a fortress for Sigismondo, lord of Rimini, and made part of the cathedral of Milan (all of its good parts). He rediscovered the ancient way of building walls and decorating interiors; he was also a marvelous sculptor. He either discovered or rediscovered how to measure the planes painters try to depict, thus helping them to paint in a way that rendered their works more lifelike. He also supplied sculptors with this same method of planes, a thing which was unknown to the Ancients. He was a master of casting and carving, and of many other things.

Donatello was a master sculptor who made numerous works in bronze and marble, both in Florence and elsewhere. In Florence, he sculpted marble pieces for the bell tower of Santa Maria del Fiore, facing the square. In the niches outside Orsanmichele, he produced the *St. George, St. Peter,* and *St. Mark,* and additional admirable works of that sort in many other places, such as Prato, Siena, Padua, etc.

Lorenzo di Bartolo [Ghiberti], an excellent sculptor, cast San Giovanni's bronze doors: the one opposite Santa Maria del Fiore and the one on the north side. He also made the bronze tomb of St. Zenobius, located inside Santa Maria del Fiore, and many other bronze figures for the niches of Orsanmichele and elsewhere.

The painter Masaccio was an extraordinary man who painted in Florence and outside the city. He died when he was about twenty-seven.[1] In Florence, he painted *St. Paul* in the Carmine, between the Serragli Chapel, where the Holy Cross is, and the chapel with the splendid painting of the life of St. Jerome. The various stories he painted in the Brancacci Chapel are magnificent; the chapel is the work of three masters, all of them good, but his work is the best. In this church he also painted that section of the cloister above the door leading into the church, and a grisaille in *terra verde* depicting Piazza del Carmine with diverse figures—all experts consider this a marvelous work. He painted throughout Florence, both in churches and for private citizens, as well as in Pisa, in Rome, and elsewhere. During his lifetime, he was considered the best of all known masters.

Fra Giovanni da Fiesole was called so because he was a friar in San Domenico. He was a superb painter. In San Marco he painted the altarpiece for the high altar, the chapter house in the first cloister—where one finds Christ on the cross flanked by thieves and many saints—and numerous other pieces for the church, especially in the friars' cells. He painted a panel, the *Coronation of Our Lady,* in the chapel of St. Giles in Santa Maria Novella; a panel, the *Last Judgment,* in the Church of the Angeli; and almost the entire tabernacle containing the altar silver in the Annunziata de' Servi. He also produced numerous works for private homes in Florence, such as side tables. He painted a panel in the sacristy of Santa Trinita depicting the deposition of Christ from the Cross. In Rome, where [Giovanni da Fiesole] died, he painted a large number of exquisite works. After becoming a friar, he never accepted money for his paintings, and whatever he had belonged to the monastery. He is buried in Rome in Santa Maria sopra Minerva in a fitting place. He never abandoned his religious duties to paint, and he led a holy life. He was born in the Mugello.

Fra Filippo [Lippi] of the Carmine was a master of painting who painted the choir chapel in the cathedral of Prato. He painted two panels for the convent of Murate in Florence, the altarpiece for the High Altar, and a panel of *St. Jerome*. He painted yet other panels for the sacristy of Santo Spirito, one of the *Annunciation* in San Lorenzo (in the Chapel of the Operai), one in the choir of Sant'Ambrogio, and many others. He also painted a chapel in Spoleto, where he died and was honorably buried.

Paolo Uccello, a master painter, painted the *Flood* in the cloister of Santa Maria Novella, the story below it, and the first two stories in the upper and lower registers as one goes down the stairs that connect the cloister to the church. He also painted other pieces in Santa Trinita and elsewhere.

Luca della Robbia was a master sculptor in bronze, marble, and clay. He was the first to discover how to glaze figures. He made many things, but in Santa Maria del Fiore in Florence one can see three fabulous works of his, namely the bronze door to the sacristy on the north side, the pulpit above it, where the organs are, and the glazed figures over the two sacristy doors—or should I say, of vitrified clay—depicting the *Resurrection of Christ* and the *Ascension*. He also produced a variety of other things for the city and elsewhere. He was a good man who led a virtuous life and had a great intellect.

1. There is an explanatory note in the margin, in what most scholars believe to be Antonio Manetti's hand, that reads, "On September 15, 1472. His brother, Lo Scheggia, told me that he was born in 1401, on the day of St. Thomas, that is to say, December 21."

32

An Account of the Great Local Artists

CRISTOFORO LANDINO

As was already pointed out in the introduction to the document by Landino in the "Literature" section of this anthology, Landino's proem to his 1481 commentary on Dante's Commedia *is a true celebration of Florentine culture. Along with the most distinguished jurists, theologians, men of letters, and merchants, Landino praised the Florentine artists who, beginning with the first half of the fourteenth century, had commonly been credited with rediscovering the elegance of ancient art. By the second half of the quattrocento, this list had grown significantly, to include experts skilled in the use of perspective: Masaccio, Donatello, and Brunelleschi. Landino's short account of the history of art shows the degree to which the endeavors of fifteenth-century Florentine intellectuals and their reworking of the image of their city were interdisciplinary.*

Source: Cristoforo Landino, *Commento di Cristoforo Landino fiorentino sopra la Comedia di Dante Alighieri poeta fiorentino*, in *Scritti critici e teorici*, ed. Roberto Cardini (Rome: Bulzoni, 1974), vol. 1, pp. 123–125.

EXCELLENT FLORENTINE PAINTERS AND SCULPTORS

We have the art of painting [left to discuss], a skill which the Ancients held in high esteem. The Egyptians claim that they invented it and that it moved to Greece from Egypt. Some Greeks, however, hold that it was invented in Sicyon, others in Corinth. The first paintings were made of a single line which followed the outline of the human body. Painters then worked with only one color; such a painting being called monochrome—that is, of a single color, since *monos* means "one" and *croma* means "color." Painting was relatively new, as Pliny writes, for at the time of the Trojan War there were not yet any painters.[1] The first painters in Greece were Aricides of Corinth and Telephanes of Sicyon, but it was Parrhasius of Ephesus who elevated and ennobled the art. Many acclaimed artists followed, among whom Apelles was the most distinguished, and he is considered unparalleled to this day. After having reached its apex, this art, like many others, nearly disappeared when Italy was enslaved. At that time, painting became completely devoid of refinement and inspiration. The Florentine Giovanni Cimabue was the first to rediscover a natural style of painting and proportion, which the Greeks called symmetry. He achieved great fame through enlivening the figures in his paintings and endowing them with a variety of expressions. He could have achieved even more fame had he not been followed by so worthy a successor as the Florentine Giotto, a contemporary of Dante.[2] Giotto was so flawless and accomplished that many have striven in vain to surpass him. Italy is filled with his works, his masterpiece being his mosaic in St. Peter's of Rome, depicting the twelve apostles in a boat, each one of whom has lifelike and vivid gestures, all different from one another, although fitting and appropriate. Out of Giotto's school, as out of the Trojan horse, came several wondrous painters, such as Maso, whose elegant work is highly praised. Stefano is commonly called the ape of nature, for he succeeded in painting whatever he set out to do. We can also see great pieces by Taddeo Gaddi. Masaccio was a distinguished artist with a pure and controlled style, always dedicated to imitating nature and making figures come alive. He certainly was as adept at perspective as anybody else in his time, and he worked with ease. He died when he was only twenty-six. Fra Filippo [Lippi]'s work was extremely skilled; he particularly excelled at multiple-figure works, in the use of color, at relief, and at any sort of adornment, whether modeled on reality or fictitious. Andrea [del Castagno], superb at drawing and relief, reveled in the challenges of art—partial views in particular. He was energetic and worked with great facility. Paolo Uccello, a good draftsman and a versatile artist, was a great master at painting animals and cities; he was skilled at partial views, for he understood perspective well. Fra Giovanni Angelico was a delightful, pious, and refined artist who worked with great dexterity. Pesello ranked above all others in painting animals. The elegant work of Pesellino followed, an excellent painter of small subjects. Filippo Brunelleschi was an architect who was also a distinguished painter and sculptor. Above all, he had an astute under-standing of perspective, so much so that some hold him to have either re-discovered it or invented it. Brunelleschi produced remarkable works of both painting and sculpture. Donatello deserves to be considered equal to the an-cient sculptors; outstandingly skilled and versatile, he was able to shape and place figures in such a way as to make them appear to be in motion. He was a great student of the Ancients, and an expert at perspective. Then there is the most worthy Desiderio [da Settignano], whose polished works were delicate, elegant, and graceful. If an untimely death had not snatched him away in his youth, his work, all experts in sculpture hoped, would have become great. Lorenzo di Bartoluccio [Ghiberti] is famous for the bronze doors of our baptis-tery. And finally, we can see superb works by Antonio Rossellino, and likewise by his brother Bernardo, a commendable architect.

1. Pli., *Nat. Hist.*, 35.15–18. Landino draws on Pliny for this brief section on ancient art.
2. Here Landino probably has in mind the verses of Dante's *Pur.*, 11.94–96, on the tran-sitoriness of glory.

33

The Beauty of Florence Surpasses
that of Ancient Athens

UGOLINO VERINO

Verino's poetic style and content matured by the time he wrote his collection Epigrams, *one of his best works by far. Here the author dismisses love poetry, which had marked his early writings, in favor of moral and religious topics. As was typical of Verino, he included poems in praise of Florence in this collection. Whereas the couplets from his* Flametta *constituted a panegyric of Florentine culture, the* Epigrams *focus on the artistic achievements of quattrocento Florence and put the city on a par with ancient Greece. Verino's selection of artists reveals his sensitivity to and familiarity with Florentine art, a common feature, as we have seen, among late quattrocento Florentine humanists.*

Source: Ugolino Verino, *De pictoribus et sculptoribus Florentinis qui priscis Graecis aequiperari possunt,* in *Poeti latini del Quattrocento,* ed. Francesco Arnaldi, Lucia Gualdo Rosa, and Liliana Monti Sabia (Milan: Ricciardi, 1964), pp. 872–874.

EPIGRAMS, 3.23

The Rhodians admired Protogenes for a single painting, which took him nearly ten years to complete. The poets write that Nicomachus, by contrast, was a rapid painter, capable of producing an excellent work in a short time. Parrhasius of Ephesus so excelled at his art that he is considered the inventor of symmetry. In the course of many centuries, ancient Greece produced these artists, all with outstanding qualities equal to their genius. But if Greece could see all the painters of our time, how highly it would praise them! Florence alone begot them all in the same age, and so wonderful are they that I would liken them to the ancient Greeks.

The two distinguished brothers, Pollaiuolo by name, are both good sculptors, but one also paints. Antonio casts bronze faces that seem to be alive, and with soft wax he molds lifelike statues. Our Verrocchio is hardly inferior to Phidias; in one respect he even surpasses him, for he both paints and casts bronze statues. Dona-tello's lifelike statues are testaments to how great a sculptor he was; and neither the Theban Scopas nor Praxiteles is superior to our Desiderio at bringing marble to life. Apelles should not be offended by being put on a par with Sandro,[1] whose name the whole world knows. Although Zeuxis of Heraclea painted the grape so well, he does not surpass the art of the Tuscan from Vinci.[2] And how could I forget to mention you, extraordinary Filippo, offspring of a painter:[3] you cer-tainly deserve to be ranked in first place. It would take too long, and this is not the right time, to name all those Florentines whose fame and work will never perish.

Although on a much larger scale, the same epideictic goal as in Flametta *2.45 animates the three books of Verino's most renowned text,* Description of the City of Florence. *The verses of the first book address the history of the city from its origins to the author's time, placing particular emphasis on Florence's military victories. Book 2 celebrates dis-tinguished Florentines in fields from literature to art, jurisprudence, medicine, and reli-gion. Book 3 sketches the history and the deeds of the most important Florentine families.*

In his celebration of Florentine art, Verino presents his fellow citizens' unparalleled success as inextricably tied to the city's growth in the political and economic sphere. It need not surprise us, then, that Verino's praise of the Florentine artists ends with a eulogy of both the prominent mercantile families of the city and the palaces they built. He concludes with an invitation to other Florentine writers to celebrate their common patron Piero de' Medici.

Source: Ugolino Verino, *De illustratione urbis Florentiae* (Florence: Landini, 1636), pp. 43–48.

DESCRIPTION OF THE CITY OF FLORENCE

Book 2

Having described the victories of the Tuscan lion and briefly narrated his deeds of old, I shall name the many illustrious sons of Florence, reporting who they were, the arts at which they have excelled, and the time in which they flourished. No other city can claim so many men of outstanding genius so deeply inflamed by love for Minerva. Pope Boniface VIII was right to consider the Florentines the fifth element of the world, after seeing so many of them come to Rome as ambassadors of kings.

O glory of the supreme heaven, Virgin Mother of Christ, support my present undertaking. O Muses, goddesses of poetry, send me your blessings so that future ages will not forget these famous men, and posterity will remember them. It is your prerogative to bestow eternal praise upon those who have accomplished worthy deeds and therefore deserve to be remembered in the future. . . . [4] Fortune never betrays him who strives with all his zeal, and this is why Florence has flourished. The deeds it has accomplished in the course of the centuries have made it so, and it has received an appropriate name from a good omen. It placed white lilies on Sulla's banner, and its people raised the standard with the red cross that has saved mankind from eternal death; it is a symbol much feared by the infernal Styx deep in the abyss below. Tuscany rears a bold animal not kept in cage: it is the proud emblem of a lion placed by the city gates, the lion being the animal all other animals obey as their king.

The people of Florence, moreover, venerate the one who is next to Christ in the heavenly court, he who, as the word of God proclaims, was superior to all men and the most holy among them: John the Baptist. They have chosen him as the patron saint of their city. Even pagans celebrate his sacred feast, and his name is honored in every region of the world. Under the protection of such a saint, the Florentines' liberty will always be safe, if they continue to keep themselves free from sin.

How can I begin to list all the illustrious descendants of Sulla who excelled in the arts sacred to Attic Minerva? Giotto revived painting. Owing to his great fame as a painter, Gaddo immortalized his family's name, as did the renowned Fabius.[5] Filippo painted such realistic figures so skillfully that one might believe that Apelles of Cos had come back to life. While Filippo is second to no Greek or Latin artist, Leonardo da Vinci perhaps surpasses them all. He, however, was never satisfied with his works, and like Praxiteles, barely managed to complete a painting in ten years. The ability to paint excellent works quickly, by contrast, made the Ghirlandaio brothers famous; and Sandro should not be deemed less worthy than Zeuxis in painting, although the latter depicted grapes so well that he deceived even birds. The Pollaiuolo brothers are as deserving of praise, but of the two, Antonio is much more famous for his additional ability to cast bronze statues. Gherardo was quite a versatile artist: he was the first to teach the

Etruscans how to glaze pottery and how to animate mosaics with lifelike figures.[6] The Tuscan Verrocchio, O Lysippus, is not at all your inferior; from him,
as if from a wellspring, all artists have learned their craft. Verrocchio had many
pupils, all of whom he taught so well that now their names are renowned in
every Italian city. You too, Perugino, have been able to create Apelles' colors
and depict living faces in your paintings. Phidias' ivory is alive and his statues
speak; yet if you saw the lifelike figures by the Etruscan Donatello you would
not really know to whom to give the crown. Desiderio is not inferior to Praxiteles, but a cruel death took him in his prime. The doors around the temple of
the angelic John the Baptist are one of the world's wonders—they seem to be
alive.[7] Who could ever grow tired of looking at this work cast in solid bronze
by a sculptor of Sulla's stock? Primacy in sculpting has passed from the ancient
Greeks and Romans to the Florentines. If you saw the marble of the temple
consecrated to the Virgin and its refined mosaics so uniquely adorned, you
would think you were at the Mausoleum;[8] you would certainly stare in awe at
the works that decorate this building. What can I say about Filippo Brunelleschi, master in the art of architecture, whose dome, a work of immense
magnitude, rises toward the heavens? Nothing is superior to this dome, not
even the seven wonders of the world. Every traveler arriving in the city of the
flower admires the marble houses and the churches textured against the sky,
swearing that there is no place more beautiful in all the world.

What can I say about the immense building, or about the imposing construction of square stones on a hill south of the city that rises toward the stars?[9]
How can I properly describe the paved and spacious streets, designed in such a
way that the traveler's journey is impeded neither by mud when it rains nor by
dust during the summer, so that his shoes are never dirtied? How can I sufficiently praise the grand temple supported by majestic columns consecrated to
the Holy Ghost[10] or the Church of San Lorenzo erected by the pious Medici or
the convent of San Marco where the Muses dwell? San Marco contains so
many thousands of volumes written by the Greek and Latin fathers that it
could rightly be called the archives of sacred doctrine. There is, moreover, a
magnificent palace of massive stones being built at present in the center of the
city in eternal commemoration of Filippo Strozzi.[11] What can one say about
the great Cosimo's magnificent palace,[12] or about the four large bridges crossing the Arno, the river which runs through the city before flowing into the
Tyrrhenian Sea? Even more beautiful than the city is the countryside around it,
an expanse studded with elegant stone villas and so large that not even double

the length of the city walls could embrace it. Seeing the house of the Sassetti at Montughi, one would believe it to be the palace of a king. And how could I conveniently commemorate the Medici's superb villas at Careggi and Trebbio, or the one they built on the hill of Fiesole? One would certainly think these villas were Lucullus' renowned palaces. The one Lorenzo started on the hill of Caiano, moreover, has no equal. The path leading up to it is so well made that the rider has the impression of being on the plain, moving comfortably with every step. The villa's construction, however, was interrupted after Lorenzo's death. What can I say, finally, of the town of Sesto and its exquisite villas? One would think he was in Baiae on the splendid shores embellished by the Romans—the rulers of the world—with their summer villas and baths of Arcadian marble, traces of which still remain.

Florence's cultivated fields are in no way inferior to its villas. Why bother listing the fruits of this region, the most fertile [of all Italy]? Tuscan wines are as good as those of Falernus, and the most divine nectar cannot compete with the grapes of Trebbiano. These wines, moreover, are not harmful to either the stomach or the head; they are the only wines that doctors permit their patients to drink. Nowhere else can one find such a varied abundance of fruits, nor should one deem this a mere consequence of a favorable climate; it is just as much the product of the zealous peasant and the persevering farmer who make the soil yield such crops. By patiently cultivating the tranquil hills around the city walls, [the farmer] not only beautifies the landscape, but renders the fields as fertile as the gardens of the Phaeacian Alcinous.

1. Botticelli.
2. Leonardo.
3. Filippino Lippi.
4. Here Verino praises famous pious Florentines. See the translation of these hexameters in the "Religion" section of this anthology.
5. Gaddo Gaddi, father of Taddeo. Verino is alluding to the Roman historian Quintus Fabius Pictor ("the painter").
6. This Gherardo must be Gherardo del Fora, who was truly a versatile artist, famous as both an illuminator and a mosaicist. It is odd that Verino ascribes to him, rather than to Luca della Robbia, the invention of glazing.
7. Ghiberti's bronze doors for the baptistery of Florence.
8. Emperor Hadrian's mausoleum in Rome.
9. The Church of San Miniato al Monte.
10. The Church of Santo Spirito.

11. He is referring to the construction of Palazzo Strozzi, which commenced in 1489. Benedetto da Maiano was its first architect; he was succeeded by Cronaca, who continued working on the palace through 1504, after which construction on the building was interrupted and resumed several times by different architects.
12. The Medici Palace in Via Larga, designed by Michelozzo.

34

An Artistic Vade Mecum for the City of Florence

FRANCESCO ALBERTINI

Most of the scanty information on the life of Francesco Albertini is drawn from the prefaces to his three extant works. Born in Florence in the second half of the fifteenth century, he studied music and poetry and is known to have been a pupil of Domenico Ghirlandaio. He was a canon of San Lorenzo from 1493 to 1502; then he moved to Rome to join the entourage of Fazio Santori, cardinal of Santa Sabina. He died in Rome between 1517 and 1521.

Albertini's most famous work is the Opusculum de mirabilibus novae et veteris urbis Romae *(1510), which was reprinted four times within the first half of the six-teenth century. Written at the request of Cardinal Della Rovere, the nephew of Julius II, the text is divided into two parts. The first section is a reworking of the most popular medieval guides to the monuments of ancient Rome, especially the well-known* Mira-bilia Urbis, *whose lack of well-documented information elicited a complaint from the cardinal. The second section illustrates the modern buildings of the city that were being completely renovated through the patronage of the church. In the appendix to the work, Albertini included a panegyric of the cities of Florence and Savona, the latter being the birthplace of Pope Julius II, to whom the work is dedicated. The same editor, Jacopo Mazzocchi, also published a brief guide written by Albertini for King Emanuel of Portugal's visit to Italy. The booklet, as the title suggests (*Septem mirabilia orbis et urbis Romae et florentinae civitatis*), gives a list of the seven wonders of the world, followed by a very brief description of the main monuments of Rome and Florence.*

Albertini is also the author of the first city guide devoted entirely to Florence, Memoriale di molte statue et picture sono nella inclyta ciptà di Florentia *(1510).* Dedicated to one of his friends, Bartolomeo Sinibaldi, a Florentine sculptor better known as Baccio da Montelupo, the *Memoriale* emphasizes the artistic and cultural primacy of Florence and aims to provide a handy yet complete presentation of its main monuments. In his guide, Albertini takes great care to inform the reader about the dimensions of the buildings, the materials that have been used for their construction and their decoration, the names of the artists, and the cost of the works. Unlike the Latin hexameters of Verino's De illustratione urbis Florentiae, *the prose text by Albertini was meant to be a guide for a wide readership, especially for travelers to the city. Albertini's* Opusculum *and* Memoriale *show how, by the beginning of the sixteenth century, the archaeological studies promoted by quattrocento humanists and their interest in the figurative arts had brought about an innovative outlook on artistic literature. Vasari's* Lives, *written in 1550 and revised in 1568, would soon provide another significant testament to this change.*

Source: Francesco Albertini, *Memoriale di molte statue et picture sono nella inclyta ciptà di Florentia per mano di sculptori et pictori excellenti moderni et antiqui* (Florence: Tubini, 1510).

THE FLORENTINE PRIEST FRANCESCO ALBERTINI SALUTES BARTOLOMEO DA MONTELUPO, SCULPTOR, AND WISHES HIM PEACE

You asked me to write about painting. This is a legitimate request, and one I feel I must fulfill, for we are old friends, we are both Florentines, and I highly admire your expertise in this field. Every cultured mind must know about painting, for sculpture and painting give man great pleasure, education, and abundant fruits. Painting is an essential [skill] not only to artists but to geographers and sailors.[1] It is the most excellent of all the arts, for it is instructive to both the learned and the unlettered. I therefore urge you to dedicate yourself to it fully, in order to become acquainted with nature, which no other art can imitate as well as painting does. What else can I say? Painting can make things that do not exist seem as if they do, and sometimes it has been able to deceive not only birds and fierce animals but even expert artists.

I have thus decided to satisfy your request and to write to you about many worthy works by ancient and modern artists who have left traces of themselves through famous paintings and sculptures in our illustrious city of Florence. They are all Florentines except one, and they have brought great prestige not only to their noble homeland but also to Rome, Venice, Naples, Milan, and other cities in Italy, France, Spain, and Hungary. Since our city is divided into four main quarters and has four beautiful stone bridges crossing the magnificent River Arno, I shall divide this guide of mine into four sections. I shall mention the paintings in the churches and buildings of each quarter, and in so doing, I shall fruitfully spend my time here in my beautiful homeland.

Since I have left my books in Rome and I shall not be staying here long, I shall not write in verse; besides, my poetry is not particularly refined. I have yet to finish writing *The Marvels and the Beauties of Florence.* As for the booklet on the ancient monuments of Rome and some buildings of Florence that I dedicated to Julius II, I do not think it necessary to translate it into the vernacular. In order to please you, however, I shall make an abridged version of all three chapters in the vernacular. To appease people who do not know Latin, I shall also translate into the vernacular all the chapters of the booklet that I wrote for the most pious king of Portugal. You will be greatly pleased with my nearly fifteen other works, each in the vernacular. I wish I could satisfy all the requests I receive. At any rate, I shall follow the teaching of the Gospel, which says, "I shall give to everyone who asks me."[2]

As I am not an expert in painting, dear Bartolomeo, and as the proverb says, a blind man cannot discourse on color, I have confronted all the aforementioned subjects by resorting to trustworthy men and ancient texts. I hope that whoever reads this work of mine will correct my mistakes and forgive my presumptuousness for having discussed a subject beyond my limited capabilities. The short time available to me and my profession will excuse me. I have embarked upon this task out of obedience, because of the affection I have felt for you ever since early childhood, and because of your lengthy stay in Venice, where you have left your traces in marble and bronze pieces deserving of great commendation. It is to God, who lives and reigns eternally, that we must give thanks for these works and virtues [of yours and of other Florentines].[3]

Florence, August 30, 1510.

The Quarter of San Giovanni and Its Environs

In the quarter of our patron St. John the Baptist, prophet and saint, is a most renowned and opulent temple dedicated in his honor. It was built before the incarnation of Christ upon beautiful columns, as one can still see, under the direction of Julius Caesar, Gnaeus Pompey Macrinus, Albinus, and other noble Romans, whom Rome's consuls and senators had sent to Florence with a number of skilled architects. They dedicated this glorious temple to Mars, whose marble statue they placed right in the middle [of the building], atop a marble column. Our pious Christian fellow citizens later moved this column to the central door facing Donatello's marble statue of St. John, replacing it with the one that we see today supporting Donatello's statue *Wealth and Abundance* in the Mercato Vecchio. The temple was built when the sign of Mars was in the ascendant, as one can see in the rich and ancient pavement artfully decorated with different kinds of marble. Close to the planets and the signs of the zodiac is a palindrome that reads as follows: "En giro torte sol ciclos et rotor igne."[4]

I shall but mention the myriad worthy and admirable things added to this temple by our Christian citizens, such as the rich and beautiful mosaics—the work of excellent masters depicting stories from the Old and New Testaments, the beautiful fonts, the marble choir, the gilded statues of bronze and marble, the three gorgeous bronze doors gilded in a manner beyond compare in all of Italy. The first two are the work of Lorenzo Ghiberti, a most excellent sculptor; it took him forty years or more to make them. Vittorio, his son, made the jambs and the decorative frieze around the ancient door opposite the Misericordia.[5] In this temple, there is Donatello's St. Mary Magdalen, as well as his bronze tomb for Pope John [XXIII], the marble ornaments for which were made by his students. There is also a silver-gilded altar; it is a fine work, with a statuette of St. John by Antonio Pollaiuolo at the center, and various rich and admirable stories in middle relief produced by other masters. On top of the altar there is a high cross made of precious silver and decorated with beautiful figures. There are also eight large silver candlesticks, the golden rose donated by the pope, and many vases and reliquaries with figures and enamels by skilled artists. In the same temple, one can also see the forefinger of John the Baptist, with which he pointed toward the Savior, saying, "Look, the Lamb of God."[6] This is the only part of the whole body that was not damaged by the fire; it is adorned with gold, silver, and pearls. I shall not now talk about the arm of St. Philip and other richly decorated relics of the saints, especially that most adorned reliquary from Constantinople with the Mysteries of the Passion of Christ, and the Holy Cross, adorned with gold, precious stones, and other well-wrought materials.

Santa Maria del Fiore

The cathedral of Santa Maria del Fiore is commonly called Santa Reparata. I shall not even begin to sing this church's praises, for without seeing it in all its detail, one could never conceive of such a marvel. It is still under construction, with two million gold pieces and more than six hundred thousand florins spent on it up until now. This sumptuous building is made of square stones, and its perimeter measures 782 2/3 braccia. The church, whose length measures 260 braccia, is detached from all other buildings; its exterior—the work of excellent sculptors—is decorated with various types of marble, marble statues, and porphyries. There is, most important, Donatello's first giant[7] by the door where Nanni di Banco produced a marble relief of the Assumption above Domenico Ghirlandaio's mosaic of the Annunciation. The façade has three statues by Donatello: a seated evangelist;[8] one who is bending; and on the corner, the figure of an old man. To tell you the truth, however, I find this façade, which Lorenzo wanted to improve, lacking in both order and proportion. I have made a model of it, and before I leave Florence, God willing, I shall show it to you. I hope it will not disappoint you; if anything, I shall give many people reason to comment, especially the envious, who will wonder, "How can he be well-read if he has not gone to school? We do not even know his name! Through sleeping and loafing about, one cannot become great." They do not know that for many years I attended the public lectures of Poliziano, Landino, and Filippo,[9] those most erudite men. In the six months I spent at the court of Bologna, moreover, I did not idle away my time, and I have also read passages from the treatises on architecture by Vitruvius and Leon Battista Alberti. In the papal palace there is even a door I designed. I shall let them talk while I carry out my project. Great public works demand great attention to detail.

Let us return to architecture, and let us turn our attention especially to the cathedral of Florence, adorned with marbles, mosaics, and marble pavements. There are two sacristies in the church, each with two pairs of organs. Donatello sculpted one of them,[10] as well as making the marble font in the sacristy and the bronze chest in the chapel of St. Zenobius. The other organs were adorned by Luca della Robbia, who made the door of the new sacristy.

I shall but mention the crucifix in the choir, the marble bust of Giotto by Benedetto da Maiano, the grisaille in terra verde by Paolo Uccello, the white fresco by Andrea [del Castagno], the crosses and the silver candlesticks, the beautiful vases made by excellent artists, the four Gospels bound in silver. The height of the testudinate dome with a double vault is 144 braccia, not counting the marble lantern that measures thirty-six braccia, and the magnificent gilded copper globe is four and a half braccia high. The beautiful marble bell tower is 144 braccia high, adorned with various friezes and fine statues. Donatello made the four tall statues facing the piazza, and the two that face the Door of the Canons.

San Lorenzo

In ancient times the Church of San Lorenzo was called Ambrosiana, for in it St. Zenobius hosted St. Ambrose. This beautiful church has been entirely renovated from the foundations up by the architect Filippo Brunelleschi, under the patronage of the renowned and noble house of the Medici. It is 144 braccia long, and in it are countless inlaid stones and massive single-stone columns. There is also a coffered ceiling adorned with various colors and fine gold, and a most elegant two-story cloister 104 braccia long with attractive residences for the canons and the chaplains. I shall but mention the fact that underneath this church there is another church whose length and width are similar to the one above, with chapels, a choir, and beautiful tombs, especially the one of Cosimo de' Medici and those of other noble citizens. There is a large banner in this church that the Florentine people commissioned from Taddeo Gaddi; it hangs from the vault of the dome. In the chapel of the Operai, there is a panel by Filippo [Lippi] of the Carmine, and another one sketched in the chapel of St. Andrew. Donatello sculpted the four great saints up above in the tabernacles; he is also responsible for the two bronze pulpits for the Gospel and the Epistles.

Desiderio [da Settignano] sculpted the marble tabernacle with its ornaments, except for the Christ above the chalice, which you sculpted, along with the crucifix and the angels of the high altar, when I was sacristan of this church. I shall not even mention the things you have made in other churches, as that would be utterly superfluous.

In the sacristy—a marvelous and richly decorated building—there are the stories of the four evangelists and other saints in middle relief and two bronze doors, all works of Donatello. I shall but mention the other marbles, tombs, the marble *Christ Child* by Desiderio, the altar on which Filippo Brunelleschi carved the figure of Abraham, and the font by Rossellino. In the same sacristy there is the bronze tomb by Andrea Verrocchio of Piero and Giovanni de' Medici, adorned with various marbles and porphyries. I shall not linger over the great silver cross and the cross of fine jasper, the vases, the reliquaries, and the paraments, all brilliantly executed by great masters.

There are countless pieces from ancient Rome in the courtyard of the Medici Palace (as there are in the Pazzi courtyard), a fountain by Rossellino, and a bronze Hercules. In the houses of the Martelli, the Braccesi, and the architect Giuliano da San Gallo there are numerous ancient Roman pieces. I shall but mention those superb pieces by the ancient Polycleitos which are in the Ghiberti residence, along with a beautifully engraved marble vase, which Lorenzo Ghiberti had brought to him from Greece.

Santa Maria Maggiore

Pope Pelagius II consecrated the ancient church of Santa Maria Maggiore. He also consecrated Santa Maria Ughi. In Santa Maria Maggiore there is a panel by Masaccio,[11] with a predella and an arch by Paolo Uccello; next to these works is a tabernacle by Andrea [del Castagno].

San Barnaba

In San Barnaba one can see a large panel by Botticelli, and other paintings. The church and the convent of San Giuliano are nearby; above the door of the church there is a crucifix with four figures by Andrea [del Castagno].[12]

San Marco

The great monastery and church of San Marco, built primarily by the Medici family, contain many noteworthy things. The Dominican friar Giovanni [Fra Angelico] made the altarpiece and the frescoes of both the chapter house and the cloister. There are panels by the Dominican friar Bartolomeo, by Sandro [Botticelli], and by Piero Pollaiuolo (depicting the crucifix above the Blessed Antonino); I know that Pollaiuolo made the wood one.

Annunziata

The Church of the Annunziata is sacred and beautiful. It has vases, gold and silver statues with votive offerings, and wax statues—all made by excellent artists. The rich, adorned, and holy chapel dedicated to the Virgin—whose head the devout artist found miraculously painted[13]—was built by the Medici family, who had it decorated with marbles and magnificently sculpted columns.[14] The silver cupboard ornaments are by Fra Giovanni [Angelico].[15] I shall not go into detail about the cloisters with their stunning frescoes. The paintings in the chapel of St. Nicholas are by Taddeo Gaddi. The paintings in the two chapels toward the cloister in semicircular tabernacles are by Andrea del Castagno; these resemble the ones Andrea painted in the chapel of St. Mary Magdalen de' Medici and in various places in the church in which he is buried.[16] Filippo [Lippi] started the altarpiece, but it was Pietro [Perugino] who finished it after the former's death. In the nearby Chapel of San Sebastiano de' Pucci there is a very fine panel by Piero Pollaiuolo,[17] and a panel by Domenico Ghirlandaio at the Innocenti.[18]

Santa Maria Maddalena dei Cistercensi

The beautiful and ornate convent of the Cistercians has numerous paintings by respected and excellent masters, such as Domenico Ghirlandaio, Lorenzo di Credi, and Piero Pollaiuolo, who painted the chapter house in the first cloister.

Gli Angeli

The holy and beautiful Convento degli Angeli has a number of panels by Fra Lorenzo, a monk of that order.[19] In the second cloister there are works by Masaccio.

Santa Maria Nuova

Pope Eugenius IV consecrated the holy church of Santa Maria Nuova in the year in which the council was held in Florence, attended by the Greek emperor.[20] The chapel of the high altar was made in part by Andrea del Castagno, and in part by Domenico Veneziano, although some figures were done by Alessio Baldovinetti. In this church there are two panels by Fra Filippo [Lippi] and one by a Flemish artist.[21] Fra Bartolommeo's *Judgment, St. Michael* by Domenico Ghirlandaio, and numerous other notable things are also in the cloister.

The Quarter of Santa Maria Novella and Its Environs

Santa Maria Novella is a wonderful church 168 braccia long, adorned with marbles and paintings. In the first cloister there are stories from Genesis: that of Adam and Eve and the one of Noah are by Paolo Uccello. The second cloister, which is 120 braccia long, has a beautiful chapel near the Sala pontificale[22] with drawings by Leonardo. In this church there is a large panel by Cimabue next to the beautiful crucifix by Filippo Brunelleschi and the *Trinity* by Masaccio. Domenico Ghirlandaio's chapel behind the main altar and the Strozzi Chapel by Filippino [Lippi] are marvelous works, indeed. I shall but mention Sandro Botticelli's *Magi* between the doors and *Saints Cosmas and Damian* by Giottino in the chapel of St. Lawrence.

In the Church of San Pancrazio there are paintings by Filippino [Lippi], Mariottino [Albertinelli], and other modern masters.

Santa Trinita

The Church of Santa Trinita is decorated with ancient mosaics and exquisite paintings. The Sassetti Chapel has a panel by Domenico Ghirlandaio, right next to the sacristy with a piece by Fra Filippo [Lippi] and one by Gentile da Fabriano. I shall but mention Paolo Uccello's paintings between the doors next to the *Mary Magdalen,* which was started by Desiderio.[23]

The Church of Ognissanti has ancient paintings, a St. Augustine by Domenico Ghirlandaio, and a St. Jerome by Sandro [Botticelli].

In San Miniato fra le Torri is a panel by Andrea [del Castagno] and a St. Christopher ten braccia high, which Piero Pollaiuolo painted outside the door.

Orsanmichele

The ancient and towering building of the oratory of Orsanmichele is detached from all the other constructions in that area. It is made of square stones and adorned with bronze and marble statues. Its magnificent tabernacle is decorated with precious stones that cost more than 20,000 ducats. Originally, the building was a public granary which cost more than 86,000 ducats. *St. Peter, St. Mark,* and *St. George* are by Donatello, who also carved the marble niche where Andrea Verrocchio's bronze statues of Christ and St. Thomas are placed. Lorenzo Ghiberti sculpted the bronze statues of St. John the Baptist, St. Matthew, and St. Stephen. Nanni di Banco made the group of four statues and the St. James. In the interior of the church there is a St. Bartholomew by Lorenzo di Credi and works by other modern artists.

The Quarter of Santa Croce and Its Environs

Santa Croce is a grand and ancient church; its length measures two hundred braccia. The marble façade is decorated with a bronze statue of Bishop St. Louis [of Toulouse] by Donatello, who produced numerous works for the magnificent Pazzi Chapel, together with Luca della Robbia and Desiderio [da Settignano]. In the second cloister, which is ninety-two braccia long and seventy braccia wide, Andrea [del Castagno] painted *The Flagellation of Christ.* In the chapter house built by the Medici family, there is a panel by Fra Filippo with the predella by Francesco Peselli. Angelo Gaddi constructed the main chapel. A painting of the Assumption by Domenico Ghirlandaio is in the large Baroncelli Chapel. Taddeo Gaddi also constructed the chapel of St. Andrew and produced many other works in this church, such as *St. Francis Resuscitating a Child Fallen off the Balcony* and the *Exposure of the Body of Christ* above the doors, next to the tomb made by Desiderio [da Settignano]. Taddeo also made the tabernacle outside, opposite the hospital of Santa Croce; he is buried in the cloister of this church. Giotto worked on the two chapels between the high altar and the sacristy, namely that of St. John and that of St. Francis. The large crucifix which points in the direction of Fiesole is by Cimabue, whereas the wooden crucifix next to Pietro's [Perugino's] panel is by Donatello, who also made the stone Annunciation. I shall but mention the beautiful pulpit by Benedetto da Maiano, next to Antonio Rossellino's marble tomb with the Virgin opposite the cycle *St. Paulinus, Bishop of Nola* by Domenico Ghirlandaio.

Convents of Sant'Ambrogio and Murate

The Church of Sant'Ambrogio is ancient and holy. It contains panels by Fra Filippo, who also painted two splendid panels at Murate, where one can see the scenes from [the life of] St. Jerome by Domenico Ghirlandaio. I shall but mention the convent of San Jacopo and the Spedale dei Tintori, where one can see paintings by excellent masters. The same is true of Santa Verdiana, where the Medici family constructed numerous buildings.

San Piero and Other Churches

The Church of San Piero Maggiore has panels by various masters; its marble tabernacle of the sacrament is by Desiderio.

The altarpiece in San Pietro Scheraggio is by Fra Lorenzo [Monaco]. This church and that of Santo Stefano were built by Charlemagne.

Palazzo Maggiore

There are many works in the Palazzo Maggiore,[24] a freestanding building made of square stones with a tower 180 braccia high. The bronze David is on a finely wrought marble column on the ground floor, whereas the Judith is in the loggia.[25] The marble giant[26] is by Michelangelo, who also did the massive bronze statue of Pope Julius II in Bologna. Verrocchio sculpted the bronze David placed on the stairs. In the room with the coffered ceiling[27] there are paintings by Domenico Ghirlandaio close to Donatello's marble David. In the

Sala del Consiglio Antico [Otto di Pratica] there is a panel by Filippo [Lippi] and Verrocchio's three large canvases depicting Hercules. In the new large Sala del Consiglio Maggiore, which is 104 braccia long and forty braccia wide, there is a panel by Filippo [Lippi] as well as Leonardo da Vinci's horses, and Michelangelo's drawings.[28] In this palace one can see the admirable and ingenious clock made by Lorenzo della Volpaia that shows the course of the sun and the movement of all the planets, and the maps of the world drafted by the illuminator Vante [Attavanti]. I shall but mention the six depictions of the virtues that Piero Pollaiuolo painted in the Palazzo della Mercanzia; the seventh is by Sandro [Botticelli]. There are many other paintings in the palaces of the twenty-one guilds and in the headquarters of the forty-six confraternities.

The Quarter of Santo Spirito and Its Environs

Filippo Brunelleschi designed the beautiful Church of Santo Spirito. It is 161 braccia long, with large stone columns and a vaulted dome made of worked stone. Its sacristy is lavishly decorated; there one can see six paintings by Taddeo Gaddi and the crucifix with two figures above the door. The church has numerous works by modern masters who are in no way inferior to the Ancients. I shall but mention Andrea Sansovino's marble altar and the crucifix which Michelangelo made for the choir. Giottino made the tabernacle outside in the piazza.

Carmine and San Frediano

Santa Maria del Carmine is an ancient and holy church 143 braccia long. It has paintings by ancient masters and by Masaccio, who did the pieces above the door in the first cloister and those in the Brancacci Chapel, which he executed together with Masolino, except for *The Crucifixion of St. Peter*, which was painted by Filippino Lippi. Masolino painted the St. Peter next to the chapel decorated by Starnina, and Masaccio painted the St. Paul. The noble Soderini family—especially those two very learned brothers, the Most Reverend Francesco, bishop of Volterra, and the most illustrious Piero, gonfaloniere and duce for life—decorated the main chapel with paintings and a lavish tomb made by Benedetto da Rovezzano, who is now working on that of St. John Gualbert.[29] I shall not even begin to list the many works which Fra Filippo [Lippi] painted in this church.

The aforementioned Soderini family had the Church of San Frediano and the surrounding buildings built from the foundations up. The church has excellent paintings.

In the Church of Santa Chiara there are two excellent panels, one of which is by Lorenzo di Credi, the other by Pietro Perugino.

San Vincenzo, commonly called Annalena, is a devout monastery whose construction was carried out mostly by the Medici family. It has a panel by Fra Filippo [Lippi] and works by other painters.

In the palace of the Capponi there is the ancient porphyry statue of a lion that Lorenzo de' Medici praised highly.

Dear Bartolomeo, accomplished painters will find some of the things I have written to be superfluous. You told me, however, to put down all I had to say without going into detail. I thus deem it appropriate to write a few more words on notable things that can be found in the Florentine countryside.

San Francesco and San Miniato

The magnificent Church of San Francesco al Monte was built by the Quaratesi family; it contains paintings by great masters.

It would be impossible to say how beautifully proportioned and adorned the Church of San Miniato al Monte is. There, in fact, one finds various types of marble, mosaics, frescoes, alabaster windows with marble columns, and the exquisite marble Medici Chapel, opposite a lavishly decorated chapel that holds Antonio Rossellino's marble sepulchre of the cardinal of Portugal, a work embellished with precious stones and an impressive coffin. This chapel also has a panel by Piero Pollaiuolo; its other figures are by Alessio Baldovinetti, and those in middle relief are by Luca della Robbia. I shall but mention the magnificent choir, below which there is a marble altar with numerous relics of saints, and the wonderful sacristy decorated with works of excellent painters. In the first cloister above, Paolo Uccello painted twelve scenes.

I shall but mention the panels by Filippino [Lippi] at San Donato [agli Scopeti] and in the Church of the Campora; and I shall also merely mention the sumptuous room in Pandolfo Pandolfini's home at Legnaia, which [Andrea del Castagno] decorated with sibyls and portraits of famous Florentines.[30]

Monastery of the Ingesuati and Other Places

The first and the second cloister of the richly decorated and beautiful monastery of the Ingesuati[31] has scenes painted by Pietro Perugino, who could rightly be called Fiorentino, since he was raised here. The church also has panels by him on the first and upper floors. The altarpiece is by Domenico Ghirlandaio.

The large convent of San Gallo, built primarily by the Medici family, has a *Pietà* by Giottino and various other paintings. I shall but mention the Badia Fiesolana, erected by the Medici, which possesses paintings and excellent works in marble.

San Domenico [in Fiesole] has pieces by Fra Giovanni [Angelico] and other modern artists. The villa of the Valori, near Maiano, has ancient Roman statues. I shall but mention the villa's splendid panels and the angel by Leonardo Da Vinci. The Compagnia del Tempio has a panel by Fra Giovanni [Angelico], who also painted the main chapel in Prato. There in the piazza, one can see Donatello's marble pulpit and the belt of the blessed Virgin.[32] For brevity's sake, I shall omit numerous other notable things that can be found in other towns and villages.[33]

1. Mapmaking was a flourishing industry in Florence at that time.
2. Luke 6:30.
3. Many of the works described by Albertini are no longer extant or have been removed from their original location. In some cases we have provided short explanatory comments in the footnotes. For more detailed information on the artists and the works mentioned in the *Memoriale,* see the notes to the most recent editions of Vasari's *Lives,* especially that of Luciano Bellosi and Aldo Rossi (Turin: Einaudi, 1991); and Peter Murray's useful study, *An Index of Attributions Made in Tuscan Sources Before Vasari* (Florence: Olschki, 1959).
4. "I, the Sun, make the planets spin in a circle, and I, too, spin with fire."
5. This "ancient door" is the one fashioned by Andrea Pisano between 1330–1336. It was originally placed on the east side of the baptistery; in 1424, it was substituted with Ghiberti's first door and moved south.
6. John 1:29.
7. This may be the immense terracotta statue of Joshua which Donatello sculpted between 1410–1412. There are documents indicating that he started another massive sculpture in 1456, but both statues are lost.
8. St. John, now in the Museo dell'Opera del Duomo.
9. Probably the famous humanist Filippo Beroaldo (1453–1505), who taught rhetoric and poetry at the University of Bologna. Albertini spent some time in Bologna, as he himself informs us in the text that follows.
10. The famous choir screen, now in the Museo dell'Opera del Duomo, together with the one by Luca della Robbia.
11. It is actually by Masolino. This passage refers to a series of works whose attribution and precise arrangement within the church of Santa Maria Maggiore are still unresolved.

12. The fresco *Crucifixion with Mary, St. Dominic, St. Julian, and St. John.*

13. The highly venerated fourteenth-century Annunciation was believed to have been painted in part by an angel.

14. Cosimo de' Medici commissioned his favorite architect and friend, Michelozzo, to design the chapel.

15. These are the doors of the silver cabinet, now at the Museo di San Marco.

16. Santa Maria Nuova.

17. The *Martyrdom of St. Sebastian* by Antonio and Piero Pollaiuolo, now at the National Gallery in London.

18. The hospital for foundlings, also known as Spedale degli Innocenti. The work by Ghirlandaio Albertini mentions is *The Adoration of the Magi.*

19. Santa Maria degli Angeli was the Camaldolite monastery of Florence. Piero di Giovanni (better known as Don Lorenzo degli Angeli or Lorenzo Monaco) entered the order in 1391 and died around 1426.

20. In 1439 the council for the unification of the two churches was held in Florence.

21. Hugo van der Goes's *Adoration of the Shepherds,* better known as Trittico Portinari. Today it is at the Uffizi Gallery.

22. This is part of the residences built in the fifteenth century by the Florentine Republic to accommodate visiting popes and other important personages. It was commonly known as the Lateran of Florence, and the Popes Martin V and Eugenius IV spent most of their pontificates there as guests, in the years 1419–1420 and 1434–1436/1438–1443, respectively.

23. It was finished by Benedetto da Maiano. It is still in Santa Trinita, although in a different location.

24. Palazzo della Signoria, the seat of the Florentine government.

25. The two famous statues by Donatello. When Albertini wrote the *Memoriale,* Donatello's bronze David was in the courtyard of the palace.

26. The David.

27. The Sala dei Gigli.

28. Albertini is referring to Leonardo's *Battaglia d'Anghiari* and Michelangelo's *Battaglia di Cascina.*

29. Started in 1505, it was completed in 1513.

30. One of the numerous fifteenth-century cycles devoted to the celebration of Florence's illustrious citizens.

31. The monastery of San Giusto alle Mura abandoned by the Gesuati in 1529.

32. The famous Pulpit of the Girdle.

33. Albertini ends the work with a poem of about ninety verses, which we omit. He admits that he included the poem "in order to leave no part of the page blank."

10. Giotto's bell tower (K).

11. The Florence baptistery (S).

12. Leon Battista Alberti's façade, Church of Santa Maria Novella (K).

13. The Church of San Miniato al Monte (K).

14. Michelozzo's Medici Palace, in the center of Florence (K).

15. The Strozzi Palace, designed by Benedetto da Maiano and Il Cronaca (K).

16. Domenico di Michelino, *Dante and His Poem,* cathedral of Florence (S).

17. Botticelli's *Adoration of the Magi*. Uffizi Gallery, Florence (K). In his life of Botticelli, Vasari writes that the old man holding out his hands toward the Christ Child is Cosimo de' Medici, while the young man in the white gown offering his gift on the right of the painting is Giuliano de' Medici, Lorenzo's brother. Scholars are uncertain about the identification of the other figures. The kneeling man next to Giuliano in the center-foreground is thought to be Piero de' Medici. The kneeling man with a cap and curly hair to the right of Piero and Giuliano is often identified as Giovanni, Cosimo's second son. Next to Giuliano, the standing figure in the black gown with a stripe down his shoulder closely resembles Lorenzo the Magnificent, and the man on the extreme right, looking at the viewer, is usually taken to be Botticelli himself.

18. *The Execution of Savonarola in the Piazza della Signoria* (artist unknown). Museo di Firenze com'era, Florence (S).

PART FIVE

Religion

35

Tuscany as the Cradle of Christianity

GIOVANNI GHERARDI

As already pointed out in the earlier introduction to this author (Part 1), Gherardi is among the last prominent representatives of a cultural tradition whose fundamental tenets derive from scholastic philosophy and from the great vernacular writers. In a unique manner, the five books of Gherardi's unfinished novel Il Paradiso degli Alberti *testify both to the author's traditionalism and to his interest in the successful diffusion of humanist ideals, some of which he readapts to support his own patriotic views. We can see an example of his stance in the passage that follows. Here Gherardi praises the culture and high moral standards of the Etruscans, the ancient inhabitants of Tuscany. He believes that the Etruscans' outstanding devotion is inherent in the very etymology of the name of the region and in the many pious customs they passed down to the Romans. In Gherardi's eyes, the piety peculiar to the Etruscans is an anticipation of the religious prominence that Tuscany was to assume after the spread of Christianity, when it became the birthplace of a number of religious orders and many saintly men.*

Source: Giovanni Gherardi da Prato, *Il Paradiso degli Alberti*, ed. Antonio Lanza (Rome: Salerno, 1975), pp. 59–62.

BOOK 2

After God's love and grace had enlightened and kindled both my fervent passion and my eager mind, in a short time my long journey had happily come to
an end, and I retired to my little room to have some rest.[1] Once sleep had
restored my body and my spirit, I started to ponder and reflect upon what I had
seen. I began to think about the Etruscans, that ancient and glorious people,
and then realized, my dear friends, that we should take great pride in being the
offspring of this renowned country of ours: its military deeds and culture, its
religion, virtue, prudence, and just government prove it to be the most noble
of all lands. The name of this magnificent country, Tuscany, itself provides clear
evidence of its religiosity. The etymology of Tuscany is *ture,* from the Latin *tus,*
which means "incense"—thus the derivation of the name Tuscia. The reason
for this is to be found in an ancient and noble Tuscan tradition: they [the
Tuscans] were the first to make frequent use of incense in their rituals, and they
have employed it ever since.

The many other peculiarities and exceptional merits of this glorious race
fall outside the scope of my work. Recall, however, the glorious people cloaked
in togas,[2] whose endless array of accomplishments seems nearly impossible.
Consult the innumerable books of famous historians, or the elegant verses of
divine poets: there you will find what this noble country [Rome] has said, in
prose and verse, regarding the learning and the wisdom of the Etruscans. I thus
believe that more than any other country in the world, Tuscany possesses and
deserves the glory of religion.

Let us leave these ancient and remote things aside for a while to discuss the
present, true, sacred, and holy religion.[3] Has Tuscany not given the whole
world numerous religious orders, whose main centers are still flourishing and
venerated in this region? Where did the saintly Romualdo undertake his endless and exceedingly tormenting penance?[4] Was it not in a dark, secluded hermitage set in the highest mountains of the Apennines, near the source of our
great River Arno? Where is the miraculous site in the barest rock where the
Word Incarnate, son of God, put the stigmata on the sacred limbs and side of
the humble Francis, thus showing to such an ardent servant the renewal of his
own holy, evangelical, and apostolic life?[5] Did this not take place on the high
and hard rock of the Verna close to the hermitage among the steep hills of the
Casentino? Does the order of Santa Maria dei Servi not still stand, which was
founded by a few chaste monks on the Asinaio, a famous mountain in the
countryside of our city?[6] Is this not also true of the holy monastery where

Giovanni Gualberto founded his most saintly order and did his surpassingly toilsome penance in the fogs of Vallombrosa?[7] What about the famous pilgrim hospice of Altopascio, which has contributed so much for such a long time?[8] Who could be so blind as to deny that all these things are true, certain, and recognized? Both in Italy and abroad one will find numerous monasteries and holy places like the ones I have mentioned. Is it not true that in almost every inhabited region of the world, schismatics, heretics, and all the fiercest enemies of this most holy faith of ours welcome and venerate with the greatest devotion the brethren of the most pure Francis? This is certainly a great thing upon which to reflect.

1. Following a common medieval topos, Book 1 of Gherardi's novel relates a miraculous voyage undertaken by the author under the guidance of his guardian angel. Back in his room, he reflects on the classical monuments he saw during his trip.
2. The Romans.
3. An example, like many others in this work, of Gherardi's traditionalist stance: he prefers not to enter into a detailed discussion of topics that would take him far from the safer, orthodox ground of Christianity.
4. The Benedictine monk who in 959 built a hermitage at Camaldoli, in the Casentino.
5. St. Francis received the stigmata on Mount Verna in the Casentino, in the province of Arezzo, in 1218.
6. Placed between the Sieve and Mugnone Rivers, Mount Asinaio (today called Mount Senario) is the seat of the monastery erected by the Romitani dei Servi di Maria.
7. Giovanni Gualberto (1009–1073) founded the Abbey of Vallombrosa in the woods in Valdarno; he was canonized in 1193 by Pope Celestinus II.
8. The hospice was built in Altopascio, in Valdinievole, near Lucca, before the end of the eleventh century.

36

Vision of the Future of Italy

ANTONIO DA RIETI

The author of the excerpt that follows is virtually unknown, except for the meager information he himself provides here. An Observant friar, Antonio preached in the Holy Land in the early 1420s, before returning to Venice, where he had the vision reported in this letter. Many fifteenth-century Florentine manuscripts include Antonio's prophecy, which was not published before the early sixteenth century. The importance of this brief text—copied in Florence on November 3, 1442, as the colophon attests—is as a valuable exemplar of the apocalyptic literature of quattrocento Florence, which was widely diffused. The Biblioteca Nazionale and other Florentine libraries possess a great number of fifteenth-century codices of prophecies, in which Florence is usually envisioned as the daughter of Rome, a daughter who will come to rescue her mother from the corruption of the clergy. In Antonio's vision, the lily will blossom in such a way that its petals will extend across all of Italy, comforting frightened people with their perfume. As with Savonarola's prophecies at the end of the century, Antonio's vision foretells the religious primacy of Florence and its future as a capital in which Christians can take shelter from heresy and violence.

The images of Antonio's text are typical of millenarian literature. Like all writers of this genre, he draws on the prophetic books of the Bible, mostly Revelation. In the notes, we have indicated the cities and the nations symbolized in Antonio's vision. Except where indicated, these interpretations also apply to the other prophetic writings included in this section of the anthology.

Source: "Copia di una visione che ebbe frate Antonio da Rieti dell'ordine dei frati di S. Francesco osservanti, la quale ebbe nell'anno 1422 nella città di Venezia e quella mandò a Fermo a maestro Ruberto dell'ordine dei frati di S. Domenico," Florence, Biblioteca Nazionale Centrale, MS. Magl. 25.344, fols. 33–36.

Jesus Christ be praised. Reverend Father Roberto, following my usual custom, I shall inform you of marvelous things that have recently happened to me. I hope you will provide me with your valued advice, as you have always done in the past.

Upon my return to Venice from Jerusalem, I stayed for some time at the convent of our order, La Vigna. We were tired from the long journey and sea voyage, and so we resolved to remain there awhile to rest. On a Monday night, twelve days after our arrival, I was sound asleep when I saw an incredible light which dazzled me as if I had fixed my eyes on the sun. I also smelled a pleasant scent and heard voices singing a sublime melody of "Glory in the highest." I had never in my life felt such intense delight. Then I said, "O hope of the miserable sinners, I beg you to call my soul to you and have me taste the sweet fruits of your garden." As I uttered these words, in the center of the light I saw a friar of your order shining like the sun with such brilliance that my eyes could barely stand to behold him. He started to speak and said to me, "True friend of Christ, dear one, you have endured great toils for the love of God. I now come to tell you things to which you must pay close attention and then reveal to all, so that they may be strengthened in their hope and faith. You have been to Jerusalem and Bethlehem and there you have preached the Word of God and the holy truth. Your efforts, however, have not brought an abundant harvest, for the fruits are still unripe and not ready to be picked. Before they mature, you will see a gigantic, horrendous, fierce serpent[1] with one human head, six serpentine ones, and a swordlike tail. It will fly over the sea and the whole of Greece, infesting them with its venom, infecting and ruining most of the trees, and will spread as far as Italy. There, as you will see, an immense falcon will arrive from the seven nests in Spain;[2] it will attack a bird of Italy and it will make its nest in that country.

Shortly before these momentous events, the lion[3] will suffer a violent fever, and later he will roar with pain from the many wounds the falcon has inflicted upon him. You will see the wolf attacking Ambrose's sheep,[4] then turning into a lamb and defending the sheep from other wolves. The lilies, more beautiful than ever before, will blossom and fill the land, their petals so large and beautiful that all the birds of Italy will take shelter under them.[5] Meanwhile, the falcon will grow so poisonous that it will be transformed into a serpent. It will then join the other serpent, and together they will assail St. Peter's successor, whose sheep will thus be dispersed and forced to take shelter under the petals of the lilies, which will put forth their stems, flowers, and leaves with a wondrous perfume so comforting that it will entice and enrapture all.

Because this comforting scent annoys and displeases every poisonous beast, as soon as the two serpents smell it, they will depart and fly over the country, ravaging it with their venom. Then, out of necessity, one will fly east and the other west to their former nests. There, the seabird[6] will have his wings partially cut off. The she-wolf[7] and her cubs will die and never reappear again. The Germans will ally with the Hungarians against the Bohemians, and the latter will stave off their attacks. In Italy, after five hundred years of peace, the cross of Christ will stretch its arms from east to west and everyone will safely rest under it. All the animals will then go to the same spring and drink together. This will last one hundred years. Afterward, many fleas and all sorts of parasites will grow on the back of the beast, causing such a stench that no one will be able to bear his brother's presence, nor the father that of his son, nor the son that of his father. A tremendous increase in heresy will overtake all nations. At that point, our great enemy, the Antichrist, will come, wreaking terrible damage through his immense malice and power. He will soon be defeated, however, as the prophets foretell, and the labors of mankind will then come to an end."

As he finished his speech, I asked him, "O divine spirit, I beg you to reveal to me who you are." He replied immediately and said, "I am St. Thomas Aquinas, before whom you have always shown great reverence." I then burst into tears and said, "O my hope and comfort, how can I remember and relate so many and diverse things?" He answered, "Do as I ordered you."

Upon hearing these last words, I awoke completely bewildered. I got out of bed, as it was already time for matins, and went to church with the others to pray. I kept on thinking to myself about what I just reported to you, and said, "Maybe this happened simply because I was tired. At times, physical tiredness makes people see things that do not exist." I thus did not talk with anybody about it for the whole day. Another night passed, and on the third night the very same thing occurred. This time St. Thomas was rather perturbed and said, "My dear friend, you do not believe my words and are not doing what I ordered you to do," and left.

Subsequently, out of respect for his command, I resolved to write everything down and reveal it to the other brothers. I informed Fra Giovanni of Recanati and Fra Piero of Ragusa, who will report the whole thing to you.

Since they are expected to be back here before the end of the month, I shall wait for your answer and excellent advice, as I have always done in the past regarding all my affairs. God willing, I shall depart once again for Jerusalem in June. God willing, I shall stay there awhile and pray to Him to bring us salvation. Farewell in the name of God, and pray for me.

1. The serpent was a common symbol for both the Turks and the Antichrist. In this context, the former interpretation is more likely to be what da Rieti intended.
2. The House of Aragon.
3. The lion represents Florence, as does the lily.
4. "Ambrose's sheep" symbolize Milan. The wolf here probably represents the Visconti.
5. The lilies symbolize Florence, especially when, as in the present case, the city appears in conjunction with the French royal family, who also took the lily as their emblem.
6. Venice.
7. It is worth noting that the she-wolf refers here to Siena, rather than to Rome.

37

A Prophecy of a New Age

This text, whose author, title, and date are unknown, not only is reported in the same manuscript as Antonio da Rieti's vision but also belongs to the same genre. The prophecy has a Franciscan resonance—like something by the Fraticelli, for instance—and is reminiscent of the thought of Joachim of Flora. The work is structured as a commentary on a vision. Once again, Rome is depicted as the den of all vice and Florence as having the responsibility for bringing peace and piety back to Italy with the help of the French royal family, the allies of the Florentines par excellence. Here, too, the political and military leadership of Florence—symbolized, as usual, by the lion and the title "daughter of Rome"—is associated with a new age of spiritual perfection and universal peace.

Source: Florence, Biblioteca Nazionale Centrale, MS. Magl. 25.344, fols. 31–32.

The she-bear of tribulation rises from her den. The swords of the philosophers clash. This stands for the teachings of the ancient prophets, sages, and astrologers, for they all appear to contend with one another. In examining them properly, however, it will become clear that they all have said the same thing. The bear represents the mother of scandalous action—more precisely, the hope of those who believe they save themselves by murdering their neighbors. She will be so thoroughly annihilated that barely even the memory of her will remain.

The whorelike she-wolf licks the blood of the she-bear, leaves her husband, and commits adultery with a strange beast. This refers to the hypocritical preachers and those who do not fight against the she-bear.

The angels shudder. They are the good people, that is, the orphans and the children who live in peace.

The birds cry. They are the ones who see things from above and the diviners of ancient times.

The lion rises and attacks the she-wolf, wounding her with his paws. That is, the aforementioned city[1] will retaliate against the she-wolf by taking all her possessions and domains.

A new bloodshed reddens the wet plain. There will be a battle between the French and the Germans in the said plain, namely in the plain of the hot springs.[2]

The city which is the daughter of Rome has become the mistress and capital of all those around. This means Florence, originally called Romolina,[3] and later named after Florin, the Roman king who founded her. The eagle will make her nest there,[4] and she will become mistress of all the western cities.

She joins forces with the Gaul and fights most valiantly. That means with the royal family of France, for in ancient times the French were called Gauls.

The wicked and the kings flee. These are the treacherous lords who have been perfidious and cruel.

Weapons will be hated, and God will bring peace from heaven to the people who live on earth. The sea will open, and from it will emerge a new crown. This means that a great power will bring peace to all Christendom.

Having risen from the bed of pain where he has lain for a long time, the lion will grow stronger. Peace will flourish, and there will be harmony among the beasts in the garden. The astrologers will be silent. The latter are the treacherous and cruel lords who have murdered out of greed. A new shepherd will come from a place other than the dominion of St. Silvester, and he will be guarded by the angels.[5] Mass will be celebrated with songs, prayers, and holy sacrifice.

---

1. That is, Florence.
2. Probably Aachen, whose Latin name is *Aquae* ("spas"): it was renowned for its hot springs.
3. "Little Rome."
4. The eagle mentioned here is more likely a symbol of Christ than of the empire.
5. This is one of the many examples attesting to the diffusion of the myth of the Angelic Pastor in the fifteenth century. The "dominion of St. Silvester" refers to the territory of the Church, whose origin goes back to the well-known and much disputed Donation of Constantine.

38

The Consecration of the Cathedral of Florence

FEO BELCARI

Feo Belcari (1410–1484) was born into an upper-middle-class family of Florentine wool merchants. He received a strict religious education, which significantly influenced his vast literary production. For many years he was in charge of the Basilica di San Lorenzo al Monte's finances. Thanks to his familiarity with the Medici, he managed to hold various important offices in the city government, and it was to the members of the powerful family that Belcari dedicated his most renowned works, the Vita del beato Giovanni Colombini *(addressed to Giovanni de' Medici in 1449) and the mystery play* Sacra rappresentazione dell'Annunziazione di Nostra Donna, *dedicated to Lucrezia Tornabuoni—mother of Lorenzo the Magnificent—and performed during Lent of 1471. Religious and moral topics characterize all Belcari's texts. Besides the above-mentioned works, he composed numerous* laudi, *two mystery plays (the famous* Sacra rappresentazione di Abraam e di Isaac suo figliuolo and Di Santo Giovanni Battista quando andò nel deserto), *and translated the* Prato spirituale *from Latin—a collection of lives of the saints written by his humanist friend Ambrogio Traversari. Belcari's prose owes much to the religious literature of the late Middle Ages, especially to the Franciscan authors, and it has been his prose, rather than his poetry, that has most interested scholars. Pietro Giordani described Belcari's prose as "an orange in January, a fruit of the fourteenth and fifteenth centuries," continuing to praise it in a letter to Giacomo Leopardi as "the most beautiful and sublime of all Italy."*

March 25, Annunciation Day, marked the beginning of the year according to the

Florentine calendar. On March 25, 1436, Pope Eugenius IV consecrated the Cathedral of Santa Maria del Fiore, whose impressive dome was nearing completion. Like some of his fellow citizens, Belcari wrote an account of this important occasion. His record, however, is quite different from those of Leonardo Bruni and Giannozzo Manetti. Bruni merely mentions the event, underscoring the great number of people who attended. Manetti, by contrast, speaks at length about the artistic beauty of the cathedral. Belcari, however, focuses on the pope's arrival at the church and on the religious ceremony. Neither Bruni nor Manetti mentions the cardinals' granting of indulgences at the request of Cosimo de' Medici, whose influence figures in the last section of Belcari's account. Belcari pays homage to his patrons, whose authority was publicly acknowledged by the pope and the cardinals—a valuable indication of Florence's prestige in the eyes of both the papacy and the lay powers of Italy.

Source: Feo Belcari, "Ricordanza che a di 25 di Marzo 1436, essendo la Domenica della Passione, si consacrò la magnifica Chiesa Cattedrale Fiorentina in questo modo," in *Lettere,* ed. Domenico Moreni (Florence: Magheri, 1825), pp. 59–63.

The Most Reverend Cardinal Orsini began the consecration of the church [Santa Maria del Fiore], continuing until the relics of the saints were placed by the altar. Then he began the consecration of the altar. The most holy Pope Eugenius IV, who had resided in Florence for thirty-one months without ever leaving the monastery of Santa Maria Novella, arrived at the church at nine in the morning. He walked on a platform two or three braccia high, decorated with rugs, drapes, tapestries, chestcloths, and other types of material. The platform had been prepared so as to protect the pontiff from the crowd, saving him the annoyance of having to walk directly on the street. It was necessary to take this measure, for more than two hundred thousand people had flocked to the city from the countryside and the towns nearby. The pope, wearing his pluvial, was accompanied by the signoria, the members of the Florentine councils, his canons, and the College of Cardinals, all of whom were dressed for the occasion. Right next to the pope walked the bishop of Piacenza, the treasurer of the papal court, the bishop of Fermo, and Cardinal Colonna. The cardinal of San Marco, who led Mass, was also part of the entourage escorting the pope, together with the patriarch of Jerusalem, bishops, and protonotaries, who were all properly dressed and wearing the white miter. The reverend cardinal of San Marcello, who was also wearing holy attire, received the pope inside the church.

After the consecration of the altar, while the cardinal of San Marco was preparing himself to sing Mass and Cardinal Orsini was lighting the twelve candles of the church, the Holy Father knighted the worthy Florentine citizen and jurist, Messer Giuliano Davanzati, who was then the standard-bearer of justice.[1] The distinguished podestà of Florence gave him the spurs, the great lord of Rimini, [Sigismondo Pandolfo] Malatesta, tied the sword around his waist, and the Holy Father pinned the precious decoration onto his chest. Mass followed, after which the cardinal of San Marco distributed indulgences for six years and six quarantines, but then yielded to the request of the noble citizen Cosimo de' Medici, who asked for indulgences up to seven years. Again, upon the request of Cosimo, the most reverend cardinal of San Marcello allowed the cardinal of San Marco to offer indulgences for ten years and ten quarantines, although he had already refused the same request previously from all the cardinals and the Florentine signoria.

Amid the rejoicing of the people, the pope finally returned to Santa Maria Novella solemnly dressed and escorted, just as he had come. It is amazing that no one was injured, despite the immense crowd, probably the largest Florence had ever seen. We should note that, contrary to the custom of the Roman Curia, the cardinals and prelates attended Mass wearing their paraments.

Although I could have easily written this account elsewhere, I decided to write it here, believing that the memory of these things will last longer in this form.[2]

1. Davanzati was a Florentine ambassador of repute who held numerous posts in the government of the city.
2. Belcari wrote his account in a manuscript he placed in the archives of the Basilica of San Lorenzo al Monte, where it remains to this day. Belcari probably considered it safer to record the event in an archival manuscript than in a private diary.

39

A History of Florentine Piety

UGOLINO VERINO

The first hexameters of Verino's second book in praise of Florence are devoted to a sketch of the most important Florentine spiritual figures. The author conflates a thousand years of local religious history into a few pages, in which he underscores the intense devotion that has characterized Florentine society from the first centuries of Christianity until the present. In doing so, Verino highlights the variety of saintly behavior exhibited by Florentine citizens throughout the ages. In this excerpt we have rendered Verino's verses into prose.

Source: Ugolino Verino, *De illustratione urbis Florentiae* (Florence: Landini, 1636), pp. 29–31.

BOOK 2

The Florentine Zenobius was bishop of this city,[1] living at the time in which the great Ambrose vanquished the rabid enemies of Christ. He distinguished himself for his genuine faith and his intolerance of heresy. Both Ambrose and Zenobius were kind shepherds who looked after their sheep responsibly. It was at that time that the pontiff of the Roman church, Damasus, sent Zenobius to Byzantium (Constantine had moved the capital of the ancient Roman Empire to the shores of Greece) to discuss matters of great importance, as he was considered an excellent orator in both Greek and Latin. Zenobius was a saintly man, renowned for his virtue, through which he was able to drive away deadly diseases and raise souls from the dark waters of Hades to the supreme heavens. Such was Zenobius, the shepherd of Florence, thanks to whom our city has fended off perfidious frauds, traps, and wicked sins.

In our time, there was Antonino,[2] celebrated as a new Thomas Aquinas because of his character, his exemplary nature, and his written works. He healed the clergy, kept the city free from corruption, and was a zealous shepherd who protected his sheep in such a way as to keep their fiercest enemy, the wolf, from capturing and slaughtering them if unattended. O Antonino, venerable father, how can my verses commemorate your noble deeds? How can I express to you, on behalf of Florence, the gratitude that you deserve? You who now dwell in heaven, please send grace to our city, save it from war, from famine, plague, and all the things harmful to feeble mankind, so that a righteous mind may thrive in a healthy body.

Andrea Corsini,[3] too, surpassed his ancestors. He was a man of noble birth and became even more noble as the shepherd of the Carmelite convent. In obedience to God's command, he left the woods and tended to the flocks of Fiesole, even though he held worldly honors in contempt. Through his words and honest deeds he educated the people, putting into practice that which he preached. Righteous acts speak louder than eloquence, and this is why the saintly customs of the past are still remembered—that is, when the blood of Christ inflamed the Fathers' spirits, and the Church was still unfamiliar with gold.

Great is the fame of Filippo Benizzi,[4] who served the holy temple of the Servi di Maria, the most sacred in the entire city. There, one can see figures made of gold and silver, and even more made of wax, depicting the people whose prayers have been answered. He was the first to bring votive offerings to this temple.

I shall not omit you, O memorable Dominican, Giovanni,[5] who deserve greater praise than I can give. Because of your purity, your renowned saintly nature, and the splendor of your doctrine, the pope listened to you alone when the wickedness of the clergy split the church of Christ. Thanks to you, peace was finally settled at the council, and a single pope was chosen.[6]

What can I say about the greatest glory of the common people, Caterina Benincasa of Siena,[7] scion of Sulla. If I wanted to celebrate her holy life and deeds and all the miracles performed by this seraphic virgin, not even the eloquent verses of Virgil would suffice.

What age does not know the saintly nature of Villana?[8] Born into the Strada family, her voice alone drove away deadly diseases. Famous for her unique piety, she gladly gave the poor all she possessed out of love for Christ, in order to become rich in heaven.

Distinguished by her noble birth and wealth, Emiliana,[9] a virgin of the Cerchi family, became even more noble by virtue of her character. No one was superior to her in probity.

Giulia was the glory of Certaldo.[10] Whoever wishes to dwell in heaven should read her works.

If I now were to enumerate all the many virgins and angels living piously on earth and by whose prayers the city of Florence is protected, not even a whole day would suffice. Let us leave this subject, then, and hasten to mention some of our poets.

1. Born in Florence in the first half of the fourth century, Zenobius was highly esteemed in his native city, where he died in 417, after having held its bishopric for many years. He was credited with numerous miracles, and his relics were believed to have the power to heal. A local tradition holds that when his body was moved from the Church of San Lorenzo to his burial place in the ancient Florentine cathedral Santa Reparata, his body touched a withered elm, which immediately started to turn green. In memory of that episode, a column was placed by the north door of the baptistery, a copy of which still stands.

2. St. Antonino Pierozzi was one of the most prominent spiritual figures of the fifteenth century. He was born in Florence in 1389 and in 1405, following Giovanni Dominici's advice, he joined the Dominicans. He held important offices within his order: he was elected prior of the convent of Cortona in 1420, vicar general of the first Dominican convent in Lombardy in 1433, and vicar general of the Dominican convents of central and southern Italy in 1437. In 1439 he became prior of the Dominican convent of San Marco in Florence, where he was appointed bishop in 1445 by Pope Eugenius IV, who disregarded the candidates proposed by the Medici in favor of this more independent and combative personality. During his bishopric, Antonino frequently defended the liberty of the Florentine church from the designs of the Medicean faction. Antonino was also known for his numerous writings, most of which aimed to educate the faithful on spirituality. Among his renowned works are *Opera a ben vivere*, *Regola di vita cristiana*, and *Confessione volgare;* his epistles are collected in the *Summa theologica*, and his *Chronicon* is a voluminous work that covers the history of the world from the Creation to the author's time.

3. Born at the beginning of the fourteenth century, St. Andrea Corsini entered the monastery of the Carmine in Florence while still quite young. He held various important offices in the Florentine monastery and within his order (he was also elected superior of the Carmelites in Tuscany), before being appointed bishop of Fiesole in 1349. According to legend, before being elected bishop, he was living a secluded life in a hermitage, and a vision eventually induced him to accept the appointment. He died in 1374.

4. St. Filippo Benizzi (b. Florence, August 15, 1233; d. Todi, August 23, 1285) studied medicine and philosophy in Paris and Padua. He worked as a doctor in Florence, but in 1253 he abandoned that profession to join the Servites. He was appointed general of the order in 1267. Under his guidance, the Servites went through a phase of considerable growth. He was also a peacemaker in the struggles between Guelphs and Ghibellines.

5. Giovanni di Domenico Banchini (1355–1419), better known as Giovanni Dominici, entered the Dominican monastery of Santa Maria Novella in 1373, thereby disappointing his family, who wanted him to continue as a silk merchant in his father's business. He studied in Pisa and Paris, but the greatest influence on his spiritual education, as he himself writes, was the example of St. Caterina da Siena, whom he met in Florence. He was prior of Santa Maria Novella from 1385 to 1387 and did fundamental reform work in the Dominican order in the province of Venice during the last decade of the fourteenth century. He attained considerable popularity as a preacher in northern Italy, a fame that certainly contributed to his election as vicar general of the reformed convents of Italy in 1393. He left Venice in 1399 and returned to Florence, where he was elected vicar of Santa Maria Novella. His popularity was augmented by the success of his sermons. Between 1401 and 1403 he composed his most famous text, the *Regola del governo di cura familiare,* followed by the *Lucula noctis,* a work written to oppose Salutati's defense of the growing humanistic interest in classical literature. In 1405 he founded the monastery of San Domenico in Fiesole, and in the following years he fervently supported the candidacy of Gregory XII during the Schism. He participated in the Council of Constance, and in 1418 Pope Martin V sent him to Bohemia to fight the Hussite heresy.

6. Verino is referring to Dominici's participation in the Council of Constance.

7. Born around 1347 to humble parents, St. Caterina da Siena is one of the most renowned women saints of the Middle Ages. Her early biographers claim that she had her first mystical experience at the age of six, when she had a vision of Christ. After this vision she pronounced her vow of chastity. In 1364, she became the first woman to enter the Dominican third order. Caterina soon showed herself to be someone who was involved with the events of her time and willing to be close to the people. We can observe this aspect of Caterina's personality in her letters, the contact she had with Pope Gregory XI, her political involvement, and the itinerant apostolate she undertook. Her most important political mission took place in 1376, when she visited Gregory XI in Avignon to discuss various momentous matters, among them the revolt of the Italian cities against the papacy and the organization of the crusade. Upon her return to Italy, Caterina founded the convent of Santa Maria degli Angeli in Rome and then moved to Florence, where she tried to reconcile the Guelph and Ghibelline factions. She spent the last years of her brief life (she died at thirty-three) promoting the reformation of the Church and supporting the candidacy of Urban VI to the papal throne.

8. Villana, the wife of the wealthy Rosso Benintendi, enjoyed great popularity during her lifetime and throughout the fifteenth century, as attested to by a passage in St. Antonino's *Chronicon.* Contrary to what Verino claims, she was a member of the Delle Botti family, although it is possible that she was related to the Stradas on her mother's side. She soon became renowned for her mortification of the flesh, her many visions, and the help she gave to the poor. She died in 1360 and was buried in the Dominican

church of Santa Maria Novella, where her relics are still venerated by Florentines. Each year, on the last Sunday of January, a large crowd attends the ceremony in which the two shrines containing her miracle-working relics are placed on her tomb in a chapel at Santa Maria Novella.

9. Blessed Emiliana (or Umiliana) Cerchi (1219–1246) first became famous for her charitable activities as a young married woman. After her husband's death, Emiliana refused to marry again, thus going against the will of her family. Having been deprived of her dowry and having suffered all sorts of cruelty from her relatives, she retired to a small room in the tower of the Cerchi palace and spent the last seven years of her life in continual meditation and prayer. She was wrongly credited by her first biographer, Vito da Cortona, with having been the first Florentine woman to enter the Franciscan tertiary order. Emiliana enjoyed great popularity during her lifetime, and immediately after her death, evidence shows, a cult was devoted to her.

10. Born at the beginning of the fourteenth century, Giulia da Certaldo took her vow of seclusion in 1342 as an Augustinian tertiary sister. From then on, she spent her life in a small cell of the Church of Santi Michele e Giacomo at Certaldo, where flowers miraculously started to grow after her arrival. She was continually visited by the faithful, and as soon as she died in 1372, Giulia's relics, credited with possessing healing powers, were venerated.

40

A Guide to Florence's Holy Sites

DOMENICO DA CORELLA

Domenico di Giovanni da Corella (1403–1483) is a rather obscure figure who has attracted little attention from scholars. He spent most of his life at the Church of Santa Maria Novella, of which he became prior in 1436, while he was vicar general of the Dominican order, a post he kept from 1415 until 1453. Starting in 1428, he taught theology at the University of Florence; and in 1469 he was asked to lecture on Dante's Commedia. *Corella was linked to Ficino and the local humanists, an association reflected in his erudition and his style; he falls into the broad category of fifteenth-century Florentine authors who wrote patriotic texts in praise of the Medici. He celebrates the powerful family in the third book of his* De origine urbis Florentiae, *a long poem (of more than six thousand verses) that narrates the history of the city from its founding through the arrival of Charles of Anjou in 1267. Corella dedicated his most famous text, the* Theotocon *("mother of God"), to Piero de' Medici.*

The Theotocon *is divided into four books of Latin couplets, comprising a life of Mary followed by a description of the main religious buildings in Rome and in Tuscany (primarily the churches dedicated to the Virgin). As Creighton E. Gilbert notes (in* Italian Art, *p. 149), "This is the first such guide that goes beyond architecture to other works of art"; lavish decorations, more than the buildings' external appearance, seem to elicit Corella's admiration. The last book of the* Theotocon *is entirely devoted to Florentine churches, an urban itinerary that leads the reader through the religious sites of a city whose piety is second only to that of Rome, the spiritual capital of the Western world. Apart from the explicit intention of offering the first biography in verse of the Virgin and paying homage to Cosimo's son Piero, Corella's* Theotocon *is a true commemoration of the artistic beauty of Florence and the religiosity of its people. We have translated his verse into prose.*

Source: *Magistri Iohannis Dominici theologi florentini ordinis predicatorum* Theotocon, Biblioteca Nazionale Centrale, Florence, MS. Conv. Sopr. G.2.8768, fols. 1–2 and 66–77.

PROEM

Devout worshipper of the Virgin Mother who gave birth to the loving king of the world, O Piero, receive this book that I have just devoted to her. I believe that you, O noble offspring of Cosimo, will welcome whatever derives from love for her, to whom you give so many lavish offerings. Please accept this brief work I have composed, whose first part will report the untainted life of the pure Virgin, as well as her death. The second part of this book will recount the immense and eternal glory of the heavenly triumph when the Virgin received the crown of the kingdom of heaven. The third book will mention the gifts that Rome has offered her, and the temples that the Tyrrhenians have erected in her honor. The fourth will describe the temples built at great expense in our city by illustrious citizens to celebrate the Holy Mother. As a man endowed with great devotion, although deserving of a greater gift than I can give, please do not reject this new book of mine. The good Lady of Heaven will always protect you from all evil. It is her life, newly told, that shines forth in the pages of this book. Its title is *Theotocon,* and rightly so, for it takes its name from the one whom a wise synod of the past age resolved to name the Divine Mother. In her pure and fertile womb she bore the true offspring of the Father. This is the reason she received the Greek title Theotocon. Although no one before me has ever reported her deeds in verse, I am resolved to dedicate to you these short lauds that I have recently composed in a series of couplets. To you, O generous citizen, I send them; to you, a worshipper of the powerful Lady, I send them, in the hope that this book can be a new token of my love for you. Please read it with your usual serene mind, O great Piero, beacon of the city of the flower, deserving to be praised with sweet poems as one of the illustrious fathers. Always protecting you, may Mary, Blessed Mother of the eternal king and our benefactress, make you one of the blessed souls who live in the heavenly kingdom.

BOOK 4: HERE STARTS THE FOURTH BOOK, CONCERNING THE FLORENTINE CHURCHES CONSECRATED TO THE DIVINE MOTHER

It is now time for me to move from the monument to the Divine Mother,[1] to a description of the temples that have been dedicated to her at immense expense and with great devotion by the Etruscan city of Florence.

Before describing the religious buildings, Corella engages in a digression on the origins of Florence, its renowned citizens (starting with Dante and Petrarch), and the city's institutions, especially the Guelph party and its link with the Church. He also celebrates the bridges over the Arno, the churches of Orsanmichele and Santa Maria Ughi, the government palace, and the guildhalls.

The first to appear is the splendid new church whose very name[2] reveals that it, too, has been consecrated to our Divine Mother. Annexed to the church is a monastery whose beauty is probably unmatched anywhere in the world. In it, the illustrious heir of Saint Dominic resides, rendered even more illustrious by its learned brothers, such as Giovanni and Leonardo,[3] two beacons of sacred study. The former's piety was rewarded with the splendor of the halo; he passed away near the city of Buda, and there he was buried. The latter was appointed by the commune to the post of teacher; he rests in a sculpted bronze tomb near the high altar. I shall not report the names of the many other fathers that the bosom of this fertile church has nourished. Whenever the sovereign pontiff happens to visit our city, he is lodged in the beautiful rooms of this monastery. Shortly after his coronation, which was not long ago, the emperor also spent a few days here on his return trip.[4] This church is also renowned for its exquisite cloisters and the long series of stone vaults which cover it. Although its external appearance was attractive, it could not, unlike the present one, boast a beautiful façade. Inflamed with an intense love for the Holy Mother, Giovanni Rucellai paid for the entire construction with his own money. Thanks to him, the outside of the church is now embellished with a new façade of colored marble. People praise him to the heavens and duly show him their immense gratitude. To this work is also linked the glory of Battista Alberti, who managed to create it through his art and skill. He adorned the façade with fruit-laden branches that stretch above the church doors and decorated the marble with varied designs. The façade was thus renovated and rendered more beautiful, thanks to the ability of this distinguished artist. Here one also finds the tomb of the most illustrious patriarch of Constantinople, Joseph. Under his lead, Greece espoused the true faith by accepting the dogmas of the Florentine council. After leading a long and righteous life, he is now memorialized by the sepulchre built in his eternal honor. But in order to discuss other buildings, I shall not mention the remaining things that are notable about this great church. Instead, I shall turn my eyes for a moment to a small church dedicated to the Holy Virgin. In olden times, this temple was called grand, for it was, in fact, much larger in size than it is today.[5]

Having addressed my prayers to the Queen of Heaven, I now walk along the street outside the church. I soon find myself before the cathedral, built by the citizens of Florence—a time-consuming endeavor that they undertook at their own great expense. Florence named it after the flower,[6] and rightly so, in the hope that the flowering Virgin who gave birth to the divine offspring of God might flourish by virtue of the pious cult she enjoys in this place of splendor. The great dome of this temple, towering into the skies, renders the building higher than any other [in the city]. This was the work of a marvelous artist endowed with unrivaled skills, Filippo [Brunelleschi], who in our time was considered a new Daedalus. Unlike the latter, however, he did not fly with the aid of artificial feathers, but with his genius he built a vast dome of solid stone; it rises to the skies far off the ground. Neither Agrippa's work[7] nor the lighthouse of the great colossus is comparable to it, nor are any of the monuments of Rome. It certainly deserves to be considered the eighth wonder of the world. With three vaults below and only one above, it manages to stand without any supporting framework. Outside, the elegant octagonal structure of the dome has round windows, and atop it stands a splendid golden lantern. Fifteen chapels embellish the interior of the church, and its exterior is decorated with variegated marble. Here Luca della Robbia, who works both gold and bronze, skillfully made two splendid doors. The church has a magnificent tower, whose bell summons the citizens to celebrate the religious feasts. The magnificent Giotto designed it, who deserved the title of divine painter. O genius superior to all the illustrious men of his time! He was certainly on a par with Apelles the ancient painter. Wanting to give a precious gift to his homeland, he drafted the project of this most noble tower, whose sides are adorned with colored marble; there is nothing more beautiful than this the world over.

Here, in a tomb, rest the sacred bones and the head of Zenobius, the great ecclesiastic. This most holy man, whose life was filled with wonders, was once the bishop of our city. He continued to work miracles even after his death: a dying tree, for instance, started to grow green again after having touched his coffin.[8] In memory of this episode, they placed a column which now stands next to the baptistery. The baptistery was originally a temple dedicated to Mars, the god of war, but the citizens later consecrated it to St. John the Baptist. In honor of this saint, they yearly celebrate with a lavish feast, the like of which, I believe, is not to be found in rituals anywhere. They traditionally organize a parade with magnificent carts, and the whole city resounds with cries of joy. During this ritual, the citizens fill the baptistery with precious objects brought from outside, thereby enhancing its already unparalleled beauty.

Corella goes on to praise the artistic highlights of the baptistery: the mosaics, the bronze doors, and Donatello's tomb for John XXIII. Corella then mentions the seat of the Misericordia—the confraternity located next to the baptistery and the cathedral—and the churches of Santa Maria Nuova, Santa Maria degli Angeli, and Santa Apollonia. His itinerary then takes him to the Dominican monastery of San Marco.

O traveler, interrupt for a while the journey you have started out of love for the Divine Mother, and joyously enter San Marco to see the crib of our Savior, who will hear and answer your pious requests.[9] Upon entering the church, one can see a representation of the divine birth, with a sculpted image of Mary and a small one of the Christ Child. There are other figures exquisitely carved, illuminated by bright light on the right side of the cradle. It is for this reason that the feast of the three Wise Men has always been celebrated in this church.[10] Recently, Cosimo de' Medici, a most generous man, has financed the enlargement of this sacred building. Cosimo has spent vast sums of money, which he has earned from worldwide trade, on construction of sacred temples. Through this virtuous act he can be said to have surpassed all great men. Not even kings can compare with him, for through his noble deeds he has managed to dispel envy, something that even the greatest rulers rarely, if ever, achieve.

1. The fourteenth-century chapel in the cathedral of Prato, where the Virgin's holy girdle is kept.
2. Santa Maria Novella.
3. The two famous Dominican theologians Giovanni Dominici and Leonardo Dati. On the former see Verino's praise and note 5 to document 39. The latter was the brother of

Goro Dati and was renowned for his theological scholarship and scientific knowledge; he taught theology at the University of Florence in 1402–1403, and in 1414 he was elected general of the Dominican order.

4. Corella is referring to the crowning of Emperor Frederick III in March 1452. Filarete opens his *Book of Ceremonies* with the record of the emperor's stay in Florence.

5. The "small church" is Santa Maria Maggiore.

6. The Cathedral of Florence is called Santa Maria del Fiore (Holy Mary of the Flower), the lily being the symbol of the city.

7. The Pantheon.

8. On St. Zenobius and this miracle, see Verino and n. 1 to document 39.

9. Corella is referring to the Christmas cradle that has been on display at San Marco since the fifteenth century.

10. The festival of the Adoration of the Magi, annually held in Florence at Epiphany. It consisted of a procession on horseback by the Magi through the main urban sites until they reached the cradle in the Church of San Marco. Upon his return from exile, Cosimo astutely promoted this celebration for reasons of personal propaganda; he himself took part in the procession, whose progress became an opportunity to display the family's wealth and power. Such processions have also influenced such works by artists linked with the Medicean circle as Gozzoli's mural in the chapel in the Medici Palace and Botticelli's *Adoration of the Magi.*

41

A Treatise on the Florentine Government

GIROLAMO SAVONAROLA

Girolamo Savonarola, born in Ferrara in 1452, was one of the most influential and enigmatic figures of fifteenth-century Italy. Having distinguished himself as a successful preacher within the Dominican order, he met the main intellectuals of the Medici court as early as 1482 and formed a particularly close friendship with Pico della Mirandola. After the downfall of Piero de' Medici in November 1494, Savonarola became actively involved in Florentine politics; he participated in the debate concerning the creation of an anti-Medici government, as we can see in his Prediche sopra Aggeo *and other works, as well as in the document we have included here. Savonarola's prophecies on the central role that Florence was to assume in the renovation of the Church immediately made him the leader of a popular and influential movement. Although immense, his success was short-lived. Internal opposition and his excommunication by Pope Alexander VI in 1497 weakened Savonarola's position and eventually led to his execution on May 23, 1498.*

Written between January and March 1498, the Trattato sul governo della città di Firenze *attests to the intense political involvement that characterized the last part of the preacher's stay in Florence. Yielding to the request of the standard-bearer Giulio Salviati, Savonarola expounded his political program for the city in the three books of this treatise. It was Savonarola's belief that the institution of a popular government aimed at enforcing a truly Christian way of living among the Florentines would transform their community into the model of a blessed city, a New Jerusalem for the whole world to admire and imitate.*

The author's indebtedness to classical and medieval political thinkers—Aristotle and Aquinas in particular—is apparent throughout the treatise. Savonarola also relies heavily on the concepts and the values promoted during the fifteenth century by Florentine humanism. Although somewhat lacking in originality, Savonarola's work stands out as an important testimonial to the spread of ideals that civic humanism introduced into Italian culture through the elaboration of classical and scholastic teaching. At the same time, however, the text ushers in a new century marked by disruptive forces in the domains of religious and political thought.

Source: Girolamo Savonarola, *Trattato sul governo della città di Firenze*, ed. Luigi Firpo (Rome: Belardetti, 1965), pp. 435–487.

INTRODUCTION

Illustrious men of acute intellect and profound scholarship have dedicated numerous pages to the government of cities and states. I have always held, therefore, that writing additional books on such a topic would simply increase the number of works devoted to this subject, without offering anything new or useful. Your lordships, however, are not asking me at present to write a treatise on the means of governing a state or city in general but instead to write about the new government of the city of Florence, a task I deem appropriate to my position. Leaving all digressions and useless words aside, I intend to carry out this work with great concision, for I shall not reject a task I find extremely relevant to the city and its people as a whole, and proper to my office as well.

For many years, by God's will, I have preached in this city. All my sermons have been devoted to four themes I hold particularly dear: to proving, to the best of my ability, the truth of religion; to demonstrating that the simplicity of Christian life represents the highest form of knowledge; to predicting events, some of which have occurred, whereas others are about to take place; and finally, to discussing the new government of your city. I have written, thus far, a book on each of the first three subjects;[1] *On Prophetic Truth,* the most recent, has not yet been published. Regarding the last of these subjects, I must write a book in such a way as to demonstrate that the principles we preach are good and consistent both with natural reason and with Church doctrine. Although I have wanted and still wish to write this book in Latin, like the other three, its aim being to explain how, to what degree, and in which circumstances a clergyman should be involved in the politics of a state, I shall comply with your lordships' request to compose a brief treatise in the vernacular for the benefit of a greater number of readers, given that only men of letters understand Latin. Once free of present cares, with the help that omnipotent God will be willing to grant me, I shall put my hand to writing a book on this subject in Latin.

I shall first expound on the best form of government for the city of Florence and then will discuss the worst. It is true, ethically speaking, that one must destroy evil in order to exalt the good. Evil, however, is the loss of the good, and as such it cannot be understood if one ignores the good. I thus find it proper to discuss the best government first, then the worst. Third, I shall explain why the worst government should be abandoned in order to found, to better, to perfect, and to preserve the present good government of the city of Florence.

Drawing on Aristotle's Politics *and Aquinas'* De regimine principum, *Savonarola illustrates the necessity of government and laws for mankind (Book 1, chap. 1). He then shows how kingship—considered the best form of government in theory—is not suited to all peoples. Savonarola poses the problem that although a monarchy is the best kind of government, like that of God's power over the universe and as the rules of nature attest, the character and customs of certain societies render that form of government unsuitable for them (Book 1, chap. 2). Such is the case of the Florentines, who tolerate neither kingship nor aristocracy, being naturally led to favor the third form of rule contemplated by classical and medieval political thinkers: civil government.*

BOOK I, CHAP. 3: CIVIL GOVERNMENT IS THE MOST APPROPRIATE FOR THE CITY OF FLORENCE

There can be no doubt, if one pays close attention to what I have said, that if the Florentine people were to tolerate the rule of a single monarch, this man would be a wise, just, and good prince, not a tyrant. Once we examine the opinions and the ideas of erudite philosophers and theologians, however, we shall see that the Florentines, because of their nature, are not suited for this form of government. The rule of a prince—they argue—is fitting for people who are servile by nature, lacking in either courage or intelligence or both. A people that lacks intelligence, despite being physically strong, sanguine, and valorous in war, can easily be ruled by a prince. Owing to their weak intellect, such people are unable to plot against the prince, and they follow him as bees follow their queen, as we can see in people from the north.[2] Peoples like those of the Orient, by contrast, who possess a sharp and quick intellect but lack valor, are easily conquered and live quietly under the authority of a prince. Such a situation occurs even more frequently when a people lacks both courage and intelligence. Only a tyrant, however, can impose complete rule on intelligent, bold, and courageous peoples. By virtue of their intelligence, these people continually plot against their prince and carry out their conspiracies thanks to their audacity. The Italians are such a people, whose past and present history shows that the rule of a prince never lasts. We see that despite its small size, Italy is ruled by as many princes as there are cities, and the latter never live in peace.

Among the Italians, history demonstrates that the Florentines make best use of their resourceful intelligence and are bold in spirit. Although the Florentines may seem meek and exclusively devoted to their mercantile activities, they are incredibly bellicose when engaged in either a war with foreigners or civil war. Their chronicles of wars fought against powerful princes and tyrants, to whom they have never surrendered, show how they manage to defend themselves, fight, and win. The nature of this people is such that it cannot tolerate the rule of a prince, even if he be a good and perfect ruler. Evil citizens, often astute and courageous, and always more numerous and more ambitious than good citizens, try either to kill or to overthrow a prince. Princes, in turn, would have to become tyrants in order to defend their own authority. If we carefully consider the Florentine people, however, we shall see that their customs—which are as important as their character—make them unsuited not only for the rule of a prince but also for that of an aristocracy. Just as nature provides beings and objects with certain immutable predispositions—like a rock that falls and can only rise thanks to an external force—habits and customs can become natural inclinations.[3] Even evil customs are difficult to eradicate from individuals and from a people as a whole once they have become part of their nature.

The Florentines have been accustomed to civil government for a long time, so much so that this form of rule, besides suiting their nature better than any other, is also so deeply rooted in their spirit and their habits that it is difficult or nearly impossible to change them. Even the tyrants who have come to rule in Florence as of late have not attempted to wield their power in blatant ways. They have governed wisely, not forcing the Florentines to betray their nature and give up their traditions. These tyrants have preserved the city's institutions and offices, seeing to it, however, that only their friends obtained posts in the government. The structure of civil government has therefore remained intact; this is why trying to change or replace such a deeply rooted system would mean forcing the people into something against their nature. Such an attempt would probably cause immense confusion and dissent in the community, not to mention a complete loss of freedom, as history, the teacher of every art, has shown. Whenever power has come into the hands of [a few] distinguished Florentines, the community has immediately suffered from bitter discord, and they have not found peace until one faction has driven the other out and someone has become a tyrant. The sole ruler, then, has always outraged the Florentines by depriving them of their freedom and well-being by rousing them to discontent and restlessness. If the city of Florence was once divided and filled with internal dissension because of the ambition and the enmity of the leading citizens, it would be even more so today, were it not for the grace and mercy of God. It is thanks to Him that those who have been exiled by the rulers, especially since 1434, have returned to their home city. During these last years, moreover, many a hatred has been smoldering in the city on account of the wrongs committed by certain families. Had God not intervened, such hatred would have caused much bloodshed, the destruction of many families, and various struggles and civil wars within and outside the city walls. The events that recently took place upon the arrival of the king of France should have signaled the ruin of Florence to any intelligent person who witnessed them. The council and the civil government—established by God and not by men—have been the instruments of divine will by which the city through the words of its noble citizens, both men and women, has managed to defend and preserve its freedom. Considering the dangers Florence has encountered in the last three years, there is no one who would deem it to be governed and protected by anyone other than God Himself, except for one whose sins have made him lose his common sense entirely.

We can therefore conclude that because of divine will, from which the present civil government derives, and because of the reasons mentioned above, civil government is the best type of rule for Florence, although in and of itself, it is not the best type of rule. A solitary rule, a monarchy, is the most perfect form of rule, yet it is not ideal for the Florentine people. Likewise, although monastic life represents spiritual perfection, it is not the best form of living, and sometimes not even good at all, for many Christians. For this people, other ways of life are more appropriate, despite the fact that these other lifestyles might not be exemplary in and of themselves.

We have thus illustrated our first point, namely, which form of government is best for Florence. Now it is time to explicate the second point: what the worst form of government is for this city.

Savonarola proceeds to discuss how tyranny, which disregards the common good, is necessarily the worst form of government. Furthermore, the rule of a tyrant is particularly horrible in that it is the most difficult to overthrow. Given the numerous factions that could be created among citizens, tyranny, Savonarola argues, is most easily established within a community ruled by a civil type of government. As a consequence, the enactment of strict laws aimed at protecting a city from tyranny is fundamental to the life of every republic (Book 2, chap. 2).

Many topics in this treatise that portray the tyrant as the worst kind of ruler reveal Savonarola's debt to well-known classical and medieval sources. It is worth noting, however, that fifteenth-century Florentine historiography and political literature offer very important models of the evils of tyranny as well. Chapter 2, for instance, entitled, "On the Iniquity and the Vicious Qualities of a Tyrant," is filled with subtle allusions to the means—especially forms of patronage—adopted by the Medici for the establishment and preservation of their regime.

BOOK 2, CHAP. 3: ON THE GOODS OF A CITY HAMPERED
BY A TYRANT; ON TYRANNY, HARMFUL TO ALL CITIES,
ESPECIALLY TO FLORENCE

Considering the matter as Christians, if the rule of a tyrant is the worst form of government for all cities and provinces, I believe this to be particularly true in the case of Florence. All Christian governments must aim toward the blessedness promised us by Christ, given that it is not possible to attain blessedness without good Christian conduct, which is the best way of life, as we have noted elsewhere. Christians must establish their governments, both local and universal, so that their rulers are examples of good Christian living, which is superior to everything.[4] Since it is genuine piety that nourishes and fosters a Christian way of life, Christians must constantly strive to maintain, preserve, and increase their devotion, which consists not so much of superficial ceremonies, but of sincere and profound faith, as well as of good, holy, and learned clergymen—both ecclesiastics and monks. As the saints teach, no one is worse than an evil religious man, nor more harmful to true devotion, more detached from Christian living, and more injurious to any noble government. It is better to have a few good ministers than many evil ones, for the latter provoke the wrath of God against the city. As God is the origin of all good governments, evil men make Him withdraw His hand from the city; they provoke Him to deny His grace to a good government on account of the gravity and number of their sins, through which they attract many citizens and persecute the good and the just. If you read and reread the Old and New Testaments, you will find that all the persecutions of the just derive mainly from such men, and that it is because of their sins that scourges from God have struck mankind. You will also find that these evil religious men have always damaged any good government by corrupting the minds of kings, princes, and other officers.

We must therefore make sure that life in Florence follows a just rule, and that the city will be inhabited by good citizens, especially by good clergymen. Every government necessarily becomes perfect whenever piety grows and citizens increase their observance of Christianity. This happens, first of all, because God and His angels take particular care of the city. As we have often read in the Old Testament, when religion was respected and widespread, the kingdom of the Jews flourished accordingly; we read similar things in the New Testament, and about Constantine the Great, Theodosius, and other devout princes as well.

Second, a government becomes perfect thanks to the continual recitation of prayers by those appointed to religious orders, by the good citizens, and by the common prayers of a people as a whole during solemn celebrations. We read in the New Testament that it is precisely because of prayer that God has spared cities terrible dangers and given them innumerable gifts, both spiritual and material.

Third, a government becomes perfect as a result of rulers' wise decisions, which preserve kingdoms and lead to their expansion; for whenever the citizens are good, they are enlightened by God. As it is written, "Exortum est in tenebris lumen rectis corde"—that is, in the darkness of the trouble of this world, the righteous of heart is enlightened by God.[5]

Fourth, it is on account of civic unity that God graces a city, for whenever people live according to Christian law, there can be no hatred, as the very roots of hatred are removed: pride, ambition, avarice, and lechery. Moreover, wherever there is unity, there is strength. This is why, in the past, we saw small yet strongly united kingdoms become large; whereas other great kingdoms have collapsed owing to internal struggles.

Fifth, God is pleased when Christians revere justice and good laws. As

Solomon said, "Iustitia firmatur solium," justice strengthens power.[6] A kingdom in which Christian commandments are followed can increase its wealth, for the rules, which encourage frugality, could facilitate the accumulation of an immense fortune in the public revenue with which to pay soldiers and officers, maintain the poor, and fight enemies. Upon hearing about the good government of the city, furthermore, merchants and other rich men would visit it, while its neighboring peoples, being ill governed, would wish for that same type of administration. By virtue of the existing harmony and the benevolence of their allies, the city would need few soldiers; the representatives of every art, science, and virtue would be enticed to gather there; and the kingdom would gain immense treasure and territory. This would serve not only the city but the peoples of other cities as well, since they, too, would be well governed: religious observance would spread, and faith and Christian good would grow—all owing to the great glory of God and our Savior Jesus Christ, King of Kings, Lord of Lords.[7]

The rule of a tyrant, by contrast, prevents and ruins all this, for there is nothing a tyrant despises more than the worship of Christ and Christian goodwill, as they are opposed to him, and opposite drives out opposite. That is why the tyrant puts all his efforts, although covertly, into driving the true worship of Christ out of the city. If he finds any good bishop, priest, or monk, especially one who is not afraid of speaking the truth, he cautiously tries either to expel him from the city or to corrupt him with flattery and gifts. He grants benefits to bad priests, to his own ministers, and to his accomplices, favoring bad clergymen and those who flatter him. He always tries to corrupt the youth and every form of honesty within the city, as they are profoundly contrary to his nature. If this is a great, even a supreme evil in any city or kingdom, it happens to be even more so in Christian communities, especially, I believe, in Florence. The Florentines are particularly inclined to respect religion, as anyone familiar with them knows. It would be very easy, thus, in the presence of good rulers, to establish in this city a perfect expression of religiosity and enforce the most sublime principles of Christian living. There is no doubt, as we can see day after day, that, were it not for bad priests and monks, Florence would follow the way of life of the first Christians and it would be a model of piety for the whole world. Even today we see so many good Florentine citizens among the numerous good Christians being persecuted, amid impediments to Christianity both from within and outside the city, and counted among the excommunicated and those of false beliefs. May what I am about to say not offend other cities. It is impossible to name, as it does not exist, any other city in which a greater number of examples and a greater perfection of Christian life can be found than in Florence. If, therefore, amid so many persecutions and impediments Florence continues to grow and thrive by the Word of God, what would it be like if, once freed from the harmful presence of bad priests, monks, and citizens devoid of genuine religiosity, Florentines lived in Christian peace?

This further confirms the sharp intellects of its inhabitants. Everyone knows that the Florentines possess subtle minds, and we know full well what a terrible thing it would be if such minds turned to evil, especially if they did so from childhood, as their souls would then be less likely to heal and more inclined to spread sin on earth. If, conversely, they were to love one another, it would be more difficult to lead them into evil, and they would be able then to propagate and spread the good. It is therefore necessary to establish a good government in Florence with great care and allow no tyrant to exist, since we know how much harm tyranny has caused this and other cities. The numerous stratagems of tyrants have often deceived Italian princes and instigated hostility not only between neighboring cities but also between distant ones. The richer and more industrious a city, the easier it is for a tyrant to incite such hostility, which explains why tyranny has often thrown Italy into confusion.

This opinion is strengthened by the fact that tyranny cannot endure, since, as mentioned earlier, a violent ruler cannot be eternal and God permits tyranny only in order to punish and expiate the sins of a people.[8] Once these are purged, it is proper for such a government to come to an end, for once the cause has been removed, the effect must go as well. Thus, if tyranny cannot be of long duration in other cities and kingdoms, then it certainly cannot endure peacefully in Florence, as the great minds of its people would not stand for it. History has repeatedly shown that popular rebellions against rulers, or civil wars, are followed by rebellions all over Italy, thus causing many a serious evil.

For all these reasons, and for others that I omit for the sake of brevity, it appears clear that if tyranny should be removed from every city, and if it would be better to suffer any other defective rule than that of a tyrant—which causes the greatest and most numerous evils—then this is particularly true in the case of Florence. He who has properly understood the considerations of this discussion will readily perceive that there is no penalty or scourge in this world of such magnitude as the sin of one who tries, attempts, or simply desires to become a tyrant in Florence. Any conceivable punishment of the present day is inadequate to respond to such a sin; but omnipotent God, who is a just judge, will know how to punish him properly, both in this life and in the next.

*Tyranny, Savonarola argues in the first chapter of Book 3, rests upon the unjust granting of privileges and offices. In order to prevent tyranny, it is thus necessary to keep any private citizen from acquiring such authority and using it as he will. Savonarola holds that the main means of thwarting tyrannical aims is the institution of a great public council (*Consiglio Grande*), which will allow citizens to participate in the government of the city and in the election of officials. He also outlines three steps that he believes this nascent system should take immediately after its founding. First, it should impose strict laws aimed at strengthening the Great Council; second, it should severely punish any corrupt members; third, it should ensure that excessive and intricate bureaucracy will not prevent officials from accomplishing their tasks.*

In the following chapter, Savonarola offers a few more suggestions for perfecting the Florentine civil government. "Above all," he writes, "it is of fundamental importance to believe that God has ordained both the council and the government," as shown, among other things, by the divine assistance Florence has enjoyed in the last years. Savonarola preaches that the citizens should then strive to master the following virtues: fear of God, love of the common good of their city, social harmony, and justice. If, however, they do not practice these virtues and perfect their civil government, God will punish them in this life and in the next with terrible wrath, as we have already seen.

BOOK 3, CHAP. 3: ON THE HAPPINESS OF GOOD RULERS
AND THE MISERY OF TYRANTS AND THEIR FOLLOWERS

Since the present government belongs more to God than to man, citizens that follow the advice I have given and strive to perfect it with all their might and zeal for the glory of God will attain earthly, spiritual, and eternal happiness. First of all, they will be free from servitude to a tyrant (a wretched condition, as has been shown) and live in true freedom, a good more precious than gold and silver. They will be safe in their city, devoting themselves with joy and tranquillity to the management of their households and farms, and to honest earning. When God increases their profits or their honors, they will not have to be afraid of losing them. They will be free to go to the countryside or wherever they wish without having to ask the tyrant for permission. They will be free to marry off their sons and daughters as they like, celebrate weddings, enjoy leisure time, choose their friends, study the sciences and arts as they wish, and other such things—all of which will provide a secure earthly happiness.

Spiritual happiness will then follow, for nothing will prevent each and every citizen from living as a good Christian. Threats will not hinder officials from exercising justice, for everyone will be free; poverty will not force anyone to accept dishonest work, as the city, being well governed, will abound in wealth. There will be employment for all, and the poor will be able to work to support their offspring honestly. Good laws will protect the honor of women and children. Above all, religion will flourish, for God, seeing the good intentions of the people, will send them good shepherds; as the Scriptures say, "God gives shepherds to suit the people."[9] Nothing will prevent these shepherds from putting their flock out to graze, and simultaneously the number of good priests and good monks will increase, especially since bad men will not find shelter in a city of good men. Religious observance will expand so much that the city will become a paradise on earth, its citizens always rejoicing and singing psalms. Children will resemble angels and will be taught to live as both good Christians and good citizens. A government more heavenly than earthly in nature will finally be established. The joy of the good citizens will be so great that their happiness in this world will approach that of spiritual beatitude.

Then, third, citizens will not only obtain eternal happiness, but in many cases they will also increase their merits and their consequential rewards in heaven, for God grants the highest tribute to the man who rules a city well. Beatitude is, in fact, the reward of virtue, for the greater a man's virtue and more he exercises it, the greater is his reward. Since it is a greater virtue to rule oneself and others as well, especially a community or a kingdom, than simply to rule oneself alone, it follows that he who rules a community deserves the highest tribute in eternal life. As we can observe in any activity, the master receives a greater reward than the servants who follow his commands. In the army, for instance, the captain's spoils are greater than those of the soldiers; in building, the architect and the master mason receive a greater reward than the laborers. The same happens in other fields. Likewise, man's good actions honor God, and the more useful he is to those around him, the greater his merit. Thus, to govern a community well, especially one like Florence, is an accomplishment worthy of the highest praise—it pays respect to God, and by virtue of its being most useful to body, soul, and material profit, it certainly deserves the highest rewards and supreme glory. As we know, God greatly compensates one who gives alms or food. Our Savior says that on the Day of Judgment he will turn to the just and say, "Come, blessed by the Father, take possession of the kingdom prepared for you from the beginning of the world; for when I was hungry and thirsty, and when I was naked and wandering, you fed me, dressed me, and gave me shelter, and you came to visit me when I was sick. What you have done to my little ones, you have done to me."[10] If God's reward for giving alms is great, what kind of tribute will he grant the good ruler of a city who offers support to an immense number of poor and outcast, protects widows and their children, saves from the hands of powerful and wicked men those who would otherwise be victims of violence, frees the country from thieves and murderers, assists the good, preserves Christian living and religion, and provides innumerable other benefits? As like loves like, the greater the resemblance between things, the greater the love between them. All creatures are loved by God, as they are similar to Him. God, though, loves even more those who bear a greater resemblance to Him. Since he who rules a city resembles God more than his subjects do, it naturally follows that if a ruler governs justly, God will love him more than during the time when he is not governing. As he who governs is more exposed to risk and is subjected to greater toils—both physical and intellectual—than those who do not govern, it follows that he deserves an even greater reward from God.

In contrast, he who aims to be a tyrant is unhappy in this life, as spiritual afflictions and constant worries—especially the high expenses necessary to maintain his position—all keep him from enjoying his possessions. His constant desire to conquer and subdue the masses leads him to be oppressed by them, as he must attentively serve those whose benevolence he hopes to win. What is more, he lacks friends, the greatest and sweetest gift a man can enjoy in this life, as he does not tolerate anyone as his equal, oppresses everyone, and is especially hated for his evil deeds. If other wicked men show him affection, it is not out of love for him but is rooted in the hope of obtaining something from him. Under such conditions, of course, true friendship cannot exist. The hatred and the envy he inspires on account of his evil actions prevent him from attaining either fame or honor. He never feels genuine consolation without toil, because he must always think about his enemies and fear them. He thus lives in constant anxiety, distrusting even his own guards. He also suffers spiritual unhappiness because he is deprived of the grace of God and of all knowledge of Him, and because, as we have previously mentioned, he is surrounded by sin and foul men who follow him everywhere and lead him into further wicked deeds. Finally, he is also subject to eternal suffering, for tyrants are almost always incorrigible. The sins he commits are so many in number and have so stained his soul that he can hardly restrain himself from continuing to commit them. Furthermore, to return all the goods he has extorted and pay the cost of the damages he has caused would reduce him to beggary, an extremely difficult condition to accept, indeed, for such an arrogant man used to the pleasures of life. He would also be thwarted by his flatterers, who mitigate his sins by persuading him that evil is good, and by lukewarm priests who confess and absolve him, thereby convincing him that his actions are, in fact, not evil at all.[11] He is thus miserable in this world, and lives in Hell in the next—there his punishment is greater than that of other men, owing both to his own sins and to those he has led people surrounding him to commit, as well as on account of the power he has unjustly seized. As the righteous ruler receives supreme tribute, the unjust ruler is subject to extreme punishment.

All who follow a tyrant suffer the same wretched fate in this life as in the next. They lose their freedom, which is the greatest of treasures, and lose their material goods as well. Their honor, their children, and their wives become the tyrant's property. To please him and resemble him as much as possible, they imitate his sins. In Hell, therefore, they will share in his severe punishment.

Similarly, all citizens who are not satisfied with civil government, although they themselves are not tyrants, experience the same misery. They lack wealth, honor, reputation, and friendship, for good men flee their company, and only wretched, evil men hoping to better their condition will associate with them, ultimately emptying them of their riches. They do not have true friends, for these "leeches" intend only to rob them. These evil companions lead them into a thousand sins which they would not otherwise commit. They are restless, constantly agitated by hatred, envy, and slander. They live in Hell in this world and in the next.

As we have shown, the good ruler is happy and similar to God; the bad one, on the contrary, is unhappy and like the devil. Every citizen should thus avoid sin, disregard his private goals, and strive to be a good ruler in order to maintain, increase, and perfect this republic for the honor of God and for the salvation of the soul. God gave Florence this government because of the particular love He feels for this city, rendering it happy in this world and in the next, by the grace of our Savior Jesus Christ, King of Kings, Lord of Lords, who with the Father and the Holy Spirit lives and rules *in saecula saeculorum*. Amen. God be praised.

---

1. The three works are: *De simplicitate Christianae vitae* (started in November 1494), *Triumphus Crucis* (1496), and *De veritate prophetica* (1497).
2. For Savonarola's thoughts on people from the north, see Aquinas' *De regimine principum*, 4.1.
3. On habit as a second nature, see *De regimine principum*, 3.22.
4. This consideration is also drawn from *De regimine principum*, 1.14–15.
5. Psalms 112:4.

6. Proverbs 16:12.

7. Revelation 19:6.

8. The same concept is to be found in *De regimine principum*, 1.6.

9. Jeremy 3:15.

10. Matthew 25:34–36.

11. Most likely a polemical reference to the Franciscans. The word "lukewarm" is probably a reference to Revelation 3:16, "I know your deeds, that you are neither cold nor hot. I wish you were either one or the other! So, because you are lukewarm—neither hot nor cold—I am about to spit you out of my mouth."

42

An Epistle to the *Fanciulli*

PIERO BERNARDO

An unlettered layman whose early life is unknown, Piero Bernardo (1475–1502), also known as Piero Bernardino, or Piero dei Fanciulli ("of the children"), was a goldsmith by profession. As one of the most fervent supporters of the Savonarolan movement, by 1496 Bernardo acquired a position of eminence in the Florentine confraternities, which had recently been reorganized under the influence of Savonarola. More specifically, he was entrusted with the important task of preaching to the members of not just one, but three confraternities. This appointment and the esteem he soon earned enabled him to deliver an unusually large number of sermons despite his youth and lay status.

As a close disciple of the Savonarolan Fra Domenico da Pescia, Bernardo conferred with his master after having a vision in which he was singled out by God to lead the fanciulli—*children from about six to fifteen years of age—whom Savonarola had appointed to purge Florence of vice. Bernardo thus assumed this privileged position within the movement, which he was to keep until his death at Mirandola, in the castle of Giovan Francesco Pico, where he had found shelter with his fanciulli from the persecution that followed Savonarola's death. Charged with heresy and sodomy, as was routine whenever a religious man was persecuted, Bernardo was captured in August 1502 and burned at the stake after a summary trial.*

Bernardo upheld moral strictness and violently denounced secular thought; he was among the most influential spokesmen of the radical wing of the Savonarolan movement. Taking Jesus' statement in Matthew 18:3 literally ("Unless you change and become like little children, you will never enter the Kingdom of Heaven"), Bernardo believed that only the fanciulli were endowed with the innocence necessary to comprehend God's plans and carry them out. Unlike Savonarola and Domenico da Pescia, therefore, Bernardo held that only Florentine children, not the adults, could bring the city salvation.

In the epistle he addressed to the fanciulli soon after having been officially appointed their leader, Bernardo expresses Savonarola's main precepts, at times even inserting citations verbatim from Savonarola's works. As the latter prophesied, God has chosen Florence to be the center from which the religious and political renewal of the world would spring. In a militant tone, Bernardo warns his fanciulli against the dangers they will face while performing their crucial task and provides them with a series of rules that, if followed, will bring to all righteous Florentines both worldly joy and eternal bliss.

Source: "Epistola di Bernardino de' fanciulli della città di Firenze mandata a epsi fanciulli el dì di sancto Barnaba apostolo adì XI di giugno MCCCCLXXXXVII," Florence: Bartolomeo de' Libri, 1500(?), Biblioteca Nazionale Centrale, Florence, Sav. 21.

LETTER BY BERNARDINO DE' FANCIULLI TO THE
FANCIULLI ON THE DAY OF ST. BARNABAS THE APOSTLE,
JUNE 11, 1497

My beloved *fanciulli,* Jesus Christ, Our Savior, told his disciples in advance that he would be tortured and flogged, and that he would suffer an ignominious death on the cross. He also predicted that on the third day he would rise again from the dead. When the time of his passion came, his disciples abandoned Our Lord because, as it is written, "The shepherd will be beaten and the sheep will be scattered."[1] Only the holy women remained, and John, the beloved disciple. When the time of resurrection came, all the disciples were together in one place; they started doubting and saying to one another, "He said that on the third day he would rise again from the dead, but it did not happen." They kept doubting, but they should not have, for, since he had suffered all the tribulations he had predicted, they should have firmly believed that his resurrection would also have taken place just as he had said. He appeared to them and rebuked them for their lack of faith and hardness of heart. He then appeared to them again, and said, "Peace be with you!"[2] Since they did not believe their eyes, our loving Jesus said, "It is I, do not be afraid. Touch me and see; I am your Lord, alive and real. You think that I am a ghost, but here are my bones and flesh; ghosts have neither flesh nor bones,"[3] by which he implied, "See, this is I, your Lord, who have predicted all these things."

Likewise, God Almighty has predicted that all Italy, even Rome, will be turned upside down and that the Church will grow and be renewed,[4] and that the Turks, the Moors, and all other infidels will be converted. Everyone will see this, as well as the other things He has predicted—namely, that the city of Florence will become richer, more powerful, and more glorious than ever before.[5] Among all the Italian cities, God has chosen it as His own, placing there the true lamp that will shed light over all Italy and the entire world, for this is God's will and He is the king of our city. Although He is the king of the whole universe, nevertheless He is especially the king of Florence, which He has chosen as His city since it is the heart of Italy, just like the heart that gives life to all the other organs. And He predicted all these things, many years ago, so that the knowledge of them could spread everywhere.[6] So far all of His predictions have taken place, one after the other, exactly as He said they would.

Since these tribulations have come to pass, we must believe that joy, too, will come, for God is more inclined to mercy than to stern justice. Therefore, my dear fanciulli, persevere in your good way of living, for God is about to come to Italy with His ministers. We are now suffering these just tribulations, but God will make our city rise again, since, as the saying goes, in the midst of adversity, virtue is perfected. Let our adversaries do as they wish, for despite their actions, these things will come to pass, because this fire is too strong to be quenched; it has extended to all lands and sects, including that of St. Francis,[7] and therefore it cannot be quenched. Fanciulli, remember that we shall win no matter what. Many say that we do not know what is being prepared against us. I reply that they do not know what is being prepared against them in heaven. We shall win no matter what. Look at Christ's triumph, consider how all seemed to be lost when He was nailed to the cross and only few believed in Him; the Virgin Mary alone kept perfect faith. On the third day, though, so great a glory came that soon it spread over the entire world. The same will happen now, for God wants to show that everything happens according to His will alone.

Remember what I told you on All Saints' Day, November 1, 1496, when we were gathered at San Marco. After reading some passages from Revelation, we started having a lively discussion, and I told you that some things were known to you, the rest, however, to God and to His angels.[8] I also told you that we would have to fight against the lukewarm,[9] against twice as much knowledge, power, and malice, and against the harm that the lukewarm do today, for they know evil and want to do harm. Things were different in Christ's time, for back then people knew only the Old Testament, and when they did something wrong, they did not realize they had done so.[10] This is what I replied to your objections, and this is the reason I now tell you, fanciulli, that if Christ came back into this world to proclaim the truth, he would be crucified yet again.[11] I tell you, fanciulli, that hardly anything has been revealed so far, for if all were revealed, the entire world would be overcome by wonder. Pray that the Lord turns the key, for if he does, the whole world will realize it.[12]

The epistle mentions other discussions that Bernardo has had with the fanciulli during the previous year. It also narrates some of the actions performed by the fanciulli in Florence, such as processions, bonfires of the vanities, and other measures designed to fight vice. Bernardo then briefly touches on Savonarola's prophecies concerning the future of Italy, before going on to expound the decalogue the fanciulli must follow to reach moral perfection. He then speaks of the rewards that God will grant the fanciulli in heaven.

My Florentine fanciulli, who could ever separate us from Christ's love? No one, no matter who he may be. Since the doors of Hell are open, heaven, too, is open for those God has chosen. We shall see who is more powerful, the angels or the devils. Fanciulli, I invite you to the espousal, to the feast, for after all the tribulations we have already suffered and after the ones that are still to come, there will be roses and flowers. The more tribulations we suffer in this world, the more rewards Christ will give us in heaven. Prepare yourself, therefore, not only now and for St. John's Day, but also for Assumption Day in mid-August, as it is written, "He who abandons God's way will go astray."[13] It is also written that our virtues must grow and that we shall see God in the radiant church.[14]

Repent and confess your sins as you have been told, and be close to God; nobody will separate you from Him. "Who could separate us from the love of Christ? Could trouble, hardship, famine, nakedness, danger, persecution, or sword? As it is written, 'For your sake we face death all / Day long; / We are like sheep to be / Slaughtered.' No, all these things we overcome through Him who loves us. For I am convinced that neither death nor life, neither angels nor principalities nor virtues, neither the present nor the future, nor fortitude, height, depth, nor anything else in all creation, will be able to separate us from the love of God that is in Christ our Lord."[15]

Pray that God will help me observe the things I am writing to you, so that one day we may all be together in that triumphal glory to dance and praise Jesus Christ our king, who is the glory of the blessed and the eternal light. He lives and reigns with the Father and the Holy Ghost forever and ever, one single and almighty God. Amen. Nothing happens in this world without a reason.[16]

1. As he does often throughout the epistle, Bernardo does not quote verbatim from the Bible but paraphrases. For the present passage see Matthew 26:31 and Mark 14:27.

2. John 20:19 and Luke 24:36.

3. A paraphrase of Luke 24:37–39.

4. Almost a literal quotation from Savonarola's famous sermon *Ecce Gladius Domini*. See Girolamo Savonarola, *Prediche sopra i Salmi,* ed. Vincenzo Romano (Rome: Belardetti, 1969), p. 42, lines 21–22.

5. This is precisely what Savonarola predicted, verbatim, in his *Prediche sopra Aggeo,* ed. Luigi Firpo (Rome: Belardetti, 1965), p. 166.

6. This simile and the passage immediately following it are taken from Savonarola's *Compendio di rivelazione.* See Girolamo Savonarola, *"Compendio di rivelazione," testo volgare e latino e "Dialogus de veritate prophetica,"* ed. Angela Crucitti (Rome: Belardetti, 1974), p. 8, lines 23–28: "Since Florence lies at the center of Italy, just as the heart does inside the body, God chose this city and predicted that such things would spread throughout the world. This is exactly what we see taking place now."

7. For the polemic between the Savonarolan movement and the Franciscan order, see Savonarola's essay.

8. This passage is also a near-literal quotation from Savonarola's sermon *Ecce gladius Dei;* see *Prediche sopra i Salmi,* p. 60, lines 1–12.

9. Like Savonarola, Bernardo draws on Revelation 3:16 in using the word "lukewarm."

10. See Savonarola, *Prediche sopra i Salmi,* p. 60, lines 12–21.

11. This last statement is also drawn from Savonarola's *Ecce gladius Dei;* see *Prediche sopra i Salmi,* p. 60, lines 21–23.

12. See Savonarola, *Prediche sopra l'Esodo,* ed. Pier Giorgio Ricci (Rome: Belardetti, 1955), *Predica 1,* vol. 1, p. 30, lines 15–19, "Listen closely to my words: you hope that the key will be turned, but if this happens, all your secrets that are now locked up will be revealed. Therefore, be careful what you do."

13. Proverbs 19:16.

14. A reference to Revelation 21:1–4.

15. Romans 8:35–39 (with a few variations).

16. Job 5:6.

43

Two Poems on Spiritual Renewal

GIROLAMO BENIVIENI

Well-versed in both Greek and Hebrew, a self-taught musician and a scholar of Dante, Girolamo Benivieni (1453–1542) distinguished himself as a gifted poet, eliciting the attention of Lorenzo de' Medici's group of scholars. Already in his early twenties, he started to frequent the Medicean circle and demonstrate his poetic talent. His compositions followed the prevailing models of the time, especially those of Lorenzo and Poliziano, whose influence, together with that of the bucolic poets of antiquity, is clearly discernible in Benivieni's eclogues.

A turning point in Benivieni's life came in 1479, when he met Giovanni Pico della Mirandola in Florence. The close friendship that Benivieni developed with the count of Mirandola inspired him to abandon his role as a court poet and to devote himself entirely to studying Neoplatonism and producing philosophical poems. The Canzona dell'amor celeste e divino, *commented on by Pico himself, is a good example of his work at this time.*

This mystical strain in Benivieni was strengthened by the influence of Savonarola beginning in the late 1480s. Benivieni went so far as to repudiate his previous compositions as too worldly and soon became one of the most passionate followers of the spiritual renewal promoted in Florence at the time. Benivieni became in effect the official translator of Savonarola's texts, and in 1496 he translated Savonarola's treatise De simplicitate Christianae vitae *into the vernacular and the* Epistola dell'umiltà *from the vernacular into Latin.*

Savonarola's tragic downfall did not break Benivieni's fervent spirit, although events forced him to limit his open support of the Piagnoni ("Wailers"), the faction most faithful to the Dominican friar. This, however, did not stop Benivieni from publishing a commentary on his own Savonarolan works, two poems of which we include here. Always adhering to the rigid tenets of Savonarola's teaching, Benivieni devoted the last years of his life to revising and publishing his writing. He tried in vain to convince Duke Alessandro de' Medici to erect a mausoleum for Pico della Mirandola in San Marco, but he was granted his wish to have his own body buried next to his friend's in the Dominican church where the great philosopher lay.

Some of Benivieni's most interesting works, like the two poems translated here into prose, date from the final years of Savonarola's life. The first is a canzone composed for the procession of the fanciulli on Palm Sunday 1496, which Benivieni himself sang in the cathedral of Florence. The second was written for a bonfire of vanities during Lent on February 7, 1497. Both poems attempt to express the destiny of the Florentine people according to Savonarola's visions: that Florence, "the city of God," "the new Jerusalem," would become the capital of a moral cleansing that would dramatically affect the entire world. Since Benivieni commented on his own poems, we include a number of his explanatory notes (though not all of them) to help elucidate passages that may be unclear or particularly important. Benivieni himself reports having slightly altered the second poem after Savonarola's execution, to emphasize the prophet's saintliness. Benivieni's notes are those beginning with a phrase in italics.

Source: Girolamo Benivieni, *Commento sopra a più sue canzoni et sonetti dello amore et della bellezza divina* (Florence: Tubini, 1500), fols. 111v–114v and 117v–120v.

CANZONE ON THE BLISS PROMISED TO THE CITY OF FLORENCE COMPOSED AND SUNG FOR PALM SUNDAY IN THE YEAR 1496 OF OUR SALVATION

Long live Florence in our hearts, long live Florence, long live Christ your king, and long live the spouse, His daughter, and mother,[1] who is queen and guide, for it is thanks to their bounty and clemency that the day is nearing in which this city shall be made richer, more powerful, and more glorious than ever before. Such a promise or inestimable gift can never be in vain, since it is not a human tongue that utters it, but divine bounty.

O city more fortunate than all others, you are certainly more fortunate than anyone would believe, and perhaps even more than you yourself could think or hope. Although those who do not know you may deem that all honors and virtue in you are dead, there still lives in you that glorious seed within which all our hope is rightly rooted. From it, the fruit will spring, O sweet Jesus, that true gift and nourishment that you will lavish on the whole world.

You certainly can, my dear Florence, in the midst of your torments, expect salvation more than any other city rejoicing in its festivities and rich pomp.[2] Since you alone are built on sacred mountains and endowed with holy doors,[3] love your Lord more than all others! About you alone are said great and glorious things, the like of which no one has ever heard before.

Do you not know that when you were selected for such an honor, your great and holy mother uttered these words in heaven,[4] "O Florence, city which God, my son, and I love most, keep your faith, devotion, and patience alive and strong, for in them lies the power to make you forever blessed by God in heaven and always honored on earth among all cities, like the sun among the stars."

Arise, O new Jerusalem, and look; behold your glory. Pray to and worship your queen and her beloved son. In you, city of God, now prostrate and weeping, such great joy and splendor will come to adorn you and the entire world. In the days of bliss you will see devout and pious people flocking to you from every land, attracted by the scent of the holy lily.

Your sweet lily will stretch its petals beyond the borders of your reign, overshadowing your ungrateful neighbors. He who shall submit to you is blessed by God,[5] and he is damned who holds in contempt your good, your glory, and your peace. Deferring to your king's will, wait for the rending of the veil;[6] amid great stupor, all your glory will then finally shine forth.

Canzone, amid so many doubts, I do not know whether it is better and more profitable for you to speak and show yourself in public or to keep silent. If you do not reveal the gifts from God,[7] you will be deemed ungrateful; if you speak and sing, however, you, these gifts, and I shall all be mocked. Therefore, either remain inside my heart and enjoy only your own company, or, if you choose to leave, appear only in those places where people who see with our eyes can be found.[8]

A CANZONE WRITTEN TO URGE PEOPLE TO PREPARE
THEMSELVES FOR THE BLISS PROMISED TO THE
CITY OF FLORENCE

Come, here is the Lord, King of Kings,[9] arriving to see how His city is faring. Come, it is now finally time, O Florence, to open the doors of your heart.[10]

Come and worship the glory of the One who rules us from the heavens and makes our flock the most blessed, since such a shepherd tends it. Because of Him it is clear that we shall fall prey to no one.[11]

In front of Him appear two beautiful ladies; one is Piety, the other Justice. With these two sisters, who tightly embrace each other in an inseparable bond, are Peace and Bliss.[12] Holy and almighty glorious Virgin, mother, daughter, and spouse of your Son;[13] guide and queen, you make the air around you shine and angels celebrate your arrival.

Arise, O new city,[14] and as an adorned spouse, meet with your Lord who is about to arrive; show Him that you are ready to enjoy the glory and the beauty that you have been promised.[15] You alone, if you wish, can gird that sword with which you shall open the path to your immortal, divine king, receiving with Him, at last, the fruit of all your hopes.

Open, O Florence, your weakened eyes, and realize that in you alone lies your good and your glory. Love, hope, act, and believe. Fortitude and patience are what can make your memory eternal and give you a rapid victory against your enemies. The good that God will lavish on you, still so young,[16] could render your fathers blessed as well, for such a precious and great gift is not bestowed according to age.[17]

Canzone, your path must be as straight as if you were before the king who rules us all, whose holy name, honor, and divine prophet[18] are mocked by many—they hold in the greatest contempt His true and eternal judgment, as well as His laws. It is now time that all people be rewarded as they deserve, so that unbelievers may see that He is God, and atone for their errors.[19]

1. See St. Bernard's invocation to the Virgin Mary in Dante, *Par.*, 33.1–39.

2. See Revelation 17:16–17: "Woe! Woe, O great city, / Dressed in fine linen, purple and scarlet, / And glittering with gold, precious stones, and pearls! / In one hour such great wealth has been brought to ruin!"

3. "*On sacred mountains:* that is, on your blessed souls. *Endowed with holy doors*—that is, the souls of your blessed citizens, through which doors, O Florence, will descend your glory and your future happiness."

4. "*O Florence,* etc.: these are the precise words that the glorious Virgin spoke to this servant and true prophet of God, and that he reported in Latin in his *Compendio di rivelazione* exactly as he had heard them, 'Florentia Deo Domino Iesu Christo filio meo et mihi dilecta, tene fidem, insta orationibus, roborare sapientia; his enim et sempiternam salutem apud Deum et apud homines gloriam consequeris.'" See Girolamo Savonarola, *"Compendio di rivelazione," testo volgare e latino e "Dialogus de veritate prophetica,"* ed. Angela Crucitti (Rome: Belardetti, 1974), p. 110, lines 23–27.

5. "*Who shall submit to you:* whoever, of his own will, shall put himself under your most just rule, which, by then, will be entirely in God's hands."

6. "*The rending of the veil:* that is, all public and private vices and defects that now cover you, O Florence, as a thick and most filthy veil. They keep you from taking the path that leads to your future joys, and, at the same time, they hide such joys from you, making it impossible for you to see them."

7. "*The gifts from God:* that is, God's promises to this city and the bliss it has already been granted."

8. "*With our eyes:* that is, with the light of the faith."

9. Revelation 19:16.

10. "*The doors of your heart:* that is, the souls of the blessed and, more precisely, their intellect and will, for it is thanks to these two powers and virtues that, as through two doors, God comes to dwell in the soul."

11. "*We shall fall prey to no one:* this can be understood in a spiritual sense—that is, referring to Satan—or in a political sense, referring to some secular prince or lord. It is obvious that had it not been for God's hand, both would have brought the city of Florence to a wretched state."

12. For this image, Benivieni refers the reader to Psalms 85:10, "Love and faithfulness meet together; righteousness and peace kiss each other."

13. Again, a passage reminiscent of Dante, *Par.,* 33.1.

14. "*New city:* because God chose her as His favorite; He has, so to speak, rebuilt her by providing her with a new manner of living and a new way of ruling and governing."

15. See Revelation 21:2, "I saw the Holy City, the new Jerusalem, coming down out of heaven from God, prepared as a bride beautifully dressed for her husband."

16. This refers to Savonarola's *fanciulli,* whereas the "fathers" of the following line are the adult citizens, as Benivieni specifies in his commentary.

17. Unlike Piero Bernardo, Benivieni held that adult citizens could also receive God's bliss, provided they followed Savonarola's teachings.

18. Savonarola.

19. "*Unbelievers:* that is, all those who have not only disregarded the things said and predicted by this prophet as false but have also sneered at them and used them to sentence this servant of God to death."

44

The Rise and Fall of the Self-Made Prophet
Girolamo Savonarola

LUCA LANDUCCI

The most intense pages of Landucci's diary are those devoted to Savonarola and his fanciulli. In vivid and concise prose describing the main events of the Dominican friar's second stay in Florence, he first celebrates Savonarola, then expresses deep sadness at the preacher's public disavowal of his prophetic virtues. Landucci had initially welcomed the great success of the Savonarolan movement in Florence, but after its leader was excommunicated in 1497, he stopped attending the friar's sermons, though the memoirs reveal that his faith in the Dominican friar survived. Imbued with both the humanist ideals of liberty and the numerous prophecies which, throughout the quattrocento, had foretold the universal cleansing that Florence was to carry out, Landucci saw Savonarola's preaching and the acts of the fanciulli as the eagerly awaited fulfillment of such predictions. Nevertheless, like many of his fellow citizens, Landucci had to admit that his dream of seeing Florence become the new Jerusalem had finally been shattered by the tragic fate of the Dominican friar and the persecution of his followers that ensued.

Source: Luca Landucci, *Diario fiorentino dal 1450 al 1516 continuato da un anonimo fino al 1542*, ed. Iodoco del Badia (Florence: Sansoni, 1883), pp. 108–109, 123–126, 128–129, 136–137, 162–163, 172–173, 176–178.

On June 17 [1495] Fra Girolamo spoke with King Charles VIII of France at Poggibonsi.[1] People said it was thanks to him that the king had not come to

Florence. They said that the friar had urged the king to act for the sake of Florence, and had told him that God wanted him to take care of Florence, and that the whole city was on his side. They said that the friar had helped Florence and that the king had taken his advice. At that time the Florentines held the friar in such high esteem and such veneration that many men and women would have thrown themselves into the fire if he had ordered them to do so. He claimed to be a prophet, and many people believed him. . . .

On June 20 [1495] Fra Girolamo met the king again, and on the 21st he delivered a sermon in which he spoke about his dialogue with the king, reporting how the king had promised much that was good. He said that if the king did not keep his promises, he would suffer great harm and God would deprive him of his office; he would no longer be God's minister and would lose the thing he held most dear. This is what he solemnly revealed to all those present at his sermon, some thirteen or fourteen thousand people, saying that things would happen exactly as he had predicted. He also said that he had predicted things that were going to happen to the king. . . .

On February 7, 1496, the fanciulli took a veil off the head of a young woman in Via Martelli—an act which caused her relatives to protest violently. The fanciulli did that because they had been urged by Fra Girolamo to correct people who were not wearing decent clothes, or who were gamblers. When someone said, "Here come the Friar's fanciulli," every gambler, no matter how good a person he might have been, took to flight, and women behaved in the most upright manner. The fanciulli gained such respect that everyone kept away from dishonest things, and especially from the unnameable vice. In that holy time neither youths nor old people could have been heard speaking about it. But it did not last long. The wicked have proved more powerful than the good. Praise be to the Lord for having granted me the opportunity to live in that brief holy period. I pray that God will once again provide that righteous way of living. The things that happened back then prove that it was a blessed period in the history of Florence—one should meditate carefully on this fact.

On February 16, 1496, carnival started. A few days before, Fra Girolamo told the fanciulli to stop playing foolish games such as throwing stones and using firecrackers and that they should go about the city, instead, to beg and collect money for the needy. Through God's will, a change took place, and for many days the fanciulli went begging. At each street corner you could find them holding a crucifix in their pure little hands. And so it happened that during carnival the fanciulli gathered after vespers. They were divided into four groups, according to their city district. Each district displayed its banner;

the first one had a crucifix, the second an image of Our Lady, and so on. The communal trumpeters and pipers were also there, together with the guards and the city officials. While walking in procession, they all sang lauds and shouted, "Long live Christ and the Virgin Mary, our Queen!" All the fanciulli held olive branches, and this sight touched the hearts of the wise and righteous people to the point of tears: they said to one another, "Such a great and unusual thing must certainly be the work of God. These children are the ones who will enjoy the good he has promised." It was like seeing the throngs of people who gathered around Jesus in Jerusalem on Palm Sunday saying, "Blessed are you who come in the name of the Lord."[2] One can fittingly quote those words from the Bible, "From the lips of children and infants you have ordained praise."[3] There were about six thousand fanciulli or more, all of them between five or six and sixteen years of age. All the districts gathered near the Servite friars, at the loggia of the Spedale degli Innocenti, and in the piazza. From there they began the procession, first passing in front of the Church of the Annunziata and then proceeding toward San Marco. They took the typical processional route: passing by Ponte Santa Trinita before arriving in the Piazza [della Signoria]. Once they reached Santa Maria del Fiore, they gave offerings before a large crowd of men and women; the men were placed on one side, the women on the other. The ceremony was carried out with such great devotion that many were moved to tears. Indeed, nothing like this had ever been seen before. They said that the offerings amounted to many thousands of florins. There were some basins in which one could see the offerings made: gold florins, silver florins, and silver coins. Some had given veils, silver spoons, handkerchiefs, shawls, and other things. People gave selflessly. It looked as if everyone wanted to give all he or she possessed, especially the women; as if everyone wanted to make offerings to Christ and to His mother. What I am saying here is true—I witnessed these things and experienced great sweetness. Even some of my sons were in those pure and blessed groups of children.

On February 17, the first day of Lent, a large crowd of fanciulli came to Fra Girolamo's sermon in Santa Maria del Fiore. A stand for the fanciulli was placed by the wall, opposite the pulpit, just behind the section occupied by the women. Some fanciulli found places among the women. Before the sermon started, all the fanciulli who were on the stand sang sweet lauds. Then the canons began to chant the litanies, and the fanciulli responded. It was such a sweet melody that many openly let fall tears, especially the virtuous people who kept saying, "This is the work of God." The fanciulli sang every morning throughout Lent before the friar's arrival in church. Another wonder must be noted—namely, that each morning it was impossible to keep the children in bed, and they all rushed to the sermon before their mothers. . . .

On March 27, 1496, Palm Sunday, Fra Girolamo had all the fanciulli walk in procession holding olive branches in their hands and with one placed in their hair; many also carried a red cross, a span or so high. People said there must have been five thousand fanciulli or more; many little girls were also there. Behind them walked the authorities of the Florentine government and the city district officials; then all the citizens of Florence, men first and then women. No one had ever seen such a great procession; I imagine that no one, man or woman, missed this opportunity to give offerings. Generous offerings to the *Monte di pietà* were laid on an altar inside Santa Maria del Fiore. In front of the procession someone carried a tabernacle with a depiction of Christ riding the donkey upon His entrance to Jerusalem on Palm Sunday. A baldachin was held above it and the procession went through the entire city while everybody kept shouting, "Long live Christ our king." . . . .

On April 17, 1496 Fra Girolamo preached in Prato, in the Church of San Marco, and a large crowd of people poured in from both Florence and the countryside. He predicted that, after the tribulations, there would be great bliss. . . .

On the 15th [of August, 1496] Fra Girolamo preached at Santa Maria del Fiore. Because of the large crowd of people, one of the stands that had been erected for the fanciulli, which was by the door facing the baptistery, collapsed. No one was hurt, and this was considered a miracle. One must realize that there were four stands, two by the wall opposite the pulpit, one in the section occupied by the men, and one in the middle of the church, where the women stood. Because the number of the fanciulli had augmented, it had become necessary to build those stands. There was great devotion in that church, and it was marvelous to listen to those children singing. They gathered throughout the church and sang with such piety and so well that it was hard to believe that they were only children. I went there myself, many times, witnessing these children and experiencing the great spiritual sweetness. Indeed, the church was filled with angels. . . .

On February 25, 1498, Fra Girolamo preached in Santa Maria del Fiore. He kept saying that his excommunication was not valid and, as such, it should be disregarded. We should note that all his sermons have been transcribed and organized by a young notary named Ser Lorenzo Violi.[4] By documenting everything Fra Girolamo has said while at the pulpit, gathering all his epistles, and everything else he has preached and prophesied in these last years, Ser

Lorenzo has proved to be, as it were, superhuman. It is a wonder that he has done all this, and the fact that he has been able to write down every single word exactly as it has been uttered, without making any mistakes, must be regarded as a miracle, for it seems an impossible task. It was accomplished, no doubt, by divine will for the good, and it is regarded as such by righteous men.

During carnival on February 27, countless vanities, such as naked images, chessboards, heretical books, *Morganti*,[5] mirrors, and many other costly, futile objects said to be worth thousands of florins were heaped up in the Piazza della Signoria. The fanciulli did just as they had done for the procession: they held olive branches and crosses and were divided into four groups according to their city district, each district displaying tabernacles. After dinner, they burned the heap of objects. Although some of the lukewarm tried to waylay them and do other despicable things, they nevertheless succeeded in setting fire to the heap, and saw to it that everything was burned. It must be noted that the wooden frame had not been made by the fanciulli; it consisted of precious objects and of a wooden square more than twelve braccia long on each side, which had taken carpenters a numbers of days' work. It was thus necessary to have armed men guard it at night, for some of the lukewarm, certain youngsters called *Compagnacci*, wanted to damage it.

It is well known that the friar's followers so venerated him that on that morning, although it was carnival, Fra Girolamo celebrated Mass at San Marco and personally administered Holy Communion to all his friars and many thousands of men and women. He then walked with the Eucharist up to a pulpit near the church door and proceeded to walk outside with it, holding the Eucharist up in his hands for all to see, while he gave the crowd his blessing and recited prayers such as, "Save your people, O Lord,"[6] and the like. A large crowd had gathered, believing that they would see signs from God. The lukewarm mocked all this and sneered at it, saying, "He has been excommunicated and yet 'communicates' others." Although I believed in him, I, too, thought this was not right. At any rate, because he was excommunicated, I preferred not to risk being a party to his sermons any more. . . .

On April 10, 1498, at 5:30 P.M., Fra Girolamo Savonarola, together with Fra Domenico [da Pescia], was taken to the Bargello.[7] He had to be carried because the handcuffs and the fetters around his ankles kept him from being able to walk. They gave him three strappadoes; four, however, to Fra Domenico. Fra Girolamo then said, "Put me down so that I can write about my life for all of you." Imagine how the good people who wanted to lead a righteous life and believed in him reacted when they heard about the strappadoes he had suffered. They could not keep themselves from weeping, for he had taught them this prayer, "Do good to those who are good and to those who are upright in heart."[8] They could not keep themselves from bursting into tears, and prayed to God with all their might.

On April 19, 1498, in the great hall of the government palace, Fra Girolamo's confession, which he had written in his own hand, was read before the city council. We had thought he was a prophet, but instead, he confessed to not being a prophet and to never having received from God the things he had said in his sermons. He also confessed that many of the things that had taken place since he first started his prophecies had proved to be just the opposite of what he wanted the people to believe. I happened to hear the reading of this confession and was utterly surprised, quite astonished, indeed. I grieved at seeing such a great dream fall apart simply because it had been foolishly founded on a single lie.[9] I expected Florence to become a new Jerusalem, out of which the laws, the glory, and the example of a righteous life would spring, and I was longing to see the renovation of the Church, the conversion of the infidels, and the good granted their rewards. I experienced, instead, the exact opposite, and I was taught a lesson. "You work out everything, O Lord, in conformity with the purpose of your will."[10] . . . .

On May 23, 1498, a Wednesday morning, the execution of these three friars took place. They led them from the Palazzo [della Signoria] and had them walk on a platform that had been placed near the ringhiera. The Otto [di guardia] and the collegi were there,[11] as well as the papal legate,[12] the general,[13] canons, priests, and monks of various sects, and Bishop Paganotti,[14] who had been entrusted with the task of demoting the three friars. The entire ceremony was held on the ringhiera. The friars were divested of all their paraments while the various formulae proper to the ceremony were pronounced. Throughout the entire procedure, while their heads and hands were being shaved, as is typical of the demotion ceremony, it was claimed by people that Fra Girolamo was being condemned to the stake because he was a heretic and a schismatic. The demotion completed, they handed the friars over to the Otto, who immediately ordered that they be hanged and burned. They were thus taken to the cross at the end of the platform. The first one to be hanged from one of the arms of the cross was Fra Silvestro [Maruffi]. Since the rope did not choke him, it took a while before he passed away; one could hear him repeating, "O Jesus," while hanging from the cross. The second to be hanged was Fra Domenico [da Pescia], who also continually repeated, "O Jesus." The third was the friar who had been called a heretic, who did not speak in a loud voice, but softly, and that is how he was hanged. None of them addressed the crowd, and this was regarded as a very surprising thing, especially since everyone expected to see signs from God and thought that on such an occasion the friar would somehow reveal the truth. This is what was expected, especially by the righteous people, who were eagerly awaiting God's glory, the beginning of a virtuous life, the renovation of the Church, and the conversion of the infidels. They were disappointed, therefore, that neither Savonarola nor the other two made any sort of speech. As a consequence, many lost their faith.

Once all three of them had been hanged with their faces turned to the Palazzo della Signoria with Fra Girolamo in the center, the platform was finally moved away from the ringhiera, and a fire was prepared under the circular end of the platform. They placed gunpowder under it and then set it aflame. The heap burned amid a great noise of crackling and explosions. Within a few hours their bodies were completely burned, and their arms and legs fell off bit by bit. Since part of their torsos had remained attached to the chains, people threw stones to make them fall down. Being afraid that some might try to take pieces of the corpses,[15] the executioner and those in charge of the ceremony pulled the cross down to the ground and burned it with a great quantity of wood. They set fire to the corpses and saw to it that none of their remains were left. They then sent for some carts to have each speck of dust brought to the Arno. The guards escorted them to Ponte Vecchio, and from there they dumped the ashes into the river, causing every last trace to disappear. Nonetheless, a number of the faithful attempted to gather the coals floating on the water. Those who did so, however, acted in secret and with fear. No one, in fact, could either mention what had happened or speak about it without risking his life, as Savonarola's enemies wanted to extinguish all memory of the friar.

1. A village in the Florentine countryside.
2. See Matthew 21:9 and John 12:13, "Blessed is he who comes in the name of the Lord!"
3. Psalms 8:2.
4. On Violi, see the studies indicated under Landucci in the "Religion" section of the bibliography.
5. Popular chivalric books, like *Morgante* by Luigi Pulci.
6. Psalms 28:9.
7. The police headquarters.
8. Psalms 125:4.
9. Savonarola's alleged prophetic virtues.

10. Ephesians 1:11.
11. For the Eight and the Collegi, see Dati's description of the Florentine officials.
12. The Spaniard Francesco Romolino.
13. Gioacchino Turriani, Dominican general.
14. Benedetto Paganotti, bishop of Vaison and vicar of the archbishop of Florence.
15. To use them as miracle-working relics.

PART SIX

Florence Through Foreigners' Eyes

45

Metropolite Isidore's Journey
to the Council of Florence

Metropolite Isidore of Kiev left Moscow on September 8, 1437, for Ferrara to attend the council for the union of the two churches. His retinue consisted of more than a hundred people, including important Russian ecclesiastics and a considerable number of assistants. The council had been moved from Ferrara because Pope Eugenius IV needed financial support to accommodate the Byzantine and Russian ecclesiastics, and the Medici offered to provide him what he needed.

The text that follows, originally in Old Church Slavonic, is our only source of information on its anonymous author, who was a part of Metropolite Isidore's retinue. He reveals neither his assignment nor his office, but various elements lead us to believe that he was a layman. Although what he says about the council sessions in Ferrara and Florence is quite detailed, other things appealed to him much more than the debates. In Ferrara, for instance, he became fascinated with a clock tower at the papal palace. Each hour, he wrote, an angel comes out of the tower and strikes a bell, and everyone in the city can see him and hear the pealing of the bell.

Though our anonymous author was impressed by Ferrara, Florence was the city he admired most, as he himself writes in the excerpt translated here. He was particularly struck by the efficiency and cleanliness of the Spedale di Santa Maria Nuova, the first public hospital in Europe, founded in the late thirteenth century. He was also taken with the marble churches of Florence and its thriving mercantile activities.

Source: "Peregrinatio metropolitae Isidori ad Florentinum concilium," in *Acta Slavica Concilii Florentini,* ed. Jan Krajcar (Rome: Pontificium Institutum Orientalium Studiorum, 1976), pp. 25–32.

Pope Eugenius IV left Ferrara for Florence on January 16, whereas Patriarch Joseph left by boat on January 26, for the River Po was calm that day. The Russian metropolite left the next day. Ferrara and Argenta are twenty-five miles apart—seven from Argenta to Bastia, and seven from Bastia to Conselice. There we landed and continued our trip on horseback: seven miles from Conselice to Lugo, ten from Lugo to Faenza, twenty-eight from there to Marradi, and thirteen from Marradi to Borgo San Lorenzo, through which the Sieve River flows, crossed by a stone bridge. It is a pleasant town, located in a valley and surrounded by countless olive trees. Between Borgo San Lorenzo and the magnificent city of Florence there are fifteen miles; the landscape has towering, rocky mountains, and the path is extremely narrow and difficult—the wagons could not continue the trip, and we had to use mules. On these mountains, however, they produce an excellent sweet red wine.

On February 4, we reached the glorious city of Florence. Both the patriarch and the emperor arrived there on February 17. Florence is huge, and it is unlike any of the other large cities I have described so far. It has beautiful, spacious churches and high marble palaces built with great skill. An impressive and swift-flowing river called the Arno divides the city in half; it is spanned by a large bridge upon which houses have been built.[1]

There is a large hospital in Florence that is attached to a church with more than a thousand beds.[2] Each and every bed is supplied with a firm mattress and expensive sheets. For love of Christ, all these things are set up to help travelers and people from other cities or foreign countries who happen to fall sick while they are in the city. They are then taken care of, washed, and provided with food, clothes, and shoes. Those who recover their health give thanks to the city and leave praising God. In the space between the beds an altar has been built, and every day a priest leads Mass.

There is also a solid, well-built monastery of marble. It has an iron gate at the entrance and its church is dazzling.[3] There are forty chapels in the monastery, numerous relics of saints, and many paraments adorned with gold and all sorts of precious stones. Forty monks live there and never leave; laymen are strictly forbidden to visit them. One of their occupations is to sew paraments with gold and silk threads. We visited this monastery with the Bishop Abraham[4] and were able to see all these things for ourselves. The tombs of the monks who died there are within the walls of the monastery. They exhume the bones of the dead monks and place them in an ossuary to remind those who see them of their own imminent death.

Among Florentine products are damask fabric and velvet painted with gold. There is an abundance of all types of goods, including olives and olive oil. In one of the city churches there is also a magnificent painting of the Virgin Mary, in front of which are some six thousand wax statuettes recalling those who have been healed.[5] If a person has been wounded by an arrow or happens to be blind, lame, or without hands, or if a noble arrives in this city on horseback, he is depicted there in such a way as to seem alive. In these statuettes you will find each person's appearance faithfully depicted, no matter if this person be an aged or a young man, a married woman, a little girl, or a child. Every detail is included: how the person was dressed, from what disease he suffered, how he was healed, or how he was wounded.

Another thing Florence produces is scarlet textiles. We also saw trees: cedars and cypresses. The cedar is similar to the Russian pine tree. The bark of the cypress is somewhat like that of the linden, but to the touch the leaves seem more like those of the fir, although they are small, curly, and soft; its berries resemble those of the pine tree.

The cathedral of Florence is large and built of black and white marble. Right next to this church there is a bell tower made of the same white marble. We were struck by this magnificent piece of architecture. We climbed the stairs of the tower to the very top and counted 450 steps. We saw twenty-two markets in the city, and its circuit of walls is six miles long. . . . [6]

Demetrius, the emperor's brother, left the council and departed from Florence for Constantinople on May 25. On July 5 the Solemn Session was celebrated.[7] The volume containing the decisions of the council on the Holy Trinity once prepared, both Pope Eugenius IV and the Byzantine emperor John signed it, followed by all the cardinals and the metropolites.

In Florence we also had the opportunity to see silkworms and learn how silk is made.

On July 6, Pope Eugenius IV celebrated Mass and administered Holy Communion in the cathedral dedicated to the Virgin Mother. There were twelve cardinals and ninety-three bishops with him, apart from the priests and the deacons. The Byzantine emperor John was seated in the place that had been prepared for him, and from which he and the members of his court could see the celebration of the rite. The metropolites, wearing their paraments, were assigned seats. The same happened with the other clerics attending Mass: archimandrites, archivists of the patriarch, priests, deacons, and monks, all of whom were dressed according to their status. Byzantine and Russian laymen were also present. The tiers of seats were high enough to afford a view of the crowd below. The crowd was so large that many people would certainly have been crushed to death if they had been allowed to enter the church. Papal officers wearing coats of mail walked back and forth with clubs in their hands, preventing people from going inside. To keep the crowd from getting any closer, other officers holding lighted twisted candelabra blocked them.

When the Mass was over, the pope and his canons started to sing the Kyrie Eleison, after which the pope sat in the middle of the church on a raised golden throne that had been specifically prepared for him. Then they brought in the movable pulpit, which the Latin and the Byzantine representatives, Cardinal Julian [Cesarini] and the metropolite Bessarion of Nicaea, mounted, with the text containing the decrees of the council. Julian read the Latin document aloud, then the metropolite read the Byzantine one. The pope then gave his blessing to all those present. Then the papal clerics started to sing in praise of the pope, and the imperial clerics in praise of the emperor, until finally all the Latins and the whole crowd started to sing and ask the Byzantines to give them their blessing.

The emperor left the council and Florence on August 26. He was seen off with great fanfare by the cardinals, the bishops, and all the Florentines, to the sound of trumpets and flutes. Twelve men held an open canopy above him, while the two principal officers of the city government led his horse. On September 4, the pope celebrated Mass in the baptistery,[8] after which cardinals, archbishops, and bishops were elected. Isidore and twelve Byzantine metropolites dressed in their liturgical vestments were seated, while the pope, wearing the pontificals, presided over the ceremony from a golden throne. A bishop named Andrew[9] ascended the pulpit to read the bull in which the pope excommunicated the members of the Council of Basel in Switzerland for having first joined the papal council and then created their own synod, refusing to obey him. On the same day, the pope gave Isidore and Bishop Abraham his blessing for the Russian people. On September 6 we left Florence to start our journey back to Russia.

1. He is referring to the Ponte Vecchio, which even today is lined with houses and goldsmiths' workshops.

2. This is the Arcispedale di Santa Maria Nuova in the center of Florence, close to the cathedral. The author exaggerates the number of beds; in the fifteenth century the hospital disposed of about 150 beds for men and 80 for women. In some cases two patients occupied one bed, but the total number of patients would not have exceeded three to four hundred.

3. The Camaldolite monastery of Santa Maria degli Angeli.

4. Bishop Abraham of Suzdal.

5. In the Church of SS. Annunziata there is a panel of the Virgin which is said to have been miraculously painted by an angel. For more on this legend and a description of the votive offerings (the number of which our anonymous author exaggerates), see Albertini's guide.

6. Omitted here is a list of the sessions held in Florence between February 26 and May 2, 1439 (sessions 16–25).

7. This was the session in which the union of the two churches took place.

8. It was actually celebrated in Santa Maria Novella.

9. Andrew Chrysoberges, a Byzantine Dominican scholar, was the archbishop of Rhodes at the time of the Florentine council.

46

The Heir to Roman Justice

STEFANO PORCARI

We possess only scanty information on Stefano Porcari, the descendant of a noble Roman family. He served as capitano del popolo in Florence in 1427–1428, before undertaking a series of trips and missions to France and Germany. Both his friendship with Eugenius IV and his fame as an orator helped him to obtain the office of podestà in Bologna (1432), Siena (1434), and Ancona (1435). The best known episode of Porcari's life is the antipapal rebellion through which (not unlike Cola di Rienzo with his coup in the mid-fourteenth century) he tried in vain to overthrow Pope Nicholas V and establish a republic modeled on that of classical Rome. Porcari and his followers believed that Roman dignity and authority had been annihilated by the domination of the pope and the venality of his court. The conspiracy was immediately discovered; Porcari was arrested and executed on January 9, 1453. Leon Battista Alberti left a vivid account of this aborted revolution in his Commentarius de coniuractione Porcaria.*

Porcari's admiration for the political system of the Florentine state characterizes many of his orations, starting with the one he delivered on the day of his appointment as capitano del popolo—the first of the two documents we include here. According to Porcari, Florence is the Italian standard-bearer of republican liberty, whose ideals it received from its Roman founding fathers and has continued to defend down through the centuries. In Porcari's eyes, the organization of the Florentine government and the righteous conduct of this city are a true model for all Italy.

Source: Stefano Porcari, *Orazione fatta in sulla ringhiera de' priori la mattina che i nuovi signori presono l'ufficio,* in *Prose del giovane Buonaccorso da Montemagno,* ed. Giovan Battista Giuliari (Bologna: Romagnoli, 1874), pp. 1–11; and *Risposta ad un altro protesto fatto per la signoria di Firenze ai rettori ed officiali fiorentini,* ibid., pp. 95–101.

ORATION DELIVERED UPON APPOINTMENT
AS CAPITANO DEL POPOLO

O glorious and most magnificent lords, when I am in the presence of your very distinguished and generous persons or reflect upon the noble nature of this most flourishing republic, the lavish display of your fortunate people, the piety with which the crowd attends the solemn ceremony of this most holy day, and finally all the riches and the wealth of this city, I am seized with astonishment at such numerous and unusual marvels. If I were to give a proper description of all these extraordinary things in an elegant speech, it would be much easier to commence it than to conclude it. Thinking of your renowned deeds reminds me of the splendor of ancient Rome's liberty; Rome, my homeland. A particular thought, however, prevails over all other considerations: if the laws and the virtues of this city of yours could be compared to the glories of ancient Rome, they, too, would certainly be judged wondrous and outstanding.

What can I say about the exceptional intellects of your brilliant citizens? Not only do they devote themselves to their affairs at home, to the growth, the defense, and the protection of their republic, but even when abroad they excel in their education and habits. What can I possibly say about the constant and tranquil freedom you enjoy? Whenever you have been attacked by powerful dukes, mighty kings, and fierce armies, you have not only managed to avenge yourselves with unique military intelligence and genius, but have also succeeded, through great deeds and valiant forces, in making your enemies' territory the scene of the very assaults and devastation that they had employed against you. How can I describe the admirable piety you display in holy and sacred ceremonies, something so magnificent that no other nation can compare itself to you? What can I say about the pomp accompanying all the sessions of your government, or the particular modesty and dignity of your experienced officials? What about the splendid wealth of your noble citizens, or the magnificence of your churches and your private and public buildings? What can I say, finally, about all the beauties and marvels of this most flourishing country of yours and all the exceptional wonders adorning your illustrious city? They are so numerous and so great that not only would my humble intellect not suffice, but all the eloquence and fluency of the great classical orators would not even succeed in approximating [the truth].

If, therefore, I am not praising this city sufficiently, especially considering the importance of this solemn day and the distinction and nobility which this excellent city justly requires, I entreat your lordships to ascribe it not to the weakness of my intellect but to your own magnificence and unparalleled worth. For your own sake, for that of your children and your future generations, I can only urge your wise minds to preserve zealously this marvelous wealth that God's benevolence has bestowed upon you. You can do so by following two fundamental teachings that the ancient philosophers discussed. First, you must strive with great diligence and persistence to maintain this holy society of yours free from all civil dissension and struggle. Second, justice must be at the foundation of your power, for without justice nothing made by man can endure. The great damage and ruin that civil struggles have caused cities can be seen not only in the recent ills of Italy, but in the misfortunes suffered in ancient times by all foreign peoples and nations. The prosperity of an empire has never been so great, nor the cohesiveness of a country sufficiently dependable and secure, to prevent it from being ruined and disrupted by civil wars. We can find many examples in ancient history, but I shall mention only one of them, which, when it comes to mind, causes me great sadness.

Widespread civil struggles brought about the agony and ruin of Rome, whose people had previously enjoyed a prosperity unparalleled even today. The Romans had vanquished all the nations of the world, fought victoriously on every sea and in every land, remained undefeated by any foreign enemy until they were finally annihilated by their own force when they began to point their weapons at one another. Their resulting downfall was so miserable that many a vile enemy then came to invade and defeat Rome, whose very name once frightened all men alike.

I shall not mention the recent ills of Italy since they are apparent to all. You know that in our age many noble and powerful Italian cities have been miserably ruined owing to civil discord. If you are fond of the beauty and the sweetness of your liberty, if the safety of your tranquil city pleases you, if you hold dear the probity of your sons and the honor of your maidens, then, by God, support your republic with all your might, and strive to secure peace and harmony among your citizens. There is no firmer foundation for a city, nor stronger army and defense, than citizens who love one another and live in concord. O blessed and fortunate city, heaven has presented you with these qualities so that you may protect and defend yourself. Since the fruit of love and harmony is so great and, by contrast, the harm caused by civil struggles and dissent is so tremendous, I urge and entreat your wise minds to secure and maintain your republic with the utmost care, love, and loyalty. This state of yours is a unique marvel and a splendid mirror for our age; even more, it is like an abode and a refuge of peace, a holy temple of tranquillity, and a sanctuary of liberty. Realize, therefore, that external dangers can cause you only little harm, provided that internal dissent does not weaken you. This is the fundamental principle a republic must follow to secure itself; it is the basic rule of all civic life to which our ancestors have always conformed and have taught us. Without such law and order, not only human affairs, but even divine works lack joy, tranquillity, and safety.

Having considered, magnificent lords, the initial foundation of the republic, we must now briefly discuss the second step that the Ancients followed to secure civic life. This second fundamental principle concerns the great good of justice, whose divine virtue so benefits human society that we can rightly call it the basis of our ever-changing life. Try to imagine a city that lacks justice and consider all the negative effects, the harm, and the dangers that would ensue. You will then see how this entity should not be deemed a republic, but rather a wretched and deplorable state of robbery filled with every evil, sorrow, and misery conceivable. No one would be safe in such a republic, not even for a single day. The virtuous and peaceful citizen would be troubled and overrun by the haughty, the wicked, and the powerful. Forlorn and miserable widows and their innocent children would be horribly tormented by greedy and insatiable thieves. Pure and pious virgins would be torn from their distressed mothers' arms and raped. The beautifully adorned churches and the sacred altars would be profaned and looted with furious greed and inconceivable audacity. My magnificent lords, the tremendous evils that would take place in a republic lacking justice certainly exceed any possible human imagining. By contrast, wherever this holy virtue reigns, the utmost peace, tranquillity, and security are always to be found; there, all private and public spheres are safe. Such a happy land deserves to be called divine and angelic rather than earthly. I urge you to set your most worthy intellects and glorious minds to the pursuit of these virtues superior to all others—namely, civil harmony and public justice.

My magnificent lords, you cannot find virtues more useful to your country than these, nor can you attain greater and more deserved praise than by putting them into practice. These are, in fact, the two splendors of all politics—they will preserve your excellence for all eternity. Having employed these and other virtues, your magnanimous ancestors have adorned this republic with their example and the glory of their names. I need not remind you of the great prudence and care, modesty and temperance, loyalty and justice, and civil harmony with which your ancestors have governed this glorious city. Therefore, my lords, this undefeated people expects your admirable virtues to bring further glory to this flourishing[1] republic. They wish you to govern it in such a way that peace, perpetual tranquillity, unwavering justice, happiness, and safety endure.

REPLY TO AN ORATION ON JUSTICE

"Blessed is the man you discipline, O Lord, the man you teach from your law."[2] By addressing Your Excellencies with the words the prophet David uttered to God, O illustrious and most powerful lords, I am referring to him who is taught by your great prudence and is educated according to your sacred laws. Nothing could have pleased me more, in fact, than to hear what your government has just ordered of its officers, whose task it is to enforce justice by following your laws.[3]

I can rightly rejoice before so many distinguished representatives of this republic by quoting the psalmist's phrase, "How sweet are your words to my taste, sweeter than honey to my mouth! Your word is a lamp to my feet and a light for my path. I have taken an oath and affirmed it, that I will follow your righteous laws."[4] I quote this psalm in order to support my statement that the words spoken on your behalf by the most worthy standard-bearer were superb.[5] To me, your laws are like a lantern that shows my feet the way; they are a beacon to my will. I have sworn and promised myself to obey your orders and be fair with all in administering justice. I have resolved to do this from the very first day when God and nature bestowed upon me the use of intellect. My intense desire for justice, far from diminishing, has increased with age. Of all virtues, in fact, this is by far the greatest, as all laws show—not only human and divine laws, but also those of nature. Cicero, too, attests to this in the third book of his *De officiis,* where, in order to show the primacy of justice over all other virtues, he writes, "Haec enim una virtus, omnium est domina et regina virtutum," which in the vernacular is, "This alone is the sovereign mistress and queen of all virtues."[6] To the same purpose, in the fourth book of his *Ethics* Aristotle writes, "Justice is not a part of virtue, for in it all virtues are contained."[7]

The more I consider and ponder your just laws and orders, your holy ceremonies, your laudable and noble customs, the magnificent pomp adorning your distinguished assemblies, and all your other innumerable virtues, the more I am reminded of the words the Queen of Sheba said upon her visit to King Solomon, "Verus est sermo quem audivi in terra mea super sermonibus tuis et super sapientia tua. Et non credebam narrantibus mihi, donec ipsa veni, et vidi oculis meis, et probavi quod media pars mihi renuntiata non fuerat. Maior est enim sapientia tua et opera tua quam rumor quem audivi. Beati viri tui, beati servi tui et hi qui sunt coram semper te, et audiunt sapientiam tuam. Sit Dominus Deus tuus benedictus, cui complacuisti, et posuit te super thronum Israhel, eo quod dilexerit Dominus Israhel in sempiternum et constituit te regem ut faceres iudicium et iustitiam."[8] Translated into our language, this passage is as follows, "The things I heard in my own country about your words and your wisdom are true. I did not believe the reports they gave me until I finally came [here] and saw for myself, realizing that I had been told the truth only in part. Your wisdom and your deeds, in fact, are greater than I had heard. Blessed are your citizens and your servants, and those who can always enjoy your presence and benefit from listening to your wise and learned speech. Praise be to Almighty God, who has resolved to grant your city such magnificence and excellence, for He has always loved and protected it, and has chosen you as rulers to maintain justice and righteousness in this city, which is considered superior to all other Italian cities." And duly so, judging from the probity, the prudence, and the justice with which you and all the Florentines elected in the past have governed and ruled it, inspiring admiration in all the neighboring peoples and even in those abroad.

You prove to be the true sons of those illustrious ancient fathers, the Romans, who founded your glorious city—as both written sources and visual evidence attest. They bestowed upon you those virtues and customs that you have constantly fostered. This should not cause anyone to judge you less worthy, but, on the contrary, it is a reason for further praise and celebration, if one considers how glorious their empire and their kingdom were, and how great was the justice with which those noble fathers governed their republic. I know full well that you do not need to be exhorted to follow the aforementioned virtues, for I have personally witnessed that your laudable orders are obeyed and fulfilled. It is my genuine desire to follow these virtues as well, for out of intense devotion, love, and obligation I have striven to fulfill, free from all bias and with the greatest possible equity, the task to which I had been appointed by administering justice in each case. I shall continue to try to do this in the future with all my might, zeal, and perseverance.

When necessary, I shall faithfully seek your support, which has been benevolently granted me in the past. I consider myself most fortunate on account of this honorable and distinguished appointment that I have been given by your magnificent government. Keeping my hope in God's grace, in your immense liberality, and in the infinite benevolence of your generous people, I shall strive to deserve, above everything else, the love and the favor of the Florentines.

I could have delivered a much shorter speech and not bored this distinguished audience by briefly expressing my assent to the elegant discourse of your honorable podestà, but the nobility of your signoria nonetheless inspired me to say what I did. I must confess, the speech lacked the clarity befitting such refined listeners, so many notable officials, and worthy citizens; I beg you to forgive its clumsiness and consider only its sincerity. Finally, I pray to Almighty God that He preserve your just republic in supreme happiness *per infinita saecula saeculorum.*

1. A reference to the name of Florence, "the city of the flower."
2. Psalms 94:12.
3. Porcari is referring to the oath all officers had to take upon assuming office.
4. A partial quotation from Psalms 119:103–106.
5. In his inauguration speech, the standard-bearer (we have not been able to determine who it was) must have said things typical of the genre Protesti di Giustizia, such as that justice is the utmost good and that he would defend it with all his might.
6. Cic., *De off.,* 3.6.28.
7. This passage is not in the fourth book of the *Nicomachean Ethics,* but in the fifth; see Arist., *Eth. Nic.,* 5.1.15.
8. 1 Kings 10:6–9. Note that, in order to praise the Florentine signoria, Porcari does not write a literal translation of this passage, but rather changes part of its content by substituting the name of Israel with that of Florence and praising the latter as the greatest city in all Italy.

47

Bittersweet Praise of Florence

POPE PIUS II

Enea Silvio Piccolomini (1405–1464), the future Pope Pius II, was born near Siena, at Corsignano, a small village that he later transformed, after Alberti's design, into the splendid Renaissance town of Pienza. Piccolomini started a profitable career in the service of renowned ecclesiastics. Through the guidance of notable teachers such as Francesco Filelfo and his acquaintance with famous humanists such as Poggio Bracciolini, Leonardo Bruni, Antonio Panormita, and Guarino Veronese, the young ecclesiastic was introduced to the most important cultural circles of the time. In 1432 he participated in the Council of Basel (which he describes in the three books of the De gestis basileensis concilii*) as a member of the retinue of Domenico Capranica, bishop of Fermo. Later he became secretary to the antipope Felix V. It was during this period that he wrote most of his poems, of which only two collections survive,* Cinthia *and* Epigrams. *His poetics, which was grounded in a sound knowledge of the classics, won him the laurel wreath in 1442. He then entered the imperial chancellery, where he served as secretary for about a year. Here Piccolomini wrote some of his most famous works, namely the short story "Historia de duobus amantibus," the play* Chrysis, *modeled on those of Plautus, and the sardonic* De curialibus miseriis. *On April 19, 1447, Nicholas V, the first humanist pope, named him bishop of Trieste. This marked the beginning of an outstanding ecclesiastic career: Piccolomini went on to become the bishop of Siena (1450), papal legate to Bohemia, Moravia, and Austria, cardinal (1456), and finally pope (1458). During his pontificate, Pius II strove to initiate a crusade against the Turks, a project he had* *promoted with great zeal ever since his composition of* De ortu et auctoritate romani imperii *(1446). His persistent endeavors, however, did not meet with success. Paradoxically, he died in the seaport of Ancona while waiting in vain for military support from the Italian states to launch his long-projected expedition.*

Pius II's prose works are deservedly more famous than his poems. His concise style, often pervaded by a caustic sense of humor, renders his prose among the most readable in all Renaissance literature. His memoirs, which were first published in 1584 in an abridged edition, to escape censorship, provide us with an excellent example of his intense spirit and rich life. The passage we have included here is one of the last Pius II wrote. It is a description of Florence, and its wealth of detail reveals the author's great respect for this city. Florence, he agrees, is the modern capital of Tuscany, surpassing all Italian cities in prosperity, in works of art, and in the celebrity of its citizens through the ages. All this praise notwithstanding, Pius II's hostility toward the Florentines, and toward Cosimo de' Medici in particular, comes to the fore in this document. The pope's dislike of Cosimo dates back at least to the time in which the Florentine banker refused him financial support for the crusade against the Turks. Resorting to his well-known sarcasm, Pius II critiques Cosimo's rule as tyrannical. He also does not refrain from disparaging the Florentines' avarice by recounting how little money they spent to entertain him and his court during his visit to Florence in 1459.[1]

Source: Pius II, *Commentarii rerum memorabilium que temporibus suis contingerunt,* ed. Adrian van Heck (Vatican City: Biblioteca Apostolica Vaticana, 1984), pp. 149–154.

Florence, once called Fluentia after the River Arno, which flows through the middle of the city, is the current capital of Tuscany. It grew out of the ruins of Fiesole, which Totila, king of the Goths, had razed to the ground. It then gained control of Volterra, Pistoia, Arezzo, Cortona, and Pisa and managed to conquer part of the territory of Lucca. It has caused Siena great losses, although at times it has itself suffered damage from this city. Florence has been repeatedly attacked by German emperors—Henry VII camped just outside its walls and laid fierce siege to the city; he would have certainly seized it, had he not been called to Naples to fight King Robert. It was precisely on this trip that Henry VII was poisoned and died near Buonconvento. Charles IV came with his army to the gates of Florence and helped the exiled Ghibellines return to their city. Moved by the deepest of hatred, the lords of Milan repeatedly waged war on the Florentines, inflicting much damage, although they, too, suffered losses at the hands of the Florentines. Thanks to the help of the Florentines and his alliance with them, Francesco Sforza became duke of Milan. The Neapolitan kings have been at times allies, at times enemies of Florence; in certain circumstances they have even held great power in the city. Florence was for a spell ruled by the duke of Athens, whom the people later forced to flee the city. The Florentines then proclaimed their liberty, but they did not realize that just when they thought themselves finally free they had, instead, entered a much worse slavery, for they had expelled one lord only to let in many others. Florence has often been tormented by civil discord, as its most powerful citizens compete for absolute power.

Palla Strozzi, Niccolò da Uzzano, and Rodolfo Peruzzi are considered the greatest Florentines of recent times. Palla excelled in wealth, Niccolò in prudence, Rodolfo in military valor. Cosimo de' Medici opposed them and was temporarily banished after Niccolò da Uzzano was already dead. He returned to Florence during the stay of Pope Eugenius IV, who favored the Medicean faction, and while the city was in revolt, Cosimo expelled his opponents and regained his position. He had Rodolfo, Palla, and many other citizens sent into exile, from which they never returned. It is true that Rodolfo, having convinced Niccolò Piccinino to attack Florence, entered the Mugello Valley and plundered it. Eventually, however, he, too, died in exile. With a firm spirit, Palla endured his adverse fortune in Padua, where, having devoted himself to the study of philosophy until the end of his life, he died when he was almost ninety. Palla was a man who did not deserve to be banished by his fellow citizens.

Having thus eliminated his opponents, Cosimo governed the republic as he wished and amassed more money than even Croesus himself ever had. In Florence, he [Cosimo] built a palace fit for a king, restored churches, erected others, built the beautiful monastery of San Marco, whose library he filled with Greek and Latin codices, and lavishly furnished his villas. Considering these notable works, it would seem as though he had gained the respect of the citizens of Florence, but people often foster hatred for men of virtue. Some claimed that Cosimo's tyranny was not to be tolerated and strove to oppose him; some slandered him.

It was around this time that the government decided to assess the citizens' possessions. Through this procedure, which the Florentines call catasto and the Sienese *libra,* the magistrates evaluate the property of each citizen and impose a commensurate tax. Cosimo urged the government to modify the catasto, but his enemies opposed his proposal. The city called a public meeting to discuss this issue, and while [people were] assembling, armed men, who had been gathered at Cosimo's command, surrounded the piazza and made it clear that serious harm would come to those who intended to go against his wishes. The voters passed Cosimo's catasto proposal out of fear of the armed men, and of the citizens who had opposed it, some were banished, others fined. From that point on, Cosimo was never again refused anything. He became the judge of war and peace, and the ruler of the law—he was regarded not as a citizen but as the lord of the city. The government meetings were held in his house; the officials appointed to the various tasks were those he himself had chosen; he was king in all but name and retinue. This is why, Pope Pius II[2] having once asked the bishop of Orte [Niccolò Palmieri] what his opinion was regarding Florence, the bishop said that it was sad to see such a pretty young woman without a husband. Pope Pius II responded, "She lacks a husband, not a lover." By this he meant that Florence had a tyrant, not a king, in the person of Cosimo, who, like an illegitimate ruler of the city, kept the people strictly under his power. When Pius II went to Florence, Cosimo happened to be bedridden, although many believe that he pretended to be ill in order not to have to meet with the pope.

Cosimo's ancestors came to the city from the Mugello. Giovanni, his father, became a client of the Medici and took the name of that family.[3] He left a great patrimony to his sons Cosimo and Lorenzo. Cosimo succeeded in increasing the family possessions by doing business all over Europe and trading even as far away as Egypt. He was physically strong, taller than the average man, with a relaxed expression and a calm manner of speaking. His literary culture was better than most merchants', and he even knew a little Greek. He possessed great intelligence and succeeded in whatever he set his mind to. He was neither cowardly nor bold; he could easily withstand fatigue and hunger, often working through the night. He knew the events in all Italy, for many cities and lords acted on his advice. He was also well aware of what happened abroad, since he corresponded with the managers of his bank's branches around the world. Toward the end of his life, he suffered from gout, an ailment which, as he had the chance to see for himself before his death, also afflicted his sons, who succeeded him, and his grandsons. When the pope visited Florence, Cosimo was more than seventy.

At this time, Antonino the archbishop of Florence, a Dominican friar and a man deserving to be remembered, passed away. He shunned avarice and pride, utterly rejected lust, and was extremely frugal in food and drink. He did not yield to either wrath, envy, or any other passion. He excelled in the study of theology and wrote numerous books esteemed by scholars. Common people liked his preaching, although he vehemently denounced vice and succeeded in reforming the customs of both the clergy and the laity. He settled quarrels, tried to free the city from dissent, and gave the profits of the church to Christ's poor—giving nothing to his relatives and his acquaintances unless they themselves were needy. The only dishes he ever used were made out of glass or clay. He wanted the few people who were in his service to be satisfied with little and live according to the principles of philosophy. When he died, the commune paid for a solemn funeral. Nothing was found in his house except a mule and some cheap furniture. Whatever he had, he had given to the poor. All Florence rightly believed that his soul had migrated to a life of bliss. Realizing that they had been deprived of so great a father, guardian of orphans, and patron of widows, the city officials met with Pius II to ask him not to take the first candidate available to succeed Antonino, but to select a fellow citizen who could prove a worthy successor to so great a man. The pontiff praised the Florentines, for, unlike the Venetians, they did not obstinately ask for a specific prelate of their choice [to succeed the late archbishop], and he said that he would satisfy their righteous, sincere request.[4]

There have been many illustrious Florentines whose names are still known today. Dante, however, seems to have surpassed them all. In his magnificent work—in which he describes heaven, Hell, and purgatory—we can observe a nearly divine doctrine, although, as he was human, he sometimes erred. After him is Francesco Petrarch, whose equal would be hard to find if his Latin works could bear comparison with those he composed in the vernacular. I would grant Giovanni Boccaccio third place, although his writings are somewhat licentious and his style is not sufficiently refined. Then there is Coluccio [Salutati], who wrote both prose and verse befitting his time, yet uncouth for the standards of ours. The Florentine government appointed him to write official letters, and Gian Galeazzo, duke of Milan, used to say that his pen was more of a menace than the thirty troops of Florentine horsemen against which he was fighting. Salutati was a wise man and, although his prose was not elegant, he knew the rhetorical figures that stir men's minds—and most artfully resorted to them in his writings. Several years later, Leonardo [Bruni] was elected to that same post. Born in Arezzo, he was truly a gift to the city of Florence. An accomplished scholar of Greek and Latin literature, his eloquence was almost on a par with Cicero's; Bruni was praised for his numerous translations from Greek into Latin. Almost equal to him in prose, but superior in verse, was Carlo [Marsuppini], also an Aretine by birth and an honorary Florentine. Another famous figure of this city was Poggio [Bracciolini], who served for a time as papal secretary to the Roman Curia and wrote brilliant works before returning to his homeland, where he became chancellor and, soon after, surrounded by his relatives, died.

Filippo Scolari[5] is renowned among the Florentines who distinguished themselves for military prowess. He governed the kingdom of Hungary for many years, where he seemed to have more power than the king himself. Another famous name is that of Niccolò Acciaiuoli,[6] general in the Royal Sicilian army. Acciaiuoli's son[7] invaded Greece and seized Thebes and Athens, which he bequeathed to his children. The Acciaiuoli possessed these cities up to our time, when the Turkish emperor Mohammed finally conquered them. There are many other men one could recall who ennobled Florence through their wealth and glory.

Those who praise Florence mention not only its illustrious citizens, but its magnitude, surpassed only by Rome in all of Italy. They praise the thick, high circuit of walls, the cleanness of the streets and squares, which are wide and at right angles, the magnificence of the churches and the buildings, both private and public—majestic and exquisitely decorated. Of all the buildings, none is more deserving of mention than the Church of Santa Reparata, whose dome is almost as large as that of Agrippa's temple in Rome, the Pantheon. Next in importance is the palace in which the *priori* reside, and then the palace built by Cosimo. Highly admirable are also the small temple of St. John the Baptist and the church consecrated to St. Lawrence—both funded by Cosimo. People sing the praises of the bridges connecting the two sides of the city, which are separated by the Arno. They extol the large population, the elegant fashions of both men and women, the myriad stores, the farms and villas just outside the city—rich in amenities and built at no less expense than those built in the city itself—and finally, the people's intelligence, although they excel particularly at trade, an activity philosophers consider vile. The Florentines actually seem to care about money more than they should; this is why the local authorities, having collected fourteen thousand gold florins from the people to pay homage to the pope, kept the greater part for themselves and spent another part to entertain Galeazzo and his retinue.[8] They spent very little on the pontiff himself and did not organize many activities, although they brought the lions into the piazza, to have them fight with horses and other beasts, and had a tournament in which much more wine was drunk than blood spilled.

1. See Filarete's description of Pius II's visit.
2. Throughout the *Commentaries,* Pius II refers to himself in the third person.
3. This explanation of the Medici family name is false and must be interpreted as one of the many caustic remarks that Pius II directed at Cosimo.
4. Pius II is probably referring to his difference with the Venetians over the appointment of the new bishop of Padua. The Venetians, in fact, aggressively supported the election of Gregorio Correr in place of Cardinal Pietro Barbo, the candidate chosen by the pope.
5. Better known as Pippo Spano, Filippo Buondelmonti degli Scolari (1369–1426) received the title "Ispan" (count) after he freed Sigismund of Hungary from the captivity imposed by Charles III of Anjou. Spano was a general in the Hungarian army.
6. After working as a merchant in the Neapolitan branch of his father's company, Niccolò Acciaiuoli began an impressive career in the kingdom of Sicily, where he was elected seneschal in 1352. He financed the construction of the famous Carthusian monastery at Galluzzo, near Florence, where he was buried in 1365. Matteo Palmieri wrote his biography in Latin.
7. Actually Angelo's nephew, Ranieri Acciaiuoli.
8. See Galeazzo's letter (document 51).

48

A Celebration of Florentine Eloquence

LUDOVICO CARBONE

Ludovico Carbone was born in Ferrara in 1435. He is one of the most renowned pupils of Guarino Veronese, whose funeral oration he composed. The official orator of the Este court, Carbone was also a distinguished author of Latin dialogues, poems, and translations. Scholars of Italian literature usually associate his name with the Facezie, *a collection of anecdotes modeled on Bracciolini's* Liber facetiarum. *Despite the title, Carbone's* Facezie *are not particularly humorous or original. The author relies heavily on classical and humanistic sources, and leaves himself little room for creativity. Carbone demonstrates more inventive ability and greater vivacity, however, in his letters and in* De Neapolitana profectione, *a dialogue in which he describes the cities he has visited during his trip to Naples to meet Eleanore of Aragon, the future wife of Duke Ercole I, and escort her back to Ferrara. Along with the famous court poet Matteo Maria Boiardo, Carbone was a member of the retinue that left the ducal capital of Ferrara in late April 1473 with 550 horses, reaching Naples in early June after having passed through the main cities of central Italy. The Vatican library possesses the copy of the* De Neapolitana profectione *that Carbone dedicated to Frederick of Montefeltro, count of Urbino. Here, Carbone praises Florence on account of its beauty and cultural primacy, especially in the realm of eloquence. He asserts that "if God came down to earth, He would certainly speak no other language than the elegant idiom of the Florentines." His acclamation of Florence ends with the statement that if it were the seat of Ercole d'Este's power, he would gladly spend his whole life there.*

Carbone's first letter to the duke on this particular mission, which we have translated here, is a celebration of Florentine culture similar to, though shorter than, that which he offered in the De Neapolitana profectione. *Works by Florentine authors were numerous in the Este library, and rhetoric at the Ferrarese court was modeled on the orations of Salutati, Bruni, and Bracciolini. This letter by Carbone to the duke of Ferrara provides further evidence of how, in the fifteenth century, it was not only members of the Este court but Italian scholars in general who regarded Florence as a center of exceptional cultural importance.*

Source: Giulio Bertoni, *La biblioteca estense e la coltura ferrarese ai tempi del Duca Ercole I, 1471–1505* (Turin: Loescher, 1903), pp. 126–127.

Florence, May 1st, 1473

Most illustrious and excellent duke and my kind lord,

Although I have no doubt that you are already informed of the course of our journey, I think it proper to send you a brief report regarding a few matters. The Bolognese treated us with great kindness and hosted us in their most beautiful houses, decorated and adorned with many tapestries and silver, as if they all belonged to noblemen. I was unable to deliver my oration in Bologna, however, because the official appointed to preside was feeling sick—I am not sure whether he was physically sick, or whether he was mentally indisposed toward the event! I composed the following two verses in praise of the house in which I lodged, and left them there:

Long live the house of Vitali
If it shelters foreigners and welcomes guests.

The Florentines escorted us into their city with a magnificent entourage. The other day, the most prominent citizens came to meet Messer Sigismondo and take him to Mass, which was to be celebrated at Santissima Annunziata, a most devout church. Each of us, in turn, was also accompanied by someone. After Mass was over, we went to meet the government officials who were waiting for us in a lavishly decorated hall. I must confess that I had the impression of being before the Roman senate! Here I delivered my oration[1] before a large audience, who seemed pleased with my words. The Florentine signori greatly appreciated my speech, so much so that they sent a messenger to persuade me

307

to appear before them again, and give them a copy of the oration, despite my saying that I found it hard to believe that the rhetorical style of a Ferrarese could be praised by the Florentines, who are the fathers of eloquence. A member of the Florentine government, the chancellor Bartolomeo Scala, claimed to be surprised at such rhetorical ability in a Ferrarese, for my style, he thought, was similar to that of the Ancients. I certainly feel honored to have been praised by the Florentines.

You would not believe how many people there are in this city! Its population, which is greater than ever before, is said to be about 160,000. Good Lord, what a place this is, and how delightful! How ideal it is for one's studies! On my way back, I think I shall stop for a while on these pleasant hills where the Muses seem to dwell.

Before arriving in Florence, we passed through such steep and inaccessible places that one is led to believe that Nature created them to convince people to stay home rather than to travel the world.

I am sending you a copy of the oration I delivered to the Florentines so that you can judge for yourself whether their opinion about it is right or not. The mule you gave me is excellent—I have not had to dismount, even on dangerous paths. Today we shall set out for Siena.

Your most humble servant,
Ludovico Carbone

---

1. Carbone's Latin oration is transcribed in a manuscript at Florence's Biblioteca Nazionale Centrale, Magl. 7.1095, fols. 128–130, and has been edited by Lazzari. As one might expect, Carbone praises Florence for its Roman origin, its beautiful location and pleasant climate, its unyielding struggle against tyranny, and the many illustrious men who were born there. In the last part of his oration, Carbone emphasizes Ferrara's loyalty to Florence and the solid alliance that links the two cities.

49

Praise of the City Before Its Authorities

PANDOLFO COLLENUCCIO

Pandolfo Collenuccio (1444–1504), jurist, poet, and historian, is an excellent exemplar of humanist erudition. In the early 1470s, after studying law at Padua, Collenuccio returned to his native town of Pesaro to serve at the court of Giovanni Sforza. Over the next two decades he carried out important diplomatic missions and began to produce his literary works, among which is the translation of Plautus' Amphitruo *into vernacular tercets. One could justifiably assert that the staging of Collenuccio's version in Ferrara in January 1487 for the marriage of Lucrezia d'Este to Annibale Bentivoglio represented a true watershed in the history of modern theater, as it was the first time since late antiquity that this play by Plautus was performed.*

Collenuccio's diplomatic activities and culture won him the admiration of such important personalities as Angelo Poliziano and Lorenzo de' Medici. In 1490 he was asked to leave the Sforza court in Pesaro after a sixteen-month imprisonment, but Lorenzo's favor proved fundamental, as he appointed Collenuccio to the position of podestà in Florence. In his later years, Collenuccio served at the court of Ercole d'Este and carried out many important diplomatic missions on behalf of his new patron. At Ercole's request, in 1498 he began his Compendio de le istorie del Regno di Napoli, *the first attempt to offer a complete account of the history of the Neapolitan kingdom. During the same period he wrote six* Apologi—*four in Latin and two in the vernacular—which reveal his philosophical interests and sharp sense of irony. Collenuccio returned to his native town when Cesare Borgia seized Pesaro, but he was imprisoned shortly thereafter when Giovanni Sforza regained possession of the Marches. Collenuccio was executed on June 11, 1504.*

On his appointment as podestà of Florence on November 1, 1490, Collenuccio recited two poems in praise of the city where he was to serve for the next six months. Both the long poem in Latin hexameters (part of which is translated here in prose) and the vernacular canzone celebrate the Florentine love of justice. Singing of the origins of the city, its outstanding military exploits, and the fairness of its government, Collenuccio tried to impress the distinguished audience gathered in the cathedral of Santa Maria del Fiore. The second half of the poem is devoted to an encomium of Lorenzo de' Medici and Florentine piety. The final verses contain a significant reference to Plato's famous myth of the eternal rewards that await those who strive for the good of their country, a topic that, as we have seen in Matteo Palmieri's Vita civile, was not new to the culture of quattrocento Florence. Collenuccio's erudite blending of myth and history pleased the Florentines attending the ceremony, especially Lorenzo the Magnificent and the members of his circle. In a letter to Collenuccio, Poliziano congratulated him on the beautiful poem that he had recited from the pulpit of the cathedral of Florence.

Source: Pandolfo Collenuccio, "Panegyrica Silva ad Florentiae Urbis Novemviros," in *Operette morali, poesie latine e volgari,* ed. Alfredo Saviotti (Bari: Laterza, 1929), pp. 103–112.

POEM IN PRAISE OF FLORENCE RECITED
BEFORE THE CITY'S AUTHORITIES

Pure, joyful, and glorious daughter of Jove,[1] sent by the heavenly council, if you cast your pious glance upon this world, please do not maintain the indignation that you were once forced to feel, when impious and belligerent people, ignoring the beatific life, drove the gods away from the earth. Turn now to your old father, whose white temples pour forth a double flame[2] and whose laws, carved on the two tables, shine with the same gaze with which you once graced the court of the Cretan king and the borders of the Spartan general, or with the same voice with which you once spoke to the Quirites, descendants of Mars, when the frugal senate governed with scanty revenue. Entreat the Thunderer, o divine Astraea, and come speak to the Tyrrhenian princes and to this flourishing senate. Weave a poem inspired by the Muses' sacred mountain and instill it in the minds of these noble people.

Hail, beloved of the gods, hail, city greater than all prophecies, hail, supreme splendor of the land of Ausonia![3] Hail again, joyous people, whose name is known all over the world and is more blessed than any other. To remind you of your origin, my dear listeners, I shall recount the whole story again: who your forefathers were, what the reason for your name is, and what the layout of your land. Remember all this, and pay heed to my words, so that being aware of the gifts you have received from the generous gods, you may honor and preserve these truths.

There rises an enormous mountain where the great Apennine stands with his humid back and his high peaks overlooking both seas[4] from his beech-covered cliffs. Its summit, treeless, towers above Apennine himself. This steep mountain, which overlooks both the Tuscans and the Umbrians, withstands the gusts of Boreas. Its peak is covered with clouds, the first sign of an impending storm. Cotylus,[5] the shepherd, gave it his immortal name, for it was he who was turned into a mountain for having been the first of the Italic peoples to dare fight the giants' fierce rule. His fecund wife, Etruria, bore him two sons: one was given the holy name Albula,[6] the other, as a sign of calm water, the name Arno. When the oldest of the Apennine fauns,[7] their leader, who knew the destiny of many ages to come, saw the two brothers on the mountain top moving in opposite directions, he caressed his disheveled fleece in thought. Then, nodding with his pine-scented head and pointing to them, he said, "One day, this son will vanquish the Tanaïs, the Nile, and the Tagus and will rule black Indus. This other one, however, will have twelve sisters,[8] and he, more glorious than all others, will enjoy twelve honors. Fate will, it is true, grant the first extensive rule over the whole world; the second, however, will hold reins that are easier to control and will keep his conquests for a long time under a steady government."

As he finished uttering these words, he sprang up on the tips of his hoofs and hurled himself off the cliff, horned head foremost, into the midst of the Arno's sacred waters, and enlarged its bed. The first river [Tiber] went down the mountain toward the fields of Umbria and Latium; the other [Arno] was received by his mother Etruria in her sweet bosom. Immediately, the joyful band of young satyrs who lived in those woods, and groups of nymphs, led Arno over steep cliffs and through villages, until his winding course finally reached the azure arms of the Tyrrhenian Tethys[9] and merged with her. The hills of ancient Arezzo were then the first to let the river pass by, moving to the left with awe, while Fiesole moved to the right, and the walls of Pisa opened, leaving the city split ever since.

One among the Tuscan nymphs was by far superior to all others. Her mind, body, strength, and youthful, pretty face would have stunned Venus herself and made her little child turn his arrows toward his chest to be burnt by his own flames. She loved gardens, woods, fields, mountains, plants, springs, and the choir of the nymphs and bees. She also loved to tend flocks, gaze at rivers full of fish, and distance herself from crowded cities. Above all, she loved hunting and all things dear to the Muses. For hunting, she used nets, spears, snares, horns, hounds, and traps; she engaged in the Muses' arts by reciting poems, by playing the crotala, the lyre, and the reed pipe, and by dancing. They say she was the daughter of Mars and of the nymph Ianthe.[10] Her father gave Arno, her tutor, the task of finding a name that would be an imperishable sign of her virtue and her beauty. In order to know what her destiny would be, what the gods would bestow upon her, and to receive propitious omens for her name, all the rural gods were summoned. Old Ombrone, swift Bisenzio, ancient Mugnone (that brook unsuited to pastoral songs), and the neighboring oreads gathered in the sacred valley.[11] Pan, too, arrived, and then Mars, Venus, and Mercury. They took the nymph by the hand and chose a name for her with auspicious portents. Having done this, snub-nosed Pan spoke: "Born of a flourishing mother, your name will be Florence. Mars, your father, will bestow upon you weapons, armies, courage, and the ability to rule over cities and rebels. No nation will ever manage to control you and deprive you of your liberty. Your mother, on the other hand, born of Aeneas' stock, will bestow upon your flourishing offspring peace, beauty, a tranquil life, pleasant woods, fine fields, and, more than in any other age, acute intellect and eloquence. Mercury will present you with trade and with arts that will be admired by many distant nations."

This, they say, was Pan's prophecy. When he had concluded his prognostication, the gods nodded, whispered secret phrases, marked the place, and gave their assent. Soon after, armed troops consisting of descendants of Rome and their brothers born on the banks of the Tiber filled the plain of the stony Arno.[12] They scattered through the fields and immediately flashed their glittering swords, making the whole plain glint and resound, as once the voracious locusts had done upon destroying the African plains while strong winds overcast the whole sky with clouds. The uproar and the noise of the soldiers mingled with those of the horses; the clang of the Tyrrhenians' arms and the horrible sound of the instruments of war filled the entire valley and the surrounding mountains with a frightful clamor. Loud cries to the skies praised Florence—the whole area was shouting, "Florence!" They say that it was then that, for the first time, the speed of the Arno decreased, bridges were built to span it, and solid foundations were laid. The distant Alps resounded with joyous voices; the noise amazed the Ligurians and Luni,[13] proud of its seaport. Even wild and inaccessible Corsica, the gulfs of Sardinia, Elba rich in iron, and bleak, thorny Capraia heard the shouting.

Then, for the first time, the majestic Gorgona[14] raised her head from the waves and saw the winding Arno in front of her. On the land, cities abandoned their sites not only to come to crown the sacred walls of the flourishing goddess, but to submit themselves to her, to show their willingness to obey her laws, follow her customs, and present her with gifts. Fiesole was the first to arrive, descending the nearby hill; imploring, she showed her defeated sisters how to obey. Then came the bellicose and once-numerous youths of Arezzo; then Ombrone, flowing nearby and dissatisfied with his small banks, followed by Cortona, the ancient capital of the Tuscan people. As the Carthaginian general does not want to enter a war that he would certainly lose, Alphean Pisa[15] handed herself and her precious shipyard over, knowing from experience the nature of divine vengeance. Volterra, rich in metal, also came to put her long[16] neck under Florence's yoke. Finally, all the cities once founded by old Tarchon[17] came to honor her. Respecting the just pacts they had signed, they brought riches and troops and showed obedience to her laws. Since then, the wicked serpent and the forces of the Insubrians[18] have repeatedly tried in vain to conquer her and take away her military supremacy.

There is, for one, the kingdom of Naples, which joined its troops, coming from different directions, into one immense camp. Might I recall the villages they attacked with fire and the towns they seized in that unjust war, when people were frightened at having the enemy near the city walls? I shall but mention the neighboring people and the numerous times the Ligurians, too, have waged war in vain against Florence; their troops were taken prisoner along with their captain, their camps seized, and the cities they conquered they then lost again. Different lands often attacked Florence with deceit and cunning, resorting to a type of powerful fraud more violent than weaponry, devising innumerable stratagems that resulted only in groundless fears.

Mars, [Florence's] father, and his Vulcanian lover[19] wield their weapons and fight; the Roman bird[20] routs the enemies, vanquishes fraud, reveals deceit, and dispels the hundred-eyed, vicious Argus. Fortified by such omens and by so noble an origin, O fortunate Florence, you raise your head to the skies. With such divine help, you increase your sway, illuminate Italy with your illustrious name, and bestow peace upon your conquests by virtue of your just rule. This is why within you, passionate city, there are exquisite holy structures and temples dedicated to the gods. This is why you can boast palaces decorated with regal magnificence, walls erected by a great king,[21] paved streets, and impressive bridges. What can I say of your fertile soil, of the gifts that Nature has bestowed upon you, of the fresh waters, of the fields rich in crops, or of the mild climate? Your hills are covered with fruits, the peasant carefully loosening the hard soil with his plow. How can I praise your wide-roofed palaces, your country villages, your hills covered with towers, and your numerous splendid villas and estates? If a foreign traveler were to see all this at a distance from a mountaintop, he would think he was before the marquees of the Assyrian king, or a land strewn with stars, or the Cyclades arranged in a circle in the sea, or fields decorated with precious stones at the feet of small towns. How can I describe the size of this city's population, its wealth, its famous intellects, its righteous wise men who carry out with the same zeal both their private affairs and those of the state?

You, Florence, have a learned group of youths who love eloquence. You have a crowd of expert jurists who revere justice, know how to determine what is right, and can readily provide solutions to the most complicated legal dilemmas. You have citizens who explore natural causes and excavate the earth, and others who try to discern the paths of the stars by making out things invisible to the human eye. Nor do you lack for those who continually celebrate Plato and his most incisive disciple [Aristotle]. To all this one must add the innumerable arts and the many gifts which divine Apollo and Pallas, rich in virtues, lavish on the city. People come even from the most remote countries to see and purchase these things. And your poets? In such a divine council, how can I refrain from mentioning the sweet Muses? To which other city in the world has fate ever given so many poets? What other city has ever been so favored by the stars? I think all the laurels of Apollo's forest have been brought here, as have the springs celebrated by innumerable poets.[22] Here are the souls of Smyrna and Mantua,[23] here, finally, the very choir of Helicon has migrated. Neither Rome nor the Athenian lares will ever be able to boast anything greater than this. Here the Greeks and the Latins can be found together, as this city alone houses all the types of erudition mankind has ever produced. Not even if I possessed nine mouths and nine tongues and the Muses dictated to me both the rhythm and the words of the poem, O Florence, so dear to the gods, would I be able to sing your merits as you deserve.

---

1. Collenuccio is invoking Astraea, the goddess of justice, who fled the world because of mankind's contempt for her precepts. In classical mythology, her return to earth is

associated with the return of the Golden Age; see, for instance, Virgil's famous fourth eclogue, vv. 6–7.

2. From Virg., *Aen.,* 8.680–681. In Virgil this image refers to Augustus.

3. Ausonia was Italy's ancient name. It is often used, for instance, in Virgil's *Aeneid.*

4. The Tyrrhenian and the Adriatic Seas.

5. Cotylus is the Latin name of Mount Fumaiolo, where the River Tiber originates. Here Collenuccio invents a myth without precedent in either classical or humanist literature.

6. The River Tiber's ancient name. For its origin, see Ov., *Fas.,* 2.383–390.

7. Collenuccio alters the version of the myth reported by Silius Italicus, who wrote in his *Punica,* 5.7, that Faunus was Arnus' father. Collenuccio's story of the origin of Florence is partly his own creation and partly a reworking of classical sources.

8. The great twelve sisters are the twelve great Etruscan cities mentioned in ancient sources such as Livy and Dionysius of Halicarnassus. See the reference to Tarchon, and note 17.

9. The Tyrrhenian Sea. Tethys was the goddess of the sea in Greek mythology.

10. From the Greek *ianthís,* meaning "violet-colored flower." It is associated with the lily, the symbol of Florence.

11. Ombrone, Bisenzio, and Mugnone are rivers near Florence. The oreads are mountain nymphs.

12. Collenuccio is referring to the battles fought during the Social War between rebel Fiesole and the Roman troops. See Bruni's narration of these episodes.

13. The town of Luni, which today lies in Tuscany, near the border with Liguria.

14. Like Elba and Capraia, an island off the Tuscan coast. This phrase alludes to Dante, *Inf.,* 33.82–83.

15. A quotation from Virg., *Aen.,* 10.179; the epithet came from the city's founding by settlers from Pisa, in Elis, on the River Alpheus.

16. Volterra sits on a hilltop.

17. According to a well-known myth (see, for example, Strabo's *Geography* [5.2.2]), Tarchon fulfilled Tyrrhenus' order by founding twelve cities in Etruria.

18. An ancient people that lived in the region of Milan. Like the "wicked serpent," the Insubrians represent the Visconti, Florence's greatest enemies.

19. Venus. Some versions of the myth say she is the wife of Mars, others, instead, of Vulcan. Here Collenuccio is probably referring to the famous Homeric story in which Venus was Vulcan's wife and Mars' lover. The author's reference to Mars and Venus is meant to underscore, once again, the Roman origin of Florence.

20. The eagle, symbol of the Guelph party. The party's victories proved it a worthy heir to Roman military valor.

21. He refers to the legendary reconstruction of Florence by Charlemagne, another sign of Collenuccio's desire to accumulate stories that Florentine humanists had considered contradictory.

22. Parnassus' founts of poetic inspiration.

23. Homer and Virgil.

50

A Sketch of Florence and Its Domain

FLAVIO BIONDO

Not much is known about the early years of Flavio Biondo's life (1392–1463). After leaving his native town of Forlì in 1423 he met Guarino Veronese in Ferrara and later entered the entourage of Cardinal Gabriele Condulmer, the future Eugenius IV. By 1434, the year of his appointment as papal secretary, he was already one of the pontiff's most intimate confidants. During Eugenius IV's stay in Florence, he became friends with Leonardo Bruni and other prominent Florentine humanists, as evidenced in his De verbis romanae locutionis *(1435), a short treatise devoted to a topic much debated within the humanist milieu: the merits of classical Latin as opposed to those of the vernacular. Following a method free of moralistic preconceptions and religious bias, Biondo undertook the first history of medieval Europe: the thirty-two volume* Historiarum ab inclinatione romani imperii decades *(1453). His* Roma instaurata, *meanwhile, marked the beginning of a new period in the study of the topography of classical Rome, just as his* Roma triumphans *had for the knowledge of ancient magistratures.*

Italia illustrata, the first systematic description of all the regions of Italy, is considered Biondo's most important work. This text was begun in 1447 when Alfonso of Aragon commissioned Biondo to write a book on the famous Italians of the time (presumably to be modeled on Ciriaco of Ancona's Itinerarium*). It took on an altogether different format, however, inaugurating a new genre with its geographical, archaeological, and historical account of Italy. In the following passage on Florence and its surroundings, Biondo gives a brief description of the land and then refers the reader to Bruni for background on the* *origins of Florence. He emphasizes the urban renovation that was carried out at the end of the thirteenth century under the direction of Arnolfo di Cambio and discusses the monuments of Florence and its renowned citizens. Biondo emphasizes that the last hundred years have been a period of exceptional splendor for the city, as it has not only been adorned with magnificent buildings by citizens such as Cosimo de' Medici but has managed to expand its dominion and become the greatest power of Tuscany.*

Source: Flavio Biondo, *De Roma triumphante libri decem, Romae instauratae libri tres, Italia illustrata, Historiarum ab inclinato Romae imperio decades tres* (Basel: Froben, 1531), pp. 303–305.

The city of Pistoia lies in the northern part of Tuscany's most extensive plains. Catilina's army was defeated there, as many ancient authors note.[1] Leonardo Bruni claims that in 1250 Pistoia was the first of many Tuscan cities to come under the rule of the Florentines, who at that time had just freed themselves.[2] In the environs of Pistoia are Monsummano, Serravalle, Vitolino, and, a little further north, Montecatini. Two rivers, called Stella and Ombrone, flow near the walls of Pistoia, not far from each other; they also flow close to Carmignano before running into the Arno near Montelupo. The Bisenzio River flows down from the Apennines and runs alongside the walls of Prato, the richest and most beautiful village in all Tuscany. North of Prato is Murlo. Close to the small village of Calenzano runs a stream called the Marina. Finally, the Mugnone flows close by the walls of Florence.

In his *Historiae,* the celebrated Leonardo Bruni has spoken at length about the origins of Florence and the deeds of this illustrious city. I shall limit my discussion, therefore, to basic information [on the origin of Florence], assuming that it was founded by Sulla's soldiers, who were given this territory by Sulla himself. They first built their houses near the river, and it is believed that they named the city Fluentia, after the flowing of the waters. Pliny, who is the first author to mention this city, writes that the "Fluentini" lived on the banks of the Arno.[3] It is commonly held that the soldiers credited with the foundation of Florence moved to this site 667 years after Rome was founded, that is, 83 years before the coming of Jesus Christ Our Savior. Florence was repeatedly attacked by the Goths, but it has never been destroyed, either by Totila or by anyone else. This is the reason for which, contrary to some people's opinion, we doubt that it was ever rebuilt by Charlemagne, especially since in the book on the king's deeds, Alcuin, his teacher, simply writes that on his way to Rome

Charles celebrated Easter twice in Florence. Florence was once very close to being razed to the ground, but the valor of a single Florentine, Farinata degli Uberti, saved it. The people of Pisa, Siena, and other Tuscan towns had gathered at Empoli and planned to destroy Florence, but Farinata, who had already spent a long time in exile, returned to his native city, saying that he did not want Florence to suffer any damage as long as he was alive.[4]

In 1024 the population and the power of Florence increased, for the citizens of Fiesole, having been defeated, were brought to this city.[5] In that same year, Emperor Henry I built the Church of San Miniato near the city walls. In 1176, Florence was damaged by two fires that occurred one right after the other. It was around that time that the priors of the guilds and the standard-bearer of justice began to govern Florence, as they still do today. Among the first standard-bearers was a member of the noble house of Strozzi. In the year 1294 commenced the construction of the beautiful church consecrated to the glorious Virgin, which is now adorned with a stunning dome, the work of the Florentine Filippo Brunelleschi. In 1298 builders started the magnificent palace which is now the seat of the priors of the guilds. Five years later the urban area was expanded and the circuit of walls was enlarged. Florence's marble bell tower, which is perhaps the most beautiful in the world, was built thirty-one years later.

It was during this time that two famous Florentine poets flourished, Dante Alighieri and Francesco Petrarch. The latter was born of a Florentine father, who had been exiled to Arezzo. When he died he was buried in Arquà, near Padua, on the Euganean Hills. Dante was born in Florence, but died in exile in Ravenna. Later, Florence could boast Giotto, an excellent painter who deserves to be considered on a par with Apelles. It was also the home of Accursio, "the prince of jurisconsults," who wrote a famous commentary on civil law which is still used today.[6] It is also believed, although no author attests it, that the parents of Claudianus the poet were from Florence.[7] Coluccio Salutati was renowned for his eloquence, although he was educated before Cicero's rhetoric was being taught as a model. He wrote many works, which appear richer in prudence and erudition than in eloquence. Although he did not write anything, our contemporary Niccolò Niccoli was very learned and introduced many youths to the study of literature.

In the hundred years or so that have elapsed since Petrarch's death, Florence has experienced a period of great splendor. In our time, in fact, it has expanded its dominion by conquering Castrocaro, Modigliana, Nonantola, Cassiano, Portico, and other towns in Romagna. In Tuscany it has seized the ancient cities of Pisa and Cortona, Borgo San Sepolcro, and all of Casentino. All the illustrious events of the last century, however, are less important than the council that Pope Eugenius IV held for the union of the eastern and western churches. This council was immensely expensive, as the Roman church covered the travel costs of John Paleologus, the emperor of Constantinople, the patriarchs, numerous archbishops and bishops, and many other Greek scholars and nobles who attended the council. At that council, Eugenius IV succeeded in converting the Armenians, the Ethiopians, the Georgians, and the Jacobites from Libya and Asia to the Catholic faith.

Florence has never lacked for excellent men famous for their virtues, nor does it lack for them today. Above all, it now has Cosimo de' Medici, who surpasses in wealth all the other private citizens of Europe. He is renowned for his prudence, kindness, and courtesy, but what elicits the greatest praise is his love of study, especially of the works of historians. His sons, Piero, Giovanni, and Carlo, who take their father's virtue as a model, bring him great joy. Nor should one forget to mention the construction of exquisite buildings through which Cosimo has rendered Florence even more beautiful. In his famous monastery of San Marco, amid other incredible works of art, one finds the most superb library in all of Italy. The splendid vaults, the marble columns, and the building of San Lorenzo also exhibit the magnificence of this outstanding man. What can I say, moreover, about his recently built palace in Via Larga, which should be compared to the residences of the Roman princes and the greatest works of architecture of that ancient city? Having attempted to reconstruct Rome through my writings,[8] I can certainly assert that in all Rome no remains can be found, either of a large private building or of some prince's palace, which display greater magnificence than Cosimo's residence.

The knight Palla Strozzi, although in exile, is another illustrious figure; he spends his time in Padua consoling himself through the study of philosophy, as a sensible man would. Angelo Acciaiuoli,[9] himself a knight, is famous on account of his illustrious family but manages to glorify them and himself even more through his wisdom, his noble customs, and his education. Andrea Fiocchi,[10] papal secretary and Florentine canon, is a man of great eloquence; he published a useful study on magistracies. Giannozzo Manetti, an erudite scholar of both Greek and Latin, and [Leon] Battista Alberti, with his keen and versatile intellect devoted to many arts, bring substantial glory to Florence. Another notable adornment to this city is Donatello, whose genius earns him the praises bestowed on the artists of old, and who is comparable to Zeuxis of Heraclea. He can carve, as Virgil writes, "living faces out of marble."[11]

By contrast, the ancient city of Fiesole, next to Florence, stands in ruins. It is mentioned by many writers, in particular by Sallust in his *Bellum Catilinae* and by Livy in a passage on the same topic in Book 102.[12] One of the reasons for Fiesole's present bleakness is that all its inhabitants have moved to Florence, taking all their possessions with them. The stream Mugnone rises on the eastern hills of Fiesole and flows alongside the walls of Florence. Outside the city, about six miles south on the banks of the Mugnone, there is a little church called Alle Croci. I presume the name of this place derives from the fact that many dead were buried here after the tremendous rout of the Goths near Fiesole in which around two hundred thousand soldiers of King Radagasius died, as I mentioned in my *Historiae*.[13] Now, between these hills and the Apennines lies a beautiful valley—which still bears its name of olden times, Mugello—filled with towns, splendid villages, and, above all, the Medici's villa. In this region the erudite and famous doctor of the last century Dino [Del Garbo] was born.[14]

1. See, for instance, Sal., *Cat.*, 60.1–7 and Flor., *Epit. Hist.*, 2.12.11–12.
2. In September 1250, after the death of Frederick II, the Florentine popular faction defeated the nobles who had supported the emperor. The Florentine government then completely reorganized its political system. Among the changes were the creation of the college of the Dodici Anziani (Twelve elders), the division of the city into districts, and the appointment of the gonfaloni to recruit citizens for the communal army. The following year Florence seized Pistoia, forcing the local Ghibelline lords to flee the city; see Bruni, *Historiae*, vol. 2 (ed. Santini), pp. 27–28.
3. Pliny, *Nat. Hist.*, 3.5.52.
4. See Dante, *Inf.*, 10.91–93: "But I was the only one, when it was agreed / To raze the city of Florence to the ground, / To oppose the plan and stand up openly in her defense." Farinata's opposition is recorded by most Florentine historians. Giovanni Villani does so in his *Cronica*, 6.81, as does Filippo Villani in a sketch of the Ghibelline leader in his *De origine*, pp. 418–419. Notice, however, that Biondo prefers not to mention the involvement of the Florentine Ghibellines in the decision to raze the city to the ground after the Guelphs' defeat at Montaperti (1260).
5. There is no evidence of this episode, although it is true that Fiesole suffered a serious decline in power in the early Middle Ages and was finally conquered by Florence in 1125.
6. The main source of information on Accursio (often called Accursius Florentinus) is to be found in Filippo Villani's *De origine*. He was born in the countryside south of Florence between 1181 and 1185 and died around 1259–1263. After studying jurisprudence in Bologna under famous instructors such as Azzone and Jacopo Baldovini, he taught civil law and became the professor of a number of illustrious pupils, including his

son, Francesco, and the future Innocent IV, Sinibaldo Fieschi. He is the author of the famous *Glossa,* the main commentary on the *Corpus iuris civilis.*

7. Filippo Villani also records this in his *De origine.*

8. Biondo is referring to his topographic work *Roma instaurata,* also included in the Froben edition.

9. Knighted in 1415, Acciaiuoli was a staunch supporter of Cosimo de' Medici and served as Florentine ambassador on numerous important occasions during the first half of the fifteenth century. He held a variety of influential offices in the city government (he was elected standard-bearer of justice twice, first in 1448 and then in 1454), before being exiled on account of his implication in the 1466 conspiracy of Luca Pitti.

10. Andrea di Domenico Fiocchi (ca. 1400–1452) was a friend and colleague of Biondo. He was the secretary to Gabriele Condulmer, the future Eugenius IV, both during the latter's cardinalate and after his election to the papal throne. Fiocchi later became canon of San Lorenzo in Florence, and parish priest of many Florentine and Fiesolean churches. He left a work entitled *De magistratibus Romanorum* (1424), the most important study on Rome's magistratures before Biondo's *Roma triumphans,* and a series of letters to humanists and ecclesiastics linked with Eugenius IV's court.

11. Virg., *Aen.,* 6.848.

12. See Sall., *Cat.,* 24.2, 27.1, 30.1, and 30.3, and the summary of book 102 of Livy's *Historiae ab urbe condita.*

13. See Biondo's *Historiarum ab inclinato Romae imperio decadis prima,* Book 1, pp. 8–9 of the Froben edition. See also n. 13 to document 6 for information on the episode that Biondo mentions here.

14. Dino Del Garbo (ca. 1280–1327) was born into a noble Florentine family. His father, a doctor and the author of a famous text on surgery, *Chirurgia,* introduced him to the study of medicine. Del Garbo taught at Bologna, Siena, Padua, and Florence, where he distinguished himself in his scholarly commentary on Avicenna.

51

The Delights of the Medici Villa in Careggi

GALEAZZO MARIA SFORZA

Irascible and cruel, though eloquent and not devoid of interest in the arts, Galeazzo Maria Sforza seems to embody the stereotype of the Italian ruler as depicted by nineteenth-century scholars. Jacob Burckhardt considered him one of those Italian Renaissance princes who, "beautiful as angels, raised with the greatest care and educated to numerous disciplines, were subject, in their adulthood, to all the attractions of the most unlimited selfishness." Both Galeazzo's career as duke of Milan and the tragic end of his life appear to fit with Burckhardt's image. After ten years of imprudent rule, in 1476 Galeazzo was murdered on his way to Mass by three conspirators. His death significantly contributed to the disruption in political balance that, following the Peace of Lodi in 1454, had brought years of relative prosperity to the Italian states.

Galeazzo maintained the alliance with Medicean Florence that his father Francesco had established with Cosimo in the early 1430s. In 1471, the Florentine authorities welcomed Galeazzo with spectacular public events, such as the elaborate staging of Belcari's mystery play about the Annunciation in San Felice in Piazza. Galeazzo's first stay in the Tuscan city, however, was in April 1459, when he was just fifteen years old (see Filarete, document 14, for a description of the ceremonies held in his honor). He left a record of this visit in a series of letters addressed to his father. In the excerpt we include here, he tells of a delightful evening spent at the Medici villa of Careggi, where he was

entertained with song, dance, and a sumptuous dinner, served under the attentive super-
vision of Giovanni de' Medici, Cosimo's youngest son.

Source: Bibliothèque Nationale, Paris, MS. Fon. Ital. 1588, fol. 226.

Florence, April 23, 1459

Most illustrious prince, excellent lord, and dear father,
As I told you I would do in the letter I wrote you yesterday, this morning I went
to Mass. I then went to Cosimo's villa in Careggi with the Most Serene Messer
Sigismondo, the Most Serene Messer d'Este, an ambassador of King Ferdinand, [Cicco] Simonetta, and Giovanni, Cosimo's son. I visited the whole area
and was impressed with its beautiful gardens, which are truly marvelous, and
with the building itself, which has bedrooms, kitchens, halls, and all sorts of
household goods—none of the other beautiful houses of this city can even
compete with it.

I dined with all the aforementioned people, except for Giovanni, Cosimo's
son, who preferred not to sit at table with the rest of us, so that he could make
sure everyone was served properly—he did not even stop to take a bite. Immediately after dinner, Messer Sigismondo left, and I went with the others to
listen to a certain Maestro Antonio [Squarcialupi] play the lute. Your Excel-
lency must at least have heard his name, if you do not know him personally. He
sang of all your accomplishments, from the first to the most recent, interposing
a great commendation of Messer Tiberto,[1] and a celebration of myself as well.
He sang so superbly that I do not think the greatest poet or orator could repeat
his performance. All present were utterly amazed, especially the most erudite.
Besides his outstanding use of simile, the like of which is hardly to be found, I
believe, in either Lucan or Dante, his songs drew upon innumerable ancient
stories and deeds of the Romans, as well as upon other tales, poems, and, in
brief, all the nine Muses. It would be virtually impossible to express how
marvelous he was. I can only conclude by saying that everyone believed he
could not possibly have sung better.

I was then invited to a beautiful party organized by the women of Florence,
among whom were the wives of Piero and Giovanni, grown-up daughter of
Piero di Cosimo, Pierfrancesco's wife, a girl of the Strozzi family—who, if not
the most beautiful in the whole city, is certainly surpassed by only a few—and

some maidens of lesser rank. Everyone danced fine quadrilles in the Florentine manner. I left after lunch on the following day and was back in Florence around 4:30 P.M. Upon hearing that the cardinal of Burgundy had arrived, I immediately rode to meet him.

1. Tiberto Brandolini served as a condottiere to numerous lords, including Francesco Sforza. He formed part of the fifteen-year-old Galeazzo's retinue on the trip to Florence in 1459.

The amount of scholarship on Renaissance Florence is immense; a detailed bibliography on the authors and the topics discussed in the present anthology would require dozens of pages. For brevity's sake, we have decided to be selective with the texts we cite in this bibliography, and to refer the reader to the *Dizionario Biografico degli Italiani* (hereafter *DBI*). Since the *DBI* itself has, as of 1999, reached only the letter *F,* for authors from G onward we will indicate the most important studies from which the reader can obtain further bibliographical information. For particularly well-documented personalities, we will also cite articles from Vittore Branca's *Dizionario critico della letteratura italiana* (Turin: UTET, 1973), 3 vols. (hereafter *DCLI*). For primary sources, please refer to the end of the introductory paragraphs to each text; however, we will indicate English translations where available, either partial or complete. General bibliographical information for authors who appear more than once in this anthology will be given only on first occurrence.

GENERAL REFERENCES

The classic work on the history of Florence is Robert Davidsohn, *Storia di Firenze* (Florence: Sansoni, 1956–1968), 8 vols. The original German edition of this work is *Forschungen zur Geschichte von Florenz* (Berlin: Mittler, 1896–1927), 6 vols. Certainly dated, but still useful as a general introduction, is Ferdinand Schevill, *Medieval and Renaissance Florence* (New York: Harper & Row, 1961). Valuable general studies on medieval and early modern cities are Jacques Heers, *La ville au Moyen Âge* (Paris: Fayard, 1990), and Christopher R. Friedrichs, *The Early Modern City, 1450–1750* (New York: Longman, 1995). One can also find useful information and a rich bibliography in the essays collected in *Athens and Rome, Florence and Venice: City States in Classical Antiquity and Medieval Italy,* ed. Anthony Molho, Kurt Raaflaub, and Julia Emlen (Stuttgart: Steiner, 1991). Two articles published in this volume are of particular interest for the topics discussed in our anthology: Alison Brown, "City and Citizen: Changing Perceptions in the Fifteenth and Sixteenth Centuries," pp. 93–111; and Franek Sznura, "Civic Urbanism in Medieval Florence," pp. 403–418. For an introduction to town planning in the Italian Renaissance see Giorgio Simoncini, *Città e società nel Rinascimento* (Turin: Einaudi, 1974), 2 vols. On Renaissance utopias and the theme of the ideal city, see the essays in *Les utopies à la Renaissance: Colloque international (avril 1961)* (Brussels: Presses Universitaires, 1963), and the exhaustive study by Frank E. Manuel and Fritzie P. Manuel, *Utopian Thought in the Western World* (Cambridge: Harvard University Press, Belknap Press, 1982), pts. 1–3. *Utopian Thought* also includes a detailed bibliography on pp. 869–875. John K. Hayd wrote a useful survey on medieval panegyrics of cities in "Medieval Descriptions of Cities," *Bulletin of the John Rylands Library* 48 (1965–1966), pp. 308–340. Late medieval and fifteenth-century descriptions of Florence have been discussed in the studies by Giuseppina Carla Romby: *Descrizioni e rappresentazioni della città di Firenze nel secolo XV* (Florence: Libreria Editrice Fiorentina, 1976), and "La rappresentazione dello spazio: La città," in *Imago et descriptio Tusciae: La Toscana nella cartografia dal XV al XIX secolo* (Venice: Marsilio, 1993), pp. 305–359. For medieval and Renaissance views of Florence in works of art, manuscripts, and printed books, see the well-illustrated inventory offered by Attilio Mori and Giuseppe Boffito, *Firenze nelle vedute e piante: Studio storico, topografico, cartografico* (Rome: Multigrafica, 1973, anastatic reprint of the original 1926 edition). See also Daniele Mazzotta, *Firenze: L'immagine urbana dal XIV al XIX secolo* (Lecce: Capone, 1998). A recent attractive volume devoted to panoramic views of cities in Europe from the Renaissance through the nineteenth century is *Città d'Europa: Iconografia e vedutismo dal XV al XIX secolo,* ed. Cesare De Seta (Naples: Electa, 1996). See also *Cartography in Prehistoric, Ancient, and Medieval Europe and the Mediterranean,* ed. John B. Harley and David Woodward, vol. 1 (Chicago: University of Chicago Press, 1987), which also has an ample bibliography. An English translation of Marin Sanudo's *Laus urbis Venetae* can be found in *Venice: A Documentary History, 1450–1630,* ed. David Chambers, Brian Pullan, and Jennifer Fletcher (Oxford: Blackwell, 1992), pp. 4–21. For the imitation of Bruni's *Laudatio* in the panegyrics of Tudor London, see *London in the Age of Shakespeare: An Anthology,* ed. Lawrence Manley (London: Croom Helm, 1986), pp. 49–53. Marin Sanudo's two descriptions of the Venetian magistratures can be read in his *De origine, situ et magistratibus urbis Venetae,* ed. Angela Caracciolo Aricò (Milan: Cisalpino Goliardica, 1980), pp. 85–154, 240–292.

Valuable introductions to the culture of the Florentine quattrocento are the classic works by Eugenio Garin, *Italian Humanism* (Westport, Conn.: Greenwood Press, 1975), and by Vittorio Rossi, *Il Quattrocento,* rev. ed., ed. Rossella Bessi (Padua: Piccin-Vallardi, 1992). Bessi's meticulous bibliographical updating has rendered Rossi's volume an indispensable source of bibliographical information on fifteenth-century Italian authors. A concise yet excellent survey of the humanistic culture of quattrocento Florence is offered by George Holmes, *The Florentine Enlightenment, 1400–50* (London: Weidenfeld and Nicolson, 1969). Many other subjects, including that of the sciences in quattrocento Florence, are discussed in the essays gathered in the volume *Idee istituzioni scienza ed arti nella Firenze dei Medici* (Florence: Giunti Martello, 1980), in the conference proceedings col-

lected in *Florence and Italy: Renaissance Studies in Honour of Nicolai Rubinstein,* ed. Peter
Denley and Caroline Elam (London: Westfield College, 1988), and in *La Toscana al tempo
di Lorenzo il Magnifico: Politica Economia Cultura Arte—Convegno di Studi promosso dalle Università di Firenze, Pisa e Siena, 5–8 novembre 1992* (Pisa: Pacini, 1996).

The importance of the struggle between Florence and Milan and its cultural consequences are discussed in the famous study by Hans Baron, *The Crisis of the Early Italian
Renaissance: Civic Humanism and Republican Liberty in an Age of Classicism and Tyranny*
(Princeton, N.J.: Princeton University Press, 1966). A recent and useful book on the same
topic is Antonio Lanza, *Firenze contro Milano: Gli intellettuali fiorentini nelle guerre con i Visconti, 1390–1440* (Anzio: De Rubeis, 1991), which also prints a variety of Florentine texts
in the appendix. For a comparison between Milan and Florence in the Renaissance, see
the essays collected in *Florence and Milan: Comparisons and Relations,* ed. Gian Carlo Garfagnini and Craig Hugh Smyth (Florence: La Nuova Italia, 1989), 2 vols.

ORIGINS

The best archaeological and topographical study of the Roman origins of Florence is still
Mario Lopes Pegna, *Firenze dalle origini al medioevo* (Florence: Del Re, 1974). See also
Colin Hardie, "The Origin and Plan of Roman Florentia," *Journal of Roman Studies* 55
(1965), pp. 122–140. For works emphasizing the Roman origins of Florence in late medi-
eval chronicles, see Alberto Del Monte, "La storiografia fiorentina dei secoli XII e XIII,"
Bullettino dell'Istituto Storico Italiano per il Medioevo 62 (1950), pp. 175–282; Marisa Mariani,
"Il concetto di Roma nei cronisti fiorentini," *Studi Romani* 4.1 (1956), pp. 15–27, and 4.2
(1956), pp. 153–166; Ead., "La favola di Roma nell'ambiente fiorentino dei secoli XIII–
XV," *Archivio della Società Romana di Storia Patria,* series 3, 81 (1958), pp. 1–54, and Charles
T. Davis, "Topographical and Historical Propaganda in Early Florentine Chronicles and
in Villani," *Medioevo e Rinascimento* 2 (1988), pp. 33–51. Mario Salmi discusses the artistic
links between classical Rome and late medieval Florence, especially in regard to the Florentine baptistery, in his "La 'Renovatio Romae' e Firenze," *Rinascimento* 1 (1950), pp. 5–
24, as does Davis in the aforementioned article. For the study of Etruscan culture in Renaissance Florence and its importance in the shaping of the myth of the city, see Giovanni
Cipriani, *Il mito etrusco nel rinascimento fiorentino* (Florence: Olschki, 1980), which devotes
the first two chapters to the Florentine humanists of the quattrocento. For the Florentine
humanists' study of antiquities in the early quattrocento, see Roberto Weiss, *The Renaissance Discovery of Classical Antiquity* (Oxford: Blackwell, 1969). On the alleged reconstruction of the city by Charlemagne and the influence of the Carolingian element in
Florentine culture, see Sergio Raveggi, "Tracce carolinge a Firenze," in *Sulle orme di Or-
lando: Leggende e luoghi carolingi in Italia,* ed. Anna Imelda Galletti and Roberto Roda
(Padua: Interbooks, 1987), pp. 167–177. See also Patrick Gilli, *Au miroir de l'humanisme:
Les représentations de la France dans la culture savante italienne à la fin du Moyen Âge* (Rome:
Ecole française de Rome, 1997), pp. 277–343. The best contribution on the myth of Flor-
ence remains Donald Weinstein, "The Myth of Florence," in *Florentine Studies: Politics and
Society in Renaissance Florence,* ed. Nicolai Rubinstein (Evanston, Ill.: Northwestern Uni-
versity Press, 1968), pp. 15–44, republished with a few variations in his *Savonarola and Florence: Prophecy and Patriotism in the Renaissance* (Princeton, N.J.: Princeton University Press,

1970), pp. 27–66. See also Charles Bec, "Per la storia del mito di Firenze," in *Cultura e società a Firenze nell'epoca della Rinascenza* (Rome: Salerno, 1983), pp. 323–348, which revises the essay published in the volume *Lorenzo Ghiberti nel suo tempo: Atti del convegno internazionale di studi, Firenze, 18–21 ottobre 1978* (Florence: Olschki, 1980), pp. 3–27. For the myth of Florence in Dante and in the Florentine trecento, see Charles Davis, "Il buon tempo antico," in *Florentine Studies,* pp. 45–69; Raffaello Ramat, *Il mito di Firenze e altri saggi* (Florence: D'Anna, 1976), pp. 147–165, and Luca Gatti, "Il mito di Marte a Firenze e la *Pietra scema,"* *Rinascimento,* series 2, 35 (1995), pp. 210–230. A useful survey of the humanistic debate concerning the origins of various Italian cities is Philip Jack, *The Antiquarian and the Myth of Antiquity: The Origins of Rome in Renaissance Thought* (New York: Cambridge University Press, 1993), which focuses on Florence on pp. 79–86 and 110–113.

On COLUCCIO SALUTATI, see the excellent volume by Ronald G. Witt, *Hercules at the Crossroads. The Life, Works, and Thought of Coluccio Salutati* (Durham, N.C.: Duke University Press, 1983). For a concise introduction to this humanist, see the entry about him by Roberto Weiss in *DCLI,* vol. 3, and Eugenio Garin, *Portraits from the Quattrocento,* trans. Victor A. and Elizabeth Velen (New York: Harper & Row, 1972), pp. 1–29.

For an accurate general introduction to LEONARDO BRUNI, see the excellent article on him by Cesare Vasoli in *DBI,* vol. 14, and the shorter one by Paola Rigo in *DCLI,* vol. 1. See also *The Humanism of Leonardo Bruni: Selected Texts,* ed. Gordon Griffiths, James Hankins, and David Thompson (Binghamton, N.Y.: Medieval and Renaissance Texts and Studies, 1987), and the excellent collection of essays in *Leonardo Bruni cancelliere della Repubblica di Firenze: Convegno di studi, Firenze, 27–29 ottobre 1987,* ed. Paolo Viti (Florence: Olschki, 1990). There is an English translation of excerpts from Bruni's *Historiae* in *Humanism and Liberty: Writings on Freedom from Fifteenth-Century Florence,* trans. and ed. Renée Neu Watkins (Columbia, S.C.: University of South Carolina Press, 1978), pp. 30–91. The preface to the *History of the Florentine People* has also been translated and commented on by Gordon Griffiths in *The Humanism,* chap. 3. Hans Baron emphasizes the crucial importance of Bruni's *Historiae* to modern historiography in *In Search of Florentine Civic Humanism: Essays on the Transition from Medieval to Modern Thought* (Princeton, N.J.: Princeton University Press, 1988), vol. 1, chaps. 3–4.

A concise sketch of GIOVANNI GHERARDI is Lucia Nadin's entry about him in *DCLI,* vol. 2. For further information, see Antonio Lanza's introduction to his edition of the *Paradiso degli Alberti,* and Lanza, *Polemiche e berte letterarie nella Firenze del primo Rinascimento, 1375–1449* (Rome: Bulzoni, 1989), chap. 8. See also the following studies by Baron: *The Crisis,* esp. pp. 332–338, and *Humanistic and Political Literature in Florence and Venice at the Beginning of the Quattrocento* (Cambridge: Harvard University Press, 1955), chap. 1. On Cino Rinuccini and his *Invective Against Some Slanderers of Dante, Petrarch, and Boccaccio,* see Lanza, *Polemiche e berte,* chap. 1, and his edition of the text on pp. 261–267. For further information on Rinuccini's literary works, see the articles by Ronald Witt, "Cino Rinuccini's *Risponsiva alla Invettiva di Messer Antonio Lusco,"* *Renaissance Quarterly* 23.2 (1970), pp. 133–149, and Giuliano Tanturli, "Cino Rinuccini e la scuola di Santa Maria in Campo," *Studi Medievali,* series 3, 17 (1976), pp. 625–674.

On GIOVANNI CAVALCANTI, see Claudio Mutini's entry in *DBI,* vol. 12, and the one by

Claudio Varese in *DCLI,* vol. 1. See also Dale Kent, "The Importance of Being Eccentric: Giovanni Cavalcanti's View of Cosimo de' Medici's Florence," *Journal of Medieval and Renaissance Studies* 9 (1979), pp. 101–132, and Monti's introduction to his edition of *Nuova opera.*

General information on CRISTOFORO LANDINO is provided by Roberto Cardini in *DCLI,* 2. The most comprehensive studies of this humanist remain Cardini's edition of *Scritti critici e teorici* and his volume *La critica del Landino* (Rome: Bulzoni, 1973). For Landino's poem on the founding of Florence and the mythography of the Florentine territory peculiar to the poetry of the Laurentian period, see Rossella Bessi, "La suggestione del mondo classico," in *La Toscana al tempo di Lorenzo il Magnifico,* vol. 2, pp. 375–383, and Paul Murgatroyd, "Landino's *Xandra* 3.3 and Its Ancient Latin Models," *Renaissance Studies* 11 (1997), pp. 57–60. See also Manfred Lentzen's essay, "Le lodi di Firenze di Cristoforo Landino: L'esaltazione del primato politico, culturale e linguistico della città sull'Arno nel Quattrocento," *Romanische Forschungen* 97.1 (1985), pp. 36–46.

For a sketch of the life and the works of ANGELO POLIZIANO, see Emilio Bigi's entry on him in *DCLI,* vol. 3, and Garin, *Portraits,* pp. 161–189. Two recent volumes offer a comprehensive introduction to Poliziano: *Poliziano e il suo tempo: Atti del VI Convegno internazionale, Chianciano-Montepulciano, 18–21 luglio 1994,* ed. Luisa Secchi Tarugi (Florence: Cesati, 1996), and Mario Martelli, *Angelo Poliziano: Storia e metastoria* (Lecce: Conte, 1995). The only contribution we have found on his letter concerning the origins of Florence is Nicolai Rubinstein, "Il Poliziano e la questione delle origini di Firenze," in *Il Poliziano e il suo tempo: Atti del IV Convegno internazionale di studi sul Rinascimento, Firenze, Palazzo Strozzi, 23–26 settembre 1954* (Florence: Sansoni, 1957), pp. 101–110.

HISTORY AND SOCIETY

The works of Gene A. Brucker, Anthony Molho, Richard Trexler, and Richard A. Goldthwaite provide detailed and comprehensive introductions to Renaissance Florence. Brucker provides a useful survey in *Renaissance Florence* (New York: Wiley, 1969), and in *The Civic World of Early Renaissance Florence* (Princeton, N.J.: Princeton University Press, 1977). He has also collected and translated documents on the Florentine economy of the late fourteenth and early fifteenth centuries in *The Society of Renaissance Florence: A Documentary Study* (New York: Harper & Row, 1971). On the social aspects of Florentine life in the quattrocento, see the exemplary research by Richard C. Trexler, *Public Life in Renaissance Florence* (New York: Academic Press, 1980), who reports and translates excerpts from a large number of primary sources. More specifically devoted to the study of the Florentine economy are Goldthwaite's volumes *Private Wealth in Renaissance Florence: A Study of Four Families* (Princeton, N.J.: Princeton University Press, 1968) and *The Building of Renaissance Florence: An Economic and Social History* (Baltimore: Johns Hopkins University Press, 1980), and Molho's monograph on the fiscal history of early Renaissance Florence, *Florentine Public Finances in the Early Renaissance, 1400–1433* (Cambridge: Harvard University Press, 1971). A collection of essays on the Italian economy of this period is *Social and Economic Foundations of the Italian Renaissance,* ed. Anthony Molho (New York: Wiley, 1969).

As regards the institutional history of quattrocento Florence, see Nicolai Rubinstein,

The Government of Florence Under the Medici, 1434 to 1494 (Oxford: Clarendon Press, 1966), and Lauro Martines, *Lawyers and Statecraft in Renaissance Florence* (Princeton, N.J.: Princeton University Press, 1968). For the topic of Florentine historiography, see Donald Wilcox, *The Development of Florentine Humanistic Historiography in the Fifteenth Century* (Cambridge: Harvard University Press, 1969); Nancy S. Struever, *The Language of History in the Renaissance: Rhetoric and Historical Consciousness in Florentine Humanism* (Princeton, N.J.: Princeton University Press, 1970), and Erich Cochrane, *Historians and Historiography in the Italian Renaissance* (Chicago: University of Chicago Press, 1981), pp. 3–33.

Bibliography on the MEDICI is immense and growing. The classic survey of the Medici's financial power in the quattrocento is Raymond de Roover, *The Rise and Decline of the Medici Bank* (Cambridge: Harvard University Press, 1980). A laudatory biography of Cosimo has been written by Curt Gutkind, *Cosimo de' Medici: "Pater Patriae," 1389–1464* (Oxford: Clarendon Press, 1938). For other contributions on Cosimo, as well as an extensive bibliography, see *Cosimo il Vecchio de' Medici, 1389–1464: Essays in Commemoration of the 600th Anniversary of Cosimo de' Medici's Birth*, ed. Francis Ames-Lewis (Oxford: Clarendon Press, 1992). Much less studied is the figure of Cosimo's son Piero. For information on Piero de' Medici, see the conference proceedings collected in *Piero de' Medici 'il Gottoso': Kunst im Dienste der Mediceer*, ed. Andreas Beyer and Bruce Boucher (Berlin: Akademie Verlag, 1993). There are excellent studies on Lorenzo de' Medici and updated bibliographies in *Lorenzo il Magnifico e il suo mondo: Convegno internazionale di studi, Firenze, 9–13 giugno 1992*, ed. Gian Carlo Garfagnini (Florence: Olschki, 1994) and *Lorenzo the Magnificent: Culture and Politics*, ed. Michael Mallet and Nicholas Mann (London: Warburg Institute, 1996). See also the numerous essays gathered in *La Toscana al tempo di Lorenzo il Magnifico*.

The best complete English translation of LEONARDO BRUNI, *Laudatio Florentinae urbis*, is that by Benjamin G. Kohl in *The Earthly Republic: Italian Humanists on Government and Society*, ed. Benjamin G. Kohl, Ronald G. Witt, and Elizabeth B. Welles (Philadelphia: University of Pennsylvania Press, 1978), pp. 135–175. See the partial translation and useful comments by Gordon Griffiths in *The Humanism*, pp. 116–120. For an evaluation of this work by Bruni, see Hans Baron, *Humanistic and Political Literature*, chap. 4, and Baron, *The Crisis*, chaps. 9–10. See also Stefano Ugo Baldassarri's introduction to his critical edition of this text (Florence: Sismel, 2000). Pier Candido Decembrio's *Panegyric of the City of Milan* has been edited and commented on by Giuseppe Petraglione in "Il *De laudibus mediolanensium urbis panegyricus*," *Archivio Storico Lombardo*, series 4, 8 (1907), pp. 5–45, later reprinted in *Rerum italicarum scriptores*, 20.1 (Bologna: Zanichelli, 1958), pp. 1013–1025.

On GORO DATI, see the entry by Paolo Viti in *DBI*, 33, and the following studies by Hans Baron: *Humanistic and Political Literature*, chap. 3; and *The Crisis*, chap. 8. For a recent and easily available edition of Dati's *Istoria*, see the appendix to Lanza, *Firenze contro Milano*, pp. 211–298. Excellent explanatory notes on the offices described by Dati are provided by Daniele Greco's edition of the ninth book of *Istoria*, published separately under the title *Dello stato e reggimento di Firenze* (Prato: Società Pratese di Storia Patria, 1991). An English translation of Dati's private diary appears in *Two Memoirs of Renaissance Florence: The Diaries of Buonaccorso Pitti and Grego. :ɔ Dati*, ed. Gene Brucker, trans. Julia Martines (New York: Harper & Row, 1967).

Vittore Branca's introduction to his edition of the *Ricordi* offers a good overview of GIOVANNI MORELLI. See also Leonida Pandimiglio, "Giovanni di Pagolo Morelli e la continuità familiare," *Studi Medievali,* series 3, 22 (1981), pp. 129–181. On the peculiarly Florentine genre of merchants' diaries, see Brucker's introduction to the aforementioned edition of Dati's memoirs, and Vittore Branca's essay in the anthology he edited, *Mercanti scrittori: Ricordi nella Firenze tra Medioevo e Rinascimento* (Milan: Rusconi, 1986), which also contains a bibliography on this subject, pp. lxxix-lxxxiii. A practical introduction to the study of the Florentine countryside in the fifteenth century is Maria Serena Mazzi and Sergio Raveggi, *Gli uomini e le cose nelle campagne fiorentine del Quattrocento* (Florence: Olschki, 1983), which offers a long appendix of documents and useful glossaries on weights, measures, and terms mentioned in the documents they include.

On BARTOLOMEO CEDERNI and FRANCESCO CACCINI, see Kent's introductory essay to the edition he and Corti edited. Recently, many valuable studies on Florentine Renaissance festivals have been published. Among them, a significant text is Nerida Newbigin, *Feste d'Oltrarno: Plays in Fifteenth-Century Florence* (Florence: Olschki, 1997), 2 vols. For specific information on the feast of St. John, see Trexler, *Public Life,* pp. 240–263, and Heidi L. Chrétien, *The Festival of San Giovanni: Imagery and Political Power in Renaissance Florence* (New York: Lang, 1994).

For VESPASIANO DA BISTICCI, see Greco's introduction to his edition of the *Vite* and Giuseppe Maria Cagni, *Vespasiano da Bisticci e il suo epistolario* (Rome: Edizioni di Storia e Letteratura, 1969). An English translation of Vespasiano's *Vite* can be found in *Renaissance Princes, Popes, and Prelates: The Vespasiano Memoirs—Lives of Illustrious Men of the 15th Century,* trans. William G. Waters and Emily Waters (New York: Harper & Row, 1963). Although not always reliable, this translation has recently been reprinted (Toronto: Toronto University Press and Renaissance Society of America, 1997). On Poggio Bracciolini, see the articles on him by Emilio Bigi and Armando Petrucci in *DBI,* vol. 13, and by Mario Pastore Stocchi in *DCLI,* vol. 1. For further information and bibliography, see the conference proceeding in *Poggio Bracciolini, 1380–1980: Nel VI centenario della nascita* (Florence: Sansoni, 1982). A concise reconstruction of Bracciolini's search for ancient manuscripts appears in *Two Renaissance Book Hunters: The Letters of Poggius Bracciolini to Nicolaus de Niccolis,* trans. Phyllis W. G. Gordon (New York: Columbia University Press, 1974). On his activity as historian, see the works on Renaissance historiography mentioned earlier, such as Erich Cochrane's *Historians and Historiography in the Italian Renaissance,* chap. 1.

The best study on MARCO PARENTI is Mark Phillips, *The Memoir of Marco Parenti: A Life in Medici Florence* (Princeton, N.J.: Princeton University Press, 1987), which also provides various passages in English translation, including those noted in the present anthology. Marco Parenti's *Letters* have recently been edited by Maria Marrese (Florence: Olschki, 1996). Useful information on Marco Parenti is also given in Andrea Matucci's introduction to Piero Parenti, *Storia fiorentina, I: 1476–78 / 1492–96* (Florence: Olschki, 1994).

The fundamental text on GIOVANNI RUCELLAI is the *Zibaldone* edited by Alessandro Perosa, especially vol. 2 concerning Rucellai's artistic interests and patronage. On this last topic, see also Roger Tarr, "Giovanni Rucellai's Comments on Art and Architecture," *Italian Studies* 51 (1996), pp. 58–95. On the *Monte delle Doti,* see Anthony Molho, *Marriage*

Alliance in Late Medieval Florence (Cambridge: Harvard University Press, 1994), chap. 1, esp. pp. 27–79. On women in Renaissance Florence, see Christiane Klapisch-Zuber, *Women, Family, and Ritual in Renaissance Italy* (Chicago: University of Chicago Press, 1985), and the article by Elaine G. Rosenthal, "The Position of Women in Renaissance Florence: Neither Autonomy nor Subjection," in *Florence and Italy*, pp. 369–381. On the catasto, see the studies on Florentine economy cited above, and the book by David Herlihy and Christiane Klapisch-Zuber, *Tuscans and Their Families* (New Haven, Conn.: Yale University Press, 1985). For a more detailed analysis of the Florentine fiscal system and its terminology, see Ugo Procacci, *Studio sul catasto fiorentino* (Florence: Olschki, 1996). An excellent glossary of Florentine fiscal terms can also be read in Matteo Palmieri, *Ricordi fiscali (1427–1474), con due appendici relative al 1474–1495,* ed. Elio Conti (Rome: Istituto Storico Italiano per il Medioevo, 1983), pp. 281–332.

In this century, very few studies have been devoted to FRANCESCO FILARETE's life and works; the most comprehensive survey is still Trexler's introduction to his edition of the *Libro Cerimoniale.*

On BENEDETTO DEI see Roberto Barducci's entry in *DBI,* 26, Anthony Molho's preface to Barducci's edition of the *Chronicle,* and Lorenzo Böninger, "Benedetto Dei on Early Florentine History," in *Florence and Italy,* pp. 309–320.

Only recently have contributions on LUCA PULCI appeared. See Stefano Ugo Baldassarri, "Lodi Medicee in un dimenticato best-seller del Quattrocento fiorentino: Il *Driadeo* di Luca Pulci," *Forum Italicum* 32.2 (1998), pp. 375–402, and Stefano Carrai, *Le Muse dei Pulci* (Naples: Guida, 1985), chaps. 1–2. Carrai devotes the other sections of his book to Luigi and to a lesser extent to Bernardo Pulci. On Luca Pulci, see also Francesca Battera, "Le *Pìstole* di Luca Pulci e la fortuna culturale del giovane Lorenzo," in *Lorenzo the Magnificent,* pp. 177–190, and Mario Martelli, *Letteratura fiorentina del Quattrocento: Il filtro degli anni Sessanta* (Florence: Le Lettere, 1996), pp. 112–126 (on the *Driadeo*), pp. 144–155 (*Pìstole*), and pp. 16–175 (*Pìstole* and *Ciriffo*). On Luigi Pulci, the best recent study in English is Constance Jordan, *Pulci's Morgante: Poetry and History in Fifteenth-Century Florence* (Washington, D.C.: Folger Shakespeare Library, 1986). For a concise survey of Luigi's life and works, see the entry on him by Remo Ceserani in *DCLI,* 3. Much work still needs to be done on Bernardo; for an introduction to his figure and literary output, especially his religious writings, see Georges Ulysse, "Un couple d'écrivains: Les *Sacre Rappresentazioni* de Bernardo et Antonia Pulci," in *Les femmes écrivains en Italie au Moyen Âge et à la Renaissance: Actes du colloque international, Aix-en-Provence, 12, 13, 14 novembre 1992* (Aix-en-Provence, France: Publications de l'Université de Provence, 1994), pp. 51–86.

The only volume on UGOLINO VERINO is Alfonso Lazzari, *Ugolino e Michele Verino* (Turin: Clausen, 1897). For further information and bibliography, see Francesco Bausi, "Ugolino Verino, Savonarola e la poesia religiosa fra Quattro e Cinquecento," in *Studi savonaroliani: Verso il V centenario,* ed. Gian Carlo Garfagnini (Florence: Edizioni del Galluzzo, 1996), pp. 127–135. There is a recent critical edition of Verino's *Carlias* by Nikolaus Thurn (Munich: Fink, 1996). See also Francesco Bausi's excellent edition of Verino's *Epigrammi* (Messina: Sicania, 1998), with its highly informative introduction and notes.

The best commentary on ANGELO POLIZIANO's *Pazzi Conspiracy* is in Perosa's notes to his critical edition of the text. There are complete English translations with brief intro-ductions by Elizabeth B. Wells in *The Earthly Republic,* pp. 293–324, and in Renée Neu Watkins, *Humanism and Liberty,* pp. 150–183.

On ALAMANNO RINUCCINI's life and literary output, see *Lettere ed orazioni,* ed. Vito R. Giustiniani (Florence: Olschki, 1953), and, also by Giustiniani, *Alamanno Rinuccini, 1426–1499: Materialen und Forschungen zur Geschichte des florentinischen Humanismus* (Cologne: Böhlau, 1965). For a good assessment of his political thought, see Francesco Adorno, "La crisi dell'umanesimo civile fiorentino da Alamanno Rinuccini al Machiavelli," *Rivista Critica di Storia della Filosofia* 7 (1952), pp. 19–40; and Mario Martelli, "Profilo ideologico di Alamanno Rinuccini," in *Culture et société en Italie du Moyen Âge à la Renaissance: Hommage à André Rochon* (Paris: Université de la Sorbonne Nouvelle, 1985), vol. 1, pp. 131–143. A complete English translation of Rinuccini's dialogue *On Liberty* and a good intro-duction appear in *Humanism and Liberty,* pp. 186–224.

Sketches of DONATO ACCIAIUOLI can be found in D'Addario's entry on him in *DBI,* vol. 1, Garin, *Portraits,* pp. 55–117, and Margery A. Ganz, "Donato Acciaiuoli and the Medici: A Strategy for Survival in 400 Florence," *Rinascimento,* series 2, 22 (1982), pp. 33–74. See also the section on him in *Cambridge Translations of Renaissance Philosophical Texts,* ed. Jill Kraye (Cambridge: Cambridge University Press, 1997), vol. 1, pp. 47–58. For Argyropoulos' stay in Florence, see Jerrold E. Seigel, "The Teaching of Argyropoulos and the Rhetoric of the First Humanists," in *Action and Conviction in Early Modern Europe: Essays in Memory of E. H. Harbison,* ed. Theodore K. Rabb and Jerrold E. Seigel (Prince-ton, N.J.: Princeton University Press, 1969), pp. 237–260, which also contains important remarks on Rinuccini and Acciaiuoli. On Argyropoulos, see also the volume by Field on the Platonic Academy indicated in the bibliographic section on Marsilio Ficino.

For LUCA LANDUCCI, see Antonio Lanza's introduction to the anastatic reprint of Del Badia's edition of the *Diario fiorentino.* An English translation of this work, today somewhat difficult to find, is Alice de Rosen Jervis, *A Florentine Diary from 1450 to 1516: Continued by an Anonymous Writer till 1542* (New York: Dutton, 1927). On Charles VIII's entry into Florence, see Eve Borsook, "Decor in Florence for the Entry of Charles VIII of France," *Mitteilungen des Kunsthistorischen Institutes in Florenz* 1 (1961), pp. 106–122 and 217. On the agreement of Florence with the French king, see Gino Capponi, "Capitoli fatti dalla città di Firenze a dí 25 di Novembre del 1494," *Archivio Storico Italiano,* 1.1 (1842), pp. 363–375. On the institutional changes introduced by the December 2, 1494, deliberations and on the first years of the Florentine popular government, see Nicolai Rubinstein, "I primi anni del Consiglio Maggiore a Firenze (1494–1499), *Archivio Storico Italiano* 112.2 (1954), pp. 151–194, and 112.3 (1954), pp. 321–347; and Rudolf Von Albertini, *Firenze dalla repubblica al principato: Storia e coscienza politica* (Turin: Einaudi, 1995), chap. 1. For an assessment of the myth of the French monarchy in Florence and its influence on both the political and the religious milieu, see Anne Denis, *Charles VIII et les Italiens: Histoire et mythe* (Geneva: Droz, 1979); Christian Bec, "Les Florentines et la France ou la rupture d'un mythe (1494–1540)," *Il Pensiero Politico* 14.3 (1981), pp. 375–394; Cesare Vasoli, "Il mito della monarchia francese nelle profezie tra il 1490 e il 1510," in *L'aube de la Renaissance,* ed. Dario Cecchetti, Lionello Sozzi, and Louis Terreaux (Geneva: Slatkine, 1991), pp. 149–165; and Lorenzo

Polizzotto and Caroline Elam, "La unione de' gigli con gigli: Two documents on Florence, France and the Savonarolan Millenarian Tradition," *Rinascimento,* series 2, 31 (1991), pp. 239–259. For the fifteenth-century pageants performed in the Church of San Felice, see Newbigin, *Feste d'Oltrarno,* vol. 1, chap. 1. On p. 43 she discusses and translates Landucci's passage on Charles VIII's unwillingness to attend the pageant.

For a general introduction to the literary culture of fifteenth-century Florence, see the volumes by Garin, Rossi, and Holmes mentioned earlier together with the aforementioned conference proceedings on Lorenzo de' Medici. Good surveys of the humanists' attitudes toward the vernacular are offered by Mirko Tavoni, *Latino, grammatica, volgare: Storia di una questione umanistica* (Padua: Antenore, 1984), and Angelo Mazzocco, *Linguistic Theories in Dante and the Humanists: Studies of Language and Intellectual History in Late Medieval and Early Renaissance Italy* (Leiden: Brill, 1993). On the Certame Coronario, see the valuable article by Guglielmo Gorni, "Storia del Certame Coronario," *Rinascimento,* series 2, 12 (1972), pp. 135–181. For a critical edition of the texts presented at the Certame and further bibliography, see *De vera amicitia: I testi del primo "Certame coronario,"* ed. Lucia Bertolini (Modena: Panini, 1993). Philologically less precise, but still of use, is Antonio Altamura's edition of these texts, *Il Certame Coronario* (Naples: Società Editrice Napoletana, 1974). For the humanists' critical views on Dante, see Eugenio Garin, "Dante in the Renaissance," in *The Three Crowns of Florence: Humanist Assessments of Dante, Petrarca, and Boccaccio,* ed. and trans. David Thompson and Alan F. Nagel (New York: Harper & Row, 1972), pp ix–xxxiv, and Giuliano Tanturli, "Il disprezzo per Dante dal Petrarca al Bruni," *Rinascimento,* series 2, 25 (1985), pp. 199–219.

There is a complete English translation of LEONARDO BRUNI's *Lives of Dante and Petrarch* in *The Three Crowns,* pp. 57–83, later republished by Thompson in *The Humanism,* pp. 85–100. For an excerpt of Bruni's *Vita di Dante* in English translation, see *Dante: The Critical Heritage, 1314(?)–1870,* ed. Michael Caesar (London: Routledge, 1989), pp. 202–215. On Bruni's *Vite,* see the recent study by Lucia Gualdo Rosa, "Leonardo Bruni e le sue 'vite parallele' di Dante e del Petrarca," *Lettere Italiane,* 47.3 (1995), pp. 386–401. On Bruni's *Dialogi,* see David Quint, "Humanism and Modernity: A Reconsideration of Bruni's *Dialogues,*" *Renaissance Quarterly,* 38.3 (1985), pp. 423–445; Riccardo Fubini, "All'uscita dalla scolastica medievale: Salutati, Bruni, e i *Dialogi ad Petrum Histrum,*" *Archivio Storico Italiano,* 150.2 (1992), pp. 1065–1103, and Stefano Ugo Baldassarri's introduction to the critical edition of this text (Florence: Olschki, 1994). There are complete English translations of Bruni's *Dialogi* in *The Three Crowns,* pp. 19–52, and *The Humanism,* pp. 60–84. A partial version appears in *Dante: The Critical Heritage,* pp. 190–196. On the importance of the rediscovery of the Ciceronian dialogue in the Italian culture of the fifteenth century, see the exemplary research by David Marsh, *The Quattrocento Dialogue: Classical Tradition and Humanist Innovation* (Cambridge: Harvard University Press, 1980).

On GIANNOZZO MANETTI, see Alfonso De Petris's introductions to his critical editions of Manetti's *Vita Socratis et Senecae* (Florence: Olschki, 1979) and *Apologeticus* (Rome: Edizioni di Storia e Letteratura, 1982). A partial English translation of Manetti's *Lives of*

Dante, Petrarch, and Boccaccio can be found in *The Three Crowns*, pp. 90–102. Also regarding Manetti's biography of the "three crowns," as well as his cultural indebtedness to Bruni, see Stefano Ugo Baldassarri, "Un testimone dei *Dialogi* di Leonardo Bruni appartenuto a Giannozzo Manetti: Il ms. Vaticano Pal. Lat. 1598," *Interpres* 14 (1994), pp. 198–213. On Manetti's study of Hebrew, see Riccardo Fubini, "L'ebraismo nei riflessi della cultura umanistica: Leonardo Bruni, Giannozzo Manetti, e Annio da Viterbo," *Medioevo e Rinascimento*, 2 (1988), pp. 283–324. The most comprehensive study on Manuel Chrysoloras' teaching of Greek in Florence remains Giuseppe Cammelli, *I dotti bizantini e le origini dell'umanesimo*, vol. 1, *Manuele Crisolora* (Florence: Vallecchi, 1941).

On the life and works of MATTEO PALMIERI, see George M. Carpetto, *The Humanism of Matteo Palmieri* (Rome: Bulzoni, 1984), and Alessandra Mita Ferraro's introduction to her critical edition of *De captivitate Pisarum* (Bologna: Il Mulino, 1995), which also provides both an Italian translation of this text and an accurate updated bibliography on the author. For an English translation of the preface to the *Vita civile*, see *The Three Crowns*, pp. 85–89. For an English translation of Book 2 of *Vita civile*, see *Cambridge Translations*, vol. 2, pp. 149–172, trans. David Marsh.

There is a partial English translation of Poliziano's preface to the "Raccolta Aragonese" in *The Three Crowns*, pp. 105–107.

On CRISTOFORO LANDINO's appraisal of Dante, see Cardini's excellent notes to his edition of Landino's proem to the commentary on the *Commedia*, and *La critica del Landino*. See also David Thompson, "Landino's Life of Dante," *Dante Studies*, 88 (1970), pp. 119–127; Arthur Field, "Cristoforo Landino's First Lectures on Dante," *Renaissance Quarterly*, 39.1 (1986), pp. 16–48, and Giuliano Tanturli, "La Firenze laurenziana davanti alla propria storia letteraria," in *Lorenzo il Magnifico e il suo tempo*, ed. Gian Carlo Garfagnini (Florence: Olschki, 1992), pp. 1–38. There are partial English translations of Landino's proem to his commentary on the *Commedia* in *The Three Crowns*, pp. 110–131, and *Dante: The Critical Heritage*, pp. 218–226.

Garin gives a concise and readable introductory sketch of MARSILIO FICINO in *Portraits*, pp. 142–160. The main studies on Ficino remain those by Paul Oskar Kristeller, starting with his comprehensive volume, *The Philosophy of Marsilio Ficino* (New York: Columbia University Press, 1953). See also the essays collected in *Ficino and Neoplatonism*, ed. Konrad Eisenbichler and Olga Zorzi Pugliese (Ottawa: Dovehouse, 1986), and the articles by Michael J. B. Allen gathered and reprinted in *Plato's Third Eye: Studies in Marsilio Ficino's Metaphysics and Its Sources* (Aldershot: Variorum, 1995). On Ficino's academy, see Arthur Field, *The Origins of the Platonic Academy of Florence* (Princeton, N.J.: Princeton University Press, 1989). There is an English translation of Ficino's praise of Dante inserted in Landino's proem to his commentary on the *Commedia* in *The Three Crowns*, pp. 108–109. On Pico della Mirandola's criticism of Dante and Petrarch, see *Prosatori latini del Quattrocento*, pp. 796–805. For an English translation of Pico's letter, see *The Three Crowns*, pp. 148–152. An English translation of Ficino's preface to his version of Dante's *Monarchia* can be found in *Dante: The Critical Heritage*, pp. 216–218. On Ficino's edition of the *Monarchia*, see Prudence Shaw, "La versione ficiniana della *Monarchia*," *Studi Danteschi* 51 (1974–1975), pp. 289–408.

ART

There are numerous surveys of Italian art in the Renaissance with entire sections on the Florentine quattrocento. For clarity, readability, and concision, we suggest the following works: Peter Murray, *The Architecture of the Italian Renaissance* (New York: Schocken Books, 1986); Ludwig H. Heydenreich, *Architecture in Italy, 1400–1500* (New Haven: Yale University Press, 1996); Peter and Linda Murray, *The Art of the Renaissance* (London: Thames and Hudson, 1966); and Charles Avery, *Florentine Renaissance Sculpture* (London: John Murray, 1996). Still valued is the interdisciplinary research by André Chastel, *Art et humanisme à Florence au temps de Laurent le Magnifique* (Paris: Presses Universitaires de France, 1959). A highly readable and informative text on the monuments of quattrocento Florence is Eve Borsook, *The Companion Guide to Florence* (London: Collins, 1966), which emphasizes the link between art and politics. On the humanists' assessment of the arts, see Michael Baxandall, *Giotto and the Orators: Humanist Observers of Painting in Italy and the Discovery of Pictorial Composition, 1350–1450* (Oxford: Oxford University Press, 1971). Important sources are available in English translation in *Italian Art, 1400–1500: Sources and Documents*, ed. Creighton E. Gilbert (Evanston, Ill.: Northwestern University Press, 1992), and in the original form in *Letteratura artistica dell'età dell'umanesimo: Antologia di testi, 1400–1520*, ed. Gianni Carlo Sciolla (Turin: Giappichelli, 1982).

The best study to date devoted to FILIPPO VILLANI is still the article by Giuliano Tanturli, "Il *De viri illustri di Firenze* e il *De origine civitatis Florentie et de eiusdem famosis civibus* di Filippo Villani," *Studi Medievali*, series 3, 14.1 (1973), pp. 833–881.

The classic study on LORENZO GHIBERTI is Richard Krautheimer's *Lorenzo Ghiberti* (Princeton, N.J.: Princeton University Press, 1956). Useful essays are collected in *Lorenzo Ghiberti nel suo tempo: Atti del convegno internazionale di studi, Firenze, 18–21 ottobre 1978* (Florence: Olschki, 1980). On Ghiberti's *Commentaries*, see Krautheimer, chap. 20, and Morisani's introduction to his edition of this text. The entire *Second Commentary* is available in English translation in *Italian Art, 1400–1500*, pp. 76–88. A detailed analysis of the *Third Commentary*—with a long introduction, German translation, and updated bibliography—is Klaus Bergoldt, *Der dritte Kommentar Lorenzo Ghibertis* (Weinheim: Acta Humaniora, 1988).

For a concise introduction to LEON BATTISTA ALBERTI, see the articles by Cecil Grayson in *DBI* I and *DCLI* I. A recent comprehensive volume on Alberti is Mark Jarzombek's *On Leon Baptista Alberti: His Literary and Aesthetic Theories* (Cambridge, Mass.: MIT Press, 1989). A general yet helpful introduction to Alberti's artistic output is Joan Gadol, *Leon Battista Alberti: Universal Man of the Early Renaissance* (Chicago: University of Chicago Press, 1969). For a brief analysis of *On Painting*, see D. R. Edward Wright, "Alberti's *De pictura:* Its Literary Structure and Purpose," *Journal of the Warburg and Courtauld Institutes* 47 (1984), pp. 52–71, which duly stresses the innovative features of this text. Two excellent English translations of this work of Alberti are available, one by John R. Spencer (New Haven: Yale University Press, 1966), the other by Cecil Grayson (Harmondsworth: Penguin Books, 1991).

On ANTONIO MANETTI and his *Vita di Filippo Brunelleschi,* see the introductions to the editions of this text by Domenico De Robertis and Giuliano Tanturli (Milan: Il Polifilo, 1976), and by Carlachiara Perrone (Rome: Salerno, 1992). For a complete English translation of this work and an excellent introductory essay, see Howard Saalman's critical edition of *The Life of Brunelleschi,* trans. Catherine Enggass (University Park, Pa.: Pennsylvania State University Press, 1970). On Manetti's culture and literary interests, see the three articles by Domenico De Robertis collected in his *Editi e rari: Studi sulla tradizione letteraria tra Tre e Cinquecento* (Milan: Feltrinelli, 1978), in the section entitled "Lo scrittoio di Antonio Manetti," pp. 183–230. For a comprehensive survey of Brunelleschi's production, see Eugenio Battisti, *Filippo Brunelleschi: The Complete Work* (New York: Rizzoli, 1981). For a discussion of the artist's relations with Florentine literary circles, see Giuliano Tanturli, "Rapporti del Brunelleschi con gli ambienti letterari fiorentini," in *Filippo Brunelleschi: La sua opera e il suo tempo* (Florence: Centro Di, 1980), vol. 1, pp. 125–144. English translations of fifteenth-century sources on Brunelleschi are in *Brunelleschi in Perspective,* ed. Isabelle Hyman (Englewood Cliffs, N.J.: Prentice Hall, 1974).

Peter Murray offers a valuable analysis and an English translation of the anonymous text entitled *Notable Men in Florence Since 1400* in "Art Historians and Art Critics," *Burlington Magazine* 99 (1957), pp. 330–336.

On CRISTOFORO LANDINO's artistic appraisal, see Michael Baxandall, "Alberti and Cristoforo Landino: The Practical Criticism of Painting," in *Convegno nel V centenario di Alberti, Roma-Mantova-Firenze, 25–29 aprile 1972* (Rome: Accademia Nazionale dei Lincei, 1974), pp. 143–154.

An excerpt of UGOLINO VERINO's poem in praise of the best Florentine artists of the fifteenth century has been translated into English and briefly commented on by Gilbert in *Italian Art, 1400–1500,* pp. 192–193.

On FRANCESCO ALBERTINI, see José Ruysschaert's article in *DBI* 1 and Peter Murray's short note to his anastatic reprint of the 1510 Florentine edition of Albertini's *Memoriale* in *Five Early Guides to Rome and Florence* (Farnborough, England: Gregg, 1972). For detailed information on the works mentioned by Albertini, in some cases useful to their identification, see Peter Murray, *An Index of Attributions Made in Tuscan Sources Before Vasari* (Florence: Olschki, 1959), and an excellent recent Italian edition of Vasari's *Vite* by Luciano Bellosi and Aldo Rossi (Turin: Einaudi, 1991).

Charles Trinkaus offers a detailed and erudite study of the humanists' attitude toward religion in *In Our Image and Likeness,* 2 vols. (Chicago: University of Chicago Press, 1970) For a wider survey, see *The Pursuit of Holiness in Late Medieval and Renaissance Religion: Papers from the University of Michigan Conference,* ed. Charles Trinkaus and Heiko A. Oberman (Leiden: Brill, 1974), and *Christianity and the Renaissance: Image and Religious Imagination in the Quattrocento,* ed. Timothy Verdon and John Henderson (Syracuse, N.Y.: Syracuse University Press, 1990)—both volumes contain numerous essays devoted to Florence. On the earliest Christian communities in Florence and the first centuries of the Florentine Church, see the essays collected in *Le radici cristiane di Firenze,* ed. Anna Benvenuti, Franco Cardini, and Elena Giannarelli (Florence: Alinea, 1994). Although centered on the figure of Sant'Antonino, Peter Francis Howard's recent book offers an ample study of religion in quattrocento Florence: *Beyond the Written Word: Preaching Theology in the Florence of Archbishop Antoninus, 1427–1459* (Florence: Olschki, 1995). For information on Florentine charitable institutions, see John Henderson, *Piety and Charity in Late Medieval Florence* (Oxford: Claredon Press, 1994), which also provides an extensive bibliography. Roberto Bizzocchi, *Chiesa e potere nella Toscana del Quattrocento* (Bologna: Il Mulino, 1987), is focused on the organization of the Church in Tuscany and on the clergy's relationship with local political powers. For a general notion of the relationship between the Curia and the Medici in the first decades of the quattrocento, see George Holmes, "How the Medici Became the Pope's Bankers," in *Florentine Studies*, pp. 357–380, and, in the same volume, Peter Partner, "Florence and the Papacy in the Earlier Fifteenth Century," pp. 381–402; and David S. Peterson, "An Episcopal Election in Quattrocento Florence," in *Popes, Teachers, and Canon Law in the Middle Ages*, ed. James S. Sweeney and Stanley Chodorow (Ithaca, N.Y.: Cornell University Press, 1989), pp. 300–325. On the Florentine ecclesiastical council, see the classic study by Joseph Gill, *The Council of Florence* (Cambridge: Cambridge University Press, 1959), and the numerous conference proceedings in *Firenze e il Concilio del 1439: Convegno di Studi, Firenze, 29 novembre–2 dicembre 1989*, ed. Paolo Viti (Florence: Olschki, 1994), 2 vols. For some foreign accounts of the council see *Les "Mémoires" du Grand Ecclésiarque de l'Eglise de Constantinople Sylvestre Syropoulos sur le concile de Florence, 1438–1439*, ed. Valérien Laurent (Paris: Editions du Centre National de la Recherche Scientifique, 1971), and Jan Krajcar, "Simeon of Suzdal's Account of the Council of Florence," *Orientalia Christiana Periodica*, 39.1 (1973), pp. 103–130. On Florentine millenarianism in the quattrocento see Cesare Vasoli, "L'attesa della nuova era in ambienti e gruppi fiorentini del Quattrocento," in *L'attesa dell'età nuova nella spiritualità della fine del Medioevo* (Todi: Accademia Tudertina, 1962), and Cesare Vasoli, "Movimenti religiosi e crisi politiche dalla Signoria al Principato," in *Idee istituzioni scienza ed arti nella Firenze dei Medici*, pp. 47–81. See also Weinstein's fundamental study *Savonarola and Florence: Prophecy and Patriotism in the Renaissance* (Princeton, N.J.: Princeton University Press, 1970).

On FEO BELCARI, see the articles by Mario Marti in *DBI* 7 and *DCLI* 1. On his religious writings and his relationship with the Medici, see Martelli, *Letteratura fiorentina*, pp. 20–46. For an excellent survey of Florentine mystery plays in the fifteenth century, and of Belcari's religious literary production, see Nerida Newbigin, *Nuovo corpus di Sacre Rappresentazioni fiorentine del Quattrocento edite e inedite tratte da manoscritti coevi o ricontrollate su di essi* (Bologna: Commissione per i testi di lingua, 1983). Newbigin has also published several of Belcari's texts. Some of Belcari's sonnets have been published in *Lirici toscani del '400*, ed. Antonio Lanza (Rome: Bulzoni, 1973), vol. 1, pp. 211–240. Manetti's description of the consecration of the cathedral of Florence in 1436 has been edited by Eugenio Battisti as an appendix to his article "Il mondo visuale delle fiabe," *Archivio di Filosofia*, 1.2–3 (1960), pp. 310–320. Bruni's brief account of the same episode can be found in his *Rerum suo tempore gestarum commentarius (aa. 1378–1440)*, ed. Carmine Di Pierro (Città di Castello: Lapi, *Rerum italicarum scriptores* vol. 19.2–3, 1926), p. 453. On the various dedications of this church and its crucial importance in the history of late medieval and early Renaissance Florence, see the study by Mary Bergstein, "Marian Politics in Quattrocento Florence: The Renewed Dedication of Santa Maria del Fiore in 1412," *Renaissance Quarterly* 44.4 (1991), pp. 673–719.

On DOMENICO DA CORELLA, see Stefano Orlandi, *"Necrologio" di S. Maria Novella* (Florence: Olschki, 1955), vol. 1, pp. 304–315, who also publishes excerpts from the *Theotocon* in vol. 2, pp. 503–511. See also the brief entry by Pier Giorgio Ricci in the *Enciclopedia Dantesca* (Rome: Istituto della Enciclopedia Italiana, 1970), vol. 2, p. 551, and the article by Francesco Bausi, "Un'inedita descrizione delle giostre fiorentine del 1469 e del 1475," *Medioevo e Rinascimento*, n.s., 5 (1991), pp. 63–79, which also indicates the eighteenth-century editions, either complete or partial, of Corella's *Theotocon*. For other passages of Corella's *Theotocon* than those reported in our anthology, and specifically the verses concerning the baptistery and the Church of SS. Annunziata, see *Italian Art, 1400–1500*, pp. 149–152.

Donald Weinstein's volume *Savonarola and Florence* is still deservedly regarded as a fundamental study for understanding GIROLAMO SAVONAROLA. See also Garin's sketch of Savonarola in *Portraits*, pp. 222–243. Useful recent surveys are provided by the essays collected in the already mentioned *Studi savonaroliani* and in *Girolamo Savonarola: Piety, Prophecy, and Politics in Renaissance Florence*, ed. Donald Weinstein and Valerie R. Hotchkiss (Dallas: Bridwell Library, 1994). Lorenzo Polizzotto offers a great contribution to the knowledge of Savonarola's followers in his *Elect Nation: The Savonarolan Movement in Florence, 1494–1545* (Oxford: Clarendon Press, 1994), which also contains an extensive bibliography. For a complete English translation of Savonarola's *Trattato* and a good introduction to this text, see *Humanism and Liberty*, pp. 226–260.

On PIERO BERNARDO, see the entry by Giampaolo Tognetti in *DBI* 9 and Polizzotto, *The Elect Nation*, especially pp. 117–138. On the *fanciulli*, see the volume by Polizzotto, and the article by Ottavia Niccoli, "I bambini del Savonarola," in *Studi savonaroliani*, pp. 279–288, as well as the bibliography given there.

Cesare Vasoli gives a general overview of GIROLAMO BENIVIENI in *DBI* 8. Weinstein has translated part of the fifth stanza of Benivieni's first canzone included in our anthology and has briefly commented on this poem in "The Myth of Florence," pp. 18–19, later reprinted in his volume *Savonarola and Florence*, pp. 30–31. Most studies on Benivieni have been devoted to his canzone *De Amore;* see Sears Jayne, "Benivieni's Christian Canzone," *Rinascimento*, series 2, 24 (1984), pp. 153–180, and Olga Zorzi Pugliese, "Variations on Ficino's *De Amore:* The Hymns to Love by Benivieni and Castiglione," in *Ficino and Renaissance Neoplatonism*, pp. 113–121. On his eclogues, see the extensive study by Francesca Battera, "Le ecloghe di Girolamo Benivieni," *Interpres* 10 (1990), pp. 133–223.

On the Savonarolan LORENZO VIOLI, see Gian Carlo Garfagnini's introduction to his edition of Violi's *Giornate* (Florence: Olschki, 1986), and the article by Armando Verde, "Ser Lorenzo Violi 'secretario' del Savonarola," *Memorie Domenicane* n.s., 18 (1987), pp. 381–399. On Florentine prophecies concerning the French king's arrival in Italy, see the articles previously cited in the bibliographical references on Landucci. The study by Polizzotto and Elam mentioned there also includes a letter (pp. 254–255) by Violi on Savonarola's prophecies regarding Charles VIII's role in the spiritual renewal of Florence.

FLORENCE THROUGH FOREIGNERS' EYES
A general survey of travels and travel literature in the Middle Ages is Norbert Ohler's *Medieval Traveller* (Woodbridge: Boydell, 1989); unfortunately, the English translation of this book does not retain the bibliography contained in the original German edition,

Reisen im Mittelalter (Munich: Artemis, 1986), and in the Italian version, *I viaggi nel Medio Evo* (Milan: Garzanti, 1988). As regards Florence, there is no single book specifically devoted to the accounts of visitors to the city in the Renaissance. The only studies on this topic concern eighteenth- and nineteenth-century travelers; for an accurate bibliography, see the article by Cesare De Seta, "L'Italia nello specchio del 'Grand Tour,' " in *Storia d'Italia,* vol. 5, *Il paesaggio,* ed. Cesare De Seta (Turin: Einaudi, 1982), pp. 127–263. For information and introductory remarks on the presence of foreigners in quattrocento Florence, see Lucia Sandri, "Stranieri e forestieri nella Firenze del Quattrocento attraverso i libri di ricordi e di entrata e uscita degli ospedali cittadini," in *Forestieri e stranieri nelle città basso-medievali: Atti del Seminario Internazionale di Studio, Bagno a Ripoli (Firenze), 4–8 giugno 1984* (Florence: Salimbeni, 1988), pp. 149–161.

On ISIDORE OF KIEV, see Krajcar's introduction to his edition of the *Peregrinatio* and his article "Metropolitan Isidore's Journey to the Council of Florence: Some Remarks," *Orientalia Christiana Periodica* 38.2 (1972), pp. 367–387. Günther Stökl gives a useful commentary in the introduction to his German translation of the *Peregrinatio* in *Europa im XV. Jahrhundert von Byzantinern Gesehen,* vol. 2 (Vienna: Byzantinische Geschichtsschreiber, 1954). On the participation of the Russian ecclesiastics in the Florentine council and their impressions of the city, see also Newbigin, *Feste d'Oltrarno,* vol. 1, pp. 3–7, which translates Abraham of Suzdal's beautiful description of a fifteenth-century Florentine pageant.

The best study on STEFANO PORCARI is Massimo Miglio's " 'Viva la libertà et populo de Roma'—Oratoria e politica: Stefano Porcari," in *Paleographica, diplomatica et archivistica: Studi in onore di Giulio Battelli* (Rome: Edizioni di Storia e Letteratura, 1979), vol. 1, pp. 381–428. See also Anna Modigliani, *I Porcari: Storie di una famiglia romana tra Medioevo e Rinascimento* (Rome: Roma nel Rinascimento, 1994). There is an English translation of Alberti's account of Porcari's conspiracy in *Humanism and Liberty,* pp. 107–115.

For English biographies of PIUS II, see Cecilia Ady, *Pius II* (London: Methuen, 1913), and Rosamond J. Mitchell, *The Laurels and the Tiara* (Garden City, N.Y.: Doubleday, 1962); see also the entry by Gioacchino Paparelli in *DCLI* 3, and Garin's *Portraits,* pp. 30–54. Essays on diverse aspects of Pius II's personality and literary works are collected in *Pio II e la cultura del suo tempo: Atti del primo convegno internazionale—1989,* ed. Luisa Rotondi Secchi Tarugi (Milan: Guerrini e Associati, 1991). Luigi Totaro presents a valuable study of the pope's life based on the reading of his *Commentaries,* in *Pio II nei suoi "Commentari"* (Bologna: Pàtron, 1978). A commendable partial English translation of this vast work of Pius II has been made available by Florence A. Gragg under the title *Memoirs of a Renaissance Pope: The Commentaries of Pius II,* ed. Leona C. Gabel (New York: Putnam, 1959). For a complete English translation, see *The Commentaries of Pius II* (Northampton, Mass.: Smith College, 1937–1957).

On LUDOVICO CARBONE, see the entry by Lao Paoletti in *DBI* 19. The oration Carbone delivered before the Florentine government has been edited and commented on by Alfonso Lazzari, "Un'orazione di Lodovico Carbone a Firenze," *Atti e memorie della R. Deputazione di storia patria per le provincie modenesi,* series 5, 12 (1919), pp. 187–205. On his account of his trip to Naples, see Isabella Nuovo, "Sulla struttura di un dialogo di Ludovico Carbone (il *De Neapolitana profectione*)," *Annali della Facoltà di Lettere e Filosofia dell'Università di Bari* 2 (1978), pp. 93–112.

On PANDOLFO COLLENUCCIO, see the entries by Eduardo Melfi in *DBI* 27 and by Claudio Varese in *DCLI* 1, and Paolo Paolini's "Aspetti letterari del Collenuccio storico," *Italianistica* 17.1 (1988), pp. 49–77, which discusses primarily the style and the structure of his *Compendio de le Istorie del Regno di Napoli.* The best study on this humanist remains Claudio Varese, "Pandolfo Collenuccio umanista," *Studia Oliveriana* 4–5 (1956–1957), pp. 7–143, which, unfortunately, alludes only in passing to the Latin poem in praise of Florence, on pp. 20–22. The only contribution to the scholarship on this poem is a brief article in Latin by Angela Minicucci, "Quae Vergiliana insint in carmine Pandulphi Collenucii Florentia inscripto," *Res Publica Litterarum* 7 (1984), pp. 155–160, which simply lists the Virgilian sources employed by Collenuccio. Poliziano's letter to Collenuccio in which the *Panegyrica Silva* is praised can be found in the seventh book of his epistolary output in *Opera* (Basel: Episcopium, 1553), pp. 98–99.

On FLAVIO BIONDO, see the excellent articles by Riccardo Fubini in *DBI* 10 and *DCLI* 1. For further information and a more recent bibliography, see Tavoni, *Latino, grammatica, volgare,* and Mazzocco, *Linguistic Theories.*

The best recent study in English on GALEAZZO MARIA SFORZA is Gregory Lubkin, *A Renaissance Court: Milan Under Galeazzo Maria Sforza* (Berkeley-Los Angeles: University of California Press, 1994). The letter from Galeazzo to his father translated in our anthology has been reproduced in part by Benjamin Buser in the second volume of his *Die Beziehungen der Mediceer zu Frankreich während der Jahre 1434–1494* (Leipzig: Humblot, 1879), pp. 347–348. A partial English translation can be found in Gutkind, *Cosimo de' Medici,* p. 219. For Galeazzo's 1471 visit to Florence and documents related to it, see Riccardo Fubini, "In margine all'edizione delle *Lettere* di Lorenzo de' Medici," in *Lorenzo de' Medici: Studi,* ed. Gian Carlo Garfagnini (Florence: Olschki, 1992), pp. 167–232.